EXCAVATING ASIAN HISTORY

EXCAVATING ASIAN HISTORY

Interdisciplinary Studies in Archaeology and History

Norman Yoffee and Bradley L. Crowell, editors

The University of Arizona Press   Tucson

The University of Arizona Press
© 2006 The Arizona Board of Regents
All rights reserved
♾ This book is printed on acid-free, archival-quality paper.
Manufactured in the United States of America

11 10 09 08 07 06   6 5 4 3 2 1

Library of Congress Cataloging-in-Publication Data
Excavating Asian history : interdisciplinary studies in
archaeology and history / Norman Yoffee and Bradley L.
Crowell, editors.
p. cm.
Includes bibliographical references and index.
ISBN-13: 978-0-8165-2418-1 (hardcover : alk. paper)
ISBN-10: 0-8165-2418-1 (hardcover : alk. paper)
1. Asia — Antiquities. 2. Archaeology and history — Asia.
3. Asia — History — Sources. I. Yoffee, Norman. II. Crowell,
Bradley L., 1970 —
DS11.E39 2006
950'.1 — dc22
2006006346

Chapters 2–8 were originally published in *Journal of the
Economic and Social History of the Orient*, copyright © Brill
Academic Publishers. Reprinted by permission. Chapters 2,
4, and 7 appeared in *JESHO* 46, no. 1 (2003), pp. 46–87;
3–45; and 88–126, respectively; chapters 3 and 6, in *JESHO*
45, no. 4 (2002), pp. 425–67 and 492–523; chapters 5 and 8,
in *JESHO* 46, no. 4 (2003), pp. 411–36 and 468–91.

CONTENTS

EXCAVATING ASIAN HISTORY

1

Historical Archaeology in Asia
An Introduction

NORMAN YOFFEE AND BRADLEY L. CROWELL

Since this volume is devoted to examining, rearranging, and otherwise breaking down the boundaries between history and archaeology in the study of premodern Asia, we consider briefly at the outset in what ways and in which disciplines archaeologists who study historic Asian societies have gone about their business. We discuss even more concisely how historians have and have not employed archaeological data and what the consequences are therefrom.

In the first place, not all archaeologists are created equal. Obviously, some archaeologists are prehistorians, that is, they work in periods for which there is no written history. Most of these archaeologists, especially in the United States, work in anthropology departments and relate their particular work within comparative frameworks. Other archaeologists, who are area specialists, may have little or no interest in cross-cultural comparisons.

Further confusing the picture are self-designated historical archaeologists. Historical archaeologists, at least in the United States, define their field mainly as the archaeology of the modern world or the archaeology of colonialism (Orser 2002, 1996), although some consider historical archaeology also to embrace the archaeology of a past culture with a literate tradition. Few Classical or Near Eastern archaeologists (including Egyptological archaeologists), however, think of themselves as historical archaeologists. This can be explained by the diverse kinds of training archaeologists receive and also the kinds of university programs or governmental or other offices in which they work.

Whereas historical archaeologists in the United States are normally trained in departments of anthropology, Classical and Near East archaeologists are usually inculcated in the areas, cultures, and (to some degree) in the languages of the area in which they work and only occasionally commune with their archaeological brethren and sistren in departments of anthropology. Anthropologists, uncharitably, tend to think of these archaeologists not as historians but as antiquarians. In most parts of the world outside the United States, of course, archaeologists (at least those who study ancient states) do think of themselves as historians, and they are trained in departments of history or in departments of archaeology. They may or may not be interested in anthropological archaeology, and text-based historians may or may not regard archaeological work as pertinent to their own investigations.

Anthropology departments in the United States usually do not employ archaeologists who work in the historical periods of the Mediterranean world or in historic Asia, although exceptions exist and are increasing in number. The long-standing exception to this rule has been Mesopotamian archaeology, and this is due to the extraordinary impact of Robert McC. Adams, who studied historic as well as prehistoric periods of Mesopotamia and had appointments in both the Department of Anthropology and the Oriental Institute at the University of Chicago (Yoffee 1997). His research in the rise of Mesopotamian civilization was undertaken in a cross-cultural framework (Adams 1966; Zettler, chapter 4, this vol.), and his pioneering use of reconnaissance survey (1981) was relevant to anthropological archaeologists working in the New World as well as in the Old World. Adams's students at the University of Chicago got excellent jobs, attracted excellent students, and today it is not uncommon for departments of anthropology to feature a Mesopotamian archaeologist who represents the archaeology of "complex societies" or Old World archaeology.

Unlike archaeologists of the Eastern Hemisphere (the Old World) who study ancient states, archaeologists of the New World who explore Mesoamerican and South American states are all anthropologists. Of course, few archaeologists outside the Americas study these ancient states. Since New World states were not thought literate (until Maya script was deciphered about twenty-five years ago), there was no problem in regarding the archaeology of the Americas as the domain of archaeologists for whom history was of little interest. Here, too, are exceptions: distinguished archaeologists who plumbed Spanish sources for information about the cultures in which Europeans found themselves (e.g., Murra 1980; Rowe 1946). Hence, New World archaeologists were in a sense "preadapted" to the kind of historical archaeology we are discussing for Asia.

This situation has changed slowly as anthropological archaeologists have became more historical, and historical archaeologists have become more anthropological. First, one towering figure, V. Gordon Childe, beginning in the 1930s, studied the rise of Mesopotamian and other states and attempted to explain their evolution and the roles of urbanism and literacy in them (e.g., 1950). Childe's contemporaries, however, such as Grahame Clark, tended to avoid the archaeological study of ancient states. His *World Prehistory, an Outline* (1961) attempted to bring together data on prehistoric sequences all over the world but stopped at the time when writing and written history appeared. Andrew Sherratt's edited volume *The Cambridge Encyclopedia of Archaeology* (1980), with a foreword by Grahame Clark, however, remedied the situation by inviting chapters on historic states as well as prehistoric cultures.

As anthropological archaeologists (or archaeological anthropologists) began to study the evolution of ancient states as a general problem, they increasingly needed to incorporate the obviously relevant findings about Harappan, Chinese, and other early states of the Old World beyond the familiar examples of Mesopotamia and Egypt. Arguably inspired by this work on early states, archaeologists began to investigate later states in Asia, too (see Trautmann and Sinopoli, chapter 6, this vol.).

Figures of transcending importance opened the historical traditions of Asian archaeology to new perspectives, both in comparative analysis and in historical perspectives. For Chinese archaeology, K.-C. Chang, who taught at Yale and then Harvard, brought Chinese archaeology, both in the prehistoric periods and in ancient states, to the attention of non-Chinese-speaking archaeologists (e.g., 1980). He also trained many archaeologists in the West, including Chinese archaeologists, and had an enormous influence in China itself. As the study of Shang dynasty oracle bones progressed, Chang and his students took on board the new decipherments. Historians of China became aware of the contributions of archaeology to the understanding of the Shang and its predecessors, which were tendentiously characterized as "dynasties" by historians of the Han dynasty. More recently, archaeologists have studied Zhou and later states in China (Li, chapter 7, this vol.).

No anthropological scholars like Adams or Chang existed for farther reaches of East and Southeast Asian archaeology, however, and the hold of archaeological historians who wrote highly particularistic studies was strong. Nevertheless, traditions for research in art and architectural history in Southeast Asia are now leading to interest in historical archaeology in the region (Lape, chapter 8, and Stark, chapter 9, both in this vol.).

In South Asia, both British and Indian archaeologists pioneered work at the cities of Mohenjo-Daro and Harappa, so a certain interest in the earliest states of South Asia entered the literature of the evolution of ancient states and civilizations (Possehl 2002, 1999). Again, in recent years, much archaeological work has also been done on early historic states of the Maurya-Gupta period and the medieval period of South Asia (Trautmann and Sinopoli, chapter 6, this vol.). Such studies have taken on urgency as claims and counterclaims of the antiquity of Hindu culture rage in the subcontinent, and archaeologists have become entangled in modern controversies whether they like it or not. Those doing historical archaeology can hardly evade the politics of how the past is used in the present.

For the study of ancient Egypt, only a few archaeologists have been trained in anthropological method and theory, although the number is growing (Lustig 1997). The works of Bruce Trigger (1983) and Barry Kemp (1989) are notable, and David O'Connor (e.g., 1990) and his students are active contributors to anthropological conferences and journals. Egyptian archaeologists such as Kathryn Bard (1994) and Janet Richards (2005) have applied prehistoric archaeological methods to their investigations of mortuary remains and social stratification. There is, of course, no dearth of archaeological studies of ancient Egypt in the dynastic periods, and Egyptological archaeologists, mainly embedded in area studies departments and museums, tend to communicate more broadly with their historian colleagues.

For the study of ancient Israel and the Islamic Middle East, the influence of anthropological archaeologists has been slower. This is not because archaeologists of "region X" (Israel, Palestine, southern Levant, Syro-Palestine) are not concerned with history, but because they often seem preoccupied with how the historicity of the biblical text affects matters of faith. Although the issue of how religious truth claims might or might not be accommodated with secular analysis is far from trivial, proving the Bible true (or false) is not a question that anthropological archaeologists have found appealing (e.g., Vaughn and Killebrew 2003; Finkelstein 2005; see chapter 3, this vol.). Let one extended example suffice.

In the Hebrew Bible, the polity of Edom is described in various sources as a mighty state, usually the enemy of Israel and Judah. Edom lay just east of the Wadi Arabah, southeast of the Dead Sea (figure 1.1), in the area later known as Nabataea, whose most famous city was Petra. According to the Hebrew Bible, at the time after the Exodus, the king

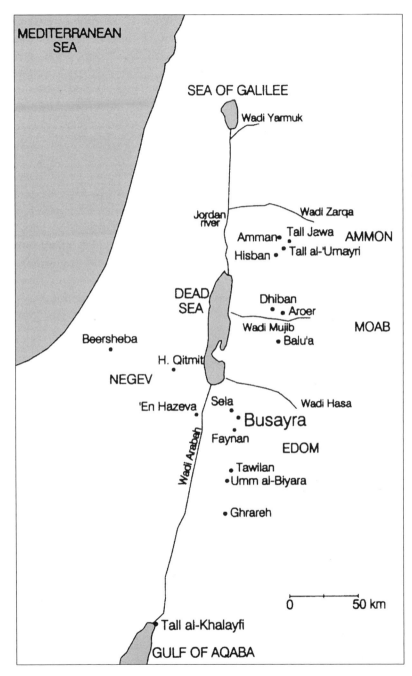

Figure 1.1 Map of the southern Levant during the Iron Age (Bienkowski 2002, fig. 1.1)

of Edom gathered his citizens to fight the Israelites. In subsequent centuries, the Edomites continued to battle with David and Solomon. The time of these relations was ostensibly the twelfth through tenth centuries BC.

Recently, archaeologists have investigated intensively the area of the Wadi Arabah, the homeland of Edom (Crowell 2004). The area was settled in the late second millennium and the early first millennium BC near copper resources that were then exploited throughout the Iron Age.[1] This region was the focus of early settlement in Edom during the eleventh through the ninth centuries BC. In the eighth century BC, in the climate of Assyrian expansion into the area and especially the increased amount of trade that flowed though the area, a few towns appeared in the highlands to the east of the Arabah. The largest of these small settlements was Busayra, which had an area of 8.16 hectares (Bienkowski 2002). Within the walls of Busayra was a structure one might call a modest "palace" (figure 1.2) and a nearby temple. Such leadership as may have existed was presumably based in the traditional kinship hierarchy.

Edom was a formidable neighbor of ancient Israel and Judah only because they were themselves minor kingdoms, working out their own destiny in the world of much larger powers, especially Egypt and Assyria (and later Babylonia). Enemies were naturally mighty instruments of the god of Israel, who alternately punished Israel when it was unfaithful to the word of the Lord and were the objects of Israel's military successes when Israel was an obedient servant of the Lord (Na'aman 1995; Mullen 1992; Machinist 1976). Historians of biblical times must incorporate archaeological evidence, and archaeologists need to frame their research of historical periods with knowledge of the biases of the textual representations of the time.

For the Islamic Middle East, there is simply little tradition of archaeological research outside the art history tradition (Whitcomb 2004). Anthropological archaeologists investigate the region mostly for evidence of early villages and for the evolution of early states; for Classical archaeologists, the Hellenistic period has been of great interest. The succeeding dynasties of Parthians and Sasanians, then the early Islamic periods, have been mainly the province of historians, with only a few archaeologists working in these historical times. This is certainly unfair, since there is a great deal of interesting historical archaeology to be done. For example, Robert Adams (1981) demonstrated that salinization in Mesopotamia did not present a grave problem until the mid-first millennium AD. This was the time when strong, centralized states began

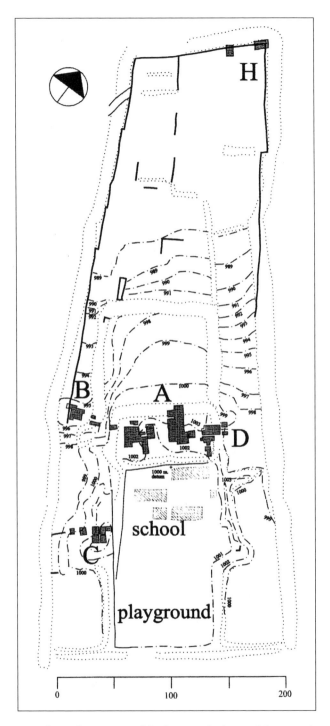

Figure 1.2 Plan of Busayra, with the temple located in area A and the palace in area C (Bienkowski 2002, fig. 1.2)

unprecedented irrigation schemes in the lower Tigris-Euphrates River valley, abandoned long-observed practices of fallow, and ruined the landscape. The ancient states of Mesopotamia were simply not powerful enough to build such great irrigation systems and did not attempt to ignore local knowledge of how to cultivate large surpluses of grain in Mesopotamia.

As Johns notes (chapter 5, this vol.), historical archaeology in the Islamic Middle East can profitably investigate the rise of traditions, the coalescence of communities around languages and beliefs, and the extensions of these communities and belief systems on a very large scale.

We cite one other work to end this brief overview of the history of relations between archaeologists and historians who study Asian history, and that is Eric Wolf's *Europe and the People Without History* (1982). The powerful message of this book to both archaeologists and historians is that the lives of certain people in literate society were either not recorded by them or were recorded by those who wished to depict them in certain ways. Of course, this message was nothing new to archaeologists of the modern world, who study the material culture of colonialism in the States (or "postmedieval archaeology" in the United Kingdom). These archaeologists routinely document the lives of Chinese railway workers, African traditions on plantations, and the small things, forgotten (Deetz 1966), that allow new interpretations of American lives and deeds.

Whereas ancient historians (like Hollywood producers) had once tended to think of archaeologists as obsessed with the golden objects of ancient elites, archaeologists had willfully regarded ancient historians as interested only in the archives of the ruling or elite classes. Although these views — never more than caricatures — now seem to be curiosities in the history of scholarship, it is still rare to find instances of integrated research using both archaeological and historical data. As we argue in this introduction, it is ironically the turn toward anthropology by archaeologists of Asian states that has advanced the practice of historical archaeology.

An analogous situation exists in historical studies of Asia in which social and economic inquiries based on archival research provide new opportunities for historical archaeologists. For example, the *Journal of the Economic and Social History of the Orient* (*JESHO*) was created in the late 1950s, under the influence of the *Annales* school of historians, to explore dimensions of history outside literary narratives, the lives of great men, and politics. Social and economic history for *JESHO* includes, among other things, studies of the distinctiveness of rural life, the economy outside palaces and temples, and social hierarchies beneath the veneer of literary descriptions of court life and those quite apart from any courts. *JESHO* has also, intermittently, explored the nonwritten evidence from the past since archaeologists in the field, no less than historians immersed in archives, study the organization of settlements, domestic conditions, craft production, trade and technology, and modes of consumption. Indeed, historical archaeologists of all species claim that important aspects of social life seldom find their way into any text, and these aspects of social and economic history have been and continue to be relevant to *JESHO*'s readership, which is mainly historians.

Although history and archaeology have the same object, namely the elucidation of the past, historians of Asia have been slow in appreciating the extent to which modern archaeologists have worked in periods in which there are texts. Indeed, historians have sometimes characterized historical archaeology as an expensive way to illustrate what is already known from texts, and a skeptical historian once commented that one word is worth a thousand pictures. In order to show, by means of case studies, how modern archaeologists have been investigating historical social and economic organizations, *JESHO* commissioned seven essays to explore the relations between history and archaeology in the study of premodern Asia.

These essays consider "biases" in both historical and archaeological data that may occasion rival claims to knowledge by archaeologists and historians. To the seven essays originally published in three issues of *JESHO* (vol. 45, issue 4 [2002]; vol. 46, issues 1 and 4 [2003]), and which have been revised and better illustrated for this volume, we have added two essays of commentary. One, by Miriam Stark, who works in both island and mainland Southeast Asia, mainly considers the chapters on eastern Asia, whereas the other, by Philip Kohl, who investigates societies in the Middle East and Central Asia, focuses on the chapters on western Asia, although both commentaries include discussions on all chapters in this volume. Bringing together the essays that appeared over several issues and also including commentaries on them allows readers to appreciate the considerable work and new directions of research on premodern Asia.

The conclusion is clear: Historians of premodern Asia (and elsewhere) cannot ignore the findings of archaeology. It is a matter of discussion and debate, however, how modern training in the disciplines of history and archaeology can incorporate methods and data from the other field. Disciplinary walls must be lowered, and teams of experts need to form to advance the knowledge of the history of Asia (and naturally other areas of the planet, too) from the earliest documented periods until today. The chapters in this volume present demonstrations of how research has been and must continue to be structured, how disciplinary limitations can be transcended through collaborative work, and how "Asia," which is both a natural and an artificial category, can serve as a model for historical archaeology elsewhere.

Notes

We thank Alexander Joffe for suggestions that have improved this introduction.

1. Thomas E. Levy and his team have recently surveyed this area and excavated several key sites (Levy et al. 2003, 2004). Radiocarbon dates show that settlement began at Khirbat an-Nahas in the eleventh century BC, and a fortress was built at the site in the tenth century BC.

Bibliography

Adams, Robert McC. 1966. *The Evolution of Urban Society: Early Mesopotamia and Prehispanic Mexico*. Chicago: Aldine.

———. 1981. *Heartland of Cities: Surveys of Ancient Settlement and Land Use on the Central Floodplain of the Euphrates*. Chicago: University of Chicago Press.

Bard, Kathryn. 1994. *From Farmers to Pharaohs: Mortuary Evidence for the Rise of Complex Society in Egypt*. Sheffield, UK: Sheffield Academic Press.

Bienkowski, Piotr. 2002. *Busayra Excavations by Crystal M. Bennet 1971–1980*. British Academy Monographs in Archaeology 13. Oxford: Oxford University Press.

Chang, Kwang-chi. 1980. *Shang Civilization*. New Haven, Conn.: Yale University Press.

Childe, V. Gordon. 1950. "The Urban Revolution." *Town Planning Review* 21:3–17.

Clark, Grahame. 1961. *World Prehistory, an Outline*. Cambridge: Cambridge University Press.

Crowell, Bradley L. 2004. "On the Margins of History: Social Change and Political Development in Iron Age Edom." PhD diss., University of Michigan, Ann Arbor.

Deetz, James. 1966. *In Small Things Forgotten: The Archaeology of Early American Life*. New York: Anchor Press/Doubleday.

Finkelstein, Israel. 2005. "Archaeology, Bible, and the History of the Levant in the Iron Age." In *Archaeologies of the Middle East: Critical Perspectives*, ed. S. Pollock and R. Bernbeck, 207–22. Oxford: Blackwell.

Kemp, Barry. 1989. *Egypt: The Anatomy of a Civilization*. London: Routledge.

Levy, Thomas E., Russell B. Adams, James D. Anderson, Mohammad Najjar, Neil

Smith, Yoav Arbel, Lisa Soderbaum, and Adolfo Muniz. 2003. "An Iron Age Landscape in the Edomite Lowlands: Archaeological Surveys along the Wadi al-Ghuwayb and Wadi al-Jariya, Jabal Hamrat Fidan, Jordan, 2002." *Annual of the Department of Antiquities of Jordan* 47:247–77.

Levy, Thomas E., Russell B. Adams, Mohammad Najjar, Andreas Hauptmann, James D. Anderson, Baruch Brandl, Mark A. Robinson, and Thomas Higham. 2004. "Reassessing the Chronology of Biblical Edom: New Excavations and 14 C Dates from Khirbat en-Nahas (Jordan)." *Antiquity* 78:865–79.

Lustig, Judith, ed. 1997. *Anthropology and Egyptology: A Developing Dialogue.* Sheffield, UK: Sheffield University Press.

Machinist, Peter. 1976. "Literature as Politics: The Tukulti-Ninurta Epic and the Bible." *The Catholic Biblical Quarterly* 38:455–82.

Mullen, E. T. 1992. "Crime and Punishment: The Sins of the King and the Despoliation of the Treasuries." *The Catholic Biblical Quarterly* 54:231–48.

Murra, John. 1980. *The Economic Organization of the Inka State.* Greenwich, Conn.: JAI Press.

Na'aman, Nadav. 1995. "The Deuteronomist and Voluntary Servitude to Foreign Powers." *Journal for the Study of the Old Testament* 65:37–53.

O'Connor, David. 1990. *Ancient Egyptian Society.* Pittsburgh: Carnegie Mellon University Press.

Orser, Charles. 1996. *A Historical Archaeology of the Modern World.* New York: Plenum.

———, ed. 2002. *Encyclopedia of Historical Archaeology.* London: Routledge.

Possehl, Gregory. 1999. *The Indus Age: The Beginnings.* Philadelphia: University of Pennsylvania Press.

———. 2002. *The Indus Civilization: A Contemporary Perspective.* Walnut Creek, Calif.: Altamira Press.

Richards, Janet. 2005. *Society and Death in Ancient Egypt: Mortuary Landscapes of the Middle Kingdom.* Cambridge: Cambridge University Press.

Rowe, John. 1946. "Inca Culture at the Time of the Spanish Conquest." In *Handbook of South American Indians,* vol. 2, ed. J. Steward, 198–410. Washington, D.C.: Smithsonian Institution.

Sherratt, Andrew, ed. 1980. *The Cambridge Encyclopedia of Archaeology.* Cambridge: Cambridge University Press.

Trigger, Bruce, ed. 1983. *Ancient Egypt: A Social History.* Cambridge: Cambridge University Press.

Vaughn, Andrew, and Ann Killebrew, eds. 2003. *Jerusalem in Bible and Archaeology: The First Temple Period.* Atlanta: Society for Biblical Literature.

Whitcomb, Donald, ed. 2004. *Changing Social Identity with the Spread of Islam:*

Archaeological Perspectives. Oriental Institute Seminars, no. 1. Chicago: Oriental Institute, University of Chicago.

Wolf, Eric. 1982. *Europe and the People Without History*. Berkeley: University of California Press.

Yoffee, Norman. 1997. "Robert McCormick Adams: An Archaeological Biography." *American Antiquity* 62:1–15.

2

Berenike Crossroads
The Integration of Information

WILLEMINA Z. WENDRICH, ROGER S. BAGNALL,

RENÉ T. J. CAPPERS, JAMES A. HARRELL,

STEVEN E. SIDEBOTHAM, AND ROBERTA S. TOMBER

The dichotomy of history and prehistory suggests that historical information by definition is "textual information." The insight that more often than not texts give biased and incomplete information is now generally accepted, and it seems that a more balanced historiography is in place, in which textual and archaeological evidence are used to balance the representation of past periods. Textual evidence in the form of inscriptions, ostraka, papyri, and graffiti is, however, also archaeological evidence and should be studied using the same methods as other archaeological finds. The taphonomic processes (depositional and postdepositional) result in an often erratic survival. The textual materials we find in excavations are the result not only of deliberate decisions in antiquity on what to write down, what to save, and what to discard, but also of later human intervention and of natural processes of decay. These processes provide an unpredictable selection, which often results in the ironic situation that what was discarded in antiquity is what survives today. Primary textual finds thus are an integral part of the archaeological record, in contrast to what perhaps could be called secondary textual finds: texts that have survived in copy, as part of textual corpora of much later dates than the originals. These mostly literary, historical, or geographic texts served a specific purpose that might have changed over time from invaluable source of practical information to canonical textual corpus and finally to important historical source. Both primary and secondary textual sources are considered here in relation to our ongoing effort to understand life and work in the Greco-Roman harbor town of Berenike.

The Study of Berenike's Role in the Long-Distance Trade

Berenike was one of the Egyptian Red Sea emporia in the long-distance trade among the Mediterranean, Arabia, Africa south of the Sahara, and the Indian Ocean basin (see figure 2.1). The existence of a harbor by the name of Berenike was known from Classical texts such as Pliny the Elder's late first-century AD *Natural History* (hereafter cited as NH; Ball 1950; Pliny the Elder 1952, 1962). Additional sources include Agatharchides' second-century BC *On the Erythraean Sea* (hereafter OES; Agatharchides 1989; Huntingford 1980); Diodoros Siculus' first-century BC *Library of History* (hereafter LH; Murphy 1989; Siculus 1961); Julius Solinus' early third-century AD *Collection of Memorabilia* (hereafter CM; Solinus 1895); Strabo's late first-century BC or early first-century AD *Geography of Strabo* (hereafter G or *Geography*; Strabo 1959, 1961, 1966); archives found elsewhere in Egypt, such as the Nikanor archive (hereafter NA; Fuks 1951; Meredith 1956); and an anonymous first-century AD merchant's handbook, the *Periplus of the Erythraean Sea* (hereafter *Periplus* or PME [*Periplus Maris Erythraei*]; Casson 1989; Huntingford 1980; Schoff 1912; see also *On Stones* [OS], Theophrastus 1956). These sources describe the character of the harbor and the goods transferred there from ship to desert caravan and vice versa.

Excavations from 1994 to 2001 have shown that the harbor town of Berenike existed for eight centuries, from the third century BC to the early sixth century AD (Sidebotham and Wendrich 1995, 1996, 1998, 1999, 2000, in press). The Berenike excavation team has a strongly international and multidisciplinary character. Because Egypt does not allow archaeological finds to leave the country, all project staff travel to the site and work in the laboratories at Berenike. This enables an interaction of specialists that, in theory, should lead to integrated results of the research. In practice, however, the pressure of work does not always allow for a leisurely comparison of results, and staff are not all on site at the same time. This chapter is, therefore, a good opportunity to explore the methodological angle, using a selection of the specialized information in discussing interpretations and deciding the central issues of the past excavation and study seasons in light of the original research questions and the subsequent excavation results. We would like to stress that this chapter draws upon the results of all expedition members and that others, not listed as coauthors, have also made extremely important contributions to the database from which this chapter draws.

For our present exposition, we choose to concentrate on a specific

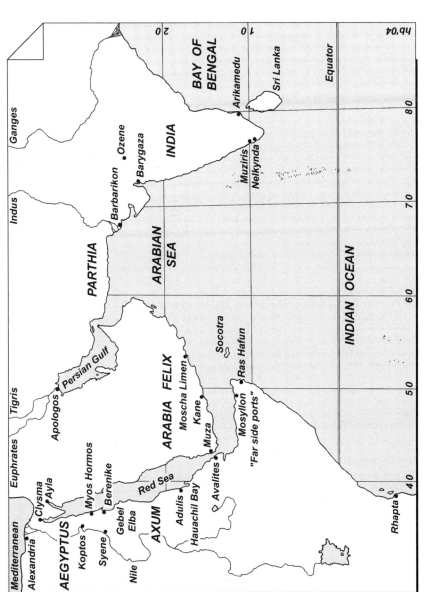

Figure 2.1 Map of the Indian Ocean basin

period and subject matter: the provenance and destination of trade commodities in the first and second centuries AD (the early Roman period). For this period, in contrast with both earlier and later layers, we have a wealth of archaeological and textual evidence. Although it has been shown that Berenike was active in the Ptolemaic period, the evidence of habitation and trade is scant (Sidebotham and Wendrich 2000). The Ptolemaic remains were robbed extensively in the later periods of occupation. During the third century AD, there is evidence for a decrease in activity in the town. The early fourth century AD was a period of expansion, during which the eastern part of the town was rebuilt and extended following the gradually receding shoreline. The general historical sources for the late Roman period, however, are not as abundant as those of the first and second centuries AD, and, therefore, the late Roman evidence from Berenike, albeit ample, is less suitable for a comparison between archaeological and historical evidence. The organic remains in the late Roman trash dumps yield important information on trade contacts in the fourth and fifth centuries AD but show a dearth of textual evidence from Berenike itself. Why the quantity of textual records in the early Roman period differs remarkably from that in the late Roman contexts is a matter of debate. Should we presume that in the fourth century, textual records were deemed less important than in the first century AD? That seems too simple a conclusion. The first-century AD trash dumps that yielded most textual evidence were located in a separate sector, away from the town itself, while the late Roman trash was excavated in residential areas, on empty plots of land, along the outside wall of a shrine and even in abandoned houses. Thus the trash deposits in the two periods indicate very different patterns of discard. The late Roman period trash dumps are very near to the areas where the refuse was produced. We probably just have not found the relevant fourth-century offices and their adjacent dumps.

The early Roman textual material has been partly published (Bagnall, Helms, and Verhoogt 2000, 2005); the tables in this chapter use the unpublished material also. Most ostraka and papyri were found in the first- and second-century AD trash dumps northwest of the main part of town. The collection comprises letters and contracts (ostraka and papyri) and a customs archive (ostraka). Together they give some insight into the organization of the trade and the movement of people and goods, as well as the mode of living in Berenike. Additional historical sources are the ostraka found in the way stations along the route from Berenike to the end of the desert route in Koptos in the Nile Valley; archives found in Koptos, such as the Nikanor archive (Fuks 1951; Meredith 1956); and the well-known literary, historical, and geographic sources mentioned at the beginning of this section.

Commodities and Containers

Berenike was a desert town on a windswept seashore, an arid coastal emporium with hardly any local food production and a lack of local raw materials. Apart from a small number of animals that could survive on the desert vegetation (sheep, goats, and camels) in an area with a limited carrying capacity, local foodstuffs would have been limited to plants such as garlic, beans, and salad greens, which could be grown in small garden plots, moistened with wastewater (Cappers 2002, 51–53). Most food (for instance, grain), water, and raw materials had to be brought in. Therefore, the goods transported by caravan from the Nile Valley to Berenike, a trip that took twelve days along a well-established route with way stations at regular intervals, were not entirely shipments for long-distance trade. A considerable part of the commodities was destined to be consumed at Berenike. Other goods passing through the Eastern Desert to Berenike were transported to provision ships as well as to Roman communities abroad. To a lesser extent, goods that came to Berenike by ship might have contained support products for a local non-Romanized population, for instance, rice to provide ships' crews with their preferred staple while waiting in port.

Water was brought in from a number of fortified wells at a distance of approximately eight kilometers from the town. Just as the caravans that traveled through the Eastern Desert brought not only goods for export but also supplies for the ships and the local inhabitants of Berenike, the water transports, probably on donkey or camel back, provided the drinking water both for the town's consumption and for provisioning the ships in sufficient quantities to allow them to reach the next place along the Red Sea shore where water could be taken in.

Trade passed through Berenike in two directions: from the Mediterranean and Egypt, goods were transferred onto Nile ships, taken by boat up the Nile to Koptos, loaded on camels, and walked through the Eastern Desert to the harbor, to be transferred there from caravan to seagoing vessel. The ships awaiting the goods would have just unloaded their commodities from India, Arabia, and Africa to be taken back to Koptos, Alexandria, and many other places in the Roman Empire. Most of this activity took place in summer months, the ships arriving with the monsoon wind from the east and up the Red Sea in early summer, while ships heading out across the Indian Ocean had to leave in late summer (PME 39, 49, 56). At a transfer harbor a certain percentage of goods are lost, partly through accidents with loading, partly because even in well-controlled circumstances, the local population seems to get access to some of the commodities, legally or otherwise. Our evidence of the extent of trade goods' availability to the local population of Berenike consists of mentions of goods in documents, of containers (wine, oil, or fish sauce amphorae), and of remains of the goods themselves. Some of these goods were apparently available in such quantities that they ended up in the trash dumps. The archaeological finds from the higher parts of Berenike show surprisingly good preservation of organic materials (Wendrich 1998). Thus, the area of the early Roman trash dump, which is located west of the town's center and at a considerable height above groundwater level, has yielded an abundance of organic evidence that includes seeds, textiles, basketry, matting, cordage, leather, animal bones, and papyri. Apart from these perishable articles are also commodities of a much more permanent character. Gems were an important commodity, and they do survive in the archaeological record. A wide variety of precious and semiprecious stones have been found in early Roman contexts in Berenike.

In this section, we make an inventory of the commodities we would expect to find in Berenike, based upon textual evidence and on the full corpus of recovered artifacts. In the discussion, we will try to explain why certain goods do not occur in the archaeological record, while others have been found in abundance but are not mentioned as a trade commodity. This enables us to define the perspective from which the texts were written, and thus gives insight into the possible biases of our textual sources. To balance the information, we look at perishable and nonperishable materials, products for local use, and trade goods.

Tables 2.1 through 2.3 inventory a selection of goods found in first- and second-century AD contexts. A summary of the archaeological context is given, and the historical context is indicated (type of source), as well as the information we have on the provenance and destination of the goods. The latter information is mainly based on textual evidence, since we do not have comparable archaeological data for the distribution of the goods around the Red Sea and in the Indian Ocean basin for all categories. Table 2.1 deals with a nonperishable good par excellence: stone. The distinction between stone for local use and as a trade good follows roughly the distinction between building stones and gemstones,

Table 2.1 Evidence for stones found in early Roman (first and second centuries AD) contexts in Berenike or in contemporary textual sources, in the order of their occurrence in the text.

Commodity: stones	Berenike finds	Textual source	Provenance (harbor)	Destination
Marble	Yes	No	Turkey (Proconnesus)	Berenike?
Rock anhydrite	Yes	No	Eastern Desert	Berenike
Rock gypsum	Yes	No	Eastern Desert	Berenike
Coral heads	Yes	No	Berenike	Berenike
Peridot	Yes	Agatharchides (OES), Diodorus (LH), *Periplus* (PME), Pliny (NH), Strabo (G)	Red Sea (Berenike)	India (Barbarikon, Barygaza, Muziris, Nelkynda)
Realgar	Yes	*Periplus* (PME), Pliny (NH)	Eastern Desert (Berenike)	India (Barygaza, Muziris, Nelkynda)
Orpiment	No	*Periplus* (PME), Pliny (NH), Theophrastus (OS)	Eastern Desert	India (Muziris, Nelkynda)
Stibnite	No	*Periplus* (PME), Pliny (NH)	Eastern Desert	India (Barygaza, Muziris, Nelkynda)
Amethyst quartz	Yes	*Periplus* (PME), "stones"	Eastern Desert (Berenike)	Africa (Mosyllon)
Green beryl (emerald)	Yes	*Periplus* (PME), "stones"; Pliny (NH); Strabo (G)	Eastern Desert (Berenike)	Africa (Mosyllon)

Table 2.1 Continued

Commodity: stones	Berenike finds	Textual source	Provenance (harbor)	Destination
Alabaster gypsum ("true" alabaster)	No	Diodorus (LH)	South Arabia	Egypt or Mediterranean
Obsidian	Yes	Periplus (PME), Pliny (NH)	Ethiopia/Eritrea	Egypt or Mediterranean
Turquoise	No	Periplus (PME), Pliny (NH)	Sinai/NE Iran (Barbarikon)	Egypt or Mediterranean
Lapis lazuli	Yes	Periplus (PME), Pliny (NH)	NE Afghanistan (Barbarikon)	Egypt or Mediterranean
Chalcedonic quartz: banded agate, onyx, and sardonyx (cameo blanks)	Yes	Periplus (PME), Pliny (NH)	India (Barygaza)	Egypt or Mediterranean
Fluorite and/or chalcedonic quartz: agate, carnelian, or sard	Yes (quartz only)	Periplus (PME), Pliny (NH)	Iran or India (Barygaza)	Egypt or Mediterranean
Diamond, or colorless corundum	No	Periplus (PME), Pliny (NH), Theophrastus (OS)	India [diamond] or Sri Lanka [corundum] (Muziris, Nelkynḍa)	Egypt or Mediterranean

Gemstone		Source	Origin	Origin
Blue corundum (sapphire)	Yes	*Periplus* (PME), Pliny (NH), Solinus (CM)	India or Sri Lanka (Muziris, Nelkynda)	Egypt or Mediterranean
Red corundum (ruby)	No	*Periplus* (PME), "transparent gemstones of all kinds"	India or Sri Lanka (Muziris, Nelkynda)	Egypt or Mediterranean
Amethyst quartz	Yes	*Periplus* (PME), "transparent gemstones of all kinds"	India or Sri Lanka (Muziris, Nelkynda)	Egypt or Mediterranean
Citrine quartz	No	*Periplus* (PME), "transparent gemstones of all kinds"	India or Sri Lanka (Muziris, Nelkynda)	Egypt or Mediterranean
Colorless quartz	Yes	*Periplus* (PME), "transparent gemstones of all kinds"	India or Sri Lanka (Muziris, Nelkynda)	Egypt or Mediterranean
Chrysoberyl	No	*Periplus* (PME), "transparent gemstones of all kinds"	India or Sri Lanka (Muziris, Nelkynda)	Egypt or Mediterranean
Aquamarine beryl	Yes	*Periplus* (PME), "transparent gemstones of all kinds"	India or Sri Lanka (Muziris, Nelkynda)	Egypt or Mediterranean
Almandine garnet	Yes	*Periplus* (PME), "transparent gemstones of all kinds"	India or Sri Lanka (Muziris, Nelkynda)	Egypt or Mediterranean
Zircon	No	*Periplus* (PME), "transparent gemstones of all kinds"	India or Sri Lanka (Muziris, Nelkynda)	Egypt or Mediterranean
Tourmaline	No	*Periplus* (PME), "transparent gemstones of all kinds"	India or Sri Lanka (Muziris, Nelkynda)	Egypt or Mediterranean

although there are some exceptions, as we will show. Table 2.2 lists botanical commodities. Table 2.3 lists wine, oil, and fish products, based on ceramic evidence. This selection excludes a large number of goods, such as glass, beads, metal, textiles, and animal products (e.g., ivory, leopard skins, turtle shell, coral, pearls, and, of course, fish, meat, and lard as well as escargots that were imported for local consumption in Berenike).

The three categories presented in tables 2.1 through 2.3 have been selected because they give a good overview of the different types of evidence as well as the variation in sources and destinations. Gemstones are nonperishable, and their transportation is based solely on their value as trade goods. The botanical evidence is more complicated, because shipments of, for instance, wheat may have any of four functions: provisions for the population of Berenike, provisions for ships and their crews, shipments of food for the Roman traders in Africa and India, and trade commodity. Apart from this, the fact that botanical materials are perishable means that the amounts found at Berenike do not reflect the quantities that were once deposited. Archaeological evidence for spices and incense is equally dependent on the preservational circumstances for organic materials, but the rationale behind the shipment of these goods is less equivocal than for that of staple foods. The shipments of wine and oil, as outlined in table 2.3, are based upon a third body of evidence, the remains of amphorae.

Egyptian Stone Products for Local Use and Export

The Egyptian Eastern Desert was an important source for both decorative building stones and gemstones. In the early Roman period, the quarries of Mons Porphyrites and Mons Claudianus produced columns, fountain basins, and revetments that were exported to other parts of the Roman Empire. The only decorative building stone found in Berenike, however, was Proconnesian marble from the Sea of Marmara in northwestern Turkey (Harrell 1996, 111; 1998, table 4.13). The marble is not mentioned in the ancient sources concerning Berenike and was probably transported to Berenike in small quantities to decorate some of the temples and official buildings in the harbor town, rather than for export. Most of Berenike was built of coral heads collected from the nearby semifossilized reefs. Rock gypsum and the closely related rock anhydrite were also used at Berenike for ashlar blocks and other architectural elements. These materials were locally available on the peninsula just north of Berenike, Ras Benas, which shelters the harbor from the prevailing northern winds (Harrell 1996, 106–7).

Table 2.2 Evidence for botanical commodities found in early Roman (first and second centuries AD) contexts in Berenike or in contemporary textual sources.

Commodity: botanical goods	Berenike finds	Textual source	Transport	Provenance	Destination
Cereals					
Hard wheat and bread wheat (*Triticum turgidum* subsp. *durum*; *Triticum aestivum*)	Desiccated and carbonized grains	*Periplus* (PME); Nikanor (NA); O. Berenike	In bulk	Nile Valley	Berenike and India
Hulled six-row barley (*Hordeum vulgare* subsp. *vulgare*)	Desiccated and carbonized grains	*Periplus* (PME); Nikanor (NA); O. Berenike	In bulk	Nile Valley	Berenike
Rice (*Oryza sativa*)	Desiccated grains	*Periplus* (PME), not considered a grain	Small numbers	India	*Periplus*: East African ports; Roman Empire
Job's tears (*Coix lacryma-jobi*)	Desiccated fruits	No textual sources	Small numbers	India	Roman Empire
Pulses					
White lupine (*Lupinus albus*)	Desiccated seeds	No textual sources	Reasonable numbers	Nile Valley	Berenike

Table 2.2 Continued

Commodity: botanical goods	Berenike finds	Textual source	Transport	Provenance	Destination
Grass pea (*Lathyrus sativus*)	Desiccated seeds	No textual sources	Small numbers	Nile Valley	Berenike
Lentil (*Lens culinaris*)	Desiccated seeds	No textual sources	In bulk	Nile Valley	Berenike
Bitter vetch (*Vicia ervilia*)	Desiccated seeds	Nikanor (NA)	Small numbers	Nile Valley	Berenike
Faba bean (*Vicia faba*)	Desiccated seeds	No textual sources	Small numbers	Nile Valley	Berenike
Mung bean (*Vigna radiata*)	Desiccated seeds	No textual sources	Small numbers	India	Berenike or Roman Empire
Vegetables and Oil Plants					
Beet (*Beta vulgaris*)	Desiccated receptacle clusters	O. Berenike	Reasonable numbers	Nile Valley and Berenike	Berenike
Garlic (*Allium sativum*)	Desiccated bulbs and bulbel bases	No textual source	Reasonable numbers	Nile Valley and Berenike	Berenike
Caper bush (*Capparis spinosa*)	Desiccated seeds	No textual sources	Reasonable numbers	Local production	Local use

Species				Local production	Local use
Colocinth (*Citrullus colocinthus*)	Desiccated seeds	No textual sources	Reasonable numbers	Nile Valley	Berenike and export?
Watermelon (*Citrullus lanatus*)	Desiccated seeds	No textual sources	Reasonable numbers	Nile Valley	Berenike
Bottle gourd (*Lagenaria siceraria*)	Desiccated seeds	No textual sources	Reasonable numbers	Nile Valley and Berenike	Berenike
Cabbage (*Brassica* spp.)	No archaeological evidence	O. Berenike	Pickled?	Nile Valley	Berenike?
Dill (*Anethum graveolens*)	No archaeological evidence	Nikanor (NA)	Unknown	Nile Valley	Berenike?
Parsley (*Petroselinum crispum*)	No archaeological evidence	O. Berenike	Unknown	Nile Valley	Berenike?
Safflower (*Carthamus tinctorius*)	Desiccated fruits	No textual sources	Reasonable numbers	Nile Valley	Berenike?
Sesame (*Sesamum indicum*)	Desiccated seeds	Nikanor (NA); *Periplus* (PME), sesame oil	In sacks, possibly limited supply	India	Egypt
Flax (*Linum usitatissimum*)	Desiccated seeds	No textual sources	Small numbers	Nile Valley	Berenike?

Table 2.2 Continued

Commodity: botanical goods	Berenike finds	Textual source	Transport	Provenance	Destination
			Fruits and Nuts		
Fig (*Ficus carica*)	Desiccated fruits	No textual sources	Fresh? Dried? Reasonable numbers	Nile Valley	Berenike?
Hazel (*Coryllus avellana*)	Desiccated fruits	No textual sources	Reasonable numbers	Mediterranean area	Berenike?
Almond (*Amygdalus communis*)	Desiccated fruit remains	No textual sources	Reasonable numbers	Mediterranean area	Berenike?
Stone pine (*Pinus pinea*)	Desiccated and charred seeds and cone fragments	No textual sources	In bulk	Mediterranean area	Berenike and export?
Peach (*Prunus persica*)	Desiccated fruit-stone	No textual sources	Single specimen	Mediterranean area	Berenike
Pomegranate (*Punica granatum*)	Desiccated seeds	No textual sources	Small numbers	Nile Valley	Berenike?
Apple (*Malus domestica*)	Desiccated seeds	No textual sources	Small numbers	Mediterranean area and Nile Valley	Berenike?
Nabq (*Ziziphus spina-christi*)	Desiccated fruit remains	No textual sources	Fresh in bulk	Eastern Desert	Berenike

	Archaeological remains	Textual sources	Quantity	Distribution area	Periplus
Olive (*Olea europaea*)	Desiccated and charred fruit stones	*Periplus* (PME), olive oil and possibly olives (translation unclear); Nikanor (NA)	In bulk	Fayum and Mediterranean area	*Periplus*: not mentioned
Grape (*Vitis vinifera*)	Desiccated seeds	*Periplus* (PME), possibly grapes (translation unclear); O. Berenike	Fresh, bunches of grapes	Nile Valley and Mediterranean area	Berenike and export?
Sugar date (*Balanites aegyptiaca*)	Desiccated fruit remains	No textual sources	In bulk	Eastern Desert	Berenike
Doam palm (*Hyphaene thebaica*)	Desiccated fruit remains	No textual sources	In bulk	Eastern Desert	Berenike
Egyptian plum (*Cordia myxa*)	Desiccated fruits and calyxes	No textual sources	Dried? Fresh? In bulk	Nile Valley and Mediterranean area	?
Cordia nevillii/ sinensis	Desiccated fruits	No textual sources	Small numbers	Gebel Elba and southern area	Berenike?
Date (*Phoenix dactylifera*)	Desiccated and charred seeds	*Periplus* (PME)	In bulk	Arabia and India	Arabia
Balsam tree (*Commiphora* cf. *gileadensis*)	Desiccated fruits and seeds	No textual sources	Small numbers	Gebel Elba and southern area	Berenike?

Table 2.2 Continued

Commodity: botanical goods	Berenike finds	Textual source	Transport	Provenance	Destination
Coconut (*Cocos nucifera*)	Fruit fragments (endo-, meso-, and exocarp)	*Vita Apollonii*, possibly first record	Complete fruits or fruits without fibers	India	Roman Empire
Carob tree (*Ceratonia siliqua*)	Desiccated seeds	No textual sources	Reasonable numbers	Uncertain	?
Senna (*Senna alexandrina/holoseri-cea*)	Desiccated fruits and seeds	No textual sources	Reasonable numbers	Eastern Desert	Berenike?
Cocculus pendulus	Desiccated fruits	No textual sources	Small numbers	Gebel Elba and southern area	Berenike?
Pickles	Stones of peaches	O. Berenike	Pickled fruit?	Nile Valley?	Berenike?
Spices and Condiments					
Spices (unspecified)	Several	*Periplus* (PME)	Dried	East African ports	Not specified
Fenugreek (*Trigonella foenum-graecum*)	Desiccated seeds	No textual sources	Reasonable numbers	Nile Valley and Berenike	Berenike?

Cumin (*Cuminum cyminum*)	Desiccated seeds	No textual sources	Reasonable numbers	Nile Valley and Berenike	Berenike?
Black pepper (*Piper nigrum*)	Abundant evidence in trash dump and as hoard	*Periplus* (PME) Alexandrian tariff: black and white pepper	In bulk	India (Muziris, Nelkynda)	Roman Empire
Long pepper (*Piper longum*)	No archaeological evidence	*Periplus* (PME)	Dried	India (Barygaza)	Roman Empire
Saffron (*Crocus sativus*)	No archaeological evidence	*Periplus* (PME)	Dried pistils	?	*Periplus*: Arabia
Coriander (*Coriandrum sativum*)	Desiccated fruits	No textual sources	Regular supply	Berenike	Berenike
Fennel (*Foeniculum vulgare*)	Desiccated fruits	No textual sources	Reasonable numbers	Nile Valley and Mediterranean area	Berenike
Abrus	Desiccated seeds	No textual sources	Reasonable numbers	East Africa?	Roman Empire?
Incense	Indirect evidence	O. Berenike?	Resin	Ethiopia or South Arabia	Berenike, Roman Empire

Table 2.3 Ceramic vessels for the transport of wine, oil, and fish products of early Roman date (first and second centuries AD) found in Berenike or in contemporary textual sources

Commodity	Berenike finds: ceramic vessel types	Vessel Name in textual sources	Provenance	Destinations listed in the *Periplus*
Wine	Dressel 2–4; Amphores Égyptiennes 4 (Empereur 1986, figs. 2–5); Class 10 (Peacock and Williams 1986)	No clear matching vessel name	Mareotis	Not mentioned
Wine	Dressel 2–4; Class 10 (Peacock and Williams 1986)	No clear matching vessel name	Campania (Naples)	Not mentioned
Wine	Dressel 2–4 (Williams 1994); Class 10 (Peacock and Williams 1986)	No clear matching vessel name	Northern Campania	Not mentioned
Wine	Gauloise 4 (Laubenheimer 1989); Class 27 (Peacock and Williams 1986)	No clear matching vessel name	Gaul (Gallia Narbonnensis)	Not mentioned
Wine	Dressel 2–4 (Tomber 1998); Class 10 (Peacock and Williams 1986)	Ladikena: ostraka, Berenike; Nikanor archive (NA); *Periplus* (PME)	Cilicia (Laodicea ad Mare)	Adulis (PME 6); Barygaza for Ozene (PME 49)
Wine	Dressel 2–4 (Tchernia and Zevi 1972); Class 10 (Peacock and Williams 1986)	No clear matching vessel name	Tarraconensis	Not mentioned
Wine	Early variant of Gaza vessel (Majcherek 1995, pl. 4), probably present but more typical of the late Roman period	No clear matching vessel name	Gaza	Not mentioned

Wine	Vessel not identified on site	Onisian: Nikanor archive (NA)	Near Crete	Not mentioned
Wine	Class 9 (Peacock and Williams 1986; Peacock 1977)	Rhodian: ostraka, Berenike	Rhodes	Not mentioned
Wine	No vessel type correlated to textual name	Italika: ostraka Berenike; *Periplus* (PME)	Italy	Adulis (PME 6); Barygaza for Ozene (PME 49)
Wine		*Periplus* (PME)	Unknown	Avalites (PME 7); Azanian ports (PME 17); Muza (PME 24/28); Kane (PME 28); Barbarikon for Minnagar (PME 39); Barygaza for Ozene (PME 49); Nelkkynda/Muziris for Bakare (PME 56)
Wine	No vessel type correlated to textual name	Aminaia: ostraka, Berenike; Nikanor archive (NA)	Unknown	Not mentioned
Wine? (Bagnall, Helms, and Verhoogt 2000, 20)	Late Roman Amphora 3 (Riley 1981); Class 45 (Peacock and Williams 1986); probably represented in the first century, but more typical of the mid-fourth and later	Ephesia: ostraka, Berenike	Ephesus region/Meander Valley	Not mentioned

Table 2.3 Continued

Commodity	Berenike finds: ceramic vessel types	Vessel Name in textual sources	Provenance	Destinations listed in the Periplus
Wine? (Bagnall, Helms, and Ver- hoogt 2000, 20)	No vessel type correlated to textual name	Kolophonia: ostraka, Berenike; Nikanor archive (NA)		Not mentioned
Oil	Dressel 20; Class 25 (Peacock and Williams 1986; Ponsich 1988)	No clear matching vessel name	Baetica	Not mentioned
Oil	Tripolitania I or I: (Panella 1973); Classes 36-37 (Peacock ard Williams 1986); sherds generally too fragmentary to attribute to a specific form	No clear matching vessel name	Tripolitania	Not mentioned
Oil	No vessel name given	Italika: Ostraka, Berenike		Not mentioned
Oil	No vessel type correlated to textual name	Ostraka, Berenike; Nikanor archive (NA); Periplus (PME)	Unknown	Adulis (PME 6)

Product	Amphora type	Documentary reference	Provenance	
Fish products, oil	Africana I "Piccolo" (Zevi and Tchernia 1969); Class 33 (Peacock and Williams 1986)		North Africa (Tunisia, Africa Proconsularis)	Not mentioned
Fish products	Eg Classes 17-18 (Peacock and Williams 1986); probably represented by body sherds (see also Ponsich 1988)	No clear matching vessel name	Cadiz	Not mentioned
Fish? (Bagnall, Helms, and Verhoogt 2000, 21)		Epimenia: ostraka, Berenike; Nikanor archive (NA)		Not mentioned
Wine (including vinegar), fish products	Egyptian early Roman, including Amphores Égyptiennes 3 (Empereur and Picon 1989, figs. 11–12)	Ostraka, Berenike; Nikanor archive (NA)	Egypt (Nile Valley and Mareotis)	Not mentioned
Unknown	(Ballet and Vichy 1992, fig. 11)	No clear matching vessel name	Aswan	Not mentioned

Exports from Berenike concentrated on gemstones, which were mostly shipped to Arabian and African harbors. The abundance of Indian gemstones effectively closed off the Far Eastern market, with the exception of three minerals and one type of gemstone. The latter is the *chrysolithon* of the *Periplus* (PME 39, 49, and 56) and was taken to Barbarikon, Barygaza, Muziris, and Nelkynda (Casson 1989, 74–85). Pliny says *chrysolithos* is "a bright golden transparent stone [that] comes to us from Ethiopia" (NH 37, 42.126), which, for the Romans, included the southern part of Egypt's Eastern Desert and its extension into present Sudan. The *Periplus'* chrysolithon can only be the warm yellowish green peridot (the gemstone variety of olivine) from Zabargad, or St. John's, Island, eighty kilometers southeast of Berenike (Ball 1950, 281–84; Casson 1989, 190, 260; Harrell 1999, 115–16). Zabargad Island was the only known source of peridot in the Classical world (Keller 1990, 119–27; Warmington 1974, 253) and, thus, would have been an important Egyptian export during Roman times. It is odd that the *Periplus* does not refer to this mineral by its common ancient name *topazo*.

Numerous ancient writers refer to Egyptian peridot. Strabo (G 16.4.6) describes the neighborhood of Berenike and mentions the existence of *topazia* quarries on the island of Ophiodes ("snaky") that produced a "transparent stone that sparkles with golden luster (*chrysoeides*)." Strabo's account basically paraphrases that of Agatharchides (OES 5.82), which was also the source of Diodorus' nearly identical account (LH 3.39). Pliny (NH 37.32.107–9) certainly knew the Egyptian topazo and, significantly, says that topazo "is the only precious stone that is affected by an iron file, whereas all others have to be smoothed with Naxian stone [i.e., emery, a granular variety of corundum]." With a Mohs hardness of 6.5–7, peridot is softer than most other gemstones. It is clear from the above descriptions of topazo that it would not be out of line for the author of the *Periplus* to call peridot *chrysolithon* ("golden-colored stone"). Several unworked pieces and one shaped cabochon of peridot have been found at Berenike.

At Berenike the team found a few small pieces of realgar, a red mineral (AsS), which was used for paint pigment and medicine (Theophrastus 1956, 171–72; Casson 1989, 208; Harrell 1999, 116–17; Schoff 1912, 191–92). Geologically, realgar commonly occurs in gold veins, and usually in close association with orpiment and stibnite. All three minerals were exported from the numerous Roman gold mines in the Eastern Desert to India. However, no evidence was found in Berenike for orpiment and stibnite.

In ancient sources realgar is referred to as *sandarache* (PME 49, 56), while orpiment (As_2S_3), which like realgar contains arsenic, is called *arsenichon* (PME 56), *arrhenicum* (NH 34.56.178), or *arrenikon* (OS 40, 51). Stibnite (Sb_2S_3) should perhaps be identified as the *stimi* of the *Periplus* (PME 49, 56). Even though Pliny's (NH 33.33.101) description of stimi (also *stibi*) is not a good fit to this mineral, it is still probably the material referred to by the *Periplus'* author (Casson 1989, 208–9; Harrell 1999, 117; Schoff 1912, 192–93). This identification is strengthened by stimi's close association with sandarache and arsenichon in the Eastern trade, and with the close geologic occurrence of stibnite, realgar, and orpiment. All three were believed to have medicinal properties. Realgar and stibnite were exported to Barygaza, Muziris, and Nelkynda (Casson 1989, 80–85), while orpiment was shipped to Muziris and Nelkynda only (Casson 1989, 84–85).

The *Periplus* mentions export from Egypt to the African harbor of Mosyllon of *lithia*, which is the itacistic writing of *litheia* (PME 10). The term literally means "gemstones" but Schoff (1912, 26) thinks it refers to glass. This latter translation is almost certainly wrong, because the author of the *Periplus* identifies glass as *hyelos* in a list of Egyptian exports (Casson 1989, 80–81). As indicated above, it is significant that these were brought to Mosyllon, rather than to the gemstone-exporting Indian ports.

Two gemstones that Egypt surely exported, and for which Roman quarries are known, are amethyst (purple quartz, SiO_2) and emerald, the Roman *smaragdus* (green beryl, $Be_3Al_2[Si_6O_{18}]$). The amethyst quarries are in Wadi el-Hudi, 230 kilometers west of Berenike (Shaw and Jameson 1993, 84, 86, 94; Klemm, Klemm, and Murr 2002), and in Wadi Abu Diyeiba, about 300 kilometers north of Berenike, near the Roman port of Myos Hormos at Quseir (Meredith 1958, 9; Murray 1914; Harrell and Sidebotham 2004). Amethysts have been found at Berenike, but these could have come from India rather than the Eastern Desert. Emerald is by far the most abundant gemstone found at Berenike, with hundreds of crystal fragments and a few beads recovered to date. Does this indicate that it was an important trade item, or was it the only gemstone readily available to the Berenike inhabitants? The quarries of Mons Smaragdus (the mountains around wadis Sikait, Zabara, Nugrus, and Umm Kabu, about ninety kilometers northwest of Berenike [Hume 1934, 109–25; Sinkankas 1989, 542–48; Sidebotham et al. 2004; Harrell 2004]) were well known in antiquity. Several ancient authors refer to these quarries, among whom are Strabo (G 17.1.45) and Pliny (NH 37.17.65, 37.16.64 and

37.18.69). Emerald is, however, not specifically mentioned in the *Periplus*. Perhaps Pliny gives a clue to why the emeralds were apparently not exported to India, but instead to Mosyllon and perhaps minor ports along the various routes. He describes the Egyptian variety of smaragdus as "bright green, although they are rarely flawless or uniform in tint." More recent authors share this low opinion of Egyptian emeralds. For example, Smith and Phillips (1972, 308) write that the stones are mostly "cloudy and rather light in color." They were, thus, probably not a trade item to India, which had its own pale greenish blue aquamarine beryls (De Romanis 1997, 95–98; Sinkankas 1989, 445–555, 507–8; Wadia 1975, 458).

Other possible gemstones for export from Egypt are green malachite $(Cu_2CO_3[OH]_2)$ and greenish blue turquoise associated with copper deposits in the Sinai (Lucas and Harris 1962, 202–5, 400–401, 404–5). Malachite is also commonly associated with copper deposits throughout the Eastern Desert. The Sinai mines were heavily worked during the Egyptian dynastic period, but they may not have been active in Roman times. Egypt's importation of Indian turquoise, indeed, seems to indicate that they were not. No turquoise has been found at Berenike, and only one piece of malachite has been recovered.

African and Arabian Stones Encountered in Berenike

Some stones that are presented as "Arabian" by Classical authors did not necessarily originate in the Arabian Peninsula but were traded through the Arabian harbors. An example is Pliny's listing of "Arabian" varieties of *adamas*, a costly clear stone, either a clear colorless variety of corundum or diamond. The first probably came from Sri Lanka, the latter from India, but both were probably traded through Arabian ports.

A stone that probably did derive from the Arabian Peninsula was *lygdinos*, a celebrated sculptural stone, which Pliny compares to the brilliantly white marble from the Greek island of Paros, and of which he says, "in earlier times it [lygdinos] was normally imported from Arabia" (NH 36.13.62; a similar account is found in Diodorus' LH 2.52). Pliny's Arabia is almost certainly Arabia Felix, which corresponds geographically to modern Yemen (Harrell 1999, 109–10). The *Periplus* mentions *lygdos* (PME 24) and states that its provenance is Muza in South Arabia (Casson 1989, 64–65, 156). Contrary to the translation of Huntingford (1980, 34, 141) and Casson (1989, 31, 114), the lygdos mentioned in the *Periplus* may not be geologic marble (i.e., a metamorphic rock consisting largely of the mineral calcite, CaCO$_3$), but may be, rather, as Schoff (1912, 31, 114) suggests, alabaster gypsum. This is the "true alabaster," not to be confused with the Egyptian alabaster, which is a calcitic rock more correctly referred to as travertine. True alabaster is a fine-grained, massive variety of rock gypsum, which is a sedimentary rock consisting mainly of the mineral gypsum (CaSO$_4$-2H$_2$O). Although an ancient quarry for white marble reportedly exists near Marib in Yemen (Geukens 1966, B12), this country is better known for its alabaster gypsum. From at least medieval times until the present, it has been the principal decorative stone used in Yemen, with quarries near Sanaa and elsewhere (Fricke 1953, 1062; Scott 1947, 125). The lygdos of the *Periplus* may, thus, be either alabaster gypsum or, less likely, marble. The former has not been encountered in Berenike, and the presence of the latter is uncertain, unless a fragment of a well-carved platter in white marble is of Yemeni origin. The building stones in Berenike were either local rock gypsum, rock anhydrite, or Proconnesian marble imported from Turkey.

A harbor in Eritrea, Hauachil Bay, is mentioned in the *Periplus* as the source of *opsianos lithos* (PME 5; Casson 1989, 52–53). This stone is the only one mentioned in the *Periplus* that was not specifically identified as a trade item. The fact that it is mentioned at all, however, suggests that it may have been of interest to traders and, thus, a commercial commodity. It is the same material as Pliny's *opsiano* (NH 37.65.177) and *obsianae* (NH 37.76.200), about which he says (NH 36.67.196), "the stone [was] found by Obsius in Ethiopia" (De Romanis 1996, 225–39).

Opsianos lithos is clearly the black volcanic glass now known as obsidian (Ball 1950, 327; Casson 1989, 109; Harrell 1999, 115; Schoff 1912, 66). The locality mentioned in the *Periplus*, Hauachil Bay, is a well-known source of this rock (Zarins 1989, 348). Although not normally considered a gemstone, obsidian was occasionally used for jewelry and other small carved objects. Its naturally ultra-sharp edges make it especially useful for cutting blades. Numerous unworked fragments of obsidian have been found at Berenike. An alternative source of these may be areas in South Arabia.

Gemstones from India and Sri Lanka

In the early Roman period, India was the preeminent source of gemstones. The *Periplus* lists *challeanos lithos*, *sappheiros*, *onychine lithia*, *moyrrine*, adamas, *hyanchinthos*, and *lithia diaphanes pantoia*. The first came from Barbarikon (Casson 1989, 74–75). The challeanos lithos corresponds with Pliny's *callaina* and *callais*, which he says (NH 37.33.110–12) originates in the "hinterland beyond India" (see also NH 37.56.151). There is widespread agreement that the name "challeanos lithos" and its variants refer to the gemstone turquoise ($CuAl_6[PO_4]_4[OH]_8$-$4H_2O$) (Ball 1950, 285–89; Casson 1989, 194; Harrell 1999, 110; Schoff 1912, 170; Smith and Phillips 1972, 447). Wadia (1975, 460) and Warmington (1974, 255) report that turquoise was not a product of India but was probably brought to Barbarikon, where it was traded, from the well-known deposits at Madan, near ancient Nishapur in northeast Iran, that is, in Pliny's "hinterland beyond India." If turquoise was truly imported into Egypt, this is somewhat surprising, because this mineral was quarried from the Old Kingdom onward at Magharah, Serabit el-Khadim, and Bir Nasib in the southwest Sinai peninsula (Lucas and Harris 1962, 202–5, 404–5; Barron 1907). Pliny (NH 37.33.112) seems to know this when he says "some authorities say that *callainae* are found in Arabia." Perhaps the Eastern turquoise was of a superior quality, as Smith and Phillips (1972, 448) maintain, and therefore fetched a better price in the Mediterranean trade than that from the Sinai. Alternatively, perhaps the Sinai quarries were not in operation at the time the *Periplus* was written. No turquoise has so far been found at Berenike.

The sappheiros (PME 39) came from Barbarikon along with the challeanos lithos (Casson 1989, 74–75). Pliny (NH 37.39.120), in referring to *sappiri*, says, "the best is found in Persia" (see also NH 33.21.68, 37.39.119, and 37.54.139; Theophrastus' OS 23 and 37). Sappheiros is, unquestionably, the gemstone now known as lapis lazuli, although the name was apparently also occasionally applied to other opaque blue stones (Ball 1950, 291–92; Theophrastus 1956, 136–37; Casson 1989, 194; Harrell 1999, Schoff 1912, 170–71). Lapis lazuli is a medieval rendering of the Persian *lazhward*, meaning "blue" (Mitchell 1985, 110). It is a rock consisting mainly of dark blue lazurite ($[Na,Ca]_8[AlSiO_4]_6[SO_4,S,Cl]_2$) or the closely related mineral haüynite ($[Na,Ca]_{4-8}[AlSiO_4]_6[SO_4]_{1-2}$), with scattered specks of golden pyrite (FeS_2) and occasional veins and patches of white calcite ($CaCO_3$). The only known ancient source for this rock is the Kokscha Valley in northeast Afghanistan (in the eastern part of Pliny's Persia), so the port of Barbarikon would have been a place where lapis lazuli was traded (Rosen 1988, 11–13; Smith and Phillips 1972, 446–47; Warmington 1974, 251–52). Only one small unworked piece of lapis lazuli has so far been found at Berenike.

The onychine lithia (PME 48–49) came from Barygaza (Casson 1989, 80–81). Pliny (NH 37.24.90–91), in describing *onychis*, says, while the Indian onychem has several different colors, fiery red, black and that of horn, surrounded by a white layer as in an eye, and in some cases traversed by a slanting layer . . . [there is] also an Arabian *onychem* which differs from the Indian in that the latter displays a small fiery red layer surrounded by one or more white bands . . . [whereas the former] is found to be black with white bands . . . [but there is also another] Indian [onyx] that is flesh-colored, with part of it resembling the *carbunculi* [possibly red] and a part, the *chrysolithos* [i.e., yellow or perhaps yellowish green as in peridot, see above] and the *amethystiu* [i.e., purple amethyst quartz].

A complementary description of *onychion* is provided by Theophrastus (OS 31).

From these descriptions there can be no doubt that the onychine lithia of the *Periplus* is the gemstone variety of chalcedonic quartz (SiO_2) known as agate (Ball 1950; Theophrastus 1956, 127–28; Harrell 1999, 111–12; Schoff 1912, 193–94), including its subvarieties banded agate, with concentric layers of various colors; onyx, with plane-banded alternating white and dark grayish to brownish layers; and sardonyx, with plane-banded white and reddish layers. There are many sources of fine agate in India, and these have been a trade commodity from ancient times onward (Smith and Phillips 1972, 434; Wadia 1975, 460; Warmington 1974, 237–42). Warmington (1974, 259) is of the opinion that the agate Pliny referred to as "Arabian" actually came from India but was traded from some of the Arabian ports. Many pieces of onyx and sardonyx have been found at Berenike, and most of these are cut into flat, oval disks for cameos. It may be, then, that the trade in onychine lithia mentioned by the *Periplus* largely involved cameo blanks.

The *moyrrine* (PME 48) came from Barygaza along with onychine lithia (Casson 1989, 80–81). This material is probably the same as Pliny's *moyrrine* (also *murrina* and *murrhina*) that he says (NH 37.8.21–22) "come to us from the East . . . particularly within the kingdom of Parthia" (see also NH 33.2.5, 36.67.198, and 37.7.18–20). Scholars disagree over the identity of this material, but the strong consensus is that the name "mourrhine" and its variants refer either to fluorite, also known as fluorspar, or agate (Ball 1950, 215–21; Casson 1989, 206; Harrell 1999, 112–13; Loewental, Harden, and Bromehead 1949; Schoff 1912, 193–94). Roman cups and bowls in both materials are known. The properties of the material, however, as described by Pliny and other ancient writers, fit only fluorite (CaF_2), as is convincingly argued by Loewental, Harden, and Bromehead (1949). Also, it seems unlikely that Pliny would have confused *achates* (NH 37.54.139–42) and onychis with a myrrhina of agate composition. Although there are reports of fluorite deposits in Iran (Loewental, Harden, and Bromehead 1949), no ancient or modern workings are known. There are also no anciently worked deposits in India, and this led Ball (1950, 220–21) and Warmington (1974, 238–39, 259) to conclude that myrrhina from India was either agate or another form of chalcedonic quartz, such as carnelian or sard. In one passage (PME 6), the *Periplus* mentions *morrines* in the context of glassware (apparently glass imitations of stone) and says it was a product of Diospolis (Thebes) in Egypt and exported to Barbarikon (Casson 1989, 52–53, 111–12). Thus, the mourrhine imported from Barygaza is not likely to also be glass. No fluorite has been found at Berenike, but carnelian, sard, and agate are abundantly present. Occurrences of these gemstones are rare in Egypt, and the only known Roman workings are in veins of chalcedonic quartz at Stela Ridge, seventy kilometers northwest of Abu Simbel, in the Nubian Desert (Harrell and Bloxam 2004). The carnelian at Berenike commonly occurs as well-worn pebbles, and this is consistent with a provenance in Sri Lanka's famous gemstone-rich placer gravels.

The adamas (PME 56) came from Muziris and Nelkynda (Casson 1989, 84–85). Pliny (NH 37.15.55–58) recognized varieties of adamas from widely scattered localities throughout the ancient world, including Arabia and India (see also NH 37.15.60–61 and 37.76.200; Theophrastus' OS 19). It is widely agreed that adamas is either colorless corundum (Al_2O_3) or, more likely, diamond (C), both among the most precious of gemstones (Ball 1950, 242–46; Theophrastus 1956, 91–92; Casson 1989, 223; Harrell 1999, 113–14; Schoff 1912, 224–26). The name "corundum" is apparently derived from the Indian *kauruntaka*, and "diamond" is a corruption of the Greek *adamas* (Mitchell 1979, 107, 111). Pliny's detailed description of adamas fits best with diamond. In antiquity, diamonds came only from India (Ball 1950, 249–50; Smith and Phillips 1972, 26; Wadia 1975, 455–56; Warmington 1974, 236), and thus the other varieties of adamas mentioned by Pliny may be corundum, which is a more widely distributed mineral. Colorless corundum could also have come from Sri Lanka (Smith and Phillips 1972, 300), where deposits of colored varieties of this mineral (red ruby and blue sapphire) are well known (Wadia 1975, 456–57; Warmington 1974, 247–49; Herath 1975, table 19; Zwaan 1982, 66; Dissanayake and Rupansinghe 1993, table 2). No diamond or colorless corundum has been found at Berenike.

Hyanchinthos (PME 56) came from Muziris and Nelkyunda along with *adamas* (Casson 1989, 84–85). Pliny (NH 37.41.125) and Solinus (CM 30.32–33) provide useful descriptions of hyanchinthos (Ball 1950, 294) but say nothing of its source. It is generally accepted that the word "hyanchinthos" and its variants refer to the blue variety of corundum known as sapphire (Ball 1950, 294–95; Casson 1989, 223; Harrell 1999, 114; Schoff 1912, 226–27). This modern name is derived from the ancient sappheiros/sappiri, which referred to lapis lazuli and occasionally other blue stones. Blue sapphire was produced anciently on Sri Lanka (Herath 1975, table 19; Zwaan 1982, 66; Dissanayake and Rupansinghe 1993, table 2) and would have been traded in the nearby ports on the Indian mainland (Smith and Phillips 1972, 299–300; Wadia 1975, 456–57; Warmington 1974, 247–49). One unworked fragment of sapphire has been found at Berenike, and a nicely shaped double cabochon was recovered from Shenshef, thirty-five kilometers southwest of Berenike.

Lithia diaphanes pantoia (PME 56) translates as "transparent gemstones of all kinds," and these came from Muziris and Nelkynda along with the *adamas* and *hyachinthos* (Casson 1989, 84–85). It is impossible to say what stones these are, but they undoubtedly include at least some of the following gemstones that are known to have come from southern India and especially Sri Lanka: amethyst quartz, citrine quartz, colorless quartz (rock crystal), chrysoberyl, ruby corundum, aquamarine beryl, almandine garnet, zircon, and tourmaline (Ball 1950, 66–67; De Romanis 1997, 95–98; Sinkankas 1989, 445–55; Warmington 1974, 245–54). Of these minerals, the ones found at Berenike were amethyst quartz, colorless quartz, aquamarine beryl, and almandine garnet.

Botanical Commodities

In Egypt, plant remains are preserved in either charred or desiccated condition (table 2.2). The latter preservation mode especially facilitates identification, mostly to the level of species. At Berenike, due to the arid climate, desiccated botanical finds are common. A successful identification, however, depends on the degree of fragmentation and the availability of matching reference material. In an archaeobotanical context, solid plant parts such as seeds, fruits, and stem fragments of woody plants, account for the largest part of the archaeobotanical records. This will introduce bias against plant species that are traded for their fragile plant parts, such as flowers (e.g., saffron, *Crocus sativus* L.) or leaves (e.g., malabathron, *Cinnamomum* spp.). The identification of the well-preserved and diagnostic plant remains at Berenike is partly hampered by their broad scope of origin. The number of cultivated species that come into consideration is huge, as trade contacts were maintained with Africa south of the Sahara, the Arabian Peninsula, and the regions around the Indian Ocean basin. Furthermore, indirect trade contacts with the Far East, via India, were possible from the first century AD onward (Cappers forthcoming a).

Archaeobotanical research at Berenike has yielded a substantial list of cultivated plants, representing cereals, pulses, vegetables and oil plants, fruits and nuts, and spices and condiments (table 2.2). The identification of their possible area of origin and final destination is often ambiguous. To determine the area of origin is especially problematic when the distribution range of a plant species is relatively large. A complicating factor is the spread of cultivated species, such as rice and cotton, outside their area of origin, a process that was accelerated during Classical times. The destination of the plant products could have been Rome, Berenike, or any of the foreign harbors that the ships would call into (for a detailed discussion, see Cappers forthcoming b).

The number of plant species evidenced by both texts and botanical remains at Berenike is limited. Of the fifty-three botanical commodities mentioned in table 2.2, only nine meet this criterion. They are staple foods representing cereals, vegetables, and fruits. Three plant species are, so far, known only from written sources: cabbage, dill, and parsley. The absence of seeds and fruits might partly be explained by assuming that vegetative plant parts were consumed. The "pickles" mentioned in the Berenike ostraka refer perhaps to pickled peach or apricot. These perishable fruits could not have been grown in Berenike nor, when ripe, could have survived the twelve-day crossing of the Eastern Desert. Remains of peaches were, nevertheless, found in the early Roman trash dumps of Berenike. Such incongruities are also evident with respect to import and export localities of botanical commodities. In the *Periplus* a total of thirty-four items of botanical origin are mentioned with their provenance and destination. The enumeration of plant names in table 2.2 clearly demonstrates that the listing in this document is far from complete.

The fact that Berenike was located in a remote, desert environment that facilitated only local cultivation of some vegetables implies that both staple and luxury items must have been imported from other regions (Cappers forthcoming b). Most of the staple food, cereals and legumes, were obtained from the Nile Valley. Additional supplies were imported from the Mediterranean area and from more southerly located regions, including Gebel Elba, 210 kilometers south of Berenike, which receive considerable rainfall and are characterized by a different flora (i.e., Flora Sudanense).

The Mediterranean region exported not only food that keeps well, such as walnut (*Juglans regia* L.), hazel (*Corylus avellana* L.), and almond (*Amygdalus communis* L.), but also perishable food such as peaches (*Prunus persica* [L.] Batsch.), cherry plums (*P. cerasifera* Ehr.), and domestic plums (*P. domestica* L.). The less arid regions south of Berenike provided, for example, incense (*Commiphora gileadensis* [L.] C. Christ.) and the rare Ethiopian pea (*Pisum abyssinicum* Braun), which has recently been accepted as a separate species. Berenike is the only archaeological context from which this plant is presently known.

Several textual sources mention pepper as one of the main objectives of the trade with India. Three kinds of pepper are distinguished: white pepper, black pepper (respectively unripe and ripe fruits of black pepper [*Piper nigrum* L.]), and long pepper (*P. longum* L.). Long pepper grows in northern India and could have been obtained from Barygaza, whereas black pepper is native to the Malabar coast and could have been traded in Muziris and Nelkynda. Long pepper is traded as complete spikes with quite small fruits and should not be confused with black pepper, which has much larger fruits that are separated from the spike. The presence of the wrinkled outer fruit wall in most of the specimens from Berenike indicate that we most probably are dealing exclusively with black pepper. Huge quantities of black pepper have been found at Berenike, including over 7.5 kilograms of peppercorns in an Indian storage jar (see figure 2.2), representing a value equivalent to enough wheat to supply the average Roman for two years. This sharply contrasts with the scanty records from other localities within the Roman Empire: Oberaden, in Germany: twelve (Kucan 1984); Straubing, in Germany: fifty-two (Küster 1995); Hanau-Salisweg, in Germany: twelve (Kreuz 1995); Biesheim-Kunheim in France: one (Jacomet and Schibler 2001).

The dearth of pepper finds in Rome itself, perhaps the most important destination for the trade, should be explained by a combination of factors. The published botanical research from excavations at Rome is scant (Follieri 1975), and the preservational circumstances for organic materials are less favorable than in the deserts of Egypt. The large quantities of peppercorns found at Berenike are only a fraction of the large supplies that must have been temporarily stored in the town on their way to the large *Horrea piperataria* near Rome (Platner and Ashby 1929, 16.63; Rickman 1971, 104–6).

Figure 2.2   The storage jar in which 7.5 kilograms of black pepper was stored

The absence of long pepper, the price of which was 3.75 times that of black pepper according to Pliny (NH 12.14.26–28), from the archaeological record seems to indicate that this spice was not much traded, possibly because it was not much in demand or because most ships called at Indian harbors along the Malabar coast. It is striking that today's supply of black and long pepper in Near Eastern spice markets mirrors that of Classical times.

Whereas texts and archaeobotanical evidence supplement each other with respect to black pepper, written sources are silent on other Indian plants found at Berenike (see figure 2.3): coconut (*Cocos nucifera* L.), rice (*Oryza sativa* L.), amla (*Phyllanthus emblica* L.), mung bean (*Vigna radiata* [L.] Wilczek), and Job's tears (*Coix lacryma-jobi* L.). The transport of these items might, of course, be related to the presence of Indian traders in Berenike, preferring their own food above local supply, but the quality of the items suggest that they were also brought in as trade goods. The presence of many botanical items found at Berenike without Roman counterparts illustrates that trade centers such as harbors are preeminent places for studying exotic commodities for the Roman markets.

The discrepancy between the archaeobotanical evidence from Bere-nike and the written sources is not confined to commodities from India, but also exists for other botanical items. This phenomenon is explain-able by taphonomic processes and excavation strategies. Unlike written sources, botanical remains are not intentionally archived, and the re-covery of reasonably large concentrations, such as the storage jar with black pepper, is exceptional. Most of the unearthed botanical remains can be classified as waste and would have been discarded outside build-ings. Just after being deposited, much of this material would vanish as it became prey to the wind and browsing animals. Incinerating rubbish would also result in the loss of plant remains. Only when the rubbish is quickly covered with a sufficiently thick layer of new rubbish or sand would it have the opportunity to become part of the archaeobotanical archive of the site. The quality of the archaeobotanical record greatly depends on the sampling procedure. Common plant species, such as wheat, barley, and date are present in almost every sample. Rare species, on the other hand, such as amla and Ethiopian pea, have a disjunctive dispersal pattern. It is obvious that the presence of large dump areas calls for special sampling strategies to optimize the recovery of these clus-tered species.

Because archaeobotanical research in Berenike has been based on morphological features, special categories of plant products will be un-derexposed. This is true for liquids and secretions from stems, leaves, and roots (e.g., resins, gums, and oils), all of which are well represented in written sources dealing with the trade in Berenike.

An additional problem is the interpretation of plant names in writ-ten sources. For many botanical commodities from India, it is unclear which Latin or Greek names were used. Although scientific plant names are in Latin, that binomial nomenclature was introduced by Carl Lin-naeus in the eighteenth century. And even though these binomials are partly based on Greek and Latin names mentioned by Classical writers, they might deviate from their original "Classical" name. The reason is that every taxon (e.g., plant species, subspecies, or variety) may be sub-ject to remodeling, and consequently, new names may be introduced in which the assignment is determined by the International Code of Bo-tanical Nomenclature (ICBN). Because the ICBN rules in some cases re-sult in the reuse of existing names for newly defined taxa, linking old trade names with analogous modern scientific plant names may lead to wrong identifications. For the interpretation of the Latin *cuci* and the Greek *cuciofeer* in Classical texts, for example, references have been

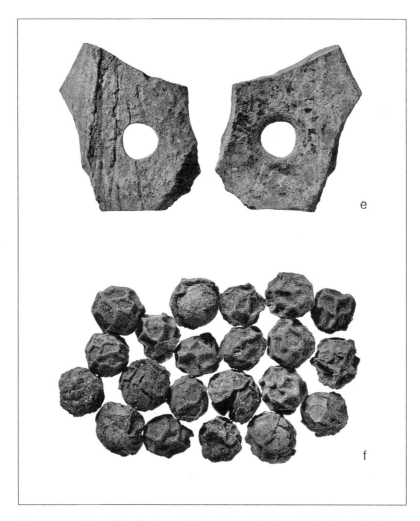

Figure 2.3 Six of the desiccated plant materials from India found in Berenike. Photographs by J. Pauptit. (a) *Phyllanthus emblica*: outside view (left) and inside view (right) of endocarp; (b) *Coix lacryma-jobi*: utricle (grass seed used as bead); (c) *Oryza sativa*: spikelet of rice in lateral view (only the upper glume is still present); (d) *Vigna radiata*: complete seeds and seeds without seedcoat; (e) *Cocos nucifera*: two perforated fruit fragments—outer side endocarp (left); inner side endocarp (right); and (f) *Piper nigrum*: fertile fruits.

made to *cucifera* and *nucifera*. Both words are used in Latin plant names, including those of palm trees. Pliny (NH 15.34.114) uses the word *cuci* for an Egyptian tree, most likely the indigenous doam palm. The legitimate scientific name for this plant is *Hyphaene thebaica* (L.) Mart., but one of its synonyms (i.e., *Cucifera thebaica* Delile) includes the original Classical term. In his translation of the *Periplus*, Schoff (1912, 99) interprets the Greek term *nauplios* (PME 17) as "palm oil," a translation which is adopted by Miller (1969, 27). Schoff reached this identification through first correcting the Greek word *nauplios* to *nargilios*, which in turn is related to the Sanskrit *narikela*, or *narikera*, and the Prakrit *nargil*. According to Schoff, this palm oil came from the coconut. He supports this interpretation by relating the Greek *cuciofeer* and the Latin *cuci* to the scientific name of the coconut (*Cocos nucifera* L.), which is not tenable. Especially for the coconut, which is conspicuous for its size, use, and taste, Romans likely used a separate name. Hohlwein (1939), citing a work by Theophrastus (4.2.7), was misled by the current scientific name for the coconut (*Cocos nucifera* L.) and interpreted κουκιόφορόν as a coconut. Warmington (1928, 217) also was of the opinion that early Classical writers mentioned the coconut. The coconut is mentioned in *Vita Apollonii* (3.5), a book on the life of Apollinius of Tyna written by Philostratus, who lived in the second century AD, but only by a brief descriptive phrase: large nuts that are dedicated to shrines (cited by Warmington 1928, 217). Warmington is correct in his interpretation that coconuts are meant, but he misjudges the context: the text is not referring to Greek temples but to Indian (family) altars dedicated to deities such as Saraswati, Dantesvari, and Khandoba. The first indisputable description of the coconut is from Cosmas Indicopleustes in his *Topographiae Christianae* (11.444.D, Wolska-Conus 1973), which is dated to AD 530. This text gives a name for the nut (Greek: *karuon indikon*, "Indian nut"; Latin: *argellia*). Of the thirty-four botanical commodities listed in the *Periplus*, twenty-three have been "identified" by conspicuous parallels in which the level of speculation is generally high. Only the eleven botanical commodities of which the identification is more or less secure have been incorporated into table 2.2.

The introduction of new botanical commodities into the Roman Empire necessitated the introduction of new plant names by the Classical authors. Such new names may contain clues when they are based on indigenous terminology, but for many, their exact identification has to be derived from the textual context. This might be a description of the morphology of the plant product, its use, or its origin. The common denominator in an enumeration also may contribute to a well-considered interpretation, but prudence is called for because modern groupings may deviate from former ones. In the *Periplus*, for example, rice is not considered a grain, nor is Berenike mentioned as a transit port for rice. Nevertheless, the import of rice in Berenike has been confirmed by archaeobotanical research. Rice could have been obtained from Socotra, or the so-called far-side ports on the northern coast of Somalia.

Amphora-Borne Products

Table 2.3 summarizes the evidence for the different products and source areas represented by the amphorae from Berenike. This includes all types of first- and second-century AD date, regardless of their findspot, and therefore includes those that may be present only residually in later deposits. There are, naturally, additional imported amphora types for which no source can be assigned.

Amphorae, the transport containers of antiquity, were used for the long-distance conveyance of liquid commodities, particularly for goods associated with and necessary to the Roman way of life. Although a diverse range of products was transported in amphorae, the most common include wine (and by-products such as *defrutum* and inferior wine known as vinegar), olive oil, and fish products (such as *garum*). The manufacture of amphorae is normally linked to the regions or estates producing their contents and in this way to the agricultural economy. Their widespread distribution relates primarily to their contents, rather than to the amphorae as objects in their own right. Many other ceramic classes, including fine tablewares, were imported into Egypt, from where they were transported to the Red Sea and eventually farther east, alongside amphorae; but whereas amphorae are considered primary objects of trade because of their contents, these objects are frequently secondary.

Amphora studies in themselves provide a complex example of the interrelationship between textual and archaeological studies because, when well preserved, many of the vessels have inscriptions relating to source, contents, weight, and so forth. These inscriptions—known as *tituli picti* or *dipinti*—can clarify many details about specific vessel types, including date, provenance, and contents. In addition, some vessels, particularly during the period being dealt with here, are stamped with the name of their maker or estate (see Peacock and Williams 1986, 9–14, for a summary). As archaeological objects, amphora sources can also be investigated through scientific analysis of the clay bodies (Bourriau,

Nicholson, and Rose 2000), the distribution patterns of the objects, and, in some cases, the discovery of production sites. Contents, too, can be scientifically investigated to detect residue absorbed into the clay wall (Serpico 2000).

The foundation for amphora typology was established by Heinrich Dressel (1899), based on the amphora inscriptions from Monte Testaccio in Rome and expanded and refined over the last one hundred years. Essentially, an amphora type is defined by the association between vessel shape and clay fabric, which in turn normally equates with a production area. Furthermore, certain shapes are associated with specific food products, providing ease of product identification in much the same way as we today associate particular bottle shapes with, for example, Coca-Cola or wine. Significantly, a one-to-one relationship does not exist between fabric (and in turn source) and shape: Instead, as already noted, certain shapes were associated with specific products, and the vessels were manufactured in a number of places and therefore in a range of fabrics. The best and most extreme example of this is Dressel's Type 2-4, which is common at Berenike. This vessel, which carried wine, is characterized by a bead rim, double-rod handle, carinated shoulder, and peg base.

Despite our extensive knowledge of amphorae, from both the textual and the archaeological evidence, the interpretation of amphora-borne commodities in the documents is not simple. In particular, whether the usage of place names refers to the source area or is generalized to refer to vessel shapes, and in turn measures, has been a matter of some debate (e.g., Bagnall, Helms, and Verhoogt 2000; Kruit and Worp 2000; Rathbone 1983): The consensus is that foreign geographic names generally refer to imported vessels and contents. Nevertheless, there is no simple resolution, and individual documents need to be evaluated. For example, the *kolophonion* appears to be used as a wine measure rather than as a direct indication of the presence of foreign wine (Bagnall, Helms, and Verhoogt 2000, 18–20), and the same may be true of the *rhodion*, a measure commonly used in Egypt in contexts where imported wine is unlikely. Given Berenike's role as an export entrepôt, however, and the presence of rhodian vessels on the site, it remains possible that at Berenike the term does refer to imported wine.

One example of the complexity of the documents relevant to the Berenike archive is the use of *italika* and *aminaia*. On the basis of the evidence available in 1983, Rathbone convincingly equated the aminaia of the Nikanor with the italika of the *Periplus*. Based on the large number of Berenike texts referring to Italian rather than Aminean wine, Kruit and

Figure 2.4   Two ostraka mentioning ladikena of wine

Worp (2000, 131–32) argued that the aminaia and italika could no longer be equated, and that the aminaia derived its name not from a place or vessel shape, but from the aminean vine. Bagnall, Helms, and Verhoogt (2000, 19–20) concluded from the Berenike texts that aminean wine was a rarer type of Italian wine and could be aminean wine from Campania.

Although there are numerous amphora types of this period found at Berenike for which a source cannot be identified, the majority of identifiable Italian ones are Dressel 2-4 vessels of Campanian origin. Rathbone (1983, 85) has identified Italy (especially Campania and central Italy), Sicily, Spain, and Syria as areas in which the Aminean vine was cultivated. Dressel 2-4 amphorae can be identified at Berenike from three of these four areas: Italy (Campania), Spain (Tarraconensis), and Syria (Laodicea ad Mare), the last matched to the *ladikena* of the Berenike ostraka (see figure 2.4). The only recurring and identifiable type of Dressel 2-4 not certainly mentioned in the documents is that from Mareotis, and it too may have contained Aminean wine (Empereur 1986).

Thus during the Roman period there is a correlation between the Dressel 2-4 and areas producing wine from the Aminean vine (see also Empereur 1986), suggesting that in these cases there was a link between vine and vessel shape (Dressel 2-4 amphorae produced elsewhere may have been intentionally creating an association with well-known wine-producing areas). At Berenike these three source areas are quantitatively represented in decreasing order by Campania, Syria, and Spain. Of these, Campania is by far the most common. Therefore, quantitatively, there is an argument to equate the aminaia with Campania, although they could also refer solely to the vessel form we call Dressel 2-4. While at present there is no positive evidence in support, it is not impossible that references to aminaia refer to local vessels, thereby not requiring further adjectival clarification.

The published documents do not provide direct evidence for the transport of Egyptian wine or other products in amphorae. Bagnall, Helms, and Verhoogt (2000, 19) have suggested that some of the wine from unspecified sources may have been Egyptian, and this is supported by the identification of the Amphores Égyptiennes 3 type at Kane (Ballet 1996) and at Ras Hafun (Smith and Wright 1988). The presence of another Egyptian type, the Dressel 2-4 wine amphorae, at Kane (Ballet 1996) is the most compelling evidence for the export of Egyptian wine via the Red Sea (see figure 2.4).

If we return to table 2.3, we see that the majority of references to wine in the *Periplus* are to unspecified types. Imported wine amphorae identified at Berenike but not specified in the documents may be subsumed within this category. However, refinement in our understanding of export will rely on interpretation of archaeological evidence from Berenike and more easterly sites (see Tomber 2005 for an overview of amphora evidence available in 1998).

There are fewer mentions of oil than wine in the *Periplus*, and the text is entirely silent regarding source area, whereas table 2.3 shows that in Berenike, oil vessels from Spain, Tripolitania, and probably North Africa can be identified in the ceramic assemblage. A single Berenike ostrakon refers to an *italikon* of oil (Bagnall, Helms, and Verhoogt 2000, 38, ostrakon no. 4). If denoting Italian oil in an Italian vessel, the text is problematic, for during this period there are no Italian amphorae found in the Eastern Desert known to have been oil containers. A more likely explanation for this, applicable to other goods as well, is the reuse of containers. The practice is common within the Eastern Desert and is documented by Berenike ostrakon no. 88, which refers to ladikena filled with local wine (Bagnall, Helms, and Verhoogt 2000, 18). Archaeologically, a similar phenomenon is indicated by a Campanian Dressel 2-4 with an intact plaster stopper stamped with the Egyptian *uraeus*, a motif common throughout the Eastern Desert (Gates forthcoming). There is no reliable method to quantify the reuse of vessels, but here the ratio of ostraka indicating primary use (export of non-Egyptian goods) to this single example of secondary use might argue that the practice was uncommon; there is no evidence either textually or archaeologically that the bulk of containers for export were reused.

References to fish products are virtually absent from the documents and can only be tenuously identified by equating the *epimenia* of Bere-nike with the Nikanor: Referring to provisions in general, this may in-clude fish (Bagnall, Helms, and Verhoogt 2000, 21). Nevertheless, the presence of Spanish amphorae associated with the exclusive use of fish products at Berenike, Myos Hormos, and Arikamedu (Will 1996) indi-cate that fish products were exported from the Red Sea to India.

On the basis of the documents (mainly the Nikanor archive), Cas-son (1989, 113–14) interpreted the Aminaean and Italian wine sent to Berenike as intended for local consumption rather than export, but the broader picture now available implies to Bagnall, Helms, and Verhoogt (2000, 16) that most of the amphora-borne commodities were destined for export. Nevertheless, these goods were without doubt available to some sectors of the Berenike population, whether officially or unoffi-cially, as seen from their presence in domestic contexts. Elsewhere in the Eastern Desert, they were available at nonport sites, including the im-perial quarries of Mons Claudianus (Tomber 1996) and Mons Porphyr-ites (Tomber 2001) and, significantly, on the Nile and on the Red Sea road at the *praesidium* of Maximianon (Brun 1996).

The Integration of Information

Although historians sometimes see archaeology as ancillary to textual sources, the work at Berenike shows that combining results from vari-ous specialists on a basis of equality results in a more balanced historical reconstruction. The tables in this chapter show a discrepancy between the textual evidence and the archaeology. Using these tables as a heu-ristic tool, by also explaining why certain commodities do not occur, or why some goods found in Berenike are not mentioned in the textual sources, our understanding of the harbor and its context is enhanced greatly.

Gemstones were an important export article from India, the Indian hinterland, and Sri Lanka. Some of these have been found in Berenike, others not. Turquoise, for instance, has not been encountered at Bere-nike. Is this a reflection of its rarity, or of the trade route? Although there are turquoise deposits in the Sinai, turquoise was imported into Egypt from northeast Iran through the harbor of Barbarikon. This was also the transit harbor for lapis lazuli, which was quarried in north-east Afghanistan. The one piece of lapis lazuli that has been found in Berenike is not a strong indication of direct contacts with Barbarikon. The rarity in Berenike of the stones said to have come through Barbarikon stands in contrast with the considerable number of cameo blanks imported through Barygaza. Fluorite, also possibly an import through this harbor, has not been encountered in the excavations.

From the evidence of the diversity in stone, it is possible to lay out a tentative trade pattern in which Barygaza seems to have been of greater importance than Barbarikon. The botanical evidence, however, suggests major contacts with the harbors of Muziris and Nelkynda, while evidence from the north is scant. The abundance of black pepper (from the south), compared with the dearth of long pepper (from the north) could be interpreted as indicative of the trade route. Muziris and Nelkynda are located opposite the Ethiopian ports and Socotra, and can be reached through a direct crossing of the Indian Ocean, rather than by a coast-hugging shipping route. The evidence from the northern gemstone trade, however, prevents a rapid and simplifying conclusion. It seems that a considerable number of ships visited or originated at the northern harbors but did not load large quantities of long pepper for transportation to Egypt. Long pepper was more expensive and perhaps less popular than black and white pepper.

The purpose of stone shipments is clear: Peridots and medicinal minerals were exported from Egypt, while the majority of gemstones were imported from India and Sri Lanka. Arabia and Africa exported attractive sculptural stone and obsidian. If we concentrate on the question of why some stones are found in Berenike but are not encountered in textual sources, then the abundant presence of green beryls from the Mons Smaragdus area stand out. It stands to reason that these low-quality beryls did not meet a demand in the Indian harbors that concentrated on gemstone export. Their presence in Berenike can be explained either by assuming that all beryls were for local use, which is unlikely since the stones found at Berenike were not worked, or by postulating that the beryls were traded in the less important harbors en route. Another possible explanation for their absence from the texts is that they did not have to travel from the Nile Valley to Berenike and thus were not part of the customs process that most of the Berenike ostraka document.

The botanical finds at Berenike do not necessarily denote trade goods but form a combination of local produce; imported goods for consumption in the harbor town, provisioning of ships, and provisioning of populations in distant harbors; and, finally, trade goods. The same is true for the oil, wine, and fish sauce, which are identified through their standardized containers.

Of the fifty-three plants listed in table 2.2, forty-six species have been found at Berenike, of which thirty-four are not mentioned in any of the textual sources. This can be partly explained by local Berenike produce, such as sugar dates, harvested in the Eastern Desert, and plants that can be grown for personal use in small garden plots. On the other hand, Berenike has yielded a considerable quantity of coconut, a species not mentioned in first- and second-century AD texts, but that is clearly not a local product. The only reference is a description of the use of coconut in India. The Nikanor archive, which lists produce that is mostly for local use in Berenike, mentions wheat, barley, bitter vetch, sesame, dill, and olive oil. The Berenike ostraka, referring to goods entering the harbor area, mention nine plants: wheat, barley, beet, onion, cabbage, parsley, pickles, grapes, and perhaps incense. The *Periplus* refers to wheat, barley, rice, sesame oil, olive oil, grape, dates, spices, black pepper, long pepper, and saffron as well as twenty-three other plant commodities of which the identification is uncertain. Thus it is clear that, not surprisingly, wheat and barley are the most important botanical bulk goods to which all textual sources make reference.

From these examples it is clear that a systematic integration of the different sources should take into account a range of biases that are the result of deposition, postdeposition, and preservation, but also of purpose and politics. Some of these biases can be countered by a well-designed sampling procedure, but for the most part they cannot be easily traced or corrected. One way of taking these biases into account in the interpretation is to specifically look for and explain evidence that does not "fit." The comparison of the different sources is particularly helpful in this procedure. The methodological problems that are involved in such a comparison have been highlighted in this chapter. Apart from the "confirmation" of textual evidence through the archaeological research, or the archaeological discovery of new textual evidence and the deeper understanding of the texts' referents, a major gain of a multidisciplinary approach is heuristic and corrective. The discrepancies between the different sources help to identify biases and prevent a simplified interpretation. The combination of evidence gives us insights that none of the categories separately could offer and enables us to give a more balanced image of the way the harbor town functioned in the organization of long-distance trade.

Although the subject matter, a study of the harbor town of Berenike in relation to long-distance trade, is the same, the four sources presented here—textual, stone, botanical, and ceramic materials—provide different kinds of information that must be balanced carefully in order to present an overall image of the emporium and the organization of the trade. On a methodological level, three caveats become apparent.

First, the interpretation of archaeological assemblages, of which locally retrieved textual evidence is a part, starts with the context. As was highlighted above, it is extremely important to understand the way objects have been deposited and preserved. While noting the occurrence or quantifying commodities, one should take into account that, for instance, each date consumed in Berenike produced a hard kernel that stood a good chance of surviving wind, animal browsing, and fire. Plants with edible seeds will have been dispersed through human or animal feces, while a considerable portion of the original botanical presence will have disappeared without trace. Peppercorns were ground before being added to food, and they were such a costly commodity that spillage was rare. The fact that peppercorns were found in the trash dumps of Berenike witnesses to the abundance of this spice. They were found charred, as part of offerings, and a large storage jar with 7.5 kilograms of peppercorns reflects deliberate storage.

Incense, as was noted in table 2.2, was not found. Nevertheless, indirect evidence for incense offerings was discovered in several of Berenike's shrines. Circular soil colorations, one of which was found on top of a small stone offering table, indicated the presence of wooden bowls. A cross section showed that the bowls were lined with a layer of sand and filled with charcoal, presumably in preparation for incense offerings.

Contrary to botanical remains, written sources are produced for future consulting, though their intended life span may be relatively short, as is the case with ostraka. Written sources are sensitive to fragmentation and fire; ink may fade in the sunlight. To gain insight into the extent and organization of the trade, a variety and a considerable number of ostraka are needed. As outlined above, to date we have not encountered a late Roman archive in Berenike. Therefore, just as with botanical remains, the sampling procedure for textual evidence is of major concern, as is the interpretation of the depositional and postdepositional processes. It is important to decide for each find why and how it became part of the archaeological record and to record whether it was an in situ discovery (archive/storage), systematically dumped waste (e.g., the Berenike ostraka "archive"), or subject to loss.

Second, in a comparison of ancient Greek or Latin with modern terminology, similar names may denote different materials or objects. Examples are the terms *sappheiros* and *sapphire* (anciently for lapis lazuli, at present for blue corundum) and *coconut*. For amphorae, the discussion on terminology focuses on the question of whether geographic terms refer to the source area of the wine, to vessel shapes, or perhaps even to standardized measures. Interweaving textual and archaeological evidence starts with careful identification of terms, based on specialists' knowledge and lexicographical study.

The third caveat is to be aware of the purpose and bias of the text material. The textual sources available for the first and second centuries AD show an interest in trade goods, economic value, and a characterization of the different markets. The goods listed in the *Periplus* are mentioned because of their attraction as trade items. The Berenike ostraka are overwhelmingly concerned with the transportation and customs process for export goods; only a scattering of texts so far deal with other subjects. Thus the Berenike ostraka give a good overview of the goods that were brought from the Nile Valley by caravan for loading aboard the ships. The relatively small quantities mentioned in the ostraka are probably attributable to the carrying capacity of the camels of an individual driver rather than to the intended use of the goods. The ostraka do not specify whether these goods were trade commodities or provisions for the ship's crew and distant populations. The Nikanor ostraka, by contrast, apparently deal heavily with the supply of the population of Berenike. Differences and similarities of commodities included and excluded may be explained to a large degree by these differences of textual origins and objectives. The physical objects and materials found at Berenike are also present for a variety of reasons: imports that represent a residue of trade and imports for local use and consumption as well as ships' provisions.

In spite of these three caveats, a multidisciplinary approach of archaeology is not only worthwhile but necessary to maximize the level of interpretation. Especially in a site such as Berenike, with preservational circumstances that do not occur in most excavations where items are found, a broad spectrum of approaches not only produces a more complete inventory but, as the occasion arises, also sheds light on problems of interpretation. It is, therefore, a challenge to the multidisciplinary-oriented archaeologist to compare the different kinds of evidence in the hope that interpretative problems are tackled and the reconstruction of the past is as complete as possible.

Thus an integration of information on textual sources, stones, botanical commodities, and ceramic evidence (to list only the Berenike specializations involved in this contribution) helps to interpret the long-distance trade but also highlights interpretative problems. The integration of archaeological and historical information sources proves to be extremely useful, but it has to be stressed that further work is necessary, especially the difficult task of quantifying the different commodities in relation to the archaeological context, in order to pronounce upon the size and extent of the freight traffic (Tomber 1993). This contribution should, therefore, be considered a work in progress, rather than the final word on the trade that came through the harbor of Berenike.

Notes

This chapter was originally published in a slightly different form in the *Journal of the Economic and Social History of the Orient* 46 (1): 46–87. Copyright © 2003 by Brill Academic Publishers. Reprinted by permission.

The Berenike project is grateful to the organizations and individuals who over the years have financially supported the work. Among these are the Humanities Research Council of the Netherlands Organization for Scientific Research (GW-NWO), the National Geographic Society, the Samuel H. Kress Foundation, the National Endowment for the Humanities, the Utopia Foundation, The Gratama Foundation, the Berenike Foundation, the Seven Pillars of Wisdom Trust, the University of Delaware, Leiden University, and the University of California at Los Angeles. During the past nine years, more than ninety persons have contributed to the work in Berenike. Here we would like to highlight in particular the work of our excellent trench supervisors, especially Shinu Abraham, Jolanda Bos, Lauren Bruning, Anne Haeckl, and Lisa Pintozzi, along with specialists Peter Francis Jr. (beads), Martin Hense (metal), Wim Van Neer (archaeozoology), André Veldmeijer (cordage), and John Peter and Felicity Wild (textiles).

Bibliography

Agatharchides. 1989. *On the Erythraean Sea/Agatharchides of Cnidus.* Trans. and ed, S. M. Burstein. London: Hakluyt Society.

Bagnall, Roger S., Christina Helms, and Arthur M. F. W. Verhoogt. 2000. *Documents from Berenike.* Vol. 1, *Greek Ostraka from the 1996–1998 Seasons.* Bruxelles: Fondation Égyptologique Reine Élisabeth.

———. 2005. *Documents from Berenike.* Vol. 2, *Greek Ostraka from the 1999–2001 Seasons.* Bruxelles: Fondation Égyptologique Reine Élisabeth.

Ball, Sydney H. 1950. *A Roman Book on Precious Stones Including an English Modernization of the 37th Booke of the Historie of the World by E. Plinius Secundus.* Los Angeles: Gemological Institute of America.

Ballet, Pascale. 1996. "De la Méditerranée à l'Océan Indien l'Égypte et le commerce de longue distance à l'époque Romaine: Les données céramiques." *Topoi* 5 (2): 809–40.

Ballet, Pascale, and Michèle Vichy. 1992. "Artisanant de la ceramique dans l'Egypte

Hellénistique et Romaine: Ateliers du Delta, d'Assouan et de Kharga." In *Ateliers de Potiers et Productions Céramiques en Egypte*, ed. P. Ballet, 109–19. Cairo: Institut Français d'Archélogie Orientale.

Barron, T. 1907. *Topography and Geology of the Peninsula of Sinai — Western Portion.* Cairo: Survey Department.

Bourriau, Janine, Paul T. Nicholson, and Pamela J. Rose. 2000. "Pottery." In *Ancient Egyptian Materials and Technology*, ed. P. T. Nicholson and I. Shaw, 121–47. Cambridge: Cambridge University Press.

Brun, Jean-Pierre. 1996. "Le praesidium Romain de Maximianon (Al-Zarqa, Egypte): Fouilles 1994–1995." *Topoi* 6 (2): 685–95.

Cappers, René T. J. 2002. "Farming in the Desert: Implications of Recent Practices for Archaeobotanical Interpretations." In *Moving Matters: Ethnoarchaeology in the Near East*, ed. W. Z. Wendrich and G. van der Kooij, 45–62. Leiden, Netherlands: Research School CNWS, School for Asian, African, and Amerindian Studies.

———. Forthcoming a. "Exotic Imports of the Roman Empire: An Exploratory Study of Potential Vegetal Products from Asia." *Africa Oecologica*.

———. Forthcoming b. "Food-prints at Berenike." *Archaeobotanical Evidence of Trade and Subsistence in the Eastern Desert of Egypt.*

Casson, Lionel. 1989. *The Periplus Maris Erythraei: Text with Introduction, Translation, and Commentary*. Princeton, N.J.: Princeton University Press.

De Romanis, Federico. 1996. *Cassia, Cinnamomo, Ossidiana: Uomini e Merci tra Oceano Indiano e Mediterraneo.* Rome: L'Erma di Bretschneider.

———. 1997. "Rome and the Notia of India: Relations between Rome and Southern India from 30 BC to the Flavian Period." In *Crossings — Early Mediterranean Contacts with India*, ed. F. De Romanis and A. Tchernia, 80–160. New Delhi: Manohar.

Dissanayake, C. B., and M. S. Rupasinghe. 1993. "A Prospector's Guide Map to the Gem Deposits of Sri Lanka." *Gems and Geology* 29 (3): 173–81.

Dressel, Heinrich. 1899. *Corpus Inscriptionum Latinorum XV (1)*. Berlin.

Empereur, Jean-Yves. 1986. "Un atelier de Dressel 2 4 en Egypte au IIIe siècle de notre ère." *BCH* 13:599–608.

Empereur, Jean-Yves, and Maurice Picon. 1989. "Les régions de production d'amphores impériales en Méditerranée Orientale." In *Amphores Romaines et Histoire Economique: Dix Ans de Recherche*, 223–48. Rome: Ecole Française de Rome.

Follieri, M. 1975. "Resti vegetali macroscopici nel collettore del Colosseo." *Annali di Botanica* 34:123–41.

Fricke, K. 1953. "Bergbau auf alabaster und gips in Jemen." *Glückauf* 89:1061–62.

Fuks, Alexander. 1951. "Notes on the Archive of Nicanor." *Journal of Juristic Papyrology* 5:207–16.

Gates, J. Forthcoming. "Amphora Stoppers." In *Berenike 2001: Report of the 2001 Excavations at Berenike and the Survey of the Egyptian Eastern Desert*, ed. S. E. Sidebotham and W. Z. Wendrich. Los Angeles: Cotsen Institute of Archaeology at UCLA.

Geukens, F. 1966. *Geology of the Arabian Peninsula — Yemen*. United States Geological Survey Professional Paper 560 (B): 1–23.

Harrell, James A. 1996. "Geology." In *Berenike 1995, Preliminary Report of the 1995 Excavations at Berenike (Egyptian Red Sea Coast) and the Survey of the Eastern Desert*, ed. S. E. Sidebotham and W. Z. Wendrich, 99–126. Leiden, Netherlands: Research School CNWS, School for Asian, African, and Amerindian Studies.

———. 1998. "Geology." In *Berenike 1996, Preliminary Report of the 1996 Excavations at Berenike (Egyptian Red Sea Coast) and the Survey of the Eastern Desert*, ed. S. E. Sidebotham and W. Z. Wendrich, 121–48. Leiden, Netherlands: Research School CNWS, School for Asian, African, and Amerindian Studies.

———. 1999. "Geology." In *Berenike 1997, Report of the Excavations at Berenike and the Survey of the Egyptian Eastern Desert, Including Excavations at Shenshef*, ed. S. E. Sidebotham and W. Z. Wendrich, 107–21. Leiden, Netherlands: Research School CNWS, School for Asian, African, and Amerindian Studies.

———. 2004. "Archaeological Geology of the World's First Emerald Mine." *Geoscience Canada* 31 (2): 69–76.

Harrell, James A., and E. G. Bloxam. 2004. "Stela Ridge Carnelian Mine, Nubian Desert." In *The Fifty-Fifth Annual Meeting of the American Research Center in Egypt — Program and Abstracts*, 52. Atlanta, Ga.: ARCE.

Harrell, James A., and Steven E. Sidebotham. 2004. "Wadi Abu Diyeiba: An Amethyst Quarry in Egypt's Eastern Desert." *Minerva* 15 (6): 12–14.

Herath, J. W. 1975. *Mineral Resources in Sri Lanka*. Economic Bulletin No. 2. Colombo: Geological Survey Department.

Hohlwein, Nicolas. 1939. "Palmiers et palmeraies dans l'Egypte Romaine." *Etudes de Papyrologie* 5:1–74.

Hume, William. F. 1934. *Geology of Egypt*. Vol. 3, pt. 1. Survey of Egypt, Ministry of Finance (later the Egyptian Geological and Mining Authority). Cairo: Government Press.

Huntingford, George W. B., trans. and ed. 1980. *The Periplus of the Erythraean Sea by an Unknown Author with some Extracts from Agatharkhides "On the Erythraean Sea."* London: The Hakluyt Society.

Jacomet, Stefanie, and Jörg Schibler. 2001. "Les contributions de l'archéobotanique et de l'archéozoologie à la connaissance de l'agriculture et de l'alimentation du site Romain de Biesheim-Kunheim." In *La frontière Romaine sur le Rhin Supérieur. À Propos des Fouilles Récentes de Biesheim-Kunheim*, ed. S. Plouin et al., 60–68. Biesheim: Ville de Biesheim.

Keller, Peter C. 1990. *Gemstones and Their Origins*. New York: Van Nostrand Reinhold.

Klemm, R., D. D. Klemm, and A. Murr. 2002. "Geoarchälogischer Survey im Wadi el Hudi." In *Festschrift Arne Eggebrecht zum 65. Geburtstagam 12. März 2000*, ed. A. Eggebrecht and B. Schmitz, 53–66. Hildescheim: Gerstenberg Verlag.

Kreuz, Angela. 1995. "Landwirtschaft und ihre ökologischen Grundlagen in den Jahrhunderten um Christi Geburt: Zum Stand der naturwissenschaftlichen Untersuchungen in Hessen." *Berichte der Kommision für Archäologische Landesforschung in Hessen* 3:59–91.

Kruit, Nico, and Klaas Worp. 2000. "Geographical Jar Names: Towards a Multidisciplinary Approach." *Archiv für Papyrusforschung* 46 (1): 65–146.

Kucan, Dusanka. 1984. "Der erste römerzeitliche Pfefferfund nachgewiesen im Legionslager Oberaden (Stadt Bergkamen)." *Ausgrabungen und Funde in Westfalen Lippe* 2:51–56.

Küster, Hansjörg. 1995. *Postglaziale Vegetationsgeschichte Südbayerns*. Berlin: Akademie Verlag.

Laubenheimer, Fanette. 1989. "Les amphores gauloises sous l'Empire: Recherches nouvelles sur leur production et leur chronologie." In *Amphores Romaines et Histoire Economique: Dix Ans de Recherche*, 105–38. Rome: Coll Ecole Française Rome.

Loewental, A. I., Donald B. Harden, and Cyril E. N. Bromehead. 1949. "Vasa Murrina." *Journal of Roman Studies* 39:31–37.

Lucas, Alfred, and John R. Harris. 1962. *Ancient Egyptian Materials and Industries*. London: Edward Arnold Publishers.

Majcherek, Grzegorz. 1995. "Gazan Amphorae: Typology Reconsidered, Hellenistic and Roman Pottery in the Eastern Mediterranean." In *Advances in Scientific Studies: Acts of the II Nieborów Pottery Workshop*, ed. J. Mlynarczyk, 163–78. Warsaw: Polish Academy of Sciences.

Meredith, David. 1956. "The Myos Hormos Road: Inscriptions and Ostraca." *Chronique d'Egypte* 31:356–62.

———. 1958. *TABVLA IMPERII ROMANI: Text for Map of the Roman Empire, Sheet no. NG36 (1:1,000,000)*. Oxford: Oxford University Press.

Miller, James I. 1969. *The Spice Trade of the Roman Empire: 29 BC to AD 641*. Oxford: Clarendon Press.

Mitchell, Richard S. 1979. *Mineral Names—What Do They Mean?* New York: Van Nostrand Reinhold.

———. 1985. *Dictionary of Rocks*. New York: Van Nostrand Reinhold.

Murphy, Edwin. 1989. *The Antiquities of Asia: A Translation with Notes of Book II of the* Library of History *of Diodorus Siculus*. New Brunswick, N.J.: Transaction Publishers.

Murray, George W. 1914. "Notes." *Cairo Scientific Journal* 8:179.

Panella, Clementina. 1973. "Appunti su un gruppo di anfore della prima, media e tarda eta imperiale." In *Ostia III: Le Terme del Nuotatore: Scavo dell'Ambiente V et di un Saggio nell'Area*, 460–633. Rome: De Luca Editore.

Peacock, David P. S. 1977. "Roman Amphorae: Typology, Fabric and Origins." In *Méthodes Classiques et Méthodes Formelles dans l'Etude des Amphores*, ed. G. Vallet, 261–78. Rome: Coll Ecole Française Rome.

Peacock, David P. S., and D. F. Williams. 1986. *Amphorae and the Roman Economy: An Introductory Guide.* New York: Longman.

Platner, Samuel B., and Thomas Ashby. 1929. *A Topographical Dictionary of Ancient Rome.* Oxford: Oxford University Press.

Pliny the Elder. 1952. *Natural History.* Vol. 9, bks. 33–35. Trans. H. Rackham. Cambridge, Mass.: Harvard University Press.

———. 1962. *Natural History.* Vol. 10, books 36–37. Trans. D. E. Eichholz. Cambridge, Mass.: Harvard University Press.

Ponsich, Michel. 1988. *Aceite de oliva y salazones de pescado.* Madrid: Complutensian University.

Rathbone, Dominic W. 1983. "Italian Wines in Roman Egypt." *Opus* 3:81–98.

Rickman, G. 1971. *Roman Granaries and Storage Buildings.* Cambridge: Cambridge University Press.

Riley, John A. 1981. "The Pottery from Cisterns 1977.1, 1977.2 and 1977.3." In *Excavations at Carthage Conducted by the University of Michigan 1977*, ed. J. H. Humphrey, 85–124. Ann Arbor: University of Michigan.

Rosen, Lissie von. 1988. *Lapis Lazuli in Geological Contexts and in Ancient Written Sources.* Jonsered: Paul Åströms Förlag.

Schoff, Wilfred H. 1912. *The Periplus of the Erythraean Sea: Travel and Trade in the Indian Ocean.* New York: Longmans Green and Co.

Scott, Hugh. 1947. *In the High Yemen.* London: John Murray.

Serpico, Margaret. 2000. "Resins, Amber and Bitumen." In *Ancient Egyptian Materials and Technology*, ed. I. Shaw, 430–74. Cambridge: Cambridge University Press.

Shaw, Ian, and Robert Jameson. 1993. "Amethyst Mining in the Eastern Desert — A Preliminary Survey at Wadi el-Hudi." *Journal of Egyptian Archaeology* 79:81–97.

Siculus, Diodoros. 1961. *Diodorus of Sicily.* Vol. 2, bks. 2–4. Trans. C. H. Oldfather. Cambridge, Mass.: Harvard University Press.

Sidebotham, Steven E., H. M. Nouwens, A. M. Hense, and J. A. Harrell. 2004. "Preliminary Report on Archaeological Fieldwork at Sikait (Eastern Desert of Egypt) and Environs in 2002–2003." *Sahara* 15:7–30.

Sidebotham, Steven E., and Willemina Z. Wendrich. 1995. *Berenike 1994: Preliminary Report of the 1994 Excavations at Berenike (Egyptian Red Sea Coast) and the Survey of the Eastern Desert.* Leiden, Netherlands: Research School CNWS, School for Asian, African, and Amerindian Studies.

———. 1996. *Berenike 1995: Preliminary Report of the 1995 Excavations at Berenike (Egyptian Red Sea Coast) and the Survey of the Eastern Desert.* Leiden, Netherlands: Research School CNWS, School of Asian, African, and Amerindian Studies.

———. 1998. *Berenike 1996: Report of the 1996 Excavations at Berenike (Egyptian Red Sea Coast) and the Survey of the Eastern Desert.* Leiden, Netherlands: Research School CNWS, School for Asian, African, and Amerindian Studies.

———. 1999. *Berenike 1997: Report of the 1997 Excavations at Berenike and the Survey of the Egyptian Eastern Desert, including Excavations at Shenshef.* Leiden, Netherlands: Research School CNWS, School for Asian, African, and Amerindian Studies.

———. 2000. *Berenike 1998: Report of the 1998 Excavations at Berenike and the Survey of the Egyptian Eastern Desert, including Excavations at Wadi Kalalat.* Leiden, Netherlands: Research School CNWS, School for Asian, African, and Amerindian Studies.

———. Forthcoming. *Berenike 1999–2000: Report of the 1999 and 2000 Excavations at Berenike and the Survey of the Egyptian Eastern Desert, including Excavations at Wadi Kalalat and Siket.* Los Angeles: Cotsen Institute of Archaeology.

Sinkankas, J. 1989. *Emerald and Other Beryls.* Prescott, Ariz.: Geoscience Press.

Smith, George F., and F. C. Phillips. 1972. *Gemstones.* New York: Pitman Publishing.

Smith, Mathew C., and Henry T. Wright. 1988. "The Ceramics from Ras Hafun in Somalia: Notes on a Classical Maritime Site." *Azania* 23:115–41.

Solinus, Caius Julius. 1895. *C. Iulii Solini—Collectanea Rerum Memorabilium* [Collection of Memorabilia]. Trans. and ed. T. Mommsen. Berlin: Weidmannsche Verlagsbuchhandlung.

Strabo. 1959. *The Geography of Strabo.* Vol. 8, bk. 17. Trans. H. L. Jones. Cambridge, Mass.: Harvard University Press.

———. 1961. *The Geography of Strabo.* Vol. 5, bks. 10–12. Trans. H. L. Jones. Cambridge, Mass.: Harvard University Press.

———. 1966. *The Geography of Strabo.* Vol. 7, bks. 15–16. Trans. H. L. Jones. Cambridge, Mass.: Harvard University Press.

Tchernia, André, and Fausto Zevi. 1972. "Amphores vinaires de Campanie et de Tarraconaise à Ostia." In *Méthodes Classiques et Méthodes Formelles dans l'Etude des Amphores*, ed. G. Vallet, 35–67. Rome: Coll Ecole Française de Rome.

Theophrastus. 1956. *On Stones.* Trans. and ed. E. R. Caley and J. F. C. Richards. Columbus: Ohio State University Press.

Tomber, Roberta S. 1993. "Long-distance Exchange: Quantitative Approaches." *Journal of Roman Archaeology* 6:144–66.

———. 1996. "Provisioning the Desert: Pottery Supply to Mons Claudinus." In *Archaeological Research in Roman Egypt*, ed. D. M. Bailey, 39–49. Ann Arbor: Journal of Roman Archaeology.

————. 1998. "'Laodicean' Wine Containers in Roman Egypt." In *Life on the Fringe: Living in the Southern Egyptian Deserts during the Roman and Early-Byzantine Periods*, ed. O. E. Kaper, 213–119. Leiden, Netherlands: Research School CNWS, School for Asian, African, and Amerindian Studies; Netherlands Flemish Institute in Cairo.

————. 2001. "Pottery." In *The Roman Imperial Quarries: Survey and Excavation at Mons Porphyrites 1994–1998*, ed. D. P. S. Peacock, 242–303. London: Egypt Exploration Society.

————. 2005. "Trade Relations in the Eastern Mediterranean and Beyond: The Egyptian-Indian Connection." In *Halicarnassus Studies*, vol. 3, *Trade Relations in the Eastern Mediterranean from the Late Hellenistic Period to Late Antiquity: The Ceramic Evidence*, ed. M. B. Briese and L. E. Vaag, 221–33. Odense: University Press of Southern Denmark.

Wadia, Darashaw N. 1975. *Geology of Egypt*. New Delhi: Tata McGraw-Hill Publishing.

Warmington, Eric H. 1928. *The Commerce Between the Roman Empire and India*. New Delhi: Munshiran Manoharlal Publishers.

————. 1974. *The Commerce Between the Roman Empire and India*. London: Curzon Press.

Wendrich, Willemina Z. 1998. "The Finds, Introduction." In *Berenike 1996: Report of the 1996 Excavations at Berenike (Egyptian Red Sea Coast) and the Survey of the Eastern Desert*, ed. W. Z. Wendrich, 148–60. Leiden, Netherlands: Research School CNWS, School for Asian, African, and Amerindian Studies.

Will, Elizabeth L. 1996. "Mediterranean Shipping Amphoras at Arikamedu, 1941–50 Excavations." In *The Ancient Port of Arikamedu: New Excavations and Researches 1989–92*, vol. 1, ed. V. Begley et. al., 317–50, Pondicherry.

Williams, David F. 1994. "Campanian Amphorae." In *Excavations at South Sheilds Roman Fort*, ed. S. Speak, 217–19. Newcastle upon Tyne: Society of Antiquaries of Newcastle upon Tyne.

Wolska-Conus, Wanda. 1973. *Cosmas Indicopleustès: Topographiae Chrétienne*. Vol. 3. Paris: Les éditions du Cerf.

Zarins, Juris. 1989. "Ancient Egypt and the Red Sea Trade—The Case for Obsidian in the Predynastic and Archaic Periods." In *Essays in Ancient Civilization Presented to Helene J. Kantor*, ed. A. Leonard, 339–68. Chicago: Oriental Institute, University of Chicago.

Zevi, Fausto, and André Tchernia. 1969. "Amphores de Byzacène au Bas-Empire." *Antiquites Africaines* 3:173–214.

Zwaan, P. C. 1982. "Sri Lanka: The Gem Island." *Gems and Geology* 18 (2): 62–71.

3

The Rise of Secondary States in the Iron Age Levant
Archaeological and Historical Considerations

ALEXANDER H. JOFFE

This chapter addresses two questions in the archaeology of the southern Levant: the nature of the rise of states during the first millennium BC, and the organization of both state and society. It attempts to delineate the external context and internal dynamics of secondary-state formation, demonstrating that polities emerged by interacting with more developed neighbors but employed new methods of integration based on collective identity, which combined elite and local concepts. Archaeology can, to a surprising extent, demonstrate the emergence of "ethnic states," that is, polities integrated by means of identity, especially ethnicity, that are territorially based (compare A. D. Smith 1998, 2000).

"Ethnic states" are not types or stages in an evolutionary scheme. Rather, they are novel and historically contingent political systems that appear in the Levant during the first millennium BC thanks to the confluence of several factors, not least of all the collapse of imperial domination and the long-standing city-state system. New forms of local identity and organization developed during the centuries of relative dislocation, which were later used in part by reemergent elites. The phenomenon has recurred periodically in the interstices between larger units such as empires, along the margins, and during periods of collapse. This approach necessarily sees the clustering of certain behaviors, symbols, and historical evidence as indicative of "ethnic" or identity-organized groups (contra Jones 1997). The extensive use of symbolism and particular forms of administration make the "ethnic state" archaeologically detectable.

Previous studies of the rise of Iron Age states, especially Israel, have been heavily oriented toward biblical accounts. Historical studies have relied almost exclusively on biblical texts, with their attendant weaknesses, while archaeological efforts traditionally attempted to compare and harmonize texts and artifacts (e.g., Wright 1962). Most of the archaeology of ancient Israel has followed the narrative of the biblical text, and even recent efforts to introduce significant revisions implicitly subordinate archaeology to this reconstruction (e.g., Dever 1997; Finkelstein 1999b). A smaller number of social science–oriented approaches have set textual and archaeological evidence against rigid models or typologies derived from neo-evolutionary theory. Generally these have succeeded only in restating older ideas (e.g., McNutt 1990; Routledge 2000; Master 2001; Levy and Holl 2002) or in reifying dubious taxonomies (Frick 1985; Jamison-Drake 1991). Even if there is a nominal advantage in situating discussions within comparative traditions, the weaknesses of "ethnographic tyranny" are well known and need not be recapitulated (Yoffee 1993).

How may a sequence of investigations be structured to avoid conditioning, consciously or otherwise, by the seeming completeness or verisimilitude of textual information? Using any text for historical reconstruction creates a paradox of priority. Texts are both "seeking and seeing" (Bagley 1992), and in a historicist tradition of archaeology, the temptation has been to use texts as the beginning and ending point of research. These are standard problems in every branch of "historical archaeology" (e.g., Andrén 1997; Paynter 2000; D. V. Armstrong 2001), made acute by the distinctive position of the Bible as a document composed over a period of centuries as canonical national literature and the centerpiece of religious faith (Rofé 1999). Since the focus of this exercise is archaeological, the discussion will not commence with a biblical reference. In methodological terms this "secular" approach seeks to tack away from texts toward archaeology (*sensu* Wylie 1989) in an effort to write "history from things" (compare Lubar and Kingery 1993).

Patterns of State Formation in the Levant

Second-millennium BC Levant was organized around competing city-states, ruled largely by headmen or mayors, some of whom regarded themselves as hereditary "princes," with a much smaller number administered by councils of elders. These were in turn under the control of the Egyptian New Kingdom empire, which increasingly assumed direct control of the Levant from its establishment, around 1500 BC, until its dissolution, about 1100 BC (Weinstein 1981). This system represented the continuation of the pattern that emerged first during the Early Bronze Age, around 3600 BC, with urbanism appearing about 3200 BC in the southern Levant, and about 2900 BC in the north (Joffe 1992; Philip 1999).

Entities and Identities in the Bronze Age

In the southern Levant there was a characteristic rising and falling of complexity "cycling" (or perhaps better, "spiraling") through episodes of village-level agropastoralism and small-scale urbanism, during which trade was an important economic component (Joffe 1993). During the second millennium BC, new ethnic elements such as Hurrians were incorporated into the overwhelmingly Semitic-speaking population (Na'aman 1994). By the Late Bronze Age, particularly after the Hyksos interlude, during which southern Levantines briefly ruled Egypt (Oren 1997), the Levant was receptive to Egyptian cultural and religious influence. Mediterranean trade was widespread and brought the Levant into contact with "palatial societies" of Cyprus, Crete, western Anatolia, and the Aegean, as well as those of states in Syria and Mesopotamia (Knapp 1990; Sherratt and Sherratt 1991).

The primary governmental institution of the Levant was the palace. During the period from 2000 to 1500 BC, ruling elites established intimate connections around the Eastern Mediterranean. Diplomatic and economic contacts created a strongly hierarchical world order that was maintained by carefully calibrated rhetoric, trade, gift exchanges, royal marriages, and warfare. Levantine states participated as the lessers, spoilers, and spoil, to the great powers of Egypt, Babylonia, Mitanni, and Hatti (Liverani 1990). The actual power of the palace varied widely throughout the Levant. In all areas, however, elite control over population was a critical problem (Bunimovitz 1994). Strategic resources such as metals formed another basis of palatial power, to the extent that on Cyprus metals were implicated in religious concepts such as symbols of patron deities (Knapp 1986). The drive for wealth necessary to maintain the appearance of legitimacy in the international system was the overriding concern of Bronze Age elites.

Other factors at work in the Late Bronze Age Levant were Egyptian taxation and corvée, geopolitical competition and warfare with the Mitannians and Hittites, and *hab/piru*, a generic term for unruly elements who rejected urban control, including villagers, nomads, and even some townsfolk (Na'aman 1986). On the margins, various nomadic Bedouin-like groups used the semiarid zones and posed occasional threats to urban-controlled settled areas (Giveon 1971). There is evidence for the generation and considerable concentration of wealth, especially at the coastal and largest inland sites, but most settlements were unfortified and rather poor. These gave Levantine city-states in the late second millennium BC a predictable brittleness and fragility.

Social identity during the second millennium BC has been a contentious subject, largely due to the paucity of references in the documentary record. Archaeological studies have suggested that material culture was frequently employed for purposes of social differentiation, in particular imported luxury items, including jewelry, pottery, and consumables. Studies of mortuary behavior, however, have succeeded only in indicating the presence of "non-Canaanites" such as Babylonians, and the archaeological identification of the presence of ethnic "Aegean" persons has been equivocal (e.g., Gittlen 1985; cf. Gonen 1992).

Palaces and ruling elites were vested with the only meaningful sets of identities above the local. Second-millennium BC elite culture was detailed and all-encompassing (Liverani 1990). For Levantine elites, the specific and demanding grammar and vocabulary of the international system defined the identities that overrode all local concerns. The terms and requirements of these asymmetrical relationships were of course defined by and for the large powers, and failure of the city-states to comprehend and submit could result in disaster. Certainly other identity concepts existed, based on kinship or "tribal" affiliation, but these are difficult to perceive in the laconic documentary evidence. In practical terms such concepts may be at work in the existence of family tombs, used over generations and supplied with enormous quantities of removable wealth (Gonen 1992), and in "patrician" houses in which extended families resided (Oren 1992).

But the ideological and economic systems of the palaces, to a far greater extent than the practical systems of local organization or even trade and communication, were the overriding components that "collapsed" at the end of the Bronze Age. Ironically, it was the persistence and reestablishment of elite communication during the Iron Age that served a dramatically different end, the development of ethnic states and their attendant ideologies.

Collapse and Transition

The Levantine city-state system began to collapse around 1200 BC, along with the Egyptian and Hittite empires. Scholars have long debated the causes, with much attention paid to the textually reconstructed predations of the Egyptian empire, repeated invasions of "Sea Peoples," and the presumed impact of Israelites and other "nomadic" groups (Sandars 1978). More recently the traditional interpretations have faltered, certainly with regard to the role of the Israelites. A more contextual interpretation sees a variety of factors at work, including the generalized collapse of palatial economies and international trade throughout the central and eastern Mediterranean, highly localized collapse of political and settlement systems, and both small- and large-scale migrations and resettlement. Egyptian weakness during the twentieth dynasty was both cause and effect, and culminated in the complete abandonment of the empire around 1150 BC. A complex array of new social and settlement forms then appeared, some of which represented new ethnicities in the process of formulation.

Some of the weaknesses of the city-state system and the Egyptian empire are outlined earlier in this chapter. The dependence on continuous circulation of prestige items and metallic wealth was a structural weakness. Cascading failures were created by the local security problems and the subsequent inability of both superpowers and local elites to extract surpluses necessary for procurement of strategic materials. Commerce conducted by entrepreneurs increasingly bypassed the palaces and undermined their wealth and authority. The development of iron metallurgy by the "sub-elites," and the dissemination of utilitarian objects outside palatial control, also contributed to the "subversion of the established order" (Sherratt 1994, 1998). New patterns of international mobility included the appearance of migrants, not least of all "Sea Peoples," who destabilized areas of Cyprus and the southern Levant (Stager 1995).

These infamous groups, largely of Aegean origins, had slowly and perhaps violently moved east to the southern Levant via Cyprus. Egyptian texts depict their land and sea invasion being successfully repulsed by Ramses III at the very borders of Egypt, after they allegedly ravaged Cyprus, Syria, the Hittite lands, and the Levant (Dothan 1982; Betancourt 2000; O'Connor 2000). Archaeological evidence, however, indicates a more complex and equivocal picture. The Hittite empire indeed collapsed, as did the Cypriot and Mycenean city-state system, largely for reasons described above, mainly in processes of localized dissolution. Little beyond the Egyptian accounts suggest that invasions or anything other than localized conflict contributed to their demise. With the notable exception of Ugarit (Yon 1992; Bonatz 1993), most of the cities of the northern Levant either continued to exist in a diminished condition or were quickly reoccupied, as were those of the central Levant and inland Syria (Liverani 1987; Caubet 1992). In the south, a few inland city-states persisted, many were abandoned, and a few others along the coast were occupied by Sea Peoples (Bietak 1993). These urban coastal sites are consistent with the area known later as Philistia, a term derived from the Egyptian term *plṣt* for one of the groups of Sea Peoples. The sites contain distinctive material culture with strong Aegean affinities that may be called "Philistine" (Dothan 1982; Stager 1995; Bunimovitz and Yasur-Landau 1996). Much of the Philistine assemblage appears specifically designed for use in the creation and maintenance of group identity, such as religion and rituals, including those related to male solidarity, and perhaps patron-client relations, such as drinking and feasting (Joffe 1999; Killebrew 2000).

Another outstanding question is that of "tribes" at the end of the Late Bronze Age (see the discussion in Routledge 2000). Much research and controversy have been predicated on the existence of tribes as understood through biblical texts. External texts do not address the existence of tribal entities that may be persuasively related to those of biblical Israel, although a variety of roughly contemporary parallel groups such as Arameans are attested in the later second millennium (Zadok 1991; Sader 2000, 64–65; Peckham 2001), along with arid-zone groups such as *Shasu* (Giveon 1971). Discussion is greatly complicated by the elaborate biblical presentation of putative relationships between various Israelite tribes and their role in religion, culture, defense, and the development of the state. These have been enthusiastically embraced by biblical scholars, as have many sociological and anthropological studies that are presumed to offer analogies for antiquity (Gottwald 1979; Overholt 1995).

It is prudent, therefore, merely to point to the relative balance between kin-based organization and mobility strategies. In the Mediterranean zones of agropastoral village settlement, ruralized society reemphasized real and fictive kinship as a means of creating bonds between families and settlements. In the semiarid zones, where resources were limited and pastoralism and other mobile strategies were always more important, the release from even nominal political constraints may have permitted "real" tribes to expand and elaborate their organization, and enter into larger confederations (LaBianca and Younker 1995; cf. Tapper 1990). But in all areas the eclipse and collapse of palatial power, the emergence of new technologies, and social and spatial reorganization, including ruralization resulting from resistance to or flight from state power on the part of villagers, were far more important factors than immigrants.

In the final analysis, what collapsed during the period around 1200–1150 BC was the international system and its interdependent network of local city-states. The end of palatial and imperial superstructures opened up spaces for local populations to shift and reconfigure, and to expand their own international contacts. The relative contribution of newcomers to disruption and growth was small, even as it loomed large in the imagination of Egyptian scribes, later biblical writers, and earlier generations of archaeologists. Local elites quickly began to assert themselves, in the same fashion as their predecessors throughout the Bronze Age, and palatial society was quickly reborn. What was different, however, was not how these new palaces were organized, but rather the size of the units over which they stood, and the differentiated identities of their societies.

Iron Age Secondary-State Formation

Several phases of state formation are apparent in the Eastern Mediterranean after 1200 BC. In each of these a similar constellation of features is found, pointing to an integrated process, similar to that of "peer polity interaction" described by Renfrew and Cherry (1986). In effect, the concept of the state and statecraft cascaded outward in a process of elite emulation and competition that took some 150 to 200 years. But it was only in a few examples, namely Israel, Judah, and perhaps Ammon and Moab, that more fully fledged "ethnic states" emerged (see figure 3.1).

The Early Phases: Phoenicia 1200–1000 BC

The first states appeared along the Mediterranean coast in what became known as Phoenicia. The primary sites were Tyre, Sidon, Beirut, Byblos, and Arwad, each separated from one another by rivers flowing west into the Mediterranean from the Lebanon range. These Canaanite city-states did not collapse entirely at the end of the Late Bronze Age but maintained social and institutional continuity across the putative boundary of 1200 BC. Previously the Syrian and Lebanese coasts had been part of the generalized province and concept of "Canaan," but after 1200 BC, an area of some two hundred kilometers, from Arwad on the Nahr el-Kebir in the north to the Plain of Akko in the south, was differentiated into "Phoenicia." This process of cultural and political differentiation may

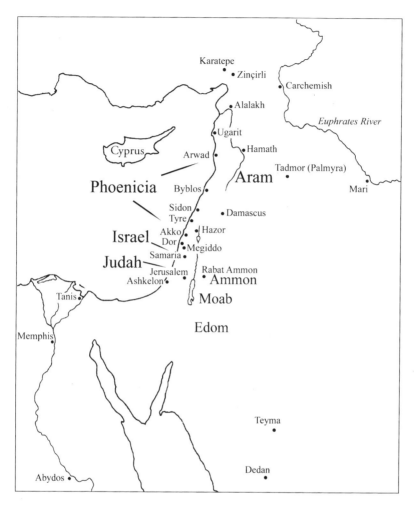

Figure 3.1   Map of the Levant in the Iron Age

be outlined to some degree (Aubet 1993, 12–16; Moscati 1993; Peckham 2001; Krings 1995).

To the north of the coastal cities, the singular entity of the kingdom of Ugarit, which had dominated much of the northern coast politically, economically, and even militarily, collapsed. Dominated politically by the Hittite empire, heavily dependent on trade with the Hittites and with Cyprus, and with demanding and top-heavy administration and elite structure, this kingdom succumbed to the multiple disruptions of the late thirteenth century BC. The end of Ugarit permitted the independence of former vassals at large sites such as Karatepe and Carchemish, a wave of renewed urbanization, and the emergence of culturally hybrid Syro-Hittite city-states across northern Syria and southeastern Anatolia (Mazzoni 1995).

To the east, the interior city-states of the Beqaa Valley and those in Syria beyond the Anti-Lebanon range had been deeply enmeshed in the Egyptian system, since they stood on the border with the Hittite sphere of influence. The withdrawal of the Egyptians and Hittites, their exactions and protections, left the interior temporarily adrift, a condition that coastal sites found highly advantageous. It is precisely in these eastern areas, notably along the Euphrates, Habur, and Orontes rivers, and in the Damascus basin, that "seminomads" from the Syrian steppe were able to enter and begin establishing themselves in an already rural environment (Sader 2000). The *ahlamu*-Arameans had long been part of the local population of Syria, associated with the area called Aram by the Assyrians, a generic designation for a wide swath from the Habur River to the Lebanon range (Nashef 1982). By the eleventh century BC, the term "Aramean" was used alone by the Assyrians, and the emergent states of the tenth century referred to themselves as *bīt*, "house of," a term reflecting the tradition of "tribal" origins and patrilineal organization (Postgate 1974; Zadok 1991).

Finally, to the south, the southern Levant was undergoing a complex situation of imperial retreat, urban decline and accompanying ruralization, and foreign settlement. Phoenicia was a semiprotected geographic entity, with an economy based on the exploitation of the sea and the mountains to the immediate east. While the central coast of Phoenicia had been heavily involved in maritime trade and the exploitation of timber products during the Bronze Age (and had perhaps even been disadvantaged by the relative strength of Ugarit), the reduction in the client base simply meant that sites could temporarily reemphasize subsistence exploitation of marine and coastal resources. But already by the reign of the Assyrian king Tiglath-Pileser I (1114–1076 BC), tribute was being sent from the Phoenician cities of Byblos, Sidon, and Arwad (Grayson 1976, 23). At the same time, Egyptian interest in Phoenician products was reemerging, as recorded in the famous report of the emissary Wen-Amun (Goedicke 1975).

In a sense, the involution of Phoenicia during the lull of imperial politics and international trade meant the reemergence of specifically coastal adaptations and identities (as measured by the crude proxy of material culture), which had prevailed during prehistory. During the Iron Age this logically bounded entity had the benefit of a very long tradition of local administration and politics. It is not surprising that a cultural and political identity such as "Phoenicia" coalesced during this period. It is critical to note, however, that this unity was cultural rather than political. Individual cities retained political autonomy under separate, named dynasties and patron deities and were never united except in dire situations. Individual Phoenician dynasties called themselves by the name of their city, Sidonian, Tyrian, Byblian, and so on. For all intents and purposes, these were simply extensions of Bronze Age concepts and practices. The very term "Phoenician" is applied not by the cultural or historical tradition of the Levantine coast, but rather by outsiders, notably Greeks. While Phoenicians must have been sufficiently distinctive in the eyes of others, they regarded themselves as "Canaanites."

As both a cultural and political concept, therefore, Phoenicia was only moderately integrated. What was new and innovative in Phoenicia were technologies and styles and their dissemination, through both Phoenician expansion and emulation. A singular technology that appeared first in Phoenicia is the alphabet. The significance of the alphabet as a means of facilitating cultural interaction by persons other than trained scribes has been much discussed, most notably in the contentious debate over the transmission of the alphabet to the Greeks (e.g., Bernal 1990; Powell 1991; Sass 1991). The alphabet was easy to learn and use on a variety of basic materials and was able to express a variety of languages with slight modifications. An information system capable of recording and codifying both prosaic data and high culture, or even generating multiple streams within historical or cultural traditions, should not be underestimated. After 1200 BC literacy became theoretically accessible to a far wider spectrum within Levantine societies.

The transmission of the alphabet is one of many Phoenician innovations that profoundly affected the rest of the Mediterranean and the Levant. Critical to Phoenicia's influence was the rapid expansion of the various city-states, ultimately leading to the establishment of colonies throughout the central and western Mediterranean. Trade relations with Greece, Sicily, Italy, and North Africa evidently began by the tenth century, with actual colonies founded slightly later (Aubet 1993). Phoenician trade with the eastern coast of Cyprus and with Egypt receded in the thirteenth and twelfth centuries but quickly reemerged in the eleventh century, with a different pattern of exports and imports than seen previously. Cypriot exports to the mainland declined, but Phoenician and other Levantine exports to Cyprus expanded considerably (Gilboa 1998; Bikai 1987). Inland participation in the new trading order was limited until the tenth century, but these regions were hardly isolated. Closer at hand, however, Phoenician city-states vied with one another for power and extended their control both inland toward the Lebanon range and to the south, into Galilee and the Plain of Akko. Major sites such as Tell Keisan and Tell Dor appear to have been under Phoenician control during the late eleventh century, although the presence of other ethnic groups is indicated by the crude proxy of ceramic types (Mazar 1994; Gilboa 1998; Lehmann 2001; cf. Stern 1998). More specialized sites such as Horvat Rosh Zayit, a small border fortress and olive oil production center, were also founded during the late eleventh or very early tenth century (Gal and Alexandre 2000).

The cultural centrality of Phoenicia and its organizational concepts to the Levant were materialized further through the arts and crafts. Among the most notable categories of material culture are ceramics, metal and ivory working, textiles, and coroplastic art (see the essays in Moscati 1988). Phoenician ceramics, painted and burnished jars and bowls, were distributed and the latter imitated widely during the tenth century BC in particular (W. P. Anderson 1990), as were the elaborate metals and ivories, reflecting complex integration of Egyptian, Syrian, and local motifs (Markoe 1985; Winter 1976). Hybrid motifs were also present on engraved seals and scarabs, which combined iconography and alphabetic inscriptions for administrative and display purposes (Gubel 1993). The ease with which Phoenician artisans adopted motifs, and perhaps underlying cultural concepts, is another distinctive feature of Levantine coastal culture glimpsed already during the third millennium BC (Joffe 1992). The dissemination of Phoenician, Syrian, and Egyptian iconography and ideas throughout the Levant was critical in exposing primarily rural areas to elite culture and organizational methods.

Despite this, Phoenicia was not a politically centralized state, nor an integrated ethnic group or nation. It was functionally interrelated by economics and many aspects of shared culture and language, but the city-states were not integrated politically and territorially. However, maintaining overall cultural distinctiveness was not a priority for elites and their states, or communities and households. The greatest significance lies in that Phoenician city-states developed organizational methods that could be tailored to distinct, local societies, and that during the early Iron Age, Phoenicia actively asserted itself over less sophisticated neighbors. These "core-periphery" relationships were hardly unique at the very end of the second millennium BC and in the initial centuries of the first. The Aramean regions of northern Syria were enmeshed in similar, if very much more complex, interactions with Phoenicia, the neo-Hittite city-states, and Assyria, as were the Urarṭian regions to the east of Lake Van, not to mention the Phrygians and Lydians of central and southern Anatolia (Zimansky 1985; Muscarella 1995). What makes the otherwise undistinguished southern Levantine periphery interesting is the emergence of progressively culturally integrated, rather small ethnic states, or better, "ethnicizing" states. (I choose the neologism "ethnicizing" precisely to indicate that the resulting ethnic states were constructions, not natural entities.)

The Early Phases: Change in the Phoenician Periphery

The period 1200–1000 BC in the southern Levant is perhaps the most closely studied and hotly debated in all Near Eastern archaeology. Despite the heavy burden placed on the archaeological data by biblical texts, new projects have created a clearer picture of shifts in settlement and organization that led to the rise of states in the southern Levant. These do not, however, appear to resemble closely the entities depicted either in the Bible or by most archaeologists.

As noted earlier, ruralization is a dominant theme at the end of the second millennium BC in the southern Levant and in inland Syria. Beginning around 1200 BC, many small rural sites were founded throughout the highlands on both sides of the Jordan River (Finkelstein 1988b, 1994). Settlements were located in upland regions suitable for carefully calibrated balances of agriculture and pastoralism. In areas of higher rainfall, agriculture, including Mediterranean crops of olives, grapes, figs, and dates, dominated, while in more arid regions, herding of ovicaprids prevailed. The differences between these two areas and their subsistence balances amounted in all cases to only a few kilometers. Typically comprising a handful to a dozen or so structures, most were open settlements. The orientation of buildings and walls seems designed to provide enclosure for livestock and at best notional defenses (Fritz 1995, 50–75). Total population density could only have numbered in the low thousands, and there is a strong gradient of settlement density decline from north to south, and from west to east (Finkelstein 1988b; Ofer 1994). The nature of settlement in southern Transjordan during this period is a matter of some controversy (Finkelstein 1995, 127–37; cf. Bienkowski 2001).

The origins of these rural settlers have been much debated, but on the available evidence of ceramic style, technology, and other material culture, including religious and ritual (Nakhai 2001, 170–76; cf. Zevit 2001, 84–85), most appear to have simply been indigenous Canaanites. The organization of new agropastoral villages, with characteristic two-story, four- or five-room farmhouses (Ji 1997), suggests complex domestic groups, probably extended families (Stager 1985). Since labor remained the key limitation for exploiting the environment, various strategies for enlarging domestic groups were likely to have been employed, including coresidence of multiple generations and siblings, matrilocal or patrilocal residence, and adoption. The manipulation of kinship also provided an important means to generate linkages between domestic groups, in order to enlarge families and create extensive webs of shared culture and reciprocal obligation within and between communities.

Religious rituals and other activities such as community feasting in the context of seasonal agricultural labor (Joffe 1999), not to mention common defense, fixed the ties and identities that held communities together. Though much has been made by some scholars of the lack of pig bones at early Iron Age sites, these do not necessarily reflect a deliberate food preference or religious prohibition so much as the difficulty in raising these animals in highland settings. But the probability that such behavior unconsciously reinforced patterns of interaction and the development of community identities should not be discounted (Hesse 1990; Hesse and Wapnish 1997).

Larger social networks were the foundation for community-wide abatement of subsistence risk. In the unpredictable environments of the Levant, and the Mediterranean as a whole, survival was contingent on creating social units that could cope with stresses such as drought through social storage and mutual obligation (Halstead and O'Shea 1989; Butzer 1996). This necessitated the creation of larger productive units, extended families, and beyond that, communities and shared culture. These, in turn, were the foundation for still larger processes of centralization, and the corollary accretion of power.

The increasing numbers of twelfth- and eleventh-century sites show trends toward site planning and social architecture (Mazar 1994). Sites became larger and more organized, with more storage facilities and social architecture, such as the extremely large structures at En Hagit and

Tell ʿEn Zippori (Dessel 1999), plausibly interpreted as civic buildings. Silos also proliferated at settlements, suggesting social storage, although how this was administered is unclear. In the northern Negev it has even been proposed that the largest site, Tell Masos, was the site of a "chiefdom" (Finkelstein 1995).

Critical to the return of states in the southern Levant are that some diminished Late Bronze Age city-states, such as Megiddo, Beth Shan, and ʿAfula, persisted into the eleventh century. Such continuities raise the possibility that at least some urban institutions and traditions remained intact. It is unclear whether elites at these sites were at the forefront of creating larger political entities, but their close proximity to Phoenicia makes it likely that they had considerable familiarity with those elite concepts and styles, through observation and trade relations over very short distances. The mechanisms and motivations for observing and emulating more sophisticated organization were extremely close at hand.

At the same time, other influences were penetrating the southern Levant. The site of Tell Hadar, for example, on the east shore of the Sea of Galilee, is a small fortified citadel used for storing agricultural products, but whose scant domestic architecture appears Aramean in design (Kochavi 1989). It is unclear whether this site was part of one of the small entities called in second-millennium-BC sources Geshur and Maacah, possibly in the process of becoming Arameanized, or was simply a southern manifestation of Aramean society (Pitard 1987, 87–89). What is certain is that this area was a frontier zone with Aram-Damascus. Even the Sea Peoples in their guise as "Philistines" were, unlike their Cypriot counterparts, becoming less distinguishable in material-culture terms from the surrounding southern Levantine culture (Dothan 1995; Iacovou 1998).

By the eleventh century BC, trends toward greater social and economic differentiation and political centralization in the southern Levant are evident. The motivation and the models for recreating states on the periphery of Phoenicia were immediate. The simplest explanation is that, as had recurred repeatedly during the Bronze Age, powerful elites, evocatively called "mafiosi" by Gilman (1990), saw it to their advantage to reorganize space, labor, and ideology in order to create more productive and exploitative social and economic structures. This was likely accomplished with an ever-shifting balance of coercions and benefits, such as violence, patronage, and the creation of new economies, as well as through social organization and ideology. The manipulation of genealogies, in all likelihood already a mechanism for establishing real and fictive kinship relations between lineages and communities, was also a long-standing means for leaders to establish their legitimacy in local, historical, and even cosmological terms (Van Seters 1983).

The question of who these elites were, however, is tantalizingly vague. Various rural headmen were likely to have been involved in the process, but it is unclear whether these were the true or only instigators. Given that urbanism and then state institutions reappear most forcefully at former city-states, with defensible locations on key trade routes and possessed of especially ample agricultural lands, two complementary suggestions may be offered. The first is that greater demographic and institutional continuity existed at major sites west of the Jordan River, as likely occurred during earlier episodes of reurbanization and the initial emergence of the state (Joffe 1993). The second is that regardless of the actual level of continuity, the economic and social centrality of key sites gave them important advantages over smaller ones in the reestablishment of social hierarchies and social differentiation. But the emergence of a rural component, with strong networks of connections, also created for the first time in the southern Levant a meaningful social counterbalance to the power of cities. The Iron Age was the uneasy fusion of both urban and rural, where loci of politics, economics, and culture were in constant tension.

The Later Phases: Israel and Its Neighbors 1000–900 BC

The tenth century BC is the pivotal period in the study of Iron Age states, and it becomes increasingly difficult to keep the biblical accounts from intruding upon the archaeological record and archaeological imagination. Predictably, the archaeological evidence is a fragmented mosaic, not easily arranged into a coherent picture.[1] It is sufficient, however, to identify the existence of a state west of the Jordan River. A series of palatial structures, and other forms of material culture, both delineate and delimit the tenth-century state (see figure 3.2).

Biblical archaeology's traditional view of the tenth century BC presumed the existence of kings named David and Solomon and revolved around insights that correlated three sets of elements from the sites of Gezer, Hazor, and Megiddo (Yadin 1958; Dever 1982; Fritz 1995, 79–96). Fortification walls, administrative buildings, and three-pier gates all show remarkable similarity in terms of design, dimension, and execution, leading to the conclusion that they were constructed by a single

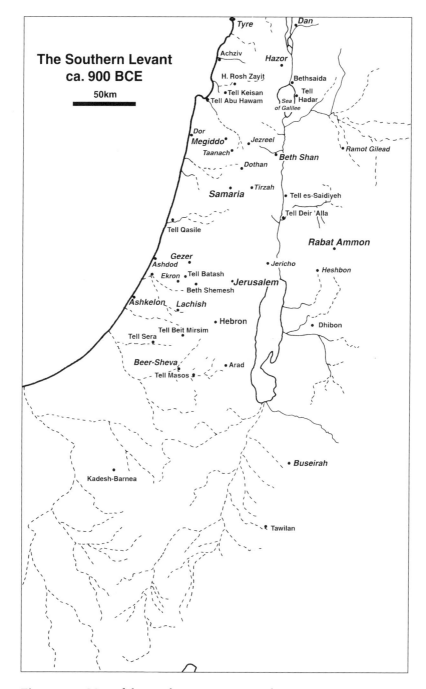

Figure 3.2 Map of the southern Levant around 900 BC

team of architects and craftsmen under the direction of a royal administration, probably Solomon's. It has become increasingly clear, however, that all these elements are not precisely contemporary. For example, the gates at Megiddo, Hazor, and Gezer were not built at exactly the same time as accompanying fortifications, which suggests that the capabilities of the organizing authorities were not especially great (Ussishkin 1980). At the same time, however, the masonry and construction styles at these sites are extremely similar, in essence employing Phoenician techniques (Shiloh 1979).

The administrative structures were not reused Late Bronze Age structures but were constructed new. Importantly, most are variants of a style called *bīt ḫilāni*, with an entranceway flanked by pillars leading to a central court. This style originated in northern Syria among Arameans with strong familiarity with neo-Hittite terms and practices (Frankfurt 1952; Reich 1992; Arav and Bernett 2000), but by the tenth century BC and afterward, it quickly became a standard template for palaces throughout western Asia, including Assyria. At Hazor and Megiddo these are the dominant structures on the sites, with only fragmentary evidence for domestic architecture (figure 3.3). But the lack of storage facilities is critical and indicates that elites occupying these structures were not primarily engaged in providing economic and social services to local communities but were concerned rather with establishing a local ideological presence and conducting political affairs. Furthermore, each site was constructed on a border, Megiddo with Phoenicia, Gezer with Philistia, and Hazor with Aram-Damascus, indicating that these were not in fact independent city-states but rather were part of a larger entity whose borders remain difficult to define. The presence of multiple palaces at these sites is difficult to understand but may even reflect competing elites within each site who were somehow subservient to the still vague center (cf. Herr 1997, 126).

Notable decorative features in these palaces are elaborate column capitals decorated with carved volutes representing palm trees. These "proto-aeolic" capitals are found not only in the southern Levant but also across the Eastern Mediterranean, particularly on Cyprus (figure 3.4). In later centuries this style decorated palaces from Moab to Etruria, used on a variety of capitals, stelae, ceramic shrines, carved ivories, and other items (Shiloh 1979). The wide dissemination of specific royal architectural and decorative styles is a strong indication that from the tenth century BC onward, a new international system was emerging, which like its Late Bronze Age predecessor had a specific grammar and syntax.

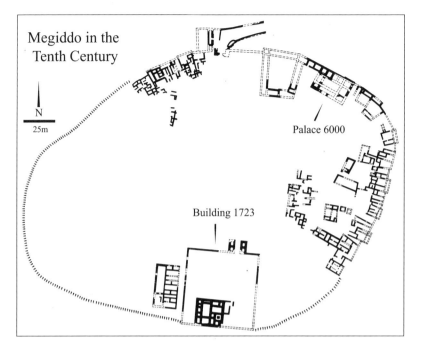

Figure 3.3 Plan of Megiddo during the tenth century BC. Palace 6000 is a bīt hilāni–style building.

Another element of the emergent "royal" culture in the tenth-century southern Levant was red burnished pottery imitating Phoenician wares. Often called "Solomonic" pottery, this assemblage was limited to open bowls and vessels and did not possess a full range of forms, for example, cooking pots or storage vessels. The assemblage was intended for use in specific social situations such as drinking and feasting. Pottery of this sort never exceeded some 15 percent of the total assemblage at any site, sometimes much lower, suggesting that it was disseminated narrowly. It was especially common in various administrative structures (Holladay 1990). Whether this was an elite assemblage manufactured from above, or a sumptuary assemblage purchased from local producers, is unclear. But the association with Phoenicia was deliberate and identified the users as associated either directly or informally with the royal establishment and its ideology. At the same time, another ceramic type, the so-called "hippo" storage jars, was widely distributed through the north, and its distribution and ceramic materials demonstrate strong commer-

Figure 3.4   Examples of "proto-aeolic" capitals from tenth-century BC Megiddo and Hazor

cial connections with Phoenicia (Alexandre 1995). The movement of actual agricultural products from the periphery to the core underpinned the export of selected ideological artifacts in the opposite direction.

A number of obvious elements, namely monumental architecture and pottery, indicate the deliberate materialization or concrete expression of a royal concept (DeMarrais, Castillo, and Earle 1996), but many more are lacking. There are few indications of the reorganization of space or labor, since the vast majority of the population remained in rural sites, little different from those of preceding centuries. Indeed, social storage continued to take place in rural society. No representational art, monumental inscriptions, or inscribed or decorated objects can be dated to the tenth century BC. Any direct discussion of royal iconography or administration is impossible, along with prosopography in general. There were not large numbers of even uninscribed seals or weights, making it difficult to discuss economic structures such as standardization and exchange. Only the construction of administrative sites suggests extraction of labor by the state. Relying therefore on negative evidence, it is reasonable to suggest that beyond architecture, there were no iconographic and administrative means for disseminating royal ideology, through a presence in the visual environment and domination of forms of business and administration. Overall, the tenth-century state seems barely integrated at all. Integration is prosaic at best, based on preexisting social and economic connections, and little suggests any meaningful level of ethnic unity.

The tenth-century state did not or could not construct a complete set of administrative and symbolic structures, but it did use elements of the emerging international style. The limited residential, administrative, and ceremonial structures show that tenth-century sites were ideological shells, where state functionaries carried on administrative and diplomatic functions. Social storage and provisioning were not used as a state service to generate allegiance. What wealth that could be extracted was channeled into materializing the state in overt ways, but not in the elaboration of a royal ideology that redefined the local political and cosmological orders to lend legitimacy to the new system (Baines and Yoffee 1998). Only the international elements gave hint of larger ideological frameworks into which new elites were connected. Royal pottery, like royal architecture, was only loosely integrated with society at large. Social organization and local religious ideology appear unchanged, with kin networks, and household cult and small open-air shrines directed at the same Canaanite deities as before (Dever 1990, 128–40). In a sense the tenth-century state was a fragile and perishable Potemkin Village, with a royal establishment that was not especially powerful.

Though a slender basis for asserting a new state, creation of a royal assemblage that projected the ideology of an emergent elite across socially diverse landscapes was common during the Iron Age. An excellent example of this is Urarṭu, where extensive and elaborate art, architecture, and material culture materialized imperial authority across a much larger area that was more ethnically diverse than the southern Levant (Zimansky 1995; A. T. Smith 1999, 2000). A meager southern Levantine parallel to this far-flung and visually rich undertaking was a network of small fortresses and caravanserai throughout the northern Negev Desert, designed to project tenth-century state authority and to defend and pacify the desert frontier. It might be as correct to say that desert fortresses were a state means of organizing the rural frontier from the outside inward. But no tenth-century inscriptions from Phoenicia, Egypt, or Mesopotamia mention a political entity called Israel or rulers called David and Solomon. To its contemporaries, the tenth-century state was probably too ephemeral to really notice as a political entity (cf. Malamat 1982).

The biblical texts speak of the capital city in Jerusalem, but the area where the royal establishment and temple may have stood cannot be excavated. Strong arguments can be made on archaeological, historical, and literary grounds that a capital existed in Jerusalem during the tenth century BC (Na'aman 1996), and the pattern of establishing new capitals either "disembedded" from or "reembedded" in preexisting geographies of power is well attested, especially in Assyria (Joffe 1998b). But the problem of Jerusalem goes to the heart of the question regarding who were the leaders of this unusual state. The biblical texts speak about the tribal structure, and how after a period of adjudicant-religious-war leaders or judges, kingship was divinely assigned to Saul and then David and his lineage. David and especially Solomon are credited with creating a state whose administrative districts defied tribal boundaries, a capital in Jerusalem, complete with palace and temple, royal cities and garrisons, and an aggressive foreign policy, all overseen by corps of administrators (Soggin 1977).

As elegant and attractive as this scenario is, the archaeological evidence suggests a far more modest state whose center remains for the moment obscure. It is difficult to even speak of kingship during the tenth century BC, only of elites with lesser or fragmentary rather than overarching forms of power, perhaps even competitive and overlapping elites, sorting out prerogatives for rule under some common, state-level framework. The literary and historical emphasis on tribes and kingship, and the documentable appearance of the latter from the ninth century onward, might indicate that such forms indeed existed in the tenth century, but this cannot be demonstrated as yet archaeologically. The adoption of elements of the international ruling style is an indication that this small, peripheral state was closely aware of the world outside its borders and the norms for elite behavior, as is later literary emphasis on the international stature of dynastic founders. In the end, the fragility of the tenth-century state, however, had unexpected effects. It stimulated both the development of even more peripheral polities and new concepts of identity. The state preceded the ethnicity.

Ethnicizing States of the Ninth Century BC

The rise of the tenth-century state was largely a function of the northern and central portions of the southern Levant becoming a periphery of Phoenician city-states and a neighbor or competitor to Aramean city-states. As noted above, Phoenician city-states were culturally integrated but politically independent. Aramean city-states were in practical terms politically independent, but texts such as the Sefire inscription suggest that some elites possessed at least a notion of ethnic-geographic integration (Grosby 1998). In contrast, the emergence of ninth-century states took place in a more complex international geopolitical situation. In the north, Phoenicia and Aram were the dominant local entities, but further afield the neo-Assyrian empire was resurgent and moving inexorably westward. One effect was to reactivate old political patterns of fight or flight, confronting elites with the choice of paying tribute or resisting individually or uniting into larger coalitions that temporarily overrode local disputes (Kuan 1995; Bar 1996). Political elites vacillated among these strategies, sometimes with success, and other times without.

Another effect was intensification of long-distance trade, including routes in the desert margins, which had diminished in importance since the evaporation of the Egyptian empire some two hundred years earlier. In Transjordan this made tribes the middlemen between villagers and pastoral nomads for transport of considerable wealth from Arabia. The archaeological evidence for the timing and extent of desert trade is still incomplete, but the appearance of *Midianite* pottery in southern Jordan and western Saudi Arabia by 1200 BC demonstrates the emergence of local groups on the far margin of the empire (Finkelstein 1988a; Parr 1992). The appearance of states east of the Jordan River during and after the ninth century, including the expansion of the Arameans along the shores of the Sea of Galilee (Arav and Bernett 2000), should be linked with new sources of wealth on an otherwise lean periphery.

The historically attested raid of Shoshenq, a non-Egyptian general who ascended to the throne and founded the twenty-second dynasty (Kitchen 1986, 72–76, 285–302; Redford 1992, 312–19; cf. Na'aman 1992) around 925 BC, has been long sought as a stratigraphic benchmark dividing the first and second stages of Iron Age states. This is also the lone synchronism between Egyptian and biblical texts, since the latter records Shoshenq's raid as taking place in the fifth year of Rehoboam, Solomon's son and successor (1 Kings 11:40). But the interest of Shoshenq demonstrates that the redeveloping urbanism of the southern Levant was a tantalizing target. As far back as the third millennium BC, Egyptian kings raided the southern Levant for short-term gains. This seems to have been Shoshenq's intent as well, although the biblical text implies that the raid was part of an effort to create a separate vassal state in Israel under Jeroboam (Wilson 2001). But the temporary reemergence of Egypt as a major state, capable of projecting its power and influence far beyond its borders, was another major factor in the emergence of still more states. Egypt represented a threat, but also an opportunity.

Given these external complexities, the tenth-century state fragmented. Regional divisions become far more apparent from the ninth century onward. West of the Jordan, the ceramic evidence indicates the bifurcation of north and south, in historical terms, Israel and Judah, along the same geographic lines displayed as far back as the late fourth millennium BC. From the ninth century onward, ceramic assemblages in these regions varied considerably, as did assemblages on either side of the Jordan River. During the Bronze Age, there was little east-west distinction in ceramic assemblages, and this persisted through the early Iron Age. After the tenth century, however, variation becomes notable, even profound, and is the best indication of social groups with very limited economic and social interaction (Amiran 1969, 191–299; Hendrix, Drey, and Storfjell 1996, 170–202). Early Iron Age integration, which consisted of local economic and social interaction in which there was little horizontal differentiation in terms of identity, language, or belief system, were confounded by political geographic factors from above. Networks of settlement, trade, marriage, and kinship were gradually severed by divergence of local interests and the emergence of local elites. By some time in the later ninth century BC, the southern Judean and Moabite states had established themselves as politically and culturally independent from the northern Israelite state. But while Philistine city-states maintained their political autonomy, they shared almost all the material culture of Judah (Gitin 1998). The creation of new ethnicities and ethnicizing states was a more powerful force than the maintenance of older ethnic concepts and political forms.

During the ninth century BC a wider range of state functions began to emerge at sites both west and east of the Jordan River. In contrast to the tenth century, the ninth century displayed a more routinized and articulated approach to rule. This is seen first of all in the design of palaces, such as at Samaria, which contain both living and administrative areas and substantial storage facilities (Crowfoot, Kenyon, and Sukenik 1942; Tappy 1992). Also constructed using Phoenician-style masonry, this palace was far larger than the border sites of Megiddo, Hazor, and Gezer, which were also rebuilt during the course of the ninth century with the notable addition of storage facilities (Holladay 1986). Unlike the tenth-century examples, the palace at Samaria was eventually elaborately equipped with sumptuary items in the Phoenician style, especially carved ivory furniture inlays and decorative items (Crowfoot and Crowfoot 1938). These items, obtainable only through elite contacts, situate the occupants not simply within the Levantine but within a broader international sphere of political style (Winter 1976; Barnett 1982, 43–55; Herrmann 2000). Other indications of the northern ruling approach are seen in the construction of additional palaces, and the production of "Samaria ware," thin, red-slipped and burnished bowls imitating Phoenician prototypes. This should be contrasted with the prosaic evidence of varied household architecture suggesting considerable ethnic diversity (Faust 2000). The façade state by necessity evolved into the rent-seeking state, but ethnic homogeneity was not an overriding goal.

The "independence" of "Judah" took place over several decades during the ninth century BC. The same considerations that had impelled the creation of the tenth-century state as a periphery that supplied Phoenicia and consumed its products, which supported a high level of urbanism and elite sumptuary behavior, now motivated elites in Judah to loosen their connections with the north. Egypt was vastly larger and wealthier than Phoenicia but had different strategic needs, primarily for buffer states. Settlement in Judah had been minimal from the twelfth through the tenth centuries, with a far lower density of settlement than in Israel, Ammon, and even Moab (Ofer 2001). The geography of Judah, with higher hills and steeper slopes that grade to desert in the east and south, was less conducive to the limited agropastoral settlement characteristic of the twelfth and eleventh centuries than was Israel in the north. Even during the tenth century BC, which experienced more extensive rural settlement, urbanism had been limited to a few "royal" outposts like Arad.

But Judah, previously a periphery to a periphery, found itself during the ninth century oriented increasingly toward Egypt. Jerusalem itself remained relatively small through the eighth century, but during the ninth century, a coherent settlement system emerged with an imposing citadel on the southeast frontier facing Egypt, Lachish; desert fortresses like Arad; and storehouse complexes in smaller towns like Beersheba, designed to protect the borders and serve as central places for economy and society. Steady growth of villages and towns took place throughout the ninth and eighth centuries with few breaks (Mazar 1997, 163). During this period, Judah began to pursue an independent economic policy, using mass-produced pottery, a distinct system of inscribed weights based on Egyptian numbers and measures (Aharoni 1966; Kletter 1998; Fox 2000, 250–68), and inscribed stamp seals and bullae, also based on Egyptian practices (Avigad and Sass 1997). Other features becoming visible in the late ninth and early eighth centuries BC include burial in bench tombs with bone repositories and headrests shaped like the hairstyle of the Egyptian goddess Hathor, which become characteristic of the south (Bloch-Smith 1992).

Among the most significant indicators of the independence of Judah are inscribed seals and bullae. More than twelve hundred Iron Age seals and impressions are known from the southern Levant, virtually all bearing some sort of inscription. The majority date to the eighth through the sixth centuries BC, but a small number show that the practice began in the ninth century or earlier. Almost all southern Levantine examples are stamp seals rather than Mesopotamian-style cylinder seals. The stamp seal, and the approach to sealing clay bullae identifying folded papyrus, parchment, or vessel tags and vessels themselves, identify the practice as being of Egyptian inspiration. The iconography of southern Levantine seals is also strongly influenced by Egypt. Winged scarabs and griffins are among the most common motifs, and even the tiny decorative element that divides the various fields is often decorated with a lotus bud (Sass 1993).

An important observation is that the overwhelming number of seals with personal names indicates a high level of literacy, at least among individuals who conducted economic transactions. This should be contrasted with contemporary neo-Assyrian seals, where inscriptions are rare (Millard 2001). The use of numerous official titles on seals also reflects a complex bureaucracy and the institution of kingship, which were deeply involved in economic oversight and military affairs (Fox 2000). The paleography of inscribed seals supports the view that scripts and dialects became distinct by the ninth century, although the persistent difficulty in classification points to their continued mutual intelligibility. Even more important, the use of theophoric elements in personal names, such as Yahweh, El, Milkom, Baʿal, and others, points to the incorporation of regional or state religion into the practices and worldview of daily society (Avigad 1987; Zadok 1988).

The identity of the elites who gradually assumed control of the Judean and Israelite states remains problematic, but by the middle of the ninth century BC, extra-biblical references give indication of who was in charge. Dating to around 850 BC, the Mesha Stele mentions the king of Israel "who oppressed Moab many days" and distinguishes him from Omri, who assumed power later. It also states that in a raid, vessels had been taken from Yahweh and given to the Moabite deity Kemosh. In further distinction from Israel, the "House of David" is mentioned as controlling a southern area that the Moabites then reclaimed in battle (Routledge 2000, 247–50). The Black Obelisk of Shalmaneser III (c. 853 BC) names and depicts Jehu, son of Omri, lying before the Assyrian king, offering gifts (Pritchard 1969, 281). Finally, the two fragments of the Tell Dan inscription (c. 805 BC) mention both the "King of Israel" and the "House of David," thus presenting fragments of royal names that have been interpreted variously (Galil 2001). These inscriptions demonstrate that two distinct political entities existed, with separate dynastic lines, whose politics can from midcentury onward be understood by triangulating archaeology, extra-biblical, and biblical evidence.

Similar to Judah, the cultural and political independence of areas to the east, some of which had been dominated by the tenth-century state, were occurring during the ninth century (Knauf 1992). Already in the eleventh century at the site of Tell ʿUmayri in Ammon, earlier fortifications were reused. In the tenth century BC, portions of the Amman Citadel were surrounded by a fortification wall, and in Moab at Hesban, a water reservoir seventeen meters on a side and seven meters deep may have already been in use. During the ninth century, the Amman Citadel became the capital of that state, and an inscription found there employs the Ammonite dialect to praise the patron deity Milkom (Aufrecht 1989, 154–63). In Moab a fortified site with public buildings was constructed at Dhibon, and a commemorative stele in the local dialect was erected by King Mesha. A series of fortresses was constructed along the southern boundary, as well as possibly a second capital, complete with a second Mesha stele (Routledge 2000, 245). Names on Moabite and Ammonite seals employ theophoric elements, which include the patron deity, and their iconography is heavily Egyptian. Ammonite political (or religious) sculpture further depicts individuals wearing the Egyptian *atef* crown. In the space of fifty or so years, these states became visible geopolitical entities with distinctive cultures.

Local and international legitimacy by the ninth century were de facto, which permitted states to begin a seemingly endless cycle of predations against one another, seeking minor territorial and demographic advantages (Donner 1977; Ahlström 1993, 601–38). These miniature states of the Iron Age also had to balance carefully their own needs with the productive capabilities of their environments, and this was especially true in Transjordan. Unlike their northern counterparts, the southern entities were not dominated by multiple and redundant palaces. A clearer relationship between the capital and the outlying districts is visible, but in Israel the redundancy of palaces has even led to the suggestion that a form of city-state organization prevailed (Finkelstein 2001). The comparative lack of conspicuous consumption and display in the south point to different strategies for ruling over different balances of agriculturists, pastoralists, traders, and nomads, necessary in more marginal and vulnerable environments.

The expensive palatial and sumptuary infrastructure in Israel suggests that taxation rather than storage was the goal. In contrast, storage was emphasized much more in the public architecture of Judah, since agricultural shortages could result in population movements and the dissolution of the state. Portable wealth, such as jewelry, was abundant, however, and points to an exit strategy for elites. The same strategy was employed in Ammon, where similar environmental conditions prevailed, as seen in the construction of fortification walls with storage spaces. There were limited expenditures on sumptuary items, but these did include elements of international political style, such as proto-aeolic column capitals and ashlar masonry. In Moab, however, an even sparser approach was adopted, reflecting the limited resources of the state, and perhaps its nature as a tribally constituted entity, namely one with a very weak king and strong ties among kin groups and villagers. Providing a buffer for agricultural production was a state prerogative, but unlike early states, daily provisioning was not an issue in the southern Levant. There is no evidence in the southern Levant for large-scale food preparation facilities such as bakeries and breweries, nor for standardized ration containers (Joffe 1998a). As with most states, those of the Iron Age were concerned primarily with their own survival. Ironically, the concept of ethnicity permitted states to limit their investments, ensuring the survival of the people.

Incomplete as they may have been, the core ethnic identities of Israel, Judah, Ammon, and Moab, were in place by the ninth century. With the addition of Edom in the eighth century, and even after the demise of Israel at the hands of Assyria in 721 BC, the southern Levant's particular adaptation—the ethnic state—became a persistent feature of the social and political landscapes of the Mediterranean and beyond. The adaptive quality of ethnicity also emerged quickly (Oded 1979; Na'aman 1995). After 721 BC, some of the Israelite population was dispersed to Assyria, but those finding refuge in Judah were integrated into society. And with the Babylonian exile, the Judean population began its transformation into Jews (Brettler 1999). In the cases of the Philistines and the Transjordanian states, however, the end of states meant the end of specific ethnic concepts such as "Edomite." Later groups, such as Nabateans, may have been their demographic but not conceptual descendants.

Identity from Above and Below

The reconstruction presented here differs in key respects from both the traditional view of the United and Divided Monarchies and the recent efforts that have revised substantially the chronology and history of the Iron Age (e.g., Finkelstein 1999a; Jamison-Drake 1991). The approach adopted here is not fundamentally historicist, seeking in the main to prove, disprove, or otherwise comment on the biblical accounts. Nor does it try to test the archaeological data against limiting models of sociopolitical evolution, which are then reflected on the biblical texts. In fairness it may be argued that the core-periphery perspective proposed here does bring a series of implications regarding sociopolitics, but that is true only because many archaeologists and especially historical sociologists discussing the topic have been determined to create generalizations where none may in fact exist (Joffe 2000, 120). But if the overt dynamics of secondary-state formation are familiar, the emergence of ethnicizing states from 1000 to 850 BC is not.

This discussion demonstrates the gradual emergence of states and distinct social identities during a period of some two hundred years. The tenth century BC saw efforts to create a state from the outside in. Rather than inventing a new identity, the tenth-century elite created a shell state that made reference outward to Phoenicia as the source of ideological legitimation. What other developments occurred at "court" or within the emerging religious establishment are unclear, but identity concepts at the lower levels remained centered on kinship and location, both intensely local and unsurprisingly regional. During the ninth-century bifurcation of north and south, and the decisive process of state formation in Moab, regions became a patchwork of small states, each striving to construct its own ethnic identity.

In their developed stages, these states perceived themselves in elite and canonical documents as having stable territorial boundaries, in which groups claiming descent from common ancestors were unified by patron deities and common dialects (Machinist 1991; Grosby 1993, 1997, 1999; Sparks 1998; cf. Routledge 2003). Royal monumental and dedicatory inscriptions consistently address or mention deities such as Melkart of Aram, Kemosh of Moab, and Milkom of Ammon. But where does ethnic identity come from? How much is by design and how much by accident, or by the law of unintended consequences? And what comes from below and what from above? Iron Age states emerged by design, in another manifestation of the ancient pattern of elites reorganizing labor, land, and ideas to their own advantage. But even mafiosi do not operate solely on the basis of coercion. Benefits, in the form of physical and nutritional security, and ideas that facilitate integration, such as a sense of safety and social cohesion, must also be real. Identity facilitates integration.

The international ruling style was one means of demonstrating an elite's impressive foreign connections, impressing upon the populace the elite's suitability for rule by making explicit statements about their international legitimacy, which have implicit subtexts about the elite's capability for locally maintaining order and fostering wealth (Helms 1993; Joffe 2000). Externally, the style expressed the regime's legitimacy and wealth to neighbors, trading partners, competitors, and potential predators. The most extreme examples of this are found in neo-Assyrian palaces, where whatever ambiguity remained for a visitor experiencing the massive architecture was dispelled utterly by the decorative art, depicting an endless series of military victories, resulting in the subjugation of enemies (Winter 1981; Russell 1991; Marcus 1995; Cifarelli 1998).

Iron Age Levantine palaces could not make such grandiose statements, and their squabbling elites had more modest practical and rhetorical goals than those of empire. Dynastic legitimacy was paramount. The earliest Assyrian and southern Levantine inscriptions, and the biblical tradition, reflect the emergence of discrete dynasties and traditions, as well as laconically record the appearance of usurpers, such as Omri, of whose ascent the Bible speaks at length. In the creation of dynastic traditions, such as the "House of David," Iron Age elites made contributions to the development of ethnicity, for these dynasties were intimately connected to religious traditions around which the state as a whole then accreted. Already in the ninth century, the king and his lineage were depicted as chosen by patron deities like Yahweh and Kemosh. The deities themselves were mostly preexisting figures, local manifestations ultimately derived from the Canaanite pantheon and given new emphasis. The relationship among deity, dynasty, and place was common during the Iron Age. The neo-Assyrian example saw the king as viceroy to the god Assur, the patron deity to the city that bore his name (Postgate 1992). To paraphrase the Sumerian King List, kingship, and god, descend from above.

But ethnic identity is not merely an elite concept foisted on the populace from on high. The new order encompassed society from above and below. The word of the god might be handed down, but on earth it encountered the quotidian dimensions of cult and kinship. With regard to the former, it is clear both from archaeology and from the Bible itself that various deities were present in Israel and Judah throughout the Iron Age. Domestic shrines, innumerable figurines and amulets, and inscriptions such as those from Khirbet el Kom and Kuntillet Ajrud (Dever 1990, 140–50), which mention Yahweh and his female consort, Asherah, make clear the worship of other deities and use of magic in a polytheistic, or at best, monolatrous, society (Zevit 2001; cf. Tigay 1986). The ascension of Yahweh and his dynasty did not preclude but incorporated these practices, which came under criticism from various prophets and reformer kings such as Josiah and Hezekiah. This process culminated by the seventh century BC with a religious and literary tradition apparently centered around an assortment of sacred texts. This is shown, for example, by the silver amulets bearing fragments of the Priestly Blessing (Numbers 6:24–26) found in a burial in Jerusalem (Yardeni 1991; Barkay 1992).

As regards kinship, although the existence of tribes remains archaeologically opaque, the existence of lineages is indicated by the texts such as the Samaria ostraka, which record deliveries of commodities to or from rural locations to the royal center (Kaufman 1982). "Houses" existed from below by the eighth century, and there is no reason to think that such organization did not emerge much earlier. Ties between various lineages might easily be construed as "tribal" in nature, particularly given the patterns of local and regional integration that existed from the twelfth century onward. The tribal concept as a means of integration would certainly have been advantageous in Ammon, Moab, and Edom, where links between settled and mobile populations had to be continually negotiated. The tribe and the house would have been ideally suited for an integrative process that enlarged the local into a master narrative of collective identity. For the household, however, retaining kinship as an organizing concept, even writ large through the ethnic mechanisms of the state, also provided an escape route in the event of social collapse.

The state and its constituent elements were the ultimate risk-abatement strategies.

Mediating all these elements was language. The divisions between dialects and scripts are apparent by the ninth century. Local dialects and local scripts reified political and social differentiation that was occurring from 1200 to 1100 BC in the dissolution of the city-state system and its economy. From 1100 to 1000 BC, dialects and scripts played a role in reintegration during the reemergence of local and regional village and town culture. And from 1000 to 900 BC, they contributed to the development of local lineages and religious traditions, and of elites with political ambitions. Scripts and dialects thus served both unity and diversity. Material culture such as pottery styles also played a role. In the active sense, material-culture styles from 1200 to 900 BC served first to differentiate the new from the old, the urban Canaanite from the new rural society, to integrate the rural into communities, and finally to differentiate and diacritically mark the regions as separate economies and loci of sociopolitical development.[2]

Once set into motion, the cultural systems described here began to assume lives of their own. Because states and ethnicities in a sense married high and low culture, no single sector was the sole mechanism for cultural transmission. The royal establishment, complete with priests and scribes, had to compete with household and village mechanisms, such as heads of local shrines and mystics. Each might espouse a different version, but the core elements of peoplehood connected to god and the land were likely shared. Another important mediating factor was the emergence of autonomous "axial" elites as semiautonomous carriers of culture, independent of rulers and with a "transcendent" view of proper government (Eisenstadt 1986). Already in the ninth century BC, the enigmatic Balaam Inscription, from Deir ʿAlla in Ammon, recounts the prophecy of Balaam, son of Beor, known from Numbers 22–24, and is written in a variant of Ammonite or Aramaic. It suggests either the presence of a prophetic tradition in Ammon or Aram, or a common tradition of such an individual in several societies (Hoftijzer and Van Der Kooij 1991). By the sixth-century Lachish letters, correspondence between a garrison commander and subordinates on the border of Egypt, there are enigmatic references to Yawheh, as well as to prophets, showing such individuals to have been well-established social phenomena (Torcyner et al. 1938). Like other oppositional features encouraging ethnic differentiation, such as warfare, these axial elites cannot yet be otherwise detected archaeologically. It is clear, however, that the historical memory did not reside solely with kings or with commoners.

Whatever their sources, unlike city-states, ethnicizing states are not simply by and for elites. With culture distributed throughout society, "the people lives on after the death of the state" (Moscati 1960, 226; cf. Aberbach 2000). Modern analyses of nationalism have tended to stress the instrumental roles of intellectuals (Kedourie 1993) or political elites and class consciousness (Hobsbawm 1993) in the promulgation of general principles and specific formulae. Other approaches emphasize the social conditions of dislocation (Gellner 1983) or the technology of dissemination (B. Anderson 1991) as key features, as well as the central role of symbols (A. D. Smith 1998; Hutchinson 2000). The present study has demonstrated elements of all these at work. The question of when or on what basis ethnic states may be defined as "proto-nations" is therefore logical but falls outside this discussion (see J. A. Armstrong 1982; Hastings 1997).

Ethnicizing States in Archaeology and History

This discussion has proposed that ethnicizing states developed in the Levant during the first millennium BC. The collapse of Bronze Age empires and their economies, and the waning of the closely connected city-state system, permitted new identities and political systems to emerge. Important elements of identity developed at the village and regional level, as did elites who quickly reconstituted town and urban life. The tenth-century state, however, typically associated with David and Solomon, invested in symbols and forms of state administration that were closely linked to reemerging Eastern Mediterranean political culture rather than local ethnicity. Only subsequently did ethnic identity begin to assume a political role, especially in the form of state cults, but also through local and axial elites outside state control. Thus, while some elements of ethnicity preceded the state, the ethnicizing state was ultimately the fusion of a number of elements. Ethnicizing states were not examples of state ethnicities, but of more subtle convergences of identity and politics.

How in the end are we to coordinate this reconstruction with biblical evidence? Should we even try? The exercise here has been to use archaeology and texts, but only those from outside the Bible, to reconstruct the development of ethnicity and state formation during the Iron Age. The much debated and ultimately ill-conceived questions regarding the "historicity" of the Bible in general, or the existence of specific individuals, such as David and Solomon, are as much literary as historical. Reconstructing history from one-sided texts is always a problem, which is compounded by the literary nature of the Bible. Neither credulity in favor or against the Bible is warranted, although the trend in recent years has been toward the latter (e.g., Thompson 1999). Such impossibly skeptical approaches founder on their own reductionism (Liverani 1999), or worse, political assumptions. The anger with which some biblical critics approach the problem, and explicitly reject archaeology's contribution, suggests that archaeology and text should perhaps remain separate domains (Halpern 1997). As much as anything else, the persistence of two monologues reflects the need for widely based research outside the confines of philology and literary criticism. The study presented here demonstrates archaeology's ability to address the political, economic, and social worlds of Iron Age states, their means of integration, and their senses of identity. Establishing these parameters independently but still alongside texts is a goal for future collaborative investigations.

Notes

This chapter was originally published in a slightly different form in the *Journal of the Economic and Social History of the Orient* 45 (4): 425–67. Copyright © 2002 by Brill Academic Publishers. Reprinted by permission.

I thank Norman Yoffee, J. P. Dessel, Rachel Hallote, Larry Herr, James Weinstein, Russell Adams, Steven Grosby, William Dever, Israel Finkelstein, and two anonymous reviewers for their help and comments.

1. Recent studies have attempted to lower the chronology of the Iron Age southern Levant by fifty to one hundred years, deliberately throwing off a web of relationships between archaeological strata, ceramic styles, and historical and literary associations (Finkelstein 1996, 1998a, 1998b, 1999a, 1999b, 2001; cf. Mazar 1997; Ben-Tor and Ben-Ami 1998). From a methodological perspective, the exercise usefully illustrates the weaknesses inherent in using texts to guide archaeological interpretation, and, in turn, the often equivocal nature of stratigraphy and ceramic dating. It also demonstrates the necessity to unpack archaeological "strata" into individually and variously dated components. Demonstrating that walls or gates or buildings may not be contemporaneous but may instead be freestanding and isolated renders less convincing the neat architectural and settlement plans (and circular reasoning) that are relied upon by archaeologists and historians alike. Whichever chronology "prevails," the question addressed here is not assigning names of kings to particular strata or buildings, but rather archaeologically reconstructing social and political processes. The reconstruction proposed here generally follows the traditional chronology but could be applied to a lower chronology as well. The social process remains largely the same. Connecting archaeological reconstructions with literary and

historical texts, explaining why various data may or may not mesh, goes beyond the immediate scope of this chapter.

    2. For a brief comparison of first-millennium BC developments in the Levant and Greece, see Joffe (2004).

Bibliography

Aberbach, David. 2000. "The Roman–Jewish Wars and Hebrew Cultural Nationalism." *Nations and Nationalism* 6:347–62.

Aharoni, Yohanan. 1966. "The Use of Hieratic Numerals in the Hebrew Ostraca and the Shekel Weights." *Bulletin of the American Schools of Oriental Research* 184:13–19.

Ahlström, Gösta W. 1993. *The History of Ancient Palestine from the Palaeolithic Period to Alexander's Conquest*. Sheffield, UK: Sheffield Academic Press.

Alexandre, Yardenna. 1995. "The 'Hippo' Jar and Other Storage Jars at Hurvat Rosh Zayit." *Tel Aviv* 22:77–88.

Amiran, Ruth. 1969. *Ancient Pottery of the Holy Land*. New Brunswick: Rutgers University Press.

Anderson, Benedict. 1991. *Imagined Communities, Reflections on the Origin and Spread of Nationalism*. London: Verso.

Anderson, William P. 1990. "The Beginnings of Phoenician Pottery: Vessel Shapes, Style, and Ceramic Technology in the Early Phases of the Phoenician Iron Age." *Bulletin of the American Schools of Oriental Research* 237:35–54.

Andrén, Anders. 1997. *Between Artifacts and Texts, Historical Archaeology in Global Perspective*. New York: Plenum.

Arav, Rami, and Monika Bernett. 2000. "The *bît hilāni* at Bethsaida: Its Place in Aramaean/Neo-Hittite and Israelite Palace Architecture in the Iron Age II." *Israel Exploration Journal* 50:47–81.

Armstrong, Douglas V. 2001. "Attaining the Full Potential of Historical Archaeology." *Historical Archaeology* 35:9–13.

Armstrong, John A. 1982. *Nations Before Nationalism*. Chapel Hill: University of North Carolina Press.

Aubet, Margarite E. 1993. *The Phoenicians and the West: Politics, Colonies and Trade*. Cambridge: Cambridge University Press.

Aufrecht, Walter E. 1989. *A Corpus of Ammonite Inscriptions*. Lewiston: The Edwin Mellen Press.

Avigad, Nachman. 1987. "The Contribution of Hebrew Seals to an Understanding of Israelite Religion and Society." In *Ancient Israelite Religion: Essays in Honor of Frank Moore Cross*, ed. P. T. Miller, P. D. Hanson, and S. D. McBride, 195–208. Philadelphia: Fortress Press.

Avigad, Nachman, and Benjamin Sass. 1997. *Corpus of West Semitic Stamp Seals*. The

Israel Exploration Society and the Institute of Archaeology. Jerusalem: The Hebrew University of Jerusalem.

Bagley, Robert W. 1992. "Changjiang Bronzes and Shang Archaeology." In *Proceedings of the International Colloquium on Chinese Art History 1991, Antiquities,
Part I*, 214–55. Taipei: National Palace Museum.

Baines, John, and Norman Yoffee. 1998. "Order, Legitimacy, and Wealth in Ancient Egypt and Mesopotamia." In *Archaic States*, ed. G. M. Feinman and Joyce
Marcus, 199–260. Santa Fe: School of American Research Press.

Bar, Jurgen. 1996. *Der assyrische Tribut und seine Darstellung: Eine Untersuchung zur
imperialen Ideologie im neuassyrischen Reich*. Kevelaer and Neukirchen-Vluyn:
Verlag Butzon und Bercker and Neukirchener Verlag.

Barkay, Gabriel. 1992. "The Priestly Benediction on Silver Plaques from Ketef Hin-
nom in Jerusalem." *Tel Aviv* 19:139–91.

Barnett, Richard D. 1982. *Ancient Ivories in the Middle East and Adjacent Countries*.
Jerusalem: The Hebrew University of Jerusalem.

Ben-Tor, Amnon, and Doron Ben-Ami. 1998. "Hazor and the Archaeology of the
Tenth Century BCE." *Israel Exploration Journal* 48:1–37.

Bernal, Martin. 1990. *Cadmean Letters: The Transmission of the Alphabet to the
Aegean and Further West before 1400 BC*. Winona Lake, Ind.: Eisenbrauns.

Betancourt, P. P. 2000. "The Aegean and the Origin of the Sea Peoples." In *The Sea
Peoples and Their World: A Reassessment*, ed. E. D. Oren, 297–303. Philadelphia:
University Museum.

Bienkowski, Piotr. 2001. "Iron Age Settlement in Edom: A Revised Framework." In
*The World of the Aramaeans II: Studies in History and Archaeology in Honour
of Paul-Eugéne Dion*, ed. P. M. M. Daviau, J. W. Wevers, and M. Weigl, 257–69.
Sheffield, UK: Sheffield Academic Press.

Bietak, Manfred. 1993. "The Sea Peoples and the End of the Egyptian Administration in Canaan." In *Biblical Archaeology Today, 1990*, ed. A. Biran and J. Aviram,
292–306. Proceedings of the Second International Congress on Biblical Archaeology, Jerusalem, June–July 1990. Jerusalem: Israel Exploration Society.

Bikai, Patricia M. 1987. *The Phoenician Pottery of Cyprus*. Nicosia, Cyprus: A. G.
Leventis Foundation.

Bloch-Smith, Elizabeth. 1992. *Judahite Burial Practices and Beliefs about the Dead*.
JSOT Sup. 123. Sheffield, UK: Sheffield Academic Press.

Bonatz, Dominik. 1993. "Some Considerations on the Material Culture of Coastal
Syria in the Iron Age." *Egitto e Vicino Oriente* 16:123–58.

Brettler, Marc Z. 1999. "Judaism in the Hebrew Bible? The Transition from Ancient
Israelite Religion to Judaism." *Catholic Biblical Quarterly* 61:429–47.

Bunimovitz, Shlomo. 1994. "The Problem of Human Resources in Late Bronze Age
Palestine and Its Socioeconomic Implications." *Ugarit-Forschungen* 26:1–20.

Bunimovitz, Shlomo, and Asaf Yasur-Landau. 1996. "Philistine and Israelite Pottery: A Comparative Approach to the Question of Pots and People." *Tel Aviv* 23:88–101.

Butzer, Karl W. 1996. "Ecology in the Long View: Settlement Histories, Agrosystemic Strategies, and Ecological Performance." *Journal of Field Archaeology* 23:141–50.

Caubet, Annie. 1992. "Reoccupation of the Syrian Coast after the Destruction of the 'Crisis Years.'" In *The Crisis Years: The 12th Century BC: From Beyond the Danube to the Tigris*, ed. W. A. Ward and M. S. Joukowsky, 123–31. Dubuque, Iowa: Kendall/Hunt.

Cifarelli, Megan. 1998. "Gesture and Alterity in the Art of Ashurnasirpal II of Assyria." *The Art Bulletin* 80:210–28.

Crowfoot, J. W., and G. M. Crowfoot. 1938. *Samaria-Sebaste II: Early Ivories from Samaria*. London: Palestine Exploration Fund.

Crowfoot, J. W., K. M. Kenyon, and E. L. Sukenik. 1942. *The Buildings at Samaria*. London: Palestine Exploration Fund.

DeMarrais, Elizabeth, Luis J. Castillo, and Timothy Earle. 1996. "Ideology, Materialization, and Power Strategies." *Current Anthropology* 37:15–31.

Dessel, J. P. 1999. "Tell 'Ein Zippori and the Lower Galilee in the Late Bronze and Iron Ages: A Village Perspective." In *Galilee Through the Centuries: Confluence of Cultures*, ed. E. Meyers, 1–32. Proceedings of the Second International Conference on Galilee in Antiquity. Winona Lake, Ind.: Eisenbrauns.

Dever, William G. 1982. "Monumental Architecture in Ancient Israel in the Period of the United Monarchy." In *Studies in the Period of David and Solomon and Other Essays*, ed. T. Ishida, 269–306. Winona Lake, Ind.: Eisenbrauns.

———. 1990. *Recent Archaeological Discoveries and Biblical Research*. The Stroum Lectures. Seattle: University of Washington Press.

———. 1997. "Archaeology, Urbanism and the Rise of the Israelite State." In *Urbanism in Antiquity, from Mesopotamia to Crete*, ed. W. E. Aufrecht et al. Sheffield, UK: Sheffield Academic Press.

Donner, Herbert. 1977. "The Separate States of Israel and Judah." In *Israelite and Judaean History*, ed. J. H. Hayes and J. M. Miller, 381–434. Philadelphia. West minster Press.

Dothan, Trude. 1982. *The Philistines and Their Material Culture*. New Haven, Conn.: Yale University Press.

———. 1995. "Tel Miqne-Ekron: The Aegean Affinities of Sea Peoples' (Philistines') Settlement in Canaan in Iron I." In *Recent Excavations in Israel, A View to the West: Reports on Kabri, Nami, Miqne-Ekron, Dor and Ashkelon*, ed. S. Gitin, 41–59. Dubuque, Iowa: Kendall/Hunt.

Eisenstadt, Samuel N. 1986. "Introduction: The Axial Age Breakthrough in Ancient Israel." In *The Origins and Diversity of Axial Age Civilizations*, ed. S. N. Eisenstadt, 127–34. Albany: State University of New York Press.

Faust, Avraham. 2000. "Ethnic Complexity in Northern Israel During the Iron Age II." *Palestine Exploration Quarterly* 132:2–27.

Finkelstein, Israel. 1988a. "Arabian Trade and Socio-political Conditions in the Negev in the Twelfth-eleventh Centuries BCE." *Journal of Near Eastern Studies* 47:241–52.

———. 1988b. *The Archaeology of the Israelite Settlement.* Jerusalem: Israel Exploration Society.

———. 1994. "The Emergence of Israel: A Phase in the Cyclic History of Canaan in the Third and Second Millennia BCE." In *From Nomadism to Monarchy: Archaeological and Historical Aspects of Early Israel,* ed. I. Finkelstein and N. Na'aman, 150–78. Jerusalem: Yad Yitzhak Ben-Zvi.

———. 1995. *Living on the Fringe: The Archaeology and History of the Negev, Sinai and Neighboring Regions in the Bronze and Iron Ages.* Monographs in Mediterranean Archaeology 6. Sheffield, UK: Sheffield Academic Press.

———. 1996. "The Stratigraphy and Chronology of Megiddo and Beth-shan in the 12th and 11th Centuries BCE." *Tel Aviv* 23:170–84.

———. 1998a. "Bible Archaeology or Archaeology of Palestine in the Iron Age? A Rejoinder." *Levant* 30:167–74.

———. 1998b. "Philistine Chronology: High, Middle or Low?" In *Mediterranean People in Transition: Thirteenth to Early Tenth Centuries BCE: In Honor of Professor Trude Dothan,* ed. S. Gitin, A. Mazar, and E. Stern, 140–47. Jerusalem: Israel Exploration Society.

———. 1999a. "Hazor and the North in the Iron Age: A Low Chronology Perspective." *Bulletin of the American Schools of Oriental Research* 314:55–70.

———. 1999b. "State Formation in Israel and Judah." *Near Eastern Archaeology* 62:35–52.

———. 2001. "The Rise of Jerusalem and Judah: The Missing Link." *Levant* 32:105–15.

Fox, Nili S. 2000. *In the Service of the King: Officialdom in Ancient Israel and Judah.* Cincinnati, Ohio: Hebrew Union College Press.

Frankfurt, Henri. 1952. "The Origin of the Bit Hilani." *Iraq* 14:120–31.

Frick, Frank S. 1985. *The Formation of the State in Ancient Israel.* Sheffield, UK: Almond Press.

Fritz, Volkmar. 1995. *The City in Ancient Israel.* Sheffield, UK: Sheffield Academic Press.

Gal, Zvi, and Yardena Alexandre. 2000. *Horbat Rosh Zayit, An Iron Age Storage Fort and Village.* Jerusalem: Israel Antiquities Authority.

Galil, Gershon. 2001. "A Re-Arrangement of the Fragments of the Tel Dan Inscription and the Relations between Israel and Aram." *Palestine Exploration Quarterly* 133:16–21.

Gellner, Ernest. 1983. *Nations and Nationalism*. Ithaca, N.Y.: Cornell University Press.

Gilboa, Ayelet. 1998. "Iron I-IIA Pottery Evolution at Dor-Regional Contexts and the Cypriot Connection." In *Mediterranean Peoples in Transition: Thirteenth to Early Tenth Centuries BCE.*, ed. S. Gitin, A. Mazar, and E. Stern, 413–25. Jerusalem: Israel Exploration Society.

Gilman, Antonio. 1990. "The Mafia Hypothesis." In *When Worlds Collide: The Indo-Europeans and the Pre-Indo Europeans*, ed. T. L. Markey and J. A. C. Greppin, 151–69. Ann Arbor: Karoma.

Gitin, Seymour. 1998. "Philistia in Transition: The Tenth Century BCE and Beyond." In *Mediterranean Peoples in Transition: Thirteenth to Early Tenth Centuries BCE*, ed. S. Gitin, A. Mazar, and E. Stern, 162–83. Jerusalem: Israel Exploration Society.

Gittlen, Barry M. 1985. "The Murder of the Merchants near Akko." In *Biblical and Related Studies Presented to Samuel Iwry*, ed. A. Kort and S. Morschauser, 63–72. Winona Lake, Ind.: Eisenbrauns.

Giveon, Raphael. 1971. *Les Bedouins Shosou des documents egyptiens*. Leiden, Netherlands: Brill.

Goedicke, Hans. 1975. *The Report of Wenamun*. Baltimore: Johns Hopkins University Press.

Gonen, Rivka. 1992. *Burial Patterns and Cultural Diversity in Late Bronze Age Canaan*. Winona Lake, Ind.: Eisenbrauns.

Gottwald, Norman K. 1979. *The Tribes of Yahweh: A Sociology of the Religion of Liberated Israel, 1250–1050 BCE*. Maryknoll: Orbis Books.

Grayson, A. Kirk. 1976. *Assyrian Royal Inscriptions, Vol. 2*. Wiesbaden, Germany: Otto Harrassowitz.

Grosby, Steven. 1993. "Kinship, Territory, and the Nation in the Historiography of Ancient Israel." *Zeitschrift für die alttestmentliche Wissenschaft* 105:3–18.

———. 1997. "Borders, Territory and Nationality in the Ancient Near East and Armenia." *Journal of the Economic and Social History of the Orient* 40:1–29.

———. 1998. "'*RM KLH* and the Worship of Hadad: A Nation of Aram?" *Aram* 7:337–52.

———. 1999. "The Chosen People of Ancient Israel and the Occident: Why Does Nationality Exist and Survive?" *Nations and Nationalism* 5:357–80.

Gubel, Eric. 1993. "The Iconography of Inscribed Phoenician Glyptic." In *Studies in the Iconography of Northwest Semitic Inscribed Seals*, ed. B. Sass and C. Uehlinger, 101–29. Fribourg and Gottingen: Editions Universitaires and Vandenhoeck Ruprecht.

Halpern, Baruch. 1997. "Text and Artifact: Two Monologues?" In *The Archaeology of Israel: Constructing the Past, Interpreting the Present*, ed. N. A. Silberman and D. Small, 311–41. Sheffield, UK: Sheffield Academic Press.

Halstead, Paul, and J. O'Shea. 1989. "Introduction: Cultural Responses to Risk and Uncertainty." In *Bad Year Economics: Cultural Responses to Risk and Uncertainty*, ed. P. Halstead and J. O'Shea, 1–7. Cambridge: Cambridge University Press.

Hastings, Adrian. 1997. *The Construction of Nationhood: Ethnicity, Religion and Nationalism*. Cambridge: Cambridge University Press.

Helms, Mary W. 1993. *Craft and the Kingly Ideal: Art, Trade, and Power*. Austin: University of Texas Press.

Hendrix, Ralph E., Philip R. Drey, and J. Bjornar Storfjell. 1996. *Ancient Pottery of Transjordan: An Introduction Utilizing Published Whole Forms*. Berrien Springs, Mich.: Institute of Archaeology, Siegfried H. Horn Archaeological Museum, Andrews University.

Herr, Larry G. 1997. "The Iron Age II Period: Emerging Nations." Archaeological Sources for the History of Palestine. *Biblical Archaeologist* 60:114–83.

Herrmann, Georgina. 2000. "Ivory Carving of First Millennium: Workshops, Traditions and Diffusion." In *Images as Media: Sources for the Cultural History of the Near East and the Eastern Mediterranean (1st Millennium BCE.)*, ed. C. Uehlinger, 267–82. Fribourg, Switzerland, and Gottingen, Germany: Editions Universitaires and Vandenhoeck.

Hesse, Brian. 1990. "Pig Lovers and Pig Haters: Patterns of Palestinian Pork Production." *Journal of Ethnobiology* 10:195–225.

Hesse, Brian, and Paula Wapnish. 1997. "Can Pig Bones Be Used for Ethnic Diagnosis in the Ancient Near East?" In *The Archaeology of Israel, Constructing the Past, Interpreting the Present*, ed. N. A. Silberman and D. Small, 238–70. Sheffield, UK: Sheffield Academic Press.

Hobsbawm, Eric J. 1993. *Nations and Nationalism Since 1780: Programme, Myth, Reality*. New York: Cambridge University Press.

Hoftijzer, J., and G. Van Der Kooij, ed. 1991. *The Balaam Text from Deir 'Alla Re-Evaluated*. Proceedings of the International Symposium Held at Leiden, Netherlands, August 21–24, 1989. Leiden: Brill.

Holladay, John S., Jr. 1986. "The Stables of Ancient Israel." In *The Archaeology of Jordan and Other Studies Presented to Siegfried H. Horn*, ed. L. T. Geraty and L. G. Herr, 103–65. Berrien Springs: Andrews University Press.

———. 1990. "Red Slip, Burnish, and the Solomonic Gateway at Gezer." *Bulletin of the American Schools of Oriental Research* 277–78:23–70.

Hutchinson, John. 2000. "Ethnicity and Modern Nations." *Ethnic & Racial Studies* 23:651–70.

Iacovou, Maria. 1998. "Philistia and Cyprus in the Eleventh Century: From a Similar Prehistory to a Diverse Protohistory." In *Mediterranean Peoples in Transition: Thirteenth to Early Tenth Centuries BCE*, ed. S. Gitin, A. Mazar, and E. Stern, 332–44. Jerusalem: Israel Exploration Society.

Jamison-Drake, D. W. 1991. *Scribes and Schools in Monarchic Judah: A Socio-Archaeological Approach*. Sheffield, UK: Sheffield Academic Press.

Ji, Chang-Ho C. 1997. "A Note on the Iron Age Four-room House in Palestine." *Orientalia* 34:387–413.

Joffe, Alexander H. 1992. "The Levant in the Third Millennium BC: Parallelisms and Divergences." Presented at the annual meeting of the American Anthropological Association, San Francisco, CA, December 1992.

———. 1993. *Settlement and Society in the Early Bronze I and II of the Southern Levant: Complementarity and Contradiction in a Small-Scale Complex Society*. Sheffield, UK: Sheffield Academic Press.

———. 1998a. "Alcohol and Social Complexity in Ancient Western Asia." *Current Anthropology* 39:297–322. With CA comment.

———. 1998b. "Disembedded Capitals in Western Asian Perspective." *Comparative Studies in Society and History* 40:549–80.

———. 1999. "Ethnicity in the Iron I Southern Levant: Marginal Notes." *Akkadica* 112:27–33.

———. 2000. "Egypt and Syro-Mesopotamia in the Fourth Millennium: Implications of the New Chronology." *Current Anthropology* 41:113–23.

———. 2004. "Athens and Jerusalem in the Third Millennium: Culture, Comparison, and the Evolution of Social Complexity." *Journal of Mediterranean Archaeology* 17:247–67.

Jones, Sian S. 1997. *The Archaeology of Ethnicity: Constructing Identities in the Past and Present*. New York: Routledge.

Kaufman, Ivan T. 1982. "The Samaria Ostraca: An Early Witness to Hebrew Writing." *Biblical Archaeologist* 45:229–39.

Kedourie, Elie. 1993. *Nationalism*. Oxford: Blackwell.

Killebrew, Ann E. 2000. "Aegean-Style Early Philistine Pottery in Canaan During the Iron I Age: A Stylistic Analysis of Mycenaean IIIC:1b Pottery and Its Associated Wares." In *The Sea Peoples and Their World: A Reassessment*, ed. E. D. Oren, 233–54. Philadelphia: University Museum.

Kitchen, Kenneth A. 1986. *The Third Intermediate Period in Egypt (1100–650 BC)*. London: Aris and Phillips.

Kletter, Raz. 1998. *Economic Keystones: The Weight System of the Kingdom of Judah*. Journal for the Study of the Old Testament, Supplement Series 276. Sheffield, UK: Sheffield Academic Press.

Knapp, A. Bernard. 1986. *Copper Production and Divine Protection: Archaeology, Ideology and Social Complexity on Bronze Age Cyprus*. Göteborg: Paul Åströms Förlag.

———. 1990. "Ethnicity, Entrepreneurship and Exchange: Mediterranean Inter-

Island Relations in the Late Bronze Age." *Annual of the British School at Athens* 85:115–53.

Knauf, Ernst A. 1992. "The Cultural Impact of Secondary State Formation: The Cases of the Edomites and Moabites." In *Early Edom and Moab: The Beginning of the Iron Age in Southern Jordan*, ed. P. Bienkowski, 47–54. Sheffield, UK: J. R. Collis Publications.

Kochavi, Moshe. 1989. "The Land of Geshur Project: Regional Archaeology of the Southern Golan (1987–1989 Seasons)." *Israel Exploration Journal* 39:1–17.

Krings, Veronica, ed. 1995. *La civilisation phénicienne et punique, Manuel de recherche*. Leiden, Netherlands: Brill.

Kuan, Jeffrey Kah-jin. 1995. *Neo-Assyrian Historical Inscriptions and Syria-Palestine*. Sheffield, UK: Sheffield Academic Press.

LaBianca, Oystein S., and Randall W. Younker. 1995. "The Kingdoms of Ammon, Moab and Edom: The Archaeology of Society in Late Bronze/Iron Age Transjordan (ca. 1400-500 BCE)." In *The Archaeology of Society in the Holy Land*, ed. T. E. Levy, 399–415. London: Leicester University Press.

Lehmann, Gunnar. 2001. "Phoenicians in Western Galilee: First Results of an Archaeological Survey in the Hinterland of Akko." In *Studies in the Archaeology of the Iron Age in Israel and Jordan*, ed. A. Mazar, 65–112. Sheffield, UK: Sheffield Academic Press.

Levy, Thomas E., and Augustin F. C. Holl. 2002. "Migrations, Ethnogenesis, and Settlement Dynamics: Israelites in Iron Age Canaan and Shuwa-Arabs in the Chad Basin." *Journal of Anthropological Archaeology* 21:83–118.

Liverani, Mario. 1987. "The Collapse of the Near Eastern Regional System at the End of the Late Bronze Age: The Case of Syria." In *Centre and Periphery in the Ancient World*, ed. M. Rowlands, M. Larsen, and K. Kristiansen, 66–73. Cambridge: Cambridge University Press.

———. 1990. *Prestige and Interest, International Relations in the Near East ca. 1600–1100 BC*. Padua, Italy: Sargon.

———. 1999. "Nuovi sviluppi nello studio della storia dell'Israeli biblio." *Biblica* 80:488–505.

Lubar, Steven, and W. Kingery. 1993. *History from Things: Essays on Material Culture*. Washington, D.C.: Smithsonian Institution Press.

Machinist, Peter B. 1991. "The Question of Distinctiveness in Ancient Israel: An Essay." In *Ah, Assyria . . . Studies in Assyrian History and Ancient Near Eastern Historiography Presented to Hayim Tadmor*, ed. M. Cogan and I. Eph'al, 196–212. Jerusalem: Magnes Press.

Malamat, Abraham. 1982. "A Political Look at the Kingdom of David and Solomon and Its Relations with Egypt." In *Studies in the Period of David and Solomon and Other Essays*, ed. T. Ishida, 189–204. Winona Lake, Ind.: Eisenbrauns.

Marcus, Michelle I. 1995. "Geography as Visual Ideology: Landscape, Knowledge, and Power in Neo-Assyrian Art." In *Neo-Assyrian Geography*, ed. M. Liverani, 193–202. Rome: Università di Roma "La Sapienza."

Markoe, Glen. 1985. *Phoenician Bronze and Silver Bowls from Cyprus and the Mediterranean*. Berkeley: University of California Press.

Master, Daniel. 2001. "State Formation Theory and the Kingdom of Israel." *Journal of Near Eastern Studies* 60:117–31.

Mazar, Amihai. 1994. "The 11th Century BC in the Land of Israel." In *Cyprus in the 11th Century*, ed. V. Karageorghis, 39–57. Nicosia, Cyprus: A. G. Leventis Foundation.

———. 1997. "Iron Age Chronology: A Reply to I. Finkelstein." *Levant* 29:157–67.

Mazzoni, Stefania. 1995. "Settlement Pattern and New Urbanization in Syria at the Time of the Assyrian Conquest." In *Neo-Assyrian Geography*, ed. M. Liverani, 181–91. Rome: Università di Roma "La Sapienza."

McNutt, Paula. 1990. *The Forging of Israel, Iron Technology, Symbolism, and Tradition in Ancient Society*. Sheffield, UK: Almond Press.

Millard, Alan J. 2001. "The Corpus of West Semitic Stamp Seals: Review Article." *Israel Exploration Journal* 51:76–87.

Moscati, Sabatino. 1960. *The Face of the Ancient Orient: Near Eastern Civilization in Pre-Classical Times*. London: Routledge and Kegan Paul.

———, ed. 1988. *The Phoenicians*. New York: Abbeville.

———. 1993. *Nuovi studi sull'indentità fenici*. Rome: Herder.

Muscarella, Oscar W. 1995. "The Iron Age Background to the Formation of the Phrygian State." *Bulletin of the American Schools of Oriental Research* 299–300:91–102.

Na'aman, Nadav. 1986. "Habiru and Hebrews: The Transfer of a Social Terms to the Literary Sphere." *Journal of Near Eastern Studies* 45:271–88.

———. 1992. "Israel, Edom and Egypt in the 10th Century BCE." *Tel Aviv* 19:71–93.

———. 1994. "The Hurrians and the End of the Middle Bronze Age in Palestine." *Levant* 26:175–87.

———. 1995. "Province System and Settlement Pattern in Southern Syria and Palestine in the Neo-Assyrian Period." In *Neo-Assyrian Geography*, ed. M. Liverani, 103–15. Rome: Università di Roma "La Sapienza."

———. 1996. "The Contribution of the Amarna Letters to the Debate on Jerusalem's Political Position in the Tenth Century BC." *Bulletin of the American Schools of Oriental Research* 304:17–27.

Nakhai, Beth A. 2001. *Archaeology and the Religions of Canaan and Israel*. Boston: American Schools of Oriental Research.

Nashef, Khaled. 1982. *Die Orts- und Gewässernamen der mittelbabylonischen und mittelassyrisch Zeit*. Repertoire Geographique des Textes Cuneiformes, Band 5. Wiesbaden, Germany: Dr. Ludwig Reichert Verlag.

O'Connor, David. 2000. "The Sea Peoples and the Egyptian Sources." In *The Sea Peoples and Their World: A Reassessment*, ed. E. D. Oren, 85–102. Philadelphia: University Museum.

Oded, Bustenay. 1979. *Mass Deportations and Deportees in the Neo-Assyrian Empire.* Wiesbaden, Germany: Dr. Ludwig Reichert Verlag.

Ofer, Avi. 1994. "'All the Hill Country of Judah': From Settlement Fringe to a Prosperous Monarchy." In *From Nomadism to Monarchy: Archaeological and Historical Aspects of Early Israel*, ed. I. Finkelstein and N. Na'aman, 92–121. Jerusalem: Yad Yitzhak Ben-Zvi.

———. 2001. "The Monarchic Period in the Judaean Highland: A Spatial Overview." In *Studies in the Archaeology of the Iron Age in Israel and Jordan*, ed. A. Mazar, 14–37. Sheffield, UK: Sheffield Academic Press.

Oren, Eliezer D. 1992. "Palaces and Patrician Houses in the Middle and Late Bronze Age." In *The Architecture of Ancient Israel*, ed. A. Kempinski and R. Reich, 105–20. Jerusalem: Israel Exploration Society.

———, ed. 1997. *The Hyksos: New Historical and Archaeological Perspectives.* Philadelphia: University Museum.

Overholt, Thomas W. 1995. *Cultural Anthropology and the Old Testament.* Minneapolis, Minn.: Fortress Press.

Parr, Peter J. 1992. "Edom and the Hejaz." In *Early Edom and Moab: The Beginning of the Iron Age in Southern Jordan*, ed. P. Bienkowski, 41–46. Sheffield, UK: J. R. Collis Publications.

Paynter, Robert. 2000. "Historical and Anthropological Archaeology: Forging Alliances." *Journal of Archaeological Research* 8:1–37.

Peckham, Brian. 2001. "Phoenicians and Aramaeans: The Literary and Epigraphic Evidence." In *The World of the Aramaeans II: Studies in History and Archaeology in Honour of Paul-Eugéne Dion*, ed. P. M. M. Daviau, J. W. Wevers, and M. Weigl, 19–44. Sheffield, UK: Sheffield Academic Press.

Philip, Graham. 1999. "Complexity and Diversity in the Southern Levant during the Third Millennium BC: The Evidence of Khirbet Kerak Ware." *Journal of Mediterranean Archaeology* 12:26–57.

Pitard, Wayne T. 1987. *Ancient Damascus.* Winona Lake, Ind.: Eisenbrauns.

Postgate, J. N. 1974. "Some Remarks on Conditions in the Assyrian Countryside." *Journal of the Economic and Social History of the Orient* 17:225–43.

———. 1992. "Land of Assur and the Yoke of Assur." *World Archaeology* 23:247–63.

Powell, Barry B. 1991. *Homer and the Origin of the Greek Alphabet.* Cambridge: Cambridge University Press.

Pritchard, James B. 1969. *Ancient Near Eastern Texts Relating to the Old Testament.* 3rd ed. with supplement. Princeton, N.J.: Princeton University Press.

Redford, Donald B. 1992. *Egypt and Israel in Biblical Times*. Princeton, N.J.: Princeton University Press.

Reich, Ronny. 1992. "Palaces and Residences in the Iron Age." In *The Architecture of Ancient Israel*, ed. A. Kempinski and R. Reich, 202–22. Jerusalem: Israel Exploration Society.

Renfrew, A. Colin, and J. F. Cherry, eds. 1986. *Peer Polity Interaction and Socio-Political Change*. Cambridge: Cambridge University Press.

Rofé, Alexander. 1999. *Introduction to the Composition of the Pentateuch*. Sheffield, UK: Sheffield Academic Press.

Routledge, Bruce. 2000. "The Politics of Mesha: Segmented Identities and State Formation in Iron Age Moab." *Journal of the Economic and Social History of the Orient* 43:221–56.

———. 2003. "The Antiquity of the Nation? Critical Reflections from the Ancient Near East." *Nations and Nationalism* 9 (2): 212–32.

Russell, John M. 1991. *Sennacherib's "Palace Without Rival" at Nineveh*. Chicago: University of Chicago Press.

Sader, Helen. 2000. "The Aramaean Kingdoms of Syria: Origin and Formation Processes." In *Essays on Syria in the Iron Age*, ed. G. Bunnens, 61–78. Louvain: Peeters.

Sandars, N. K. 1978. *The Sea Peoples*. London: Penguin.

Sass, Benjamin. 1991. *Studia Alphabetica. On the Origin and Early History of the Northwest Semitic, South Semitic and Greek Alphabets*. Orbis Biblicus et Orientalis 102. Goettingen, Fribourg.

———. 1993. "The Pre-Exilic Hebrew Seals: Iconism vs. Aniconism." In *Studies in the Iconography of Northwest Semitic Inscribed Seals*, ed. B. Sass and C. Uehlinger, 194–256. Fribourg: Universitatsverlag; Gottingen: Vandenhoeck & Ruprecht.

Sherratt, Andrew, and Susan Sherratt. 1991. "From Luxuries to Commodities: the Nature of the Bronze Age Trading System." In *Bronze Age Trade in the Mediterranean*, ed. N. H. Gale, 351–86. Jonsered: Paul Åströms Förlag.

Sherratt, Susan. 1994. "Commerce, Iron and Ideology: Metallurgical Innovation in 12th–11th Century Cyprus." In *Cyprus in the 11th Century BC*, ed. V. Karageorghis, 59–106. Nicosia: A. G. Leventis Foundation.

———. 1998. "Sea Peoples and the Economic Structure of the Late Second Millennium in the Eastern Mediterranean." In *Mediterranean Peoples in Transition: Thirteenth to Early Tenth Centuries BCE*, ed. S. Gitin, A. Mazar, and E. Stern, 292–313. Jerusalem: Israel Exploration Society.

Shiloh, Yigal. 1979. *The Proto-Aeolic Capital and Israelite Ashlar Masonry*. Jerusalem: Institute of Archaeology, Hebrew University of Jerusalem.

Smith, Adam T. 1999. "The Making of an Urartian Landscape in Southern Transcaucasia: A Study of Political Architectonics." *American Journal of Archaeology* 103:45–71.

———. 2000. "Rendering the Political Aesthetic: Political Legitimacy in Urartian Representations of the Built Environment." *Journal of Anthropological Archaeology* 19:131–63.

Smith, Anthony D. 1998. *Nationalism and Modernism*. London: Routledge.

———. 2000. *The Nation in History: Historiographic Debates about Ethnicity and Nationalism*. Hanover, NH: University Press of New England.

Soggin, J. Alberto. 1977. "The Davidic-Solomonic Kingdom." In *Israelite and Judaean History*, ed. J. H. Hayes and J. M. Miller, 332–80. Philadelphia: Westminster Press.

Sparks, Kenton L. 1998. *Ethnicity and Identity in Ancient Israel, Prolegomena to the Study of Ethnic Sentiments and Their Expression in the Hebrew Bible*. Winona Lake, Ind.: Eisenbrauns.

Stager, Lawrence E. 1985. "The Archaeology of the Family in Ancient Israel." *Bulletin of the American Schools of Oriental Research* 260:1–35.

———. 1995. "The Impact of the Sea Peoples in Canaan (1185–1050 BCE)." In *The Archaeology of Society in the Holy Land*, ed. T. E. Levy, 332–585. Leicester, UK: Leicester University Press.

Stern, Ephraim. 1998. "The Relations Between the Sea Peoples and the Phoenicians in the Twelfth and Eleventh Centuries BC." In *Mediterranean Peoples in Transition: Thirteenth to Early Tenth Centuries BCE.*, ed. S. Gitin, A. Mazar, and E. Stern, 345–52. Jerusalem: Israel Exploration Society.

Tapper, Richard. 1990. "Anthropologists, Historians, and Tribespeople on Tribe and State Formation in the Middle East." In *Tribes and State Formation in the Middle East*, ed. P. S. Khoury and J. Kostiner, 48–73. Berkeley: University of California Press.

Tappy, Ronald E. 1992. *The Archaeology of Israelite Samaria*. Atlanta: Scholars Press.

Thompson, Thomas L. 1999. *The Mythic Past: Biblical Archaeology and the Myth of Israel*. New York: Basic Books.

Tigay, Jeffrey H. 1986. *You Shall Have No Other Gods: Israelite Religion in the Light of Hebrew Inscriptions*. Atlanta: Scholars Press.

Torcyner, Harry, Lankester Harding, Alkin Lewis, and J. L. Starkey. 1938. *The Lachish Letters*. London: Oxford University Press.

Ussishkin, David. 1980. "Was the 'Solomonic' City Gate at Megiddo Built by King Solomon?" *Bulletin of the American Schools of Oriental Research* 239:1–18.

Van Seters, John. 1983. *In Search of History: Historiography in the Ancient World and the Origins of Biblical History*. New Haven, Conn.: Yale University Press.

Weinstein, James M. 1981. "The Egyptian Empire in Palestine: A Reassessment." *Bulletin of the American School of Oriental Research* 241:1–28.

Wilson, Kevin A. 2001. "The Campaign of Pharaoh Shoshenq I into Palestine." PhD diss., The Johns Hopkins University.

Winter, Irene J. 1976. "Phoenician and North Syrian Ivory Carving in Historical Context: Questions of Style and Distribution." *Iraq* 39:1–22.

———. 1981. "Royal Rhetoric and the Development of Historical Narrative in Neo-Assyrian Reliefs." *Studies in Visual Communication* 7:2–38.

Wright, G. Ernest. 1962. *Biblical Archaeology*. Revised ed. Philadelphia: Westminster Press.

Wylie, Alison. 1989. "Archaeological Cables and Tacking: the Implications of Practice for Bernstein's 'Options beyond Objectivism and Relativism.'" *Philosophy of the Social Sciences* 19:1–18.

Yadin, Yigal. 1958. "Solomon's Wall and Gate at Gezer." *Israel Exploration Journal* 8:80–86.

Yardeni, Ada. 1991. "Remarks on the Priestly Blessing on Two Ancient Amulets from Jerusalem." *Vetus Testamentum* 41:176–85.

Yoffee, Norman. 1993. "Too Many Chiefs? or Safe Texts for the 90s." In *Archaeological Theory—Who Sets the Agenda?* ed. A. Sherratt and N. Yoffee, 60–78. Cambridge: Cambridge University Press.

Yon, Marguerite. 1992. "The End of the Kingdom of Ugarit." In *The Crisis Years: The 12th Century BC From Beyond the Danube to the Tigris*, ed. W. A. Ward and M. S. Joukowsky, 111–22. Dubuque, Iowa: Kendall/Hunt.

Zadok, Ran. 1988. *The Pre-Hellenistic Israelite Anthroponymy and Prosopography*. Leuven: Peeters.

———. 1991. "Elements of Aramean Pre-History." In *Ah, Assyria . . . Studies in Assyrian History and Ancient Near Eastern Historiography Presented to Hayim Tadmor*, ed. M. Cogan and I. Eph'al, 104–17. Jerusalem: Magnes Press.

Zevit, Ziony. 2001. *The Religions of Ancient Israel: A Synthesis of Parallactic Approaches*. London: Continuum.

Zimansky, Paul E. 1985. *Ecology and Empire: The Structure of the Urartian State*. Chicago: Oriental Institute, University of Chicago.

———. 1995. "Urartian Material Culture as State Assemblage: An Anomaly in the Archaeology of Empire." *Bulletin of the American Schools of Oriental Research* 299–300:103–16.

4

Reconstructing the World of Ancient Mesopotamia
Divided Beginnings and Holistic History

RICHARD L. ZETTLER

The invention of writing in southern Mesopotamia in the late fourth millennium BC, whatever its short- or long-term consequences for that ancient civilization, radically transformed the "character and potentialities" of the archaeological record (Adams 1981, 131). It also affected the analytical methodologies of those who today labor to reconstruct the culture(s) of the land between the Tigris and Euphrates rivers (figure 4.1). The existence of an extensive corpus of texts in languages that had to be deciphered, such as Sumerian and Akkadian, stimulated a compartmentalization of praxis in which archaeologists, on the one hand, and philologists and historians, on the other, staked out their respective territories and discouraged "trespassing" (Brinkman 1984b, 170). Yet such a division of labor, however seemingly practical, has had regrettable consequences, all too often skewing reconstructions of ancient Mesopotamia's historic periods, or, more accurately, literate societies (Postgate 1984, 4). Working within a politico-historical framework derived from ancient Mesopotamian sources, archaeologists must engage documentary sources, but by and large, they are poorly trained in ancient languages and are perforce uninformed "consumers" of textual data. For their part, philologists and historians have written history from texts alone and have ignored material culture. Yet written sources have inherent limitations and document only part of the Mesopotamian past. As Miguel Civil (1980) noted more than twenty years ago, texts do not provide modern readers the background information needed to comprehend them and seldom elaborate core cultural activities, whose details would have been common knowledge. Moreover, texts are biased, reflecting, for example, the interests of urban elites. Archaeological remains have the potential to flesh out and enrich textual data and add new dimensions to text-based historical reconstructions.

Whatever the past of the field, recent efforts to meld archaeological

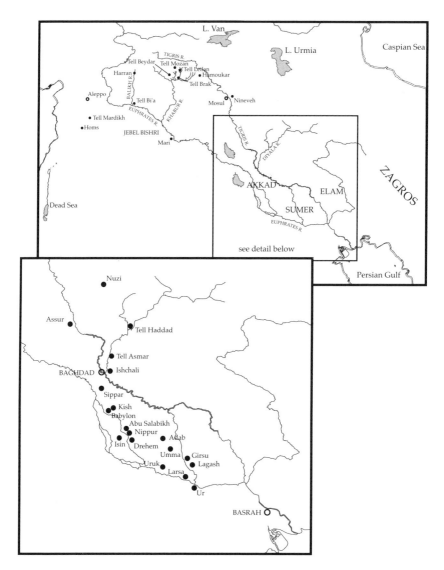

Figure 4.1   Map of places referred to in ancient Mesopotamian sources

and written sources offer hope for more holistic histories of the land between the rivers. Here I intend to explore, both in general and through
case studies, the dynamic between material culture and texts and the
interplay between archaeologists and philologists and historians in reconstructing the world of historic Mesopotamia.

Excavating Archaeologists' Role in Ancient
Mesopotamia's Historic Periods

Since its inception in the early to mid-nineteenth century, the study of ancient Mesopotamia has, in effect, recognized a division of labor between archaeologists and philologists and historians. In England, for example, Layard, Rassam, Loftus, and Taylor toiled on ruin mounds, while Rawlinson, Hincks, Smith, and others worked on the decipherment of the languages written in the cuneiform script and the publication of texts. Rawlinson displayed little or no interest in the material world Layard was uncovering, much to the archaeologist's disappointment (Reade 1993, 42; Larsen 1996, 208).

The debate concerning the role of archaeology in the study of ancient Mesopotamia's literate societies is not much in evidence in the twentieth century. A. Leo Oppenheim, long-time editor of the *Chicago Assyrian Dictionary*, seemingly relegated archaeologists to working on prehistoric periods and providing occasional illustrations of ancient Mesopotamian realia, although he did hold out some hope for synthetic research (1977, 10–11):

> The texts on clay tablets are far more valuable, far more relevant, than the monuments that have been discovered, although the latter, especially the famous reliefs on the walls of Assyrian palaces and the countless products of glyptic art, offer welcome illustration to the wealth of factual information contained on clay tablets, stelae, and votive offerings. The archaeologist's contribution toward the elucidation of the Mesopotamian past bears primarily on that crucial millennium or more which preceded the earliest written documentation (i.e., before 2800 BC), and which only field and comparative archaeologists are able to scan and to articulate through their intricate network of horizons and stratified levels. (In exceptional instances, however, and in small sites, the interplay of the archeologist and the epigrapher in Mesopotamia can yield important results.)

More recently, Robert McCormick Adams, Hans J. Nissen, and J. N. Postgate have published more balanced views. Adams (1981, 131), an anthropologist largely responsible for settlement surveys of the southern floodplain and adjacent regions, emphasized the complementarity of textual and archaeological data *stricto senso* and the role that archaeological survey could play in enriching text-based reconstructions of settlement and land use in historic periods. In publications such as his seminal *Heartland of Cities*, Adams drew heavily on specialized historical literature. Some years after its publication, he argued explicitly that social scientists and humanists (language specialists and historians) often have different research priorities and that anthropologists have to command the whole of the ancient Mesopotamian record, both texts, the "primary part" of the record for historic periods, and archaeological sources (Adams 1991, 41–42). Adams specifically advocated altered patterns of graduate education and interdisciplinary collaboration.

Nissen, an archaeologist with an extensive background in ancient languages, took a position not radically different from Adams. He stressed the limitations of textual sources and posited an independent role for archaeology in "extending" text-based history, in particular by reconstructing settlement patterns (Nissen 1983, 3–5; 1988, 2–4). Even while emphasizing the usefulness of prehistorians' methods, for example, botanical and faunal studies, he insisted on the priority of documentary evidence for reconstructing early Mesopotamian politics, society, and economy. For his part, Postgate (1984, 15; 1992, xxii–xxiii), a language specialist and historian, as well as an active field archaeologist, suggested that archaeologists and philologists could carry on a productive dialogue about the material world of early Mesopotamian society and economy.

The key problem for archaeologists, as well as for philologists and historians, researching Mesopotamia's protohistoric and historic periods (see table 4.1) is the dynamic between material culture and writing (or artifact and text). And yet, in a field with an institutionalized division of labor, integrating the two complementary data sources to produce a holistic picture is a challenge that few have taken up. The Sumerologist Thorkild Jacobsen (e.g., 1953) demonstrated a keen appreciation for the value of both strands of data. Jacobsen directed excavations at Ishchali, ancient Neribtum, in the 1930s and doubled as field epigrapher. At Nippur in 1953–54, Jacobsen produced a unique tablet catalogue that included detailed sketches showing the findspots of the tablets. Moreover, Jacobsen (1954, 1960; cf. Adams 1965, 119; 1981, xx) conceived and developed archaeological surface survey as a field method for reconstructing the ancient courses of rivers and canals. Penelope Weadock's dissertation on the *gipāru* at Ur, written under Jacobsen's supervision, was one of the first major efforts to incorporate archaeology and texts. The gipāru, located in close proximity to the ziggurat, was a building that housed the temple of Ningal, wife of the moon god, Nanna, as well as the residence and burial place of the en-priestess (Weadock 1958, 1975). Some

Table 4.1 Chronology of ancient Mesopotamia

Years (BC)	South	North
	Prehistoric or "Preliterate" Periods	
5500–4000	Ubaid[1]	
	Proto-literate Periods[2]	
4000–3100	Early, Middle, and Late Uruk	
3100–2900	Jemdet Nasr	
	Historic or "Literate" Periods	
2900–2350	Early Dynastic I (II) and III	
2334–2154[3]	Dynasty of Akkad	
2112–2004	Ur III	Old Assyrian
2017–1595	Isin-Larsa/Old Babylonian	
1530–1155	Kassite	Middle Assyrian
1157–626	Post-Kassite	Neo-Assyrian
625–539	Neo-Babylonian	
538–331	Achaemenid	

1. Corrected radiocarbon dates put the earliest phases of the Ubaid in the later half of the seventh millennium BC. See Valladas, Evin, and Arnold 1996, 382.

2. For the term "proto-literate," see Delougaz and Lloyd 1942, 8, n. 10.

3. I have maintained the conventional middle chronology dates for southern Mesopotamia's historic dynasties (Brinkman 1977).

years after Weadock's dissertation, McGuire Gibson combined artifacts, pictorial evidence, and texts in "The Mace, the Axe and the Dagger in Ancient Mesopotamia" (1964).

By the late 1970s and early 1980s, studies that explicitly sought to integrate archaeology and texts began to appear. The majority of such studies, whether by archaeologists or philologists and historians, dealt with particular buildings (or groups of buildings), attempting to establish the findspots of tablets and correlating the findspots and contents of texts. Some emerged from recent archaeological projects that meticulously recorded findspots, while others revisited older excavations, for which findspot information varied in detail. The list includes, among others, Westenholz's (1987) work on Akkadian Nippur; Zettler's (1992) analysis of the temple of Inanna under the Third Dynasty of Ur (Ur III); Ellis's (1983, 1986) study of the Old Babylonian Ishtar Kittitum temple at Ishchali; Gasche's (1989) work on the house at Tell ed-Der, Sippar Amnanum, belonging to Inanna-mansum and his son, Ur-Utu, successive lamentation priests of the goddess Annunitum; Stone's reconsideration of Nippur (1979, 1981, 1987; for critical reviews, see Charpin 1989, 1990; Postgate 1990; van Driel 1990); Charpin's (1986) detailed analysis of Ur, as well as Van De Mieroop's (1992) and Brusasco's (1999–2000) complementary studies; and Reichel's dissertation (2001a) on the Gimil-Sin temple and the Palace of the Rulers at Tell Asmar, ancient Eshnunna. Papers from a roundtable on the end of archives in Mesopotamia that appeared in 1995's *Revue d'Assyriologie* contain interesting and related studies.

Among other notable conjunctive approaches, Civil (1995), Veldhuis (1997), Tinney (1998, 1999), and others have called attention to Old Babylonian scribal exercise tablets as material artifacts and described their formal characteristics, highlighting the curricular setting of lexical and literary compositions, as well as the structure of pedagogy in early second-millennium "schools." Tanret (2002) and Robeson (2001) have expanded on their studies of largely decontextualized data, analyzing corpora of "school texts" found in situ at Nippur and Tell ed-Der. Brinkman's (1984b; also 1984a, 3–15) close scrutiny of site survey data, by and large the domain of anthropological archaeology, provided a unique politico-historical perspective on the demographics of settlement on the southern floodplain in the late second and early first millennia, roughly 1150–625 BC. Winter's (e.g., 1981, 1983, 1985, 1986, 1987, 1997) investigations of the interplay between texts and imagery, focusing primarily, though not exclusively, on Assyrian reliefs and statuary, enriched our understanding of the complexity of ancient Mesopotamian communication systems, as has Bahrani's (e.g., 1995) deconstructivist, postcolonialist approach.

Postgate's *Early Mesopotamia: Society and Economy at the Dawn of History* (1992) and Potts's *Mesopotamian Civilization: The Material Foundations* (1997) are the only syntheses that integrate archaeological and textual data. Moorey's *Ancient Mesopotamian Materials and Industries: The Archaeological Evidence* (1994) covers somewhat more restricted grounds but effectively incorporates textual information.

The segregation of academic training and practice is still deeply embedded in ancient Mesopotamian studies, as the title of the recently published *Cuneiform Texts and the Writing of History* (Van de Mieroop 1999) implies, but efforts such as those cited above have had a constructive impact on the field and prodded it to produce more holistic reconstructions. In the pages that follow, I introduce a number of case studies, successful to varying degrees, in integrating material culture and textual data.

The Inanna Temple at Nippur

The salient feature of our written sources for ancient Mesopotamia is the fact that the overwhelming majority are excavated artifacts with contexts in the three-dimensional soil matrices of archaeological sites, just like any other finds. Though texts admittedly provide information independent of context, findspots are an essential part of clay tablets' information content. The loss of context, whether through looting or through ignorance, can skew historical reconstructions (Zettler 1992, 2–3; 1996, 83–84). More constructively, however, methodical explication of findspot information can enrich our understanding of ancient Mesopotamia, both the microcosms of particular buildings or groups of buildings and the macrocosms, for example, of early Mesopotamian society and economy. My own study of the level IV Inanna temple at Nippur (Zettler 1992), reconstructed by Shulgi, second king of the Third Dynasty of Ur, will perhaps illustrate both the import and the ambiguities of putting texts in context.

Texts and Buildings

The level IV temple was poorly preserved (figure 4.2). Only its front (northwestern) wall and northeastern corner were intact; the remainder had been largely destroyed by Parthian construction activities in the second century. The building's condition prompted Richard C. Haines, Nippur's field director at the time, to write jokingly to Carl H. Kraeling, director of the Oriental Institute, in a letter dated January 25, 1956, "The [level IV] plan looks better on paper than in actuality and is a reconstructor's dream. To paraphrase, I've never seen a building where so little will look like so much after it is drawn in good black ink." Despite the state of the temple's preservation, 200 or so clay tablets; 155 clay sealings, many with impressions of inscribed seals; stamped bricks; and various other inscribed artifacts were found in primary contexts on the floors of various rooms. However, only Thorkild Jacobsen's tablet catalogue from the fourth season provided detailed notes, with plans, showing the findspots of the tablets.

My reconstruction of the functioning of rooms or complexes of rooms in the Inanna temple was based largely on criteria such as cir-

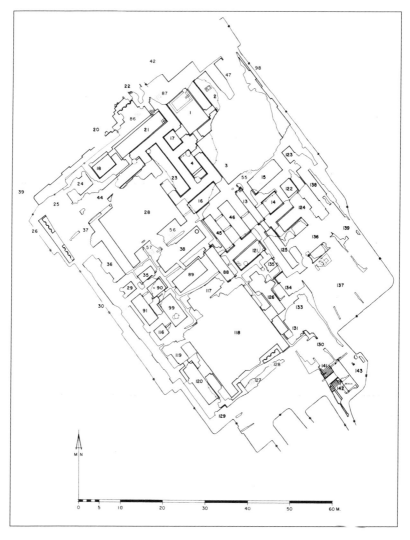

Figure 4.2 Plan of Nippur Inanna temple, level IV, showing foundations and walls as excavated

culation and room arrangement patterns (Zettler 1992, 57–90). The few tablets found in situ provided only limited insights but did help in identifying rooms in the northeastern corner of the building as the temple's chancery.

The overwhelming majority of the tablets recovered in the Inanna

Figure 4.3   Cross-section of Parthian platform, showing fill and temple walls, taken in 1955–56. Walls of levels VII–IV in foreground.

temple excavations were found in secondary contexts in the fill of a platform that the Parthians built as the substructure for their temple (Crawford 1959, 77–78). The Parthians apparently cleared the existing site of the temple roughly to the level of Shulgi's building. They then laid out a rectangular retaining wall and backfilled the soil and debris they had previously turned up (figure 4.3). Approximately 1,700 tablets were found in discrete pockets in the platform's fill, including a small number of Early Dynastic and Akkadian texts (Goetze 1968); nearly 1,000 Ur III economic texts, as well as more than 150 literary and lexical texts (see Rubio 1999); roughly 400 Isin-Larsa texts recording *sattukku* ("fixed and regular") offerings and their redistribution (Sigrist 1984); 50 or so Kassite economic texts; and a few neo-Assyrian (Goetze 1963), neo-Babylonian or Achaemenid, and Seleucid documents.

The Ur III economic texts, as well as the literary and lexical compositions, were found throughout the fill of the Parthian platform, but 90 percent came from the center of the platform. I argued that they were part of the temple's archive because a few carried the notation é-^dInanna, but also because of their prosopography and because scribal hands, as well as text type and format, could be related to tablets found in situ in the level IV building.

Analysis of the texts from the level IV building and those from the fill of the platform permitted a detailed reconstruction of the temple's economic underpinnings and its administration, demonstrating, for example, that the temple was dominated by one of Nippur's elite families, which included the successive governors of the city (Zettler 1992, 91–238). The texts also illustrate links that existed between the temple of Inanna and other temples, and detailed, for example, the economic interactions between the temple and local merchants and craftsmen (Zettler 1992, 220–31; 1990).

The Isin-Larsa texts recording sattukku offerings were found in the center of the northwestern part of the platform (Sigrist 1984, 3–6). Goetze characterized them as Ninurta temple records, and Sigrist maintained that identification (though see 1984, 191–92). Their link to the Ninurta temple derives from the priority of Ninurta (or the temple of Ninurta) in the list of offerings in one subgroup of the texts, as well as the occurrence of a Ninurta temple cult place (é-igi-šu-kalam-ma) and cult weapons (Sigrist 1984, 22, 141, 150).

Crawford (1959, 77–78) accounted for Ninurta temple records in the platform by suggesting that in the second century, the southeastern end of the Inanna temple area was preserved to a greater height than the northwestern. The Parthian builders, therefore, moved debris from the southeast to the northwest as far as needed to provide for the platform. However, not enough fill was available in the area, so they brought additional dirt from elsewhere. That soil contained the Isin-Larsa sattukku-offering texts. I built on Crawford's reconstruction, suggesting that the Ninurta temple lay north of the temple of Inanna (Zettler 1992, 16–17). Westenholz (1987, 97–98) and Gibson (1993, 15) subsequently localized the Ninurta temple on Nippur's west mound (Mound X).

In his detailed review of my book, van Driel (1995) muddied the otherwise neat picture drawn up to then. He argued that the Ur III economic texts from the platform probably included Ninurta temple records, basing his arguments on the economic ties between the Ninurta and Inanna temples in that period, as well as on the Isin-Larsa sattukku-offering texts, supposedly from the Ninurta temple, in the platform fill. Van Driel identified in particular 6 NT 398 and 6 NT 437 as Ninurta temple records. Both are sealed tablets recording the receipt of grain rations by the Inanna temple's chief administrator from the Ninurta temple's chief administrator. Such receipts would have been sealed by the recipient and then handed over to the person who disbursed the grain.

Despite van Driel's suggestion, I maintain that all the Ur III tablets from the platform are Inanna temple records. Rather than casting doubts on the attribution of the Ur III texts found in the platform, van Driel might just as readily have challenged the attribution of the Isin-Larsa sattukku-offering texts to the Ninurta temple. Their link to the Ninurta temple is highly questionable (Kraus 1985, 533–34).

If the Isin-Larsa sattukku-offering texts are not Ninurta temple records, what institution drafted them? What weight should we give to content and context in answering the question? Large numbers of tablets found together in secondary contexts commonly prove to be coherent corpora, presumably taken from a single site and redeposited. The Ur III tablets found below the Kassite floors of rooms to the south of é-dub-lá-mah courtyard at Ur provide a good example of such homogeneous tablet lots in secondary contexts (Jacobsen 1953). Where the content and attribution of a corpus of texts is questionable — as it is in the case of the Isin-Larsa sattukku-offering tablets — should not archaeological context and associated finds be weighed as factors in their identification? No one who reviewed Sigrist's publication (1984) raised context as a relevant factor in the identification of the Isin-Larsa sattukku-offering texts (see, for example, Kraus 1985, 533–34; Krebernik 1990; Postgate 1986). I see no reason, however, that those texts could not be Inanna temple records. Far from being self-sufficient households, Nippur's temples were linked economically, at least in the Ur III period, and the Inanna temple and Ninurta temple had close ties, as van Driel (1995) noted. So, too, the Inanna temple had annual expenditures characterized as sá-dug$_4$, or sattukku. If similar conditions continued into the Isin-Larsa and Old Babylonian periods (see Sigrist 1984, 191–92, and Robertson 1992 on economic ties among Nippur's temples in the Isin-Larsa and Old Babylonian periods), the sattukku-offering texts might in fact record some portion of those distributions for which the Inanna temple was responsible.

Early Mesopotamian Society and Economy

Individual buildings like the Inanna temple or groups of buildings can be used as building blocks in reconstructing Mesopotamian society and economy more generally. As one such building block, the Inanna temple stands out as the only excavated temple, with archival documentation, for the Ur III period. The Inanna temple's unique position in a period for which we have more texts than any other in Mesopotamia's long history raises critical questions about the biases of the archaeological and documentary record. Such questions about our sample are fundamental not just for reconstructing particular periods of time, but also for comparing periods and understanding long-term trends.

For example, in *The Babylonians*, Saggs repeated a long-standing "axiom" of early Mesopotamian documentary history, namely that in the Ur III period, the economy was dominated by the state and the private sector was of "little significance." With the Ur III collapse, the private sector of the economy came to have increasing importance (Saggs 1995, 95).

Several years prior to Saggs's publication, Postgate (1992, 292) had alluded to the seeming growth of the private sector of the economy in the Isin-Larsa and Old Babylonian periods. However, he eschewed such generalizations because of the difficulties of assessing the significance of biases in the documentary record. More recently, Baines and Yoffee (1998, 210) took cognizance of what they termed "systematic biases" of our documentary sources from successive periods. While allowing that biases could result from accidents of discovery, they noted that most scholars, apparently including Yoffee himself, believed that the biases in fact reflected the "cultural and organizational emphases of distinct periods and important differences between them" (Yoffee 1995, 297–98). Both Postgate and Baines and Yoffee take reasonable positions. However, a review of excavated remains of the late third and early second millennia suggest that generalizations of the sort Saggs reiterated reflect not so much "economic reality" as disparities in the archaeological and documentary record from one period to the next. Appropriately, philologists and historians are beginning to challenge Saggs's characterization at least of Ur III (see, for example, Neumann 1992; van Driel 1994; Garfinkle 2000).

Excavated Ur III remains are dominated by monumental architecture, for example, Urnamma's ziggurat complex at Ur and surrounding buildings such as the "palace," é-hur-sag, the royal mausolea, and so forth. The overwhelming majority of textual sources come from central state or provincial administrative archives (see, for example, Sallaberger 1999). Because the bulk of the tablets come from older excavations, secondary contexts (as at Ur), or illicit digging, their identification as state records is based largely on content. However, excavations at Tello (ancient Girsu) and Tell Asmar provide archaeological support for their attribution to state archives. In his eighth campaign at Tello in 1894, de Sarzec uncovered more than thirty thousand tablets in two discrete groups of rooms in the Tell des Tablettes, just south of the mound's prominence (Heuzey 1884–1912, 435–39). The tablets were in distinct rows and stacked five to six deep on low benches that flanked the walls and stood in the center of some of the rooms, as well as on the floors. In addition to the tablets, de Sarzec found a series of weights in the rooms. Inscribed pivot stones found nearby linked the rooms to the provincial governor's palace (Heuzey 1884–1912, 445; Thureau-Dangin 1898, 99–102; Cros 1914, 237–49). The tablets from Tell Asmar were associated with the Palace of the Rulers, a structure that can be traced back to the reign of Shulgi; the largest number come from the economic sector of the building north of the courtyard and palace chapel (Reichel 2001b, 114–16; 2001a, 43–56).

Only the site of Nippur has yielded archaeological and documentary sources for the Ur III period from a diversity of contexts, including the Inanna temple and houses. The University of Pennsylvania expedition uncovered burned houses that contained large numbers of tablets on the southern tip of Mound X in 1890 (Peters 1895, 453; 1904, 184–85). Peters' architectural notes include no plans, and the single photograph (Peters 1895, 453, fig. 59; 1904, following p. 188) is not particularly revealing. Moreover, while Peters noted the approximate number of tablets found day by day, he did not record tablets by findspots. Except in a few cases, we cannot determine specifically which tablets came from the houses. Nevertheless, the bulk of the roughly two thousand Ur III tablets from Penn's excavations probably came from Mound X. They stand apart from contemporary administrative records; they are often described as "private" in character (e. g., Neumann 1992; van Driel 1994); and their Sumerian shows peculiarities (Sauren 1969) that may reflect their setting outside the administrative bureaucracy.

Fifty years later the joint expedition uncovered a large, complex, and well-planned building dubbed house J on the southern tip of the east mound known as Tablet Hill, or the Scribal Quarter (McCown and Haines 1967, 43–53). John Sanders (1981, 63–65), Nippur's architect for many years, accepted the excavators' identification of the building as a house but tried to account for its size and the multiplicity of courtyards by suggesting that it served as the residence of an extended family. Heinrich (1984, 47–48) dubbed it a palace. In reanalyzing house J's architecture and artifacts, including more than twenty-seven clay sealings and seventy-five tablets, scribal exercises, and economic records, I suggested that it was more likely an official residence that served both as a house and functioned within the state or provincial administration. Its occupant, Ur-Suen, a supervisor of plowing oxen, played a role in institutional land management and agricultural production (Zettler 1991).

The limited range of excavated Ur III remains stands in marked contrast to the arguably more balanced sample of public buildings and houses for the succeeding Isin-Larsa and Old Babylonian periods. The most prominent remains dating to the first half of the second millennium include palaces at Mari (Parrot 1958, 1959), Tell Asmar (Frankfort, Lloyd, and Jacobsen 1940; Reichel 2001a), Senkereh, ancient Larsa (Parrot 1933, 1968; Margueron 1970), and Uruk,[1] as well as temples such as Ishchali's Ishtar Kittitum (Hill, Jacobsen, and Delougaz 1990; Ellis 1986). They also include substantial exposures of houses at Tell es-Sib/Tell Haddad, ancient Me-turan (Postgate and Watson 1979; Roaf and Postgate 1981; Killick and Roaf 1983; Killick and Black 1985; Cavigneaux and al-Rawi 1993); Abu Habba, or Sippar Yahrurum (Harris 1975; al-Jadir 1986; Gasche and Janssen 1997); Tell ed-Der (Gashe 1989); Nippur (Hilprecht 1903, 508–32, with plan p. 523; Geere and Fisher n.d.; Stone 1987; Franke 1987); and Ur (Woolley and Mallowan 1976; Charpin 1986; Van de Mieroop 1992; Brusasco 1999–2000). The domestic remains have provided a wealth of artifacts, including a large number of clay tablets, economic-administrative and legal, as well as literary and lexical texts. For example, several houses uncovered on Tablet Hill by the University of Pennsylvania in January through February 1900 yielded approximately seventeen thousand tablets and fragments (Haynes 1899–1901), while area TA house F, uncovered in 1951–52, had one thousand to fifteen hundred fragments (see, most recently, Robeson 2001). Tell ed-Der's Ur-Utu house contained some two thousand texts and fragments (de Meyer, Gasche and Tanret 1984, 21–25; van Lerberghe 1991).

Given the disparity in the distribution of our archaeological and documentary sources attributable to the late third millennium and the first half of the second millennium, comparisons between society and economy under the Ur III and Isin-Larsa–Old Babylonian periods appear futile. Postgate (1992, 292) may be right in suggesting that we leave "time and future excavations" to provide additional data before we draw any conclusions as to long-term trends in early Mesopotamian society and economy, at least for the third and early second millennia.

In terms of methodology, my study of the temple of Inanna highlighted the problems involved in integrating disparate data sets. Where large numbers of finds including clay tablets and other inscribed artifacts are found in situ on floors in well-preserved architectural contexts, architecture, small finds, and written documentation can be exploited to reconstruct a detailed and coherent picture of the functioning of rooms, complexes of rooms, or whole buildings. Where such conditions do not exist, as in the case of the Inanna temple, with large numbers of tablets found in secondary contexts, the analyses of archaeological and written sources tend to become discrete efforts. The secondary contexts from which the majority of the tablets found in the course of the Inanna temple excavations, whether from Ur III or later, introduce a degree of uncertainty in their identification and links to particular institutions. That uncertainty, in its turn, highlights the more substantial ambiguities unprovenanced texts raise.

Whatever its implications for our understanding of the functioning of a temple building, the Inanna temple highlighted the biases of the text-archaeological record, even for richly documented periods and their relevance for understanding the longue durée of Mesopotamian history. And the recent (re)discovery of records from Garshanna, a rural estate near Umma belonging to Shu-Kabta, a general and physician, and his presumed wife, Simat-Ishtaran, a sister of the Shu-Suen, fourth Ur III ruler, only reemphasizes the gaps in our knowledge (Owen 2002). While we may never be able to redress the biases of our data, we can at least include a palliative assessment of the representativeness of the archaeological and documentary sample in historical accounts.

Climate Change and the Collapse of Late Third Millennium BC Historic Dynasties

For the last ten years or so, Harvey Weiss, an archaeologist, Marie-Agnès Courty, a soils scientist, and various collaborators working at Tell Leilan in northeastern Syria have argued that an abrupt climate change occurred around 2200 BC and lasted for several centuries. Its characteristics included aridification, a radical increase in airborne dust, cooling, disappearance of forests, land degradation, possible alterations in seasonality, and flow reductions in the area's four major river systems due to reduced or displaced Mediterranean westerlies and Indian monsoons (Weiss et al. 1993; Weiss 2000a, 83–84). Climatic deterioration led to area-wide abandonments and the displacement of populations, both settled and transhumant, including Hurrians, Gutians, and Amorites. It precipitated the collapse of the dynasty of Akkad's imperial economy, dependent on the dry farming production of the Khabur, and led inexorably to the collapse of that dynasty. Gutians then seized at least parts of its weakened southern Mesopotamian core territory (Weiss et al. 1993, 1002). While the succeeding Third Dynasty of Ur reunited the cities of the south, aridification and reduced river flow made even irrigation agriculture unstable. Resulting scarcities engendered the painstaking bureaucratic accounting procedures commonly cited as a hallmark of Ur III (Weiss 2000a, 88–89). At the same time, migrations of populations from the north, including the Amorites against whom Shulgi and later Shu-Suen built walls (Sallaberger 1999, 159, 169), continued and are reflected in archaeological surface survey data (Weiss 2000a, 88–89). These movements caused disruptions and further stressed scarce resources, leading to agricultural and economic collapse. Weiss added that one possible explanation for the failure of Ur III agriculture is suggested by an "arid flicker" in the Greenland ice core record (Weiss 2000a, 89).

The abrupt climate change Weiss postulated was not an isolated phenomenon but caused disruptions — including social collapse — in an area stretching from the Aegean and Egypt to the Indus. De Menocal (2001) recently excerpted Weiss's data and historical scenario in his more general review of responses to prolonged environmental stresses, such as multidecadal-to-multicentury droughts in both the Old and New Worlds.

Weiss based his reconstruction of paleoclimate on proxy indicators such as soil micromorphological data from Tell Leilan and other sites in the Khabur, lake and marine cores, and the Greenland Ice Sheet Project 2 ice core (Weiss et al. 1993, 999–1002; Weiss 2000a, 78–83). He has attempted to meld a varying array of written sources and archaeological data to build a "consilience of inductions" to support his historical reconstruction and his understanding of the impact of abrupt climate change (Weiss 2000b, 209–11).[2]

In dealing with written sources, Weiss has employed questionable translations of Sumerian terms and drawn unsupportable inferences from literary texts. For example, he has cited references to natural disasters — drought, wind turbulence, harvest collapse, Euphrates flow reductions and "flaming potsherds" — in compositions such as the Curse of Akkade (CA), the Lamentation over the Destruction of Ur (LU) and the Lamentation over the Destruction of Sumer and Ur (LSUr) to support abrupt climate change (Weiss 1997, 719; Weiss 2000b, 209–11). He particularly emphasized Pascal Attinger's (1984, 117) implausible reconstruction of the phrase "flaming potsherds raining from the sky" in CA (1.175), presumably because CA's composition around the time of Ur III, shortly after the supposed onset of drought (Cooper 1983, 11–12), would give it substantial historical weight. He interpreted the phrase "flaming potsherds" as suggestive of volcanic activity, postulated at the time he was writing to have provoked the abrupt change in climatic conditions.

Weiss lamented the fact that philologists had generally dismissed references to natural disasters as "poetic metaphor." Yet, he failed to acknowledge that Assyriologists have expressed strong methodological reservations about using literary compositions to reconstruct the history of the periods they purport to describe. Liverani (1993), for example, argued that the historiographic traditions concerning Sargon and Naram-Suen cannot be used in writing the history of the dynasty of Akkad. They were really meaningful only within the political debates of the eras in which they were composed, namely, the Isin-Larsa and Old Babylonian periods. Michalowski (1989, 9–10) and Tinney (1995, 1996, 7–8) were more categorical in arguing that compositions such as CA, LU, and LSUr are not meaningful records of historical events, but literary constructions. They cannot be mined for historical data, at least in the absence of supporting sources. As Tinney (1995, 2; but see Westenholz 1999, 20–24) noted, the most effective approach to both historical inscriptions and literary reworkings is "to examine texts with a view to learning not what they tell us about the events they purport to describe, but what they tell us about themselves and the reasons for describing these events in a given way."

Weiss's climate-triggered developments and the link to the dynasty of Akkad raises the thorny problem of third-millennium BC chronology. Weiss based his date of 2200 for abrupt climate change on radiocarbon dates (Weiss et al. 1993), and recent determinations provide a calibrated date of 2280–2040 BC from the end of the Akkadian occupation at Tell Leilan (Forrest et al. 2004). Yet, the chronology of Mesopotamia's early historically attested dynasties is "alarmingly flexible" (Reade 2001, 1). Absolute chronology is still based largely on textual sources, in particular later copies of astronomical observations, such as those made of Venus during the reign of Ammiṣaduqa, Hammurabi's fourth successor and penultimate king of the first dynasty of Babylon. If the Venus observations are reliable (see, for example, Huber 2000; Gurzadyan 2000), the observations provide a series of possible dates—dubbed the high, middle, and low chronologies—for the end of Hammurabi's dynasty. The high chronology puts its denouement at 1651, the middle at 1595, and the low at 1531. King and year name lists, dated administrative texts, and royal inscriptions, then, permit the reconstruction of an unbroken succession of Mesopotamian rulers from the first dynasty of Babylon to the beginnings of the Ur III. The absolute date of Sargon's dynasty depends, in large part, on the number of years assigned to the so-called Guti interregnum, that is, the time between Sharkalisharri's death and Urnamma's succession. Sources such as the Sumerian King List insert a period of chaos and two kings of Akkad, the fourth dynasty of Uruk, Gutian kings, and the fifth dynasty of Uruk into the interregnum, and give it 80–120 years (Jacobsen 1939). Hallo has more convincingly argued that the period should be no more than 40 (or 50) years (1971, 713–14).

In his placement of the dynasty of Akkad, Weiss has adopted the middle chronology Brinkman outlined in his appendix to Oppenheim's *Ancient Mesopotamia* (1977, 335–48), with the eighty years he assigned to the Gutian interregnum. The middle chronology, however, has been adopted more out of convenience than conviction and is under attack, with various scholars arguing strongly in favor of a low(er) chronology for various reasons (Boese 1982; Gasche et al. 1998; Reade 2001), with Ur III shifted accordingly. While such shifts in absolute chronology still leave the dynasty of Akkad and Ur III within the period of prolonged drought Weiss has posited, they nevertheless affect the details of his historical scenario.

Finally, Weiss has not demonstrated his central contention, namely that the dynasty of Akkad was *economically dependent* on the Khabur as its "breadbasket." More generally, in espousing the causality of climate change, Weiss neglected the possible role of other factors in the dynasty of Akkad's downfall. In doing so, he exaggerated the extent of abandonment in northern Mesopotamia and overstated the weight of survey data for documenting the "mass migration" of northern populations into the south.

Economic Dependence

In describing the genesis of the Akkadian "empire," Weiss argued that by late Early Dynastic III, the population of the southern floodplain had reached its limits. Under Sargon's successors, increasing demand led inexorably to the "imperialization" of northern Mesopotamia's rainfall-based agricultural production (Weiss and Courty 1993, 147). While the successive kings of the dynasty of Akkad, whose capital city probably lay on the northeast fringes of the floodplain (Wall-Romana 1990; but see Westenholz 1999, 31–43), may well have perceived the Khabur as their "backyard," Weiss has not documented the large-scale transport of grain from the north to the south (or the necessity of such shipments). He initially argued that grain shipments moved down the Khabur and the Euphrates to Akkad, citing an Old Akkadian sealed clay bulla with a short notation referencing a boat (?) as proof (Weiss and Courty 1993, 148, n. 73; Mallowan 1937, 151 and pl. XIIIB; Gadd 1937, 178; Loretz 1969, no. 68). While river transport would make sense for heavy cargoes, no evidence exists to corroborate Weiss's hypothesis. Subsequently, Weiss suggested that grain moved overland from the Khabur to Nineveh and then to Akkad on packasses. Weiss based this assertion on a mistranslation of a line from the Curse of Akkad,[3] but more important, he failed to demonstrate that overland transport was economically viable. Equids engaged in hard work over an extended period of time need both grain and straw and chaff, as well as water, to be fed adequately (Engels 1978, 126–27; Jordan 1905, 367–78, esp. 374–78). Given maximum loads of one hundred kilograms, the donkeys transporting the grain over the twenty- to thirty-day trip Weiss envisioned would have consumed the bulk of their cargoes.

The Collapse of the Dynasty of Akkad and Its Aftermath

For at least the end of the fourth and much of the third millennia BC, the southern Mesopotamian floodplain was divided into thirty or so competing city-states (or shifting coalitions of city-states), each with its particular traditions but sharing a common cultural identity (Postgate 1992, 34). Rulers of various city-states periodically claimed an ill-defined hegemony expressed in the honorific "King of Kish." Conventional accounts suggest that Sargon, whose origins are shrouded in myth, but who was a high-ranking functionary of Ur-Zababa, king of the city-state of Kish, ended this state of affairs (Westenholz 1999, 29–59). He founded a new capital city (Akkad) and defeated Lugalzagesi, king of Umma, who dominated the disparate cities of the south and expressed claims to wider-ranging hegemony (Bauer 1998, 493–95). Sargon united the cities of the floodplain, north and south, and initiated a program of imperial expansion that climaxed under his grandson, Naram-Suen, though our evidence for Akkadian contacts with distant lands, particularly when stripped of modern commentaries, is sparse at best (Michalowski 1993, 73). The Akkadian or Sargonic dynasties collapsed under Naram-Suen's successor. However, the last two dynasts stabilized the political situation and ruled a much-reduced realm for nearly forty years. Historians have generally attributed the collapse of the dynasty of Akkad to various factors. Glassner (1986, 1994), for example, suggested that wars of succession led to political troubles.

Yoffee (1991, 46–49; 1995, 292–94) argued that unification of the formerly independent city-states of the southern floodplain created an inherently unstable polity, generating an "uneasy" power sharing between local elites and royal appointees that was particularly apparent in the redistribution of provincial lands to royal officials and the requisitioning of labor and resources. Signs of internal instability were also evident in rebellions by city-states at the death of one ruler and the accession of his successor. In addition, Yoffee argued that external factors probably also contributed to the dynasty of Akkad's collapse. The dynasty was "overextended," and the projection of military power in distant regions "galvanized" local populations, inducing them to form alliances and conduct "guerilla" operations against the Akkadians. The Gutians were eventually successful in penetrating the core of the "empire."

Whatever the factors involved, with the disintegration of Akkad's power, the southern city-states reasserted their independence, probably during the reign of Sharkalisharri (Sallaberger 1999, 132–34). Urnamma and his son, Shulgi, eventually succeeded in reuniting the city-states of the floodplain and building a highly structured bureaucratic state, centered on Ur. The Ur III kings campaigned extensively in the mountains to the north and northeast and one time against Anshan (Malyan) to the southeast (Sallaberger 1999, 156–59). They set up a militarized buffer zone east of the Tigris (Steinkeller 1991, 24–33) and built walls to block access to the floodplain from the north and west (Sallaberger 1999, 159). The Ur dynasts used royal marriages to cement relations with more distant polities (Sallaberger 1999, 151–61; Durand 1985, 156–57; Boese and Sallaberger 1996; Sharlach 2001).

Early in the reign of Ibbi-Suen, the Ur III's power collapsed, and the southern city-states again asserted their independence (Sallaberger 1999, 174–78). Ibbi-Suen was left in effective control only of territory around his own capital. Texts document grain shortages and staggering inflation, as well as famine. Amorites threatened on the northwestern frontier, but Elamites eventually administered the dynasty's deathblow.

The reasons for Ur III's collapse remain elusive. Jacobsen and Adams suggested that salinization led to the substitution of barley for wheat and diminishing surpluses, presumably under natural conditions of agriculture on the floodplain (Jacobsen and Adams 1958). Adams (1981, 151) argued that maximization of agriculture would have led to shortened fallow periods and salinization. However, Powell (1985) has challenged, if not necessarily disproved, their assertions. Yoffee (1995, 294–96) cited long-standing centrifugal tendencies of the southern city-states. He likewise pointed to the "unproductive, gigantic bureaucracy" as a contributory factor, a factor Hallo (1971) and Postgate (1992, 42) had earlier cited. Yoffee also dismissed later Mesopotamian traditions—and some modern accounts—that Amorite incursions were responsible for the dynasty's fall (Kamp and Yoffee 1980; Yoffee 1991, 50–51). More recently, Sallaberger (1999) noted the coincidence between a textually documented increase in the percentage of land cultivated in the Lagash-Girsu area, the floodplain's breadbasket, from late in the reign of Shulgi to the early years of Ibbi-Suen (Civil 1991, 39–40, 43), and the decline in production (or at least lack of grain). Sallaberger (1999, 176–77) postulated that ecological dynamics, such as river shift or salinization, led to the dynasty's collapse.

Weiss (1997, 719) has chided text-based historians for failing to grapple with his reconstruction of the genesis of the Akkadian empire, abrupt climate change, and its wide-ranging impact. Yet Weiss himself has not taken into account the longue durée of early Mesopotamia history. The norm of political organization in early Mesopotamia was the city-state. Periods of unification under the dynasty of Akkad, Ur III, or even Hammurabi and Samsuiluna represent anomalous eras that briefly lasted (Michalowski 1991, 46). Those polities, in effect, contained the seeds of their own destruction. The dynasty of Akkad, for example, had inherent structural weaknesses, perhaps exacerbated by expansionist policies; its disintegration can be readily explained using textual sources.

Moreover, the dynasty of Akkad's fall did not lead to social collapse, but led to the reemergence of normative political organization. The southern cities reasserted their independence. If we know little about this period, it may be due more to accidents of discovery than because of widespread collapse, since the extensive French excavations at Tello yielded remains dating right through the period.

The challenge that Weiss has rightly posed for historiography is to integrate all data, whether derived from texts, excavations, or geomorphology and soil micromorphology, into narratives of the ancient Mesopotamian past. Even so, perhaps the disintegration of the dynasty of Akkad and its successors is a far less interesting problem than understanding the processes that sparked unification in the first place (see Michalowski 1991).

Late Third-Millennium BC Abandonment of
the Khabur and Northern Mesopotamia

Recent work at sites such as Tell Brak and Hamoukar are pushing back the horizons of northern Mesopotamian urbanism, but excavations carried out in northern Iraq, Syria, and southeastern Turkey over the last twenty-five to thirty years have demonstrated that complex urban, literate states flourished there by the mid-third millennium BC (Schwartz 1994).

Archival texts found at Tell Mardikh (ancient Ebla) provide a glimpse of the north in the mid-third millennium BC, suggesting a political situation not radically different from that in the better-documented eighteenth and seventeenth centuries (Archi 1993, 470; Klengel 1992, 44–79). Though roughly contemporary and somewhat later texts from Mari, Tell Beydar, and Tell Brak are now fleshing out our picture of Syria in the mid-to-late third millennium, the Ebla texts suggest that by the early twenty-fourth century, northern Mesopotamia was a highly urbanized society. Extensive city-states, twenty to thirty kilometers apart and encompassing on average eight hundred square kilometers each, were gradually brought through military action and treaties into larger regional entities dominated, for example, by Ebla, just south of Aleppo; Mari, located on the Euphrates near the Syria-Iraq border; and Tell Brak (Nagar), near modern Hassake (Archi 1993, 466–68; 1995, 115; 1998). In addition to Mari and Nagar (Matthews and Eidem 1993; Archi 1998; Eidem 1998; Eidem, Finkel and Bonechi 2001), the Ebla texts contain references to other important northern Mesopotamian states: Harran on the upper Balikh (Archi 1988); Emar near modern Meskene on the "big bend" of the Euphrates (Archi 1990a); and Tuttul (Tell Bi'a) at the confluence of the Euphrates and the Balikh (Archi 1990b). They also include references to an array of smaller polities linked to the more powerful states through sociopolitical and economic ties.

While transhumant populations existed in the area, the Ebla texts contain few references to nomadic pastoralists such as the Martu (Amorites), some of whom appear to have existed in the area of Ibal, not far from modern Homs, and in the Jebel Bishri, along the west bank of the Euphrates between the confluences of that river and the Balikh and Khabur (Archi 1985, 1993, 470; Bonechi 1991, 71–73).

Weiss and collaborators argue that the 2200 BC abrupt climate change radically altered northern Mesopotamia's urban landscape, leading to a widespread abandonment across the regions. For example, they initially noted that drought led to the abandonment of Tell Leilan and estimated that the intensively surveyed Tell Leilan region suffered a net loss of roughly 182 hectares of built-up site area, or a displacement of 14,000 to 28,000 persons (Weiss et al. 1993, 1002). Whatever the situation around Tell Leilan, archaeological remains and textual documentation reveal that their picture is exaggerated. Large parts of the Khabur and northern Mesopotamia continued to be occupied in the late third millennium BC (for a summary, see Oates, Oates, and McDonald 2001, 392–94). For example, though the archaeological data have not been fully published, Tell Mozan, ancient Urkesh (Buccellati and Kelly-Buccellati 1996, 1), near Amuda to the east of Tell Leilan, continued to be occupied and was part of the Hurrian "kingdom of Urkesh and Nawar" (Matthews and Eidem 1993, 203–05; Salvini 1998, 108–111).

The recently published final report on the third-millennium BC remains at Tell Brak, Nagar, a center of Akkadian imperial administration, indicates that the whole of the site (forty to sixty hectares) continued to be occupied in the post-Akkadian period (Oates, Oates and McDonald 2001, 392–94). Arguably more important, the Brak excavations have established for the first time a well-stratified and dated corpus of pottery, with distinctive post-Akkadian ceramics and links to the big bend of the Euphrates that can be used to identify late third-millennium remains at other sites.

To the east in northern Iraq, miscellaneous artifacts document continued occupation at Kuyunjik, ancient Nineveh, in the post-Akkadian era (Gut, Reade, and Boehmer 2001). For example, the University of California at Berkeley's "gully cut" (Area KG) on the northeast side of Kuyunjik yielded post-Akkadian pottery in trash deposits outside the city's walls (McMahon 1998). Though textual references to Nineveh are not common in the Ur III administrative records, the few references that do exist attest to Nineveh's continued importance (Wilcke 1988; Sallaberger 1999, 161; Whiting 1982, 173–78; and, Zettler, in press).

Population Movements from North to South

Weiss (2000a, 88–89) cites data from settlement surveys of the southern floodplain as documenting a large-scale influx of northerners into the south in the "post-Akkadian Ur III time." However, Weiss's representation of the chronological precision of survey data, and the ex-

tent to which the results can be used for wide-ranging historical reconstructions, are highly questionable (see, for example, Adams and Nissen
1972, 37).

The problems with survey data for the late third and early second
millennia BC relate broadly to the ceramic indicators for the early historic dynasties. Adams specifically noted the problem of distinguish-
ing Early Dynastic from Akkadian, Akkadian from Ur III, and Ur III
from Isin-Larsa in surface collections. In presenting his results, he in fact
lumped together settlements dating to Ur III and the succeeding Isin-
Larsa periods (Adams 1981, 142–43). Adams accepted the fact that his
survey results lacked a fine-tuned chronology, but he saw the deficiency
as a trade-off for his "study's emphasis on wide geographic coverage and
hence rapidity of application" (Adams and Nissen 1972, 37–39; Adams
1981, 143).

Adams calculated total assumed site areas of 1,659 hectares for the
late Early Dynastic, 1,416 hectares for the Akkadian, 2,725 hectares for
the Ur III and Isin-Larsa periods, and 1,791 hectares for the Old Babylonian period. The Ur III and Isin-Larsa periods together cover about 330
years, and not all the sites he recorded would have been occupied at the
same time. Although the difference between total area occupied in the
Ur III and Isin-Larsa periods and the areas occupied in the preceding
Akkadian and following Old Babylonian periods must be understood
within these considerations, Adams argued that there was a "sharp increase in the numbers of sites in every size category" for the late third
and early second millennia BC (Adams 1981, 143).

However, since Adams completed his surveys, excavations have considerably refined our knowledge of the ceramic sequence for Mesopotamia's early historic dynasties, making it possible to reassess the time
range of the ceramic indicators he used for the Akkadian, Ur III and
Isin-Larsa, and Old Babylonian periods (see Adams 1965, 127–29; 1981,
170–71; Adams and Nissen 1972, 103–4). In general, the index fossils
Adams used for the Akkadian period are late Akkadian, Ur III, and early
Isin-Larsa in date (see Gibson and McMahon 1995). Adams' Ur III–Isin-
Larsa period falls largely in the Isin-Larsa period (Gibson and McMahon
1995, 16).

In short, the "sharp increase in the numbers of sites in every size category" that Adams documented occurred presumably in the early second millennium BC, after the time of the putative large-scale migrations
from north to south that Weiss postulated as a cause for the end of the

Ur III state. The factors behind the increase in the numbers of sites remain open to question.

Weiss's work at Tell Leilan over the last ten years or so and, in particular, the data he has adduced for late third millennium BC abrupt climate change, its impact on dry farming production and settlement in the Khabur drainage basin, as well as its contributory role in the disintegration of the dynasty of Akkad, have contributed significant insights to our understanding of the dynamics of the relationship between northern and southern Mesopotamia, a theme that he initiated with his work at Tell Leilan. In particular, his explanation of the dynasty of Akkad as politically dominant and economically dependent on the Khabur's dry farming production has turned conventional pictures of the surplus-producing, irrigation-based agricultural regime of the southern floodplain on its head. Yet perhaps his reconstruction of the genesis of the Akkadian empire is not so far-fetched. Whether the population of the southern floodplain had reached its limits by late Early Dynastic III times remains questionable. However, Akkad's location on the northeastern periphery of the southern floodplain would have put the Khabur in its backyard geographically and made the Khabur a critical economic resource. Perhaps, as Weiss himself concluded, the "jejune" cuneiform record for early historic Mesopotamia missed, among others, the "structure and goals of Akkadian imperialism" (Weiss 2000a, 91–92).

On a broader methodological level, Weiss has called particular attention to geomorphological and soil micromorphological lake and marine cores as data sources critical for reconstructing natural and anthropogenic phenomena. And his insistence on integrating information derived from those sources with archaeological and textual data at least aims at holistic historical reconstruction, even if his attempts to fully articulate hard climatological data with inconsistent documentary and archaeological records are still far from convincing (Reycraft and Bawden 2000, 7).

Mesopotamian Subsistence: Archaeological and Historical Perspectives

Mesopotamia has been described as the world's first urban civilization and dubbed the "heartland of cities" (Adams 1981). Surface surveys, despite their limitations, provide coarse demographic data, suggesting that in the latter part of the Early Dynastic period, roughly 80 percent of the population lived in urban settlements forty hectares (about one hundred acres) or more in area, while a mere 10 percent lived in nonurban settlements smaller than four hectares (ten acres). The urban population remained disproportionately high through the mid-second millennium BC (or Old Babylonian period), though the percentage of the population living in small settlements had increased threefold by that time (Adams 1981, 138). At least until recently with the initiation of salvage projects, archaeologists working in Mesopotamia have focused their efforts largely on urban sites. For example, until the Hamrin Dam salvage project began in 1977, the major excavations in Iraq were Seleucia, Sippar (Abu Habba), Tell ed-Der, Nippur, Isin, Larsa, Uruk (Wark), and al-Hiba (Lagash). Abu Salabikh was the only relatively small site under excavation (Postgate 1977). As might be expected, our textual corpora, too, whether excavated or looted, derive largely from urban centers.

Weiss's work on abrupt climate change has forcefully reminded us that however urban in character Mesopotamian civilization was, it was founded on highly productive irrigation and dry farming agriculture, complemented by animal — primarily sheep and goat — husbandry and the exploitation of wild animals in marginal areas (Zeder 1994). Lexical and literary, as well as legal and administrative-economic texts, provide a wealth of data on subsistence activities. The canonical recension of the lexical series HAR-ra = *hubullu* includes lists of trees; wooden objects; reeds and reed objects; clays and pottery; hides and leather objects; domestic and wild animals; cuts of meat; stones; plants, including vegetables; birds and fish; textiles; geographic terms; and food and drink (Civil 1995, 2311; Oppenheim 1977, 247). The didactic literary composition known as the *Farmer's Instructions* describes how to cultivate cereals from the spring flood season in April–May, through tilling and sowing, until the end of the harvest the following spring (Civil 1994). The large number of Ur III administrative texts from Tello provide substantive insights about how at least the "great organizations," that is, temples and palaces, organized cereal production, as well as data on seeding rates, yields (for example, see Maekawa 1984), animal husbandry (Maekawa 1983), and horticulture (e.g., Zettler 1992, 134–37).

However rich the data, textual sources have not been effectively used in reconstructing ancient Mesopotamian subsistence activities. Those who publish texts have all too often been wholly engrossed in "essential philological preliminaries of copying and translating the texts, and establishing the grammar and lexicon of the languages involved" (Postgate 1984, 1), and often oblivious to the material world. I. J. Gelb's "Sumerian and Akkadian Words for 'String of Fruit'" represents a case in point. In a sidebar to his article, Gelb (1982) argued that the Sumerian term *hashur* should be translated "apricot," not "apple." He based his argument, at least in part, on the fact that apricot trees grow well on the southern alluvium and appeared to be a much more important fruit in modern Iraq than apples (apples grow optimally at higher altitudes). Gelb also noted that apricots, dried or fresh, were more likely than apples to have been strung on strings, as hashur is commonly characterized in texts. In the last paragraph of his article, Gelb observed that he should know better than to get drawn into the debate about the identification of the names of fruit trees. Shortly after Gelb mailed his draft, he discovered a note on food remains from the Royal Cemetery of Ur that included small crab apples cut in half when fresh, threaded on a string, and dried (Ellison et al. 1978, 167–77). He eventually wrote a short addendum to his work that effectively refuted his own conclusion (Gelb 1982, 484).

So, too, philologists have commonly assumed that the textual record is broadly representative and mirrors the totality of ancient Mesopotamia. Oppenheim's observation on the consumption of fish illustrates such a perspective (1977, 46):

> The fish in rivers, swamps, lakes, and the sea were used on a large scale as food dried or preserved in salt only up to the middle of the second millennium BC, and that with markedly decreasing frequency. The economic texts up to the early Old Babylonian period enumerate large quantities of a variety of fish in contexts that indicate the importance of the fishing industry for the community. The lexical texts corroborate the popularity of fish with their endless lists of fish names. Late and Assyrian texts, however, rarely speak of fish and fishing. The word fisherman even came to denote, in neo-Babylonian Uruk, a lawless person.

Oppenheim's contention that ancient Mesopotamians ate less and less fish over time is counterintuitive and seems implausible in a riverine environment like southern Mesopotamia. Postgate's (1987, 125–27) not dissimilar observation about another comestible illustrates the possible explanations for the presence or absence of foods or other commodities in the textual record. Postgate noted that fruit, common in Ur III administrative texts, largely disappears in sources of the succeeding Isin-Larsa and Old Babylonian periods. He suggested, on the one hand, that fruit might no longer have been grown or imported (was less commonly grown and imported) because of the deterioration in the administration of irrigation after Ur III's disintegration. Fruit trees were particularly dependent on irrigation. Alternatively, he argued that the relative rarity of fruit might be due to multiple biases in the textual record for the earlier second millennium. Postgate concluded that the rarity of fruit was probably a reality, but his argument was based on an absence of evidence, and his discussion highlights the value of archaeological—in particular faunal and botanical—remains in enriching text-based observations on subsistence.

The Sumerian Agricultural Group (SAG), an informally constituted and elastic body set up in the early 1980s, demonstrated the utility of interdisciplinary collaboration among botanists, archaeobotanists, archaeologists, ethnoarchaeologists, cuneiformists, and others with practical experiences in elucidating the real world of early Mesopotamian subsistence activities. Over the course of its existence, SAG had six summer meetings, discussing cereals, pulses and oil seeds, alliaceous vegetables, cucumbers, fruit trees, irrigation and cultivation techniques, and domestic animals (Powell 1999). The proceedings of the meetings were published with exemplary speed in the *Bulletin of Sumerian Agriculture*. Though its editors, J. N. Postgate and Marvin Powell, initially bemoaned the fact that SAG served more to cast doubt on conventional translations given in Assyriological literature than to establish convincing alternatives, the wide range of information that SAG brought to bear on subsistence problems was groundbreaking.

SAG's first meeting brought together cuneiformists with a group of archaeobotanists. Though all the contributions, however seemingly basic, were highly informative, Naomi F. Miller's (1984a) short paper, excerpted from her then recently completed dissertation on the botanical remains from Malyan (Miller 1982), and G. C. Hillman's (1984) lengthier contribution stand in interesting contrast. Miller argued that carbonized seeds in the archaeological record derived largely from the use of dung fuel, and she subsequently expanded her argument in various articles (Miller 1984b; Miller and Smart 1984). Hillman (1984, 1985) elaborated his own suggestion put forth a few years earlier (1981) that carbonized plant remains resulted from the deliberate burning of crop-processing debris. Miller and Hillman continue to disagree (e.g., Miller 1996; Hillman et al. 1997), but Miller's work has alerted archaeologists, philologists, and historians alike that charred botanical remains from archaeological sites, particularly those in areas where alternative fuel sources were lacking, more likely reflect patterns of animal rather than human consumption. Though the context and content of samples are critical factors in determining the sources of charred botanical remains (Miller 1997b: 103–4; 1997a), even carbonized clean barley stored in jars could be intended as winter fodder for animals.

SAG's meeting on irrigation and cultivation techniques, held at Leiden in 1987, brought together archaeologists, archaeobotanists, an anthropologist (Robert C. Hunt) who studied irrigation and hydraulic management in parts of the world as diverse as Mexico and Egypt, and irrigation engineers from British consulting firms with experience of traditional (1950s) irrigation systems in Iraq. One important question raised was the relevance of traditional irrigation technologies to understanding early Mesopotamian irrigation systems. The question was stimulated by the Sumerian term *nag-ku5*, discussed by Steinkeller (1988) and Waetzoldt (1990) among others. The nag-ku5 is a lateral reservoir or pond to which excess flood waters could be diverted. In southern Mesopotamia the floods of the Tigris and Euphrates come at the time of the spring harvests and therefore pose distinct challenges for farmers. Though not the nag-ku5's primary function, once the floods had subsided, stored excesses could be used for irrigation (Civil 1994, 132–34). As Postgate (1988, ix) noted, nag-ku5s do not correspond to any elements of the traditional irrigation system; so, we perhaps have to reckon with an ancient irrigated landscape somewhat or perhaps even radically different from that of the 1950s.

Parenthetically, though not included in the *Bulletin of Sumerian Agriculture*, Miguel Civil presented a preliminary edition of the *Farmer's Instructions* at the Leiden meeting. Discussions with participants and subsequent detailed comments from some in attendance doubtless enriched the published edition that appeared some years later. Civil's *Farmer's Instructions* (1994) stands as a paradigm for the reconstruction of the realia of ancient Mesopotamian subsistence from textual sources.

The last of SAG's annual meetings in 1990 and 1993 focused on domestic animals, in particular, caprids and cattle, and were enlivened by the participation of Edward Ochsenschlager. While taking part in the excavations at al-Hiba, on the edges of the marshes near Shatra in southern Iraq, from 1968 to 1990, Ochsenschlager had been able to conduct informal ethnoarchaeological work in nearby villages, and he contributed papers on sheep (1993a) and village weavers (1993b), as well as on water buffalo (Ochsenschlager and Gustav 1995), at the meetings.

Ochsenschlager's papers document the sort of small-scale animal husbandry that probably existed in ancient Mesopotamia, if outside the purview of cuneiform records, and doubtless offered a healthy dose of reality to discussions, as the organizers intended. Among other observations, Ochsenschlager described the use of dung, often mixed with straw (or in the case of water buffalo, straw and crushed reeds), as fuel, corroborating Miller's suggestion offered nearly ten years earlier. He also described the winter fodder-feeding of animals with barley. Ochsenschlager noted that for four months of the year, when little or no pasturage exists, sheep have to be grain fed, normally two handfuls of barley twice a day. The period during which the animals have to be grain fed can be shortened to two or three months for those with land on the edge of the marsh or with irrigated ground. The lack of sufficient pasturage, which results in prolonged and costly supplemental feeding of animals, provides a major limitation on the growth of sheep herds. Ochsenschlager's observations on winter grain feeding and constraints on herd size support the underpinnings of recent efforts to integrate animals into reconstructions of human occupation and agricultural production, particularly for the dry farming and more marginal areas of northern Mesopotamia (e.g., Miller 1997a; Danti 2000; Wilkinson 2000).

Miller's (2000) investigation of plant ornaments on Pu-abi's diadem (figure 4.4) from the Early Dynastic Royal Cemetery of Ur recently confirmed the utility of SAG's interdisciplinary approach to the natural world of ancient Mesopotamia for elucidating even long-standing enigmas. The diadem was found in Pu-abi's tomb chamber; it had apparently been on a wooden table to the left of her bier, near her head. Woolley described the find as follows in his final report on the excavations (1934, 89).

> There were thousands of very small lapis lazuli beads which lay against a strip of white powdery material the fibrous texture of which suggested leather; this must have been the background to which the beads were sewn. Against this blue field there had been attached small ornaments of gold which in spite of the decay of the background still kept their order and to some extent their spacing and so could be replaced with tolerable accuracy. There are four pairs of animal figures, stags, bearded bulls, gazelles, and rams, small eight-petalled rosettes, ears of wheat, clusters of three pomegranates with their leaves, plants with stems of gold leaf over silver, and with gold, lapis, or carnelian pods, palmettes of twisted gold wire, the last found always inverted and so apparently hanging downwards.

Figure 4.4   Pu-abi's "diadem"

In Woolley's reconstruction, the so-called "ears of wheat" and "plants with stems of gold leaf over silver, and with gold, lapis, or carnelian pods" were affixed to the bead backing in an upright position, despite the fact that the loops suggested that they were dangling ornaments. Woolley likely restored the pieces as he had seen them in the ground but was no doubt influenced by his interpretation of some of the ornaments as "ears of wheat." Seeing the two components of the diadem as "dangling ornaments," Miller noted that the "ears of wheat" were more likely hanging inflorescences, and their morphology suggested the inflorescence of a date palm, a "much-branched spadix," probably describing the male flowering branch. Miller suggested that the ornament was probably to be identified with the Sumerian term *á-an šu-ša-lá*.

The identification of the "plants with stems of gold leaf over silver, and with gold, lapis, or carnelian pods" as the fruiting inflorescence of a date palm followed from the recognition of the identity of the "ears of wheat." Miller noted that the plants resembled a "bunch of some sort of fruit" and suggested that their ellipsoidal shape was consistent with dates. Since dates ripen from the tip toward the main step, the carnelian bead at the tip of the ornament would represent the first ripe date of the bunch. Dates were found in the Royal Cemetery, and Miller noted the close connection in Sumerian mythology between dates, the goddess Inanna, and fertility.

Miller likewise corrected Woolley's identification of the third plant ornament as pomegranates, identifying them as apples based on the morphology of the fruit and leaves. She noted that some species of apples have several fruits in terminal clusters like those on Pu-abi's diadem. Though the significance of apples remains to be investigated, dried apples on strings were found in the graves in the Royal Cemetery.

Though Pu-abi's "diadem" was probably not a diadem but several discrete items, likely part of a coordinated ensemble of jewelry (Pittman 1998, 92–94), Miller has taken the first and biggest step—namely, plausibly identifying the plants—in elucidating the meaning of the imagery. Her work challenges colleagues, archaeologists and archaeozoologists, art historians and philologists alike, to weigh in with a comprehensive explication of the symbolism of the ornaments that had graced Ur's queen in her life.

Challenge for the Future

Historic Mesopotamia has been an established focus of research in universities for more than a hundred and fifty years now. In the mid-nineteenth century, philological and literary studies, as a well-established and respectable part of the academic tradition (Larsen 1996, 147), held the dominant hand in efforts at reconstructing the ancient cultures of the land between the rivers. Archaeology, then in its infancy, could offer, as Oppenheim (1977, 10) would have it, little more than "welcome illustration to the wealth of factual information contained on clay tablets." The segregation of academic training and practice that is a product of the field's nineteenth-century roots remains today a deeply embedded part of its past. Nevertheless, over the last twenty-five years efforts have been made toward producing more holistic histories that integrate archaeological and textual data. The case studies in this chapter remind us that neither archaeologists nor philologists and historians can afford to think and work in rigidly bounded confines (at least not without paying a price that skews the ancient past). Clay tablets come out of the ground and have contexts in the archaeological record that are integral to their interpretation. Assessing the representativeness of our sample of that one strand of evidence is critical to the reconstruction of long-term trends in ancient Mesopotamian history. At the same time, as both Harvey Weiss's discussion of abrupt climate change and SAG forcefully reiterate, bringing together all available strands of data can challenge long-held translations or historical scenarios and markedly enrich our picture of the ancient past. While the nature of the data and analytical methodologies, research problems, and complexities of interpretation in the two fields are perhaps too demanding for any one person to be equally an archaeologist and a philologist and historian, broader academic training that makes archaeologists informed consumers of textual data and encourages philologists and historians to grapple with the survey data, site reports, and so forth, as well as collaborative efforts such as those that SAG and Hermann Gasche and colleagues (Gasche et al. 1998; Gasche and Tanret 1998) have fostered, can go some distance toward promoting a dialogue that can invigorate our reconstruction of historic Mesopotamia. Furthermore, even inferences about preliterate Mesopotamia depend on a holistic historical archaeology of Mesopotamia, since cuneiform sources provide a rich source of analogies on which prehistorians are fundamentally dependent (see, for example, Andrén 1998, 131–34; Postgate 1992, xxii).

Notes

This chapter was originally published in a slightly different form in the *Journal of the Economic and Social History of the Orient* 46 (1): 3–45. Copyright © 2003 by Brill Academic Publishers. Reprinted by permission.

1. The Sinkashid Palace of Uruk has been published piecemeal. For a summary description, see Heinrich (1984, 63–66). For a detailed bibliography, see Finkbeiner (1993, 117–19), and for additional text publications, see Sanati-Müller (1993, 1994, 1995, 1996, 2000a, and 2000b), and Blocher (2000).

2. Note that Marie-Agnès Courty (1998, 1999, 2001) has changed her interpretation of the Tell Leilan and Abu Hjeira soil micromorphological data, as well as its dating, and broadened her analyses to include other archaeological sites and natural soils across Syria. She now argues that the data point to an explosive cosmic collision involving a high-energy air blast, high-speed ejection of dust plumes, wide dispersion of atmospheric aerosols, violent swirls, sand and hail storms, and devastating rains, and places it somewhere in the 2600–2300 BC time range.

3. Weiss cited CA 1.50, part of the opening section of the composition that describes Akkad's rise; it portrays Akkad's patron deity, Inanna, as opening the city's gates and all the lands, bringing agricultural produce and exotic goods to her. The text reads, "Elam and Subir carried goods [to/for her, that is, Inanna] like packasses, or, literally, donkeys loaded with sacks" (Cooper 1983, 53; Attinger 1984). Weiss changed the translation to "Elam and Subir carried goods to her with packasses." The Sumerian does not support the translation "on or with packasses."

Bibliography

Adams, Robert McC. 1965. *Land behind Baghdad*. Chicago: University of Chicago Press.

————. 1981. *Heartland of Cities*. Chicago: University of Chicago Press.

————. 1991. "Contexts of Civilizational Collapse." In *The Collapse of Ancient States and Civilizations*, ed. N. Yoffee and G. L. Cowgill, 20–43. Tucson: University of Arizona Press.

Adams, Robert M., and Hans J. Nissen. 1972. *Uruk Countryside*. Chicago: University of Chicago Press.

Andrén, Anders. 1998. *Between Artifacts and Texts*. Trans. Alan Crozier. New York and London: Plenum.

Archi, Alfonso. 1985. "Mardu in the Ebla Texts." *Orientalia* 54:7–13.

————. 1988. "Harran in the III Millennium BC" *Ugarit Forschungen* 20:1–8.

————. 1990a. "Imar au IIIeme millénaire d'apres les archives d'Ebla." *M.A.R.I.* 6:21–38.

————. 1990b. "Tuttul-sur-Balih à l'age d'Ebla." In *De la Babylonie à la Syrie en passant par Mari*, ed. Ö. Tunca, 197–207. Liège: Université de Liège.

————. 1993. "Fifteen Years of Studies on Ebla: A Summary." *Orientalistische Literaturzeitung* 88:461–71.

————. 1995. "Gli Archivi reali e l'organizzazione istituzionale e amministrativa protosiriano." In *Ebla. Alle origini della civiltà urbana*, ed. P. Matthiae, F. Pinnock, and G. Scandone Matthiae, 112–19. Milan: Electa.

————. 1998. "The Regional State of Nagar according to the Texts from Ebla." *Subartu* 4 (2): 1–16.

Attinger, Pascal. 1984. "Remarques à propos de la 'Malédiction d'Accad.'" *Revue d'Assyriologie* 78:99–121.

Bahrani, Zainab. 1995. "Assault and Abduction: The Fate of the Royal Image in the Ancient Near East." *Art History* 18:363–82.

Baines, John, and Norman Yoffee. 1998. "Order, Legitimacy, and Wealth in Ancient Egypt and Mesopotamia." In *Archaic States*, ed. G. M. Feinman and Joyce Marcus, 199–260. Santa Fe: School of American Research Press.

Bauer, Josef. 1998. "Der vorsargonische Abschnitt der mesopotamischen Geschichte." In *Mesopotamien. Späturuk-Zeit und Frühdynastische Zeit*, ed. P. Attinger and M. Wäfler, 431–585. Orbis Biblicus et Orientalis 160/1. Freiburg: Universitätsverlag.

Blocher, Felix. 2000. "Texte aus dem Sînkāšid-Palast. Zehnter und elfter Teil: Die Siegelabrollungen." *Baghdader Mitteilungen* 31:177–80.

Boese, Johannes. 1982. "Zur absoluten Chronologie der Akkad-Zeit." *Wiener Zeitschrift für die Kunde des Morgenlandes* 74:33–55.

Boese, Johannes, and Walther Sallaberger. 1996. "Apil-kin von Mari und der Könige der III. Dynastie von Ur." *Altorientalische Forschungen* 23:24–39.

Bonechi, Marco. 1991. "Onomastica dei testi di Ebla: nomi propri come fossili-guida?" *Studi Epigrafici e Linguistici* 8:59–79.

Brinkman, J. A. 1977. "Mesopotamian Chronology of the Historical Period. In A. Leo Oppenheim." *Ancient Mesopotamia*. Rev. ed. Completed by Erica Reiner, 335–48. Chicago: University of Chicago Press.

———. 1984a. *Prelude to Empire*. Babylonian Society and Politics, 747–626 BC. Philadelphia: Babylonian Fund, University of Pennsylvania Museum.

———. 1984b. "Settlement Surveys and Documentary Evidence: Regional Variation and Secular Trend in Mesopotamian Demography." *Journal of Near Eastern Studies* 43:169–80.

Brusasco. P. 1999–2000. "Family Archives and the Social Use of Space in Old Babylonian Houses at Ur." *Mesopotamia* 34–35:3–174.

Buccellati, Giorgio, and Marilyn Kelly-Buccellati. 1996. "The Royal Storehouse of Urkesh: The Glyptik Evidence from the Southwestern Wing." *Archiv für Orientforschung* 42–43:1–32.

Cavigneaux, Antoine, and Farouk al-Rawi. 1993. "New Sumerian Literary Texts from Tell Haddad (Ancient Me-Turan): A First Survey." *Iraq* 55:91–105.

Charpin, Dominique. 1986. *Le clergé d'Ur au siècle d'Hammurabi (XIXe–XVIIIe siècles av. J. C.)*. Genève-Paris: Librairie Droz.

———. 1989. "Un Quartier de Nippur et le probleme des écoles à l'époque paléo-babylonienne." *Revue d'Assyriologie* 83:97–112.

———. 1990. "Un Quartier de Nippur et le probleme des écoles à l'époque paléo-babylonienne (suite)." *Revue d'Assyriologie* 84:1–15.

Civil, Miguel. 1980. "Les Limites de l'information textuelle." In *L'Archéologie de l'Iraq de début de l'époque néolithique à 333 avant notre ère*, ed. M. T. Barrelet, 225–32. Paris: Éditions du Centre National de la Recherche Scientifique.

———. 1991. "Ur III Bureaucracy: Quantitative Aspects." In *The Organization of Power: Aspects of Bureaucracy in the Ancient Near East*, ed. M. Gibson and R. D. Biggs, 35–44. Studies in Ancient Oriental Civilizations, No. 46. Chicago: Oriental Institute, University of Chicago.

———. 1994. *The Farmer's Instructions*. Aula Orientalis-Supplementa 5. Sabadell (Barcelona): Editorial AUSA.

———. 1995. "Ancient Mesopotamian Lexicography." In *Civilizations of the Ancient Near East*, ed. J. M. Sasson et al., 2305–14. New York: Scribner.

Cooper, Jerrold S. 1983. *The Curse of Agade*. Baltimore and London: The Johns Hopkins University Press.

Courty, Marie-Agnès. 1998. "The Soil Record of an Exceptional Event at 4000 BP in the Middle East." In *Natural Catastrophes during Bronze Age Civilizations*, ed. B. J. Peiser, T. Palmer and M. E. Bailey, 93–108. Oxford: Archaeopress.

———. 1999. "The 4000 year BP Impact Event: The Birth of a Scientific Hypothesis." *The Observatory* 119:168–71.

———. 2001. "Evidence at Tell Brak for the Late ED III/Early Akkadian Air Blast Event (4kyr BP)." In *Excavations at Tell Brak, Vol. 2: Nagar in the Third Millennium BC*, ed. D. Oates, J. Oates, and H. McDonald, 367–72. Cambridge and London: McDonald Institute for Archaeological Research and British School of Archaeology in Iraq.

Crawford, Vaughn E. 1959. "Nippur, the Holy City." *Archaeology* 12:74–83.

Cros, Gaston. 1914. *Nouvelles fouilles de Tello*. Troisiéme Livraison. Paris: Ernest Leroux, Éditeur.

Danti, Michael D. 2000. "Early Bronze Age Settlement and Land Use in the Tell es-Sweyhat Region, Syria." PhD diss., University of Pennsylvania.

Delougaz, Pinhas, and Seton Lloyd. 1942. *Pre-sargonid Temples in the Diyala Region*. Oriental Institute Publications 58. Chicago: University of Chicago Press.

Driel, G. van. 1990. "Old Babylonian Nippur." *Bibliotheca Orientalis* 47:559–78.

———. 1994. "Private or Not-so-private: Nippur Ur III Files." In *Cinquante-deux réflexions sur le proche-Orient Ancien, offertes en homage à Leon De Meyer*, ed. H. Gasche, M. Tanret, C. Janssen, and A. Degraeve, 181–92. Leuven: Peeters.

———. 1995. "Nippur and the Inanna Temple during the Ur III Period." *Journal of the Economic and Social History of the Orient* 38:393–406.

Durand, Jean-Marie. 1985. "La Situation historique des Sakkanakku: nouvelle approche." *M.A.R.I.* 4:147–72.

Eidem, Jesper. 1998. "Nagar." In *Reallexikon der Assyriologie*, Bd. 9, Lfg. 1/2, ed. D. O. Edzard, 75–77. Berlin and New York: Walter de Gruyter.

Eidem, Jesper, Irving Finkel, and Marco Bonechi. 2001. "The Third Millennium Inscriptions." In *Excavations at Tell Brak, Vol. 2: Nagar in the Third Millennium BC*, ed. D. Oates, J. Oates, and H McDonald, 99–105. Cambridge and London: McDonald Institute for Archaeological Research and British School of Archaeology in Iraq.

Ellis, Maria deJong. 1983. "Correlation of Archaeological and Written Evidence for the Study of Mesopotamian Institutions and Chronology." *American Journal of Archaeology* 87:497–507.

———. 1986. "The Archive of the Old Babylonian Kittitum Temple and Other Texts from Ischali." *Journal of the American Oriental Society* 106:757–86.

Ellison, Rosemary, Jane Renfrew, Don Brothwell and Nigel Seeley. 1978. "Some Food Offerings from Ur, Excavated by Sir Leonard Woolley, and Previously Unpublished." *Journal of Archaeological Science* 5:167–77.

Engels, Donald W. 1978. *Alexander the Great and the Logistics of the Macedonian Army*. Berkeley: University of California Press.

Finkbeiner, Uwe. 1993. *Uruk. Analytische Register zu den Grabungsberichten Kampagnen 1912/13 bis 1976–77*. Berlin: Gerb. Mann Verlag.

Forrest, Francesca deLillis, Lucia Mori, Thomas Guilderson and Harvey Weiss. 2004. "The Akkadian Administration on the Tell Leilan Acropolis." Poster Presentation. 4th International Congress on the Archaeology of the Ancient Near East. Berlin, March 29–April 3.

Franke, Judith A. 1987. "Artifact Patterning and Functional Variability in the Urban Dwelling: Old Babylonian Nippur, Iraq." PhD diss., University of Chicago.

Frankfort, Henri, Seton Lloyd and Thorkild Jacobsen. 1940. *The Gimil-Sin Temple and the Palace of the Rulers at Tell Asmar*. Oriental Institute Publications 43. Chicago: University of Chicago Press.

Gadd, C. J. 1937. "Tablets from Chagar Bazar." *Iraq* 4:178–85.

Garfinkle, Steven J. 2000. "Private Enterprise in Babylonia at the End of the Third Millennium BC." PhD diss., Columbia University.

Gasche, Hermann. 1989. *Babylonie au 17e siècle avant notre ère: approche, archéologique, problèmes et perspectives*. Mesopotamian History and Environment, Series II, Memoirs 1. Ghent: University of Ghent.

Gasche, Hermann, J. A. Armstrong, S. W. Cole, and V. G. Gurzadyan. 1998. *Dating the Fall of Babylon: A Reappraisal of Second Millennium Chronology*. Mesopotamian History and Environment. Series II, Memoirs 4. Chicago: University of Ghent and the Oriental Institute.

Gasche, Hermann, and Caroline Janssen. 1997. "Sippar." *The Oxford Encyclopaedia of Archaeology in the Near East*, vol. 5, 47–49. New York and Oxford: Oxford University Press.

Gasche, Hermann, and Michel Tanret, eds. 1998. *Towards a Reconstruction of the Ancient Environment in Lower Mesopotamia*. Mesopotamian History and Environment. Series II, Memoirs 5/1. Chicago: University of Ghent and the Oriental Institute.

Geere, H. Valentine, and Clarence Fisher. n.d. Notes to Accompany the Preliminary Plan of the Temple Library, Nippur. University of Pennsylvania Museum Archives. Nippur Archive. Box 16/9.

Gelb, I. J. 1982. "Sumerian and Akkadian Words for 'String of Fruit.'" In *Zikir Šumim: Assyriological Studies Presented to F. R. Kraus on the Occasion of His Seventieth Birthday*, ed. G. van Driel, 67–82, 484. Leiden, Netherlands: Brill.

Gibson, McGuire. 1964. "The Mace, the Axe and the Dagger in Ancient Mesopotamia." Master's thesis, University of Chicago.

———. 1993. "Nippur, Sacred City of Enlil, Supreme God of Sumer and Akkad." *al-Rāfidān* 14:1–18.

Gibson, McGuire, and Augusta McMahon. 1995. "Investigation of the Early Dynastic–Akkadian Transition: Report of the 18th and 19th Seasons of Excavations in Area WF, Nippur." *Iraq* 57:1–40.

Glassner, Jean-Jacques. 1986. *La Chute d'Akkadé. Le Événement et sa mémoire*. Berliner Beiträge zum vorderen Orient, 5. Berlin: Dietrich Reimer Verlag.

———. 1994. "La Chute de l'empire d'Akkade, les volcans d'Anatolie et la désertification de la vallée du Habur." *Le nouvelles de l'archéologie* 56:49–51.

Goetze, Albrecht. 1963. "Esarhaddon's Inscription from the Inanna Temple in Nippur." *Journal of Cuneiform Studies* 17:119–31.

———. 1968. "Akkad Dynasty Inscriptions from Nippur." *Journal of the American Oriental Society* 81:54–59.

Gurzadyan, Vahe G. 2000. "On the Astronomical Records and Babylonian Chronology." *Akkadica* 119–120:177–86.

Gut, Renate, Julian Reade, and Rainer Michael Boehmer. 2001. *Beiträge zur Vorderasiatische Archäologie Winfried Orthmann gewidmet*, ed. J. W. Meyer, M. Novak and A. Pruss, 74–129. Frankfurt am Main: Johan Wolfgang Goethe–Universität: Archäologisches Institut, Archäologie und Kulturgeschichte des Vorderen Orients.

Hallo, W. W. 1971. "Gutium." In *Reallexikon der Assyriologie*, Bd.3, ed. D. O. Edzard, 708–20. Berlin and New York: Walter de Gruyter.

Harris, Rivkah. 1975. *Ancient Sippar. A Demographic Study of an Old Babylonian City (1894–1595 BC)*. Istanbul: Nederlands Historisch-Archaeologisch Instituut te Istanbul.

Haynes, John Henry. 1899–1901. "IV Expedition Diary." University of Pennsylvania Museum Archives. Nippur Archive. Box 15.

Heinrich, Ernest. 1984. *Die Paläste im alten Mesopotamien*. Berlin: de Gruyter.

Heuzey, Léon. 1884–1912. "Les constructions de Tello d'apres les fouilles d'Ernest de Sarzec: Notes complémentaires." In *Découvertes en Chaldée*, ed. E. de Sarzec. Paris: Ernest Leroux, Éditeur.

Hill, Harold, Thorkild Jacobsen, and Pinhas Delougaz. 1990. *Old Babylonian Public Buildings in the Diyala Region*. Oriental Institute Publications 98. Chicago: Oriental Institute, University of Chicago.

Hillman, G. C. 1981. "Reconstructing Crop Husbandry Practices from Charred Remains of Crops." In *Farming Practice in British Prehistory*, ed. R. Mercer, 123–61. Edinburgh: Edinburgh University Press.

———. 1984. "Traditional Husbandry and Processing of Archaic Cereals in Modern Times: Part I, The Glume-wheats." *Bulletin of Sumerian Agriculture* 1:114–52.

———. 1985. "Traditional Husbandry and Processing of Archaic Cereals in Recent Times: Part II, The Free-threshing Cereals." *Bulletin of Sumerian Agriculture* 2:1–31.

Hillman, G. C., A. J. Legge, and P. A. Rowley-Conwy. 1997. "On the Charred Seeds from Epipalaeolithic Abu Hureyra: Food or Fuel." *Current Anthropology* 38:651–59.

Hilprecht, H. V. 1903. *Explorations in Bible Lands in the 19th Century.* Philadelphia: A. J. Holman.

Huber, Peter J. 2000. "Astronomy and Ancient Chronology." *Akkadica* 119-20:159–76.

Jacobsen, Thorkild. 1939. *The Sumerian King-list.* Assyriological Studies, No. 11. Chicago: University of Chicago Press.

———. 1953. "Review of Leon Legrain, Business Documents of the Third Dynasty of Ur (UET 3)." *American Journal of Archaeology* 57:125–28.

———. 1954. "Mesopotamian Mound Survey." *Archaeology* 7:53–54.

———. 1960. "The Waters of Ur." *Iraq* 22:174–85.

Jacobsen, Thorkild, and Robert M. Adams. 1958. "Salt and Silt in Ancient Mesopotamian Agriculture." *Science* 128:1251–58.

al-Jadir, Walid. 1986. "Sippar: ville du dieu soliel." *Dossiers Historire et Archéologie* 103:52–54.

Jordan, Whitman Howard. 1905. *The Feeding of Animals.* New York: The Macmillan Company.

Kamp, Kathryn A., and Norman Yoffee. 1980. "Ethnicity in Ancient Western Asia during the Early Second Millennium BC: Archaeological Assessments and Ethnoarchaeological Prospectives." *Bulletin of the American Schools of Oriental Research* 237:85–104.

Killick, Robert, and Jeremy Black. 1985. "Tell Haddad. In Excavations in Iraq, 1983–84." *Iraq* 47:220.

Killick, Robert, and Michael D. Roaf. 1983. "Tell Haddad. In Excavations in Iraq, 1981–82." *Iraq* 45:210–11.

Klengel, Horst. 1992. *Syria 3000 to 300 BC.* Akademie Verlag, Berlin.

Kraus, F. R. 1985. "Eine altbabylonische Buchhaltung aus einem Amtsarchiv in Nippur." *Bibliotheca Orientalis* 42:526–41.

Krebernik, M. 1990. "Review of René Marcel Sigrist: Les sattukku dans l'Éšumeša durant la période d'isin et Larsa." *Orientalistische Literaturzeitung* 85:410–12.

Larsen, Mogens Troelle. 1996. *The Conquest of Assyria.* London and New York: Routledge.

Lerberghe, Karel van. 1991. *Sippar Amnanum: The Ut-Utu Archive.* Mesopotamian History and Environment, Series III, Texts. 1. Ghent: University of Ghent.

Liverani, Mario. 1993. "Model and Actualization: The Kings of Akkad in the Historical Tradition." In *Akkad: The First World Empire*, ed. M. Liverani, 41–61. Padua, Italy: Sargon.

Loretz, Oswald. 1969. *Texte aus Chagar Bazar und Tell Brak*. Neukirchen-Vluyn: Verlag Butzon and Bercker Kevelaer und Neukircher Verlag.

Maekawa, Kazuya. 1983. "The Management of Fatted Sheep (udu-niga) in Ur III Girsu/Lagash." *Acta Sumerologica* 5:81–111.

————. 1984. "Cereal Cultivation in the Ur III Period." *Bulletin of Sumerian Agriculture* 1:77–96.

Mallowan, M. E. L. 1937. "The Excavations at Tall Chagar Bazar and an Archaeological Survey of the Qabur Region, Second Campaign." *Iraq* 4:91–177.

Margueron, Jean. 1970. "Larsa. Rapport préliminaire sur la quatrième campagne." *Syria* 47:261–77.

Matthews, Donald, and Jesper Eidem. 1993. "Tell Brak and Nagar." *Iraq* 55:201–8.

McCown, Donald E., and Richard C. Haines. 1967. *Nippur I: Temple of Enlil, Scribal Quarter, and Soundings*. Oriental Institute Publications 78. Chicago: University of Chicago Press.

McMahon, Augusta. 1998. "The Kuyunjik Gully Sounding, Nineveh, 1989 and 1990 Seasons." *al-Rāfidān* 19:1–32.

de Menocal, P. B. 2001. "Cultural Responses to Climate Change during the Late Holocene." *Science* 292:667–73.

de Meyer, Leon, Hermann Gasche and Michel Tanret. 1984. "Tell ed-Der. La vie en Babylonie il y a 4000 ans." *Archeologia* 195:8–25.

Michalowski, Piotr. 1989. *The Lamentation over the Destruction of Sumer and Ur*. Winona Lake, Ind.: Eisenbrauns.

————. 1991. "Charisma and Control: On Continuity and Change in Early Mesopotamian Bureaucratic Systems." In *The Organization of Power: Aspects of Bureaucracy in the Ancient Near East*, ed. M. Gibson and Robert D. Biggs, 45–57. Studies in Ancient Oriental Civilizations, No. 46. Chicago: Oriental Institute, University of Chicago.

————. 1993. "Memory and Deed: The Historiography of the Political Expansion of the Akkad State." In *Akkad: The First World Empire*, ed. M. Liverani, 69–90. Padua, Italy: Sargon.

Miller, Naomi F. 1982. "Economy and Environment of Malyan, a Third Millennium B. C. Urban Center in Southern Iran." PhD diss., University of Michigan, Ann Arbor.

————. 1984a. "The Interpretation of Some Carbonized Cereal Remains." *Bulletin of Sumerian Agriculture* 1:25–47.

————. 1984b. "The Use of Dung as Fuel: An Ethnographic Example and an Archaeological Application." *Paléorient* 10:71–79.

————. 1996. "Seed Eaters of the Ancient Near East: Human or Herbivore?" *Current Anthropology* 37:521–28.

————. 1997a. "Farming and Herding along the Euphrates: Environmental Constraint and Cultural Choice (Fourth to Second Millennium BC)." In *Subsistence and Settlement in a Marginal Environment: Tell es-Sweyhat, 1989–1995 Preliminary Report*, ed. R. L. Zettler, et al., 123–68. MASCA Research Papers in Science and Archaeology 14. Philadelphia: University of Pennsylvania Museum of Archaeology and Anthropology.

———. 1997b. "Sweyhat and Hajji Ibrahim: Some Archaeobotanical Samples from the 1991 and 1993 Seasons." In *Subsistence and Settlement in a Marginal Environment: Tell es-Sweyhat, 1989–1995 Preliminary Report*, ed. R. L. Zettler, et al., 95–122. MASCA Research Papers in Science and Archaeology 14. Philadelphia: University of Pennsylvania Museum of Archaeology and Anthropology.

———. 2000. "Plant Forms in Jewelry from the Royal Cemetery at Ur." *Iraq* 62:149–55.

Miller, Naomi F., and Tristine Lee Smart. 1984. "Intentional Burning of Dung as Fuel: A Mechanism for the Incorporation of Charred Seeds into the Archaeological Record." *Journal of Ethnobiology* 4:15–28.

Moorey, P. R. S. 1994. *Ancient Mesopotamian Materials and Industries: The Archaeological Evidence.* Oxford and New York: Clarendon Press.

Neumann, Hans. 1992. "Zur privaten Geschäftstätigkeit in Nippur in der Ur III-Zeit." In *Nippur at the Centennial*, ed. M. deJong Ellis, 161–76. Philadelphia: University of Pennsylvania Museum.

Nissen, Hans J. 1983. *Gründzüge einer Geschichte der Frühzeit des Vorderen Orients.* Darmstadt: Wissenschaftliche Buchgesellschaft.

———. 1988. *The Early History of the Ancient Near East, 9000–2000 BC.* Trans. Elizabeth Lutzeier and Kenneth J. Northcott. Chicago and London: University of Chicago Press.

Oates, David, Joan Oates, and Helen McDonald. 2001. *Excavations at Tell Brak, Vol. 2: Nagar in the Third Millennium BC.* Cambridge and London: McDonald Institute for Archaeological Research and British School of Archaeology in Iraq.

Ochsenschlager, Edward L. 1993a. "Sheep: Ethnoarchaeology at al-Hiba." *Bulletin of Sumerian Agriculture* 7:33–42.

———. 1993b. "Village Weavers, Ethnoarchaeology at al-Hiba." *Bulletin of Sumerian Agriculture* 7:43–62.

Ochsenschlager, Edward L., and Bonnie Gustav. 1995. "Water Buffalo and Garbage Pits: Ethnoarchaeology at al-Hiba." *Bulletin of Sumerian Agriculture* 8:1–9.

Oppenheim, A. Leo. 1977. *Ancient Mesopotamia*, rev. and completed by Erica Reiner. Chicago: University of Chicago Press.

Owen, David I. 2002. "Abstract: The Rural Estate of Shu-Kabta and Princess Simat-Ishtaran, Sister of Shu-Suen." 3rd International Congress on the Archaeology of the Ancient Near East. Paris. April 15–19, 2002. Abstract is available online at www.web26.net/3icaane/index.html.

Parrot, André. 1933. "La Prémiere campagne archéologique de Larsa." *Revue d'As-syriologie* 30:175–82.

———. 1958. *Le Palais. Architecture.* Mission Archéologique de Mari, 2. Paris: Librarie Orientaliste Paul Geuthner.

———. 1959. *Le Palais. Documents et Monuments.* Mission Archéologique de Mari, 2. Paris: Librarie Orientaliste Paul Geuthner.

———. 1968. "Les Fouilles de Larsa. Deuxième et troisième campagnes (1967)." *Syria* 45:205–39.

Peters, John Punnett. 1895. "University of Pennsylvania Expedition to Babylonia. III. The Court of Columns at Nippur." *American Journal of Archaeology* 10:439–68.

———. 1904. *Nippur.* 2 vols. New York and London: G. P. Putnam's Sons.

Pittman, Holly. 1998. "Jewelry." In *Treasures from the Royal Tombs of Ur,* ed. R. L. Zettler and L. Horne, 87–122. Philadelphia: University of Pennsylvania Museum of Anthropology and Archaeology.

Postgate, J. N. 1977. "Excavations in Iraq, 1976." *Iraq* 39:301–20.

———. 1984. "Cuneiform Catalysis: The First Information Revolution." *Archaeological Review from Cambridge* 3:4–18.

———. 1986. "Review of René Marcel Sigrist: Les sattukku dans l'Éšumeša durant la période d'isin et Larsa." *Journal of Semitic Studies* 31:237–38.

———. 1987. "Notes on Fruit in the Cuneiform Sources." *Bulletin of Sumerian Agriculture* 3:115–44.

———. 1988. "Introduction." *Bulletin of Sumerian Agriculture* 4:vii–xii.

———. 1990. "Archaeology and Texts—Bridging the Gap." *Zeitschrift für Assyriologie* 80:228–40.

———. 1992. *Early Mesopotamia. Society and Economy at the Dawn of History.* New York and London: Routledge.

Postgate, J. N., and P. J. Watson 1979. "Tell es-Sib. In Excavations in Iraq, 1977–78." *Iraq* 41:167.

Potts, Daniel T. 1997. *Mesopotamian Civilization: The Material Foundations.* Ithaca, N.Y.: Cornell University Press.

Powell, Marvin. 1985. "Salt, Seed and Yields in Sumerian Agriculture: A Critique of the Theory of Progressive Salinization." *Zeitschrift für Assyriologie* 75:7–38.

———. 1999. "The Sumerian Agriculture Group: A Brief History." In *Landwirtschaft im alten Orient: ausgewählte Vorträge der XLI Rencontre Assyriologique Internationale Berlin, 4–8, 7, 1994,* ed. H. Klengel and J. Renger, 11–15. Berliner Beiträge zum vorderen Orients, 18. Berlin: Dietrich Reimer Verlag.

Reade, Julian. 1993. "Hormuzd Rassam and His Discoveries." *Iraq* 55:39–62.

———. 2001. "Assyrian King-Lists, the Royal Tombs of Ur, and Indus Origins." *Journal of Near Eastern Studies.* 60:1–29.

Reichel, Clemens. 2001a. "Political Changes and Cultural Continuity in the Palace of the Rulers at Eshnunna (Tell Asmar) from the Ur III Period to the Isin-Larsa Period (ca. 2070–1850 BC)." PhD diss., University of Chicago.

———. 2001b. "Seals and Sealings at Tell Asmar: A New Look at an Ur III to Early Old Babylonian Palace." In *Proceedings of the XLVe Rencontre Assyriologique Internationale*, Part II, *Seals and Seal Impressions*, ed. W. W. Hallo and I. J. Winter, 101–32. Bethesda, Md.: CDL Press.

Reycraft, Richard Martin, and Garth Bawden. 2000. "Introduction." In *Environmental Disaster and the Archaeology of Human Response*, ed. G. Bawden and R. M. Reycraft, 1–10. Anthropology Papers No. 7. Albuquerque, N.Mex.: Maxwell Museum of Anthropology.

Roaf, Michael D., and J. N. Postgate. 1981. "Tell Haddad." In Excavations in Iraq, 1979–80. *Iraq* 43:177–78.

Robertson, John F. 1992. "The Temple Economy of Old Babylonian Nippur: The Evidence for Centralized Management." In *Nippur at the Centennial*, ed. M. deJong Ellis, 177–88. Philadelphia: University of Pennsylvania Museum.

Robeson, Eleanor. 2001. "The Tablet House: A Scribal School in Old Babylonina Nippur." *Revue d'Assyriologie* 95:39–66.

Rubio, Gonzalo. 1999. "Sumerian Literary Texts from the Time of the Third Dynasty of Ur." PhD diss., The Johns Hopkins University.

Saggs, H. W. F. 1995. *The Babylonians*. Norman: University of Oklahoma Press.

Sallaberger, Walther. 1999. "Ur III-Zeit." In *Mesopotamien. Akkade-Zeit u. Ur III-Zeit*, ed. P. Attinger and M. Wäfler, 119–414. Orbis Biblicus et Orientalis 160/3. Freiburg, Germany: Universitätsverlag.

Salvini, Mirjo. 1998. "The Earliest Evidence of the Hurrians before the Formation of the Reign of Mitanni." In *Urkesh and the Hurrians: Studies in Honor of Lloyd Costen*, ed. G. Buccellati and M. Kelly-Buccellati, 99–116. Malibu, Calif.: Undena Publications.

Sanati-Müller, Shirin. 1993. "Texte aus dem Sinkasid-Palast. Sechster Teil. Texte verschiedenen Inhalts III." *Baghdader Mitteilungen* 24:137–84.

———. 1994. "Texte aus dem Sinkasid-Palast. Siebenter Teil. Texte verschiedenen Inhalts IV." *Baghdader Mitteilungen* 25:309–40.

———. 1995. "Texte aus dem Sinkasid-Palast. Achter Teil. Texte in Zusammenhang mit Skelettresten." *Baghdader Mitteilungen* 26:65–84.

———. 1996. "Texte aus dem Sinkasid-Palast. Neunter Teil. Rohrtexte." *Baghdader Mitteilungen* 27:365–99.

———. 2000a. "Kollationen zu 'Ein Tontafelarchiv aus dem Palast des Sîn-Kāšid in Uruk' von Gerlind Mauer." *Baghdader Mitteilungen* 31:181–94.

———. 2000b. "Texte aus dem Sînkāšid-Palast. Zehnter Teil: Holztexte-Elfter Teil: Fragmentarisch erhaltene Texte." *Baghdader Mitteilungen* 31:93–176.

Sanders, John C. 1981. "Aspects of Mesopotamian Settlement Geography: An Empirical and Computer-aided Analysis of Building Forms, Room Arrangements and Circulation." Master's thesis, University of Wisconsin, Milwaukee.

Sauren, Herbert. 1969. "Untersuchungen zur Schritt- und Lautlehre der neusumerischen Urkunden aus Nippur." *Zeitschrift für Assyriologie* 59:11–64.

Schwartz, Glenn M. 1994. "Before Ebla: Models of Pre-State Political Organization in Northern Mesopotamia." In *Chiefdoms and Early States in the Near East*, ed. G. Stein and M. S. Rothman, 153–74. Madison, Wisc.: Prehistory Press.

Sharlach, Tonia. 2001. "Beyond Chronology: The Šakkanakkus of Mari and the Kings of Ur." In *Proceedings of the XLVe Rencontre Assyriologique Internationale*, Part II, *Seals and Seal Impressions*, ed. W. W. Hallo and I. J. Winter, 59–70. Bethesda, Md.: CDL Press.

Sigrist, René Marcel. 1984. *Les sattukku dans l'Ešumeša durant la période d'isin et Larsa*. Bibliotheca Mesopotamica 11. Malibu, Calif.: Undena Publications.

Steinkeller, Piotr. 1988. "Notes on the Irrigation System in Third Millennium Southern Babylonia." *Bulletin of Sumerian Agriculture* 4:73–92.

———. 1991. "The Administrative and Economic Organization of the Ur III State: The Core and the Periphery." In *The Organization of Power: Aspects of Bureaucracy in the Ancient Near East*, ed. M. Gibson and R. D. Biggs, 15–43. Studies in Ancient Oriental Civilizations, No. 46. Chicago: Oriental Institute, University of Chicago.

Stone, Elizabeth C. 1979. "The Social and Economic Organization of Old Babylonian Nippur." PhD diss., University of Chicago.

———. 1981. "Texts, Architecture and Ethnography Analogy: Patterns of Residence in Old Babylonian Nippur." *Iraq* 43:19–33.

———. 1987. *Nippur Neighborhoods*. Studies in Ancient Oriental Civilizations, No. 44. Chicago: Oriental Institute, University of Chicago.

Tanret, Michel. 2002. *Per Aspera ad Astra. L'Apprentissage du cunéiforme à Sippar-Amnanum pendant le période paléobabylonienne tardive*. Mesopotamian History and Environment, Series III, Texts 1, 2. Ghent, Belgium: University of Ghent.

Thureau-Dangin, François. 1898. "Notice sur le troisiéme collection de tablettes." *Revue d'Assyriologie* 5:67–102.

Tinney, Steve. 1995. "A New Look at Naram-Sin and the Great Rebellion." *Journal of Cuneiform Studies* 47:1–14.

———. 1996. *The Nippur Lament*. Philadelphia: University of Pennsylvania Museum.

———. 1998. "Texts, Tablets and Teaching: Scribal Education in Nippur and Ur." *Expedition* 40:40–50.

———. 1999. "On the Curricular Setting of Sumerian Literature." *Iraq* 59:159–72.

Vallades, Hélène, Jacques Evin, and Maurice Arnold. 1996. "Datation par la méthode de carbone 14 calibr. des couches Obeid 0 & I de Tell el-Oueili (Iraq)." In *Oueili:*

Travaux de 1987 et 1989, ed. Jean Lopuis Huot, 381–83. Paris: Editions recherche sur les civilisations.

Van de Mieroop, Marc. 1992. *Society and Enterprise in Old Babylonian Ur.* Berliner Beiträge zum vorderen Orients, 12. Berlin: Deitrich Reimer Verlag.

———. 1999. *Cuneiform Texts and the Writing of History.* London and New York: Routledge.

Veldhuis, Niek. 1997. "Elementary Education at Nippur: The Lists of Trees and Wooden Objects." PhD diss., University of Groningen.

Waetzoldt, H. 1990. "Zu den Bewässerungseinrichtungen in der Provinz Umma." *Bulletin of Sumerian Agriculture* 5:1–29.

Wall-Romana, Christophe. 1990. "An Areal Location of Agade." *Journal of Near Eastern Studies* 49:205–45.

Weadock, Penelope. 1958. "The Giparu at Ur: A Study of Archaeological Remains and Related Textual Material." PhD diss., University of Chicago.

———. 1975. "The Giparu at Ur." *Iraq* 37:101–28.

Weiss, Harvey. 1997. "Late Third Millennium Abrupt Climate Change and Social Collapse in West Asia and Egypt." In *Third Millennium BC Climate Change and Old World Collapse*, ed. H. Nüzhet Dalfes, G. Kukla, and H. Weiss, 711–23. Berlin and New York: Heidelberg and Springer-Verlag.

———. 2000a. "Beyond the Younger Dryas: Collapse as Adaptation to Abrupt Climate Change in Ancient Western Asia and the Eastern Mediterranean." In *Environmental Disaster and the Archaeology of Human Response*, ed. G. Bawden and R. M. Reycraft, 75–99. Albuquerque, N.Mex.: Maxwell Museum of Anthropology.

———. 2000b. "Causality and Chance: Late Third Millennium Collapse in Southwest Asia." *Subartu* 7:207–17.

Weiss, Harvey, and Marie-Agnès Courty. 1993. "The Genesis and Collapse of the Akkadian Empire: The Accidental Refraction of Historical Law." In *Akkad: The First World Empire*, ed. M. Liverani, 131–56. Padua, Italy: Sargon.

Weiss, Harvey, Marie-Agnès Courty, W. Wetterstrom, F. Guichard, L. Senior, R. Meadow, and A. Curnow. 1993. "The Genesis and Collapse of Third Millennium North Mesopotamian Civilization." *Science* 261 (5124): 995–1004.

Westenholz, Aage. 1987. *Old Sumerian and Old Akkadian Texts in Philadelphia.* Part 2. CNI Publications 3. Copenhagen: University of Copenhagen Press.

———. 1999. "The Old Akkadian Period: History and Culture." In *Akkade-Zeit u. Ur III-Zeit*, ed. P. Attinger and M. Wäfler, 15–117. Orbis Biblicus et Orientalis 160/3. Freiburg, Germany: Universitätsverlag.

Whiting, Robert M. 1982. "Tish-atal of Nineveh and Babati, Uncle of Shu-Sin." *Journal of Cuneiform Studies* 28:173–82.

Wilcke, Claus 1988. "A Note on Ti'amat-Bashti and the Goddess Sha(w)ush-(k)a of Nineveh." *Drevnii Vostok* 5:225–27.

Wilkinson, T. J. 2000. "Settlement and Land Use in the Zone of Uncertainty in Upper Mesopotamia." In *Rainfall and Agriculture in Northern Mesopotamia*, ed. R. M. Jas, 3–36. Istanbul: Nederlands Historisch-Archaeologisch Instituut te Istanbul.

Winter, Irene J. 1981. "Royal Rhetoric and the Development of Historical Narrative in Neo-Assyrian Reliefs." *Studies in Visual Communication* 7:2–38.

———. 1983. "The Program of the Throneroom of Assurnasirpal II at Nimrud." In *Essays on Near Eastern Art and Archaeology in Honor of Charles Kyrle Wilkinson*, ed. P. O. Harper and H. Pittman, 15–31. New York: Metropolitan Museum of Art.

———. 1985. "After the Battle Is Over: The Stele of the Vultures and the Beginning of Historical Narrative in the Art of the Ancient Near East." In *Pictorial Narrative in Antiquity to the Middle Ages*, ed. H. Kessler and M. S. Simpson, 11–37. Washington, D.C.: National Gallery.

———. 1986. "The King and the Cup: Iconography of the Royal Presentation Scene on Ur III Seals." In *Insight through Images: Studies in Honor of Edith Porada*, ed. M. Kelly-Buccellati, 253–68. Bibliotheca Mesopotamica, 21. Malibu, Calif.: Undena Publications.

———. 1987. "Legitimation of Authority through Image and Legend: Seals belonging to Officials in the Administrative Bureaucracy of the Ur III State." In *The Organization of Power: Aspects of Bureaucracy in the Ancient Near East*, ed. M. Gibson and R. D. Biggs, 69–116. Studies in Ancient Oriental Civilizations, No. 46. Chicago: Oriental Institute, University of Chicago.

———. 1997. "Art in Empire: The Royal Image and the Visual Dimensions of Assyrian Ideology." In *Assyria 1995*, ed. S. Parpola and R. M. Whiting, 359–82. Helsinki: the Neo-Assyrian Text Corpus Project.

Woolley, C. L. 1934. *The Royal Cemetery*. Ur Excavations, 2. London: Trustees of the British Museum and the University of Pennsylvania Museum.

Woolley, Sir Leonard, and M. E. L. Mallowan. 1976. *The Old Babylonian Period*. Ur Excavations, 7. London: Trustees of the British Museum and University of Pennsylvania Museum.

Yoffee, Norman. 1991. "The Collapse of Ancient Mesopotamian States and Civilization." In *The Collapse of Ancient States and Civilizations*, ed. N. Yoffee and G. L. Cowgill, 44–69. Tucson: University of Arizona Press.

———. 1995. "Political Economy in Early Mesopotamian States." *Annual Review of Anthropology* 24:281–311.

Zeder, Melinda. 1994. "After the Revolution: Post-Neolithic Subsistence Strategies in Northern Mesopotamia." *American Anthropologist* 96:97–126.

Zettler, Richard L. 1990. "Metalworkers in the Economy of Mesopotamia in the Late Third Millennium BC." In *Economy and Settlement in the Near East: Analysis of*

Ancient Sites and Materials, ed. N. F. Miller, 85–88. MASCA Research Papers in Science and Archaeology Supplement to vol. 7. Philadelphia: MASCA, University of Pennsylvania Museum.

———. 1991. "Nippur under the Third Dynasty of Ur. In Velles Paralles: Ancient Near Eastern Studies in Honor of Miguel Civil on the Occasion of His Sixty-fifth Birthday." *Aula Orientalis* 9:251–81.

———. 1992. *The Ur III Temple of Inanna at Nippur*. Berliner Beiträge zum vorderen Orients, 11. Berlin: Deitrich Reimer Verlag.

———. 1996. "Written Documents as Excavated Artifacts and the Holistic Interpretation of the Mesopotamian Archaeological Record." In *The Study of the Ancient Near East in the Twenty-First Century*, ed. J. S. Cooper and G. M. Schwartz, 81–102. Winona Lake, Ind.: Eisenbrauns.

———. in press. "Tishatal and Nineveh at the End of the 3rd Millennium BCE." In *If a Man Builds a Joyful House: Essays in Honor of Erle Verdun Leichty*, ed. A. Guinan et al. Groningen: Brill/STYX.

5

Archaeology and the Early History of Islam
The First Seventy Years

JEREMY JOHNS

In 1991, Judith Koren and Yehuda D. Nevo issued a methodological challenge to historians of early Islam. Koren and Nevo were encouraged to do so by their reading of the so-called "revisionist" historians, including Patricia Crone, Michael Cook, Gerald Hawting, Moshe Sharon, and John Wansbrough, whose work, Koren and Nevo believed, had completely undermined the foundations upon which the traditional positivist account of the rise of Islam had been constructed. None of the written Islamic sources for the first two hundred years of the hijra could be used as evidence for what had actually happened. Archaeology, which in any case consisted of objective facts that were always to be preferred over subjective written sources, was therefore almost the only evidence available and should be used to compose a new account of the origins of Islam that would be radically different from the traditional historical narrative. Koren and Nevo's polemical style permitted historians to dismiss the article as not worth an answer, while Nevo's unorthodox interpretation of material evidence embarrassed archaeologists into silence (figure 5.1).[1] What, it was widely asked, could have persuaded *Der Islam* to waste space in this manner?

The editor, the late Albrecht Noth, was himself one of the radical historians.[2] He, as much as any, was keenly aware of the problematic character of the Islamic literary sources.[3] This has rarely been described more judiciously and succinctly than by Stephen Humphreys (1991, 69–70):

> If our goal is to comprehend the way in which Muslims of the late 2nd/8th and 3rd/9th centuries understood the origins of their society, then we are very well off indeed. But if our aim is to find out "what really happened"—i.e., to develop reliably documented answers to modern questions about the earliest decades of Islamic societies— then we are in trouble.

The Arabic narrative sources represent a rather late crystallisation of a fluid oral tradition. These sources can become an adequate foundation for "scientific" history only when we have learned a great deal more than we presently know about this oral tradition: its origins, the social and cultural institutions by which it was shaped and transmitted, the variations and transformations it underwent in the course of transmission, the circumstances in which it was first committed to writing, the degree of alteration suffered by early written versions before they at last achieved their definitive form in the mid–3rd/9th century, etc. Questions of this kind have been discussed over and over by modern scholars, but so far their conclusions remain more in the realm of speculation than of demonstration. The evidence is such, in fact, that reasonable certainty may be beyond our grasp. . . . The first seventy years of Islamic history command our attention, therefore, not only because of the enormous interest of this period, but also because of the extraordinary methodological problems posed by our principal sources for it.

Noth, a pioneer of new methodological approaches to the Islamic literary sources, was attracted by the methodological terms of the challenge issued by Koren and Nevo, and believed that *Der Islam* should give archaeologists a chance to air their views (personal communication). A similar respect for archaeology as a sovereign discipline that is not the mere slave of history clearly informs the initiative of this volume.

Koren and Nevo were not the first to turn to archaeology for evidence in support of a radical reinterpretation of the rise of Islam. For example, in *Hagarism*, Crone and Cook (1977, 3) explored the possibility that one way around the historiographical problem posed by the Islamic sources was "to step outside the Islamic tradition altogether and start again." Although their account of the formation of Islam as a religion was based for the most part upon non-Islamic written sources, they occasionally cited archaeological evidence in corroboration of it. For example, the proposition that the original sanctuary of the primitive Muslims (*muhājirūn*) was not Mecca but Bakka (Qur'ān 3.90), an unidentified site in northwestern Arabia well to the north of Medina, was "dramatically confirmed" by the eccentric orientation (*qibla*) of the mosques excavated at Wāsiṭ (figure 5.2) and Uskāf Banī Junayd (both in Iraq).[4] *Hagarism* is perhaps now best regarded as a highly entertaining and provocative thought experiment that, "with a certain recklessness," to use the authors' own words, attempted extensive reconstruction at a time when

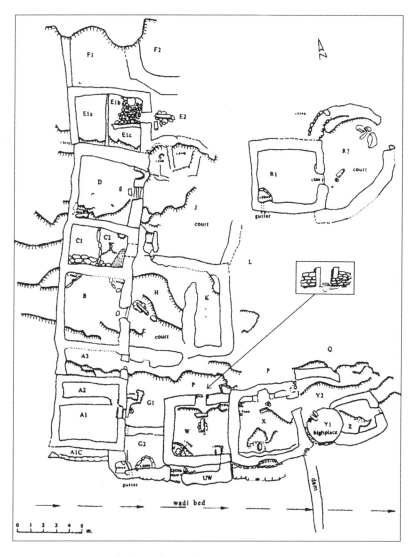

Figure 5.1 Ground plan of eighth-century (?) domestic structures from Area J at Sde Boqer (Naqab); the inset shows an elevation of a doorway (after Nevo 1990, figs. 3, 7b). Nevo interpreted such structures as part of a pagan sanctuary, analogous to the Meccan *ḥaram*; each structure (for Nevo, a ḥijr—cf. Mecca) contained shards of ceramics and glass, grinding stones, animal bones, ash, and so forth, that is, ordinary domestic refuse, which Nevo interpreted as ritually deposited fragments or *ḥaṭīm* (cf. Mecca), while he identified the jambs of the doorways as *anṣāb*, or stelae.

the task of deconstruction was still under way. The authors made no attempt to collect systematically all the evidence independent of Islamic tradition for the rise of Islam. That was left to Robert Hoyland, a pupil of Crone. Hoyland's principal concern was to survey and evaluate the non-Islamic written sources, but he did make extensive use of archaeological evidence and, in an appendix, listed all securely dated Islamic writings from the hijra to AH 72/AD 691–2, and all religious declarations attributable to caliphs from then until the fall of the Umayyads (Hoyland 1997, 545–90, 687–703). To what does this amount?

From as early as 22/643, coins, papyri, building inscriptions, tombstones, travelers' graffiti, and possibly (but probably not) a *ṭirāz* silk, were written *bism Allāh* ("In the name of God"), and some were dated according to a new calendar corresponding to the era of the hijra. Some of the formulae used are identical to those that are later characteristically Islamic—for example, *bism Allāh al-raḥmān al-raḥīm* ("In the name of God, the Merciful, the Compassionate") and *amīr al-muʾminīn* ("Commander of the Believers," i.e., the caliph)—and a phrase common in graffiti, and first securely attested in 64/683–4, also appears in the Qurʾān—*mā taqaddama min dhanbihi wa-mā taʾakhkhara* ("May God forgive him for his sins, the earlier and the later ones" Qurʾān 48.2). It is remarkable, however, that none of these early religious writings mentions either the Prophet Muḥammad or his religion, Islam. Thus, for example, the earliest tombstone of a Muslim, dated 31/651–2, from Egypt (figure 5.3), makes no reference to the Prophet, an omission that almost never occurs after 72/691–2 (el-Hawary 1930; Hoyland 1997, 689, n. 5). The first clear and detailed proclamation of Islam and of the role of Muḥammad is in the inscriptions of the Dome of the Rock, built by ʿAbd al-Malik b. Marwān (65–86/685–705) and dated 72/691–2.[5] This marks a watershed, and immediately thereafter, religious declarations become common, and only exceptionally do religious inscriptions fail to mention the Prophet. And yet, even before the reign of ʿAbd al-Malik, non-Muslim observers already perceived the Arabs to constitute a distinct religious community with Muḥammad as its leader (Hoyland 1997, 549).[6] The problem is therefore how to account for the absence of Islam and the Prophet from the archaeological record.

Absence of evidence is not evidence of absence, and it is certainly possible that new research will uncover explicit declarations of Islam earlier than 72/691–2. Possible but not, I believe, probable. All the earliest declarations of Islam are found on coins, documents, and monumental inscriptions produced by ʿAbd al-Malik and his successors. After

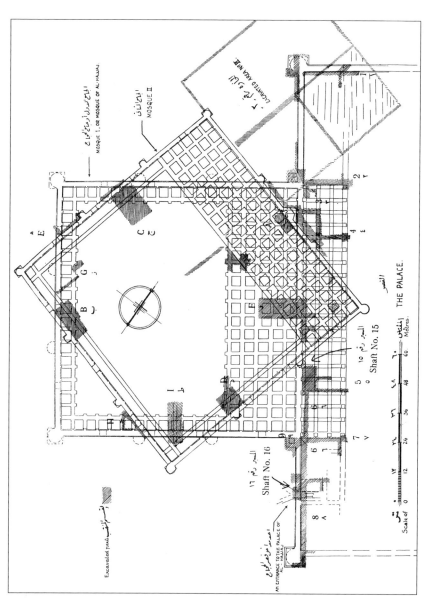

Figure 5.2 Ground plan of the excavations at Wāsit, showing Mosque I (probably AD 703), oriented on a *qibla* of 231 degrees from magnetic north (1942), lying beneath Mosque II, which is aligned on 197 degrees, close to the true *qibla* (after Safar 1945, fig. 5)

Figure 5.3 The tombstone of ʿAbd al-Raḥmān ibn Khayr al-Ḥajrī, Egypt, Jumādā II, 31/January–February 652 (after el-Hawary 1930, plate IIIb). The inscription reads: *bism Allāh al-raḥmān al-raḥīm hādhā l-qabr / li-ʿAbd al-Raḥmān ibn Khayr al-Ḥajrī allahumma ighfir lahu / wa-dkhulhu fī r raḥma minka wa-ātinā maʿahu / istaghfir lahu idhā qaraʾa hādha l-kit[ā]b / wa-qul amīn wa-kutiba hādha / l-kit[ā]b fī jum[ā]dā al-ā- / khar min sanat Iḥdā wa- / thalāthīn* ("In the name of God, the Merciful, the Compassionate. This tomb / belongs to ʿAbd al-Raḥmān ibn Khayr al-Ḥajrī. God forgive him / and admit him to Your mercy, and make us go with him. / Ask pardon for him, when reading this writing, / and say 'Amen.' This writing was written / in Jumādā / II in the year one and / thirty").

72/691–2, such media became increasingly common; before, they were extremely rare. But it is not just that coins, documents, and inscriptions are so scarce; not one single public monument built by the conquerors has yet been found that can be securely dated before the reign of 'Abd al-Malik. The earliest religious building is the Dome of the Rock itself, and a century of increasingly intensive archaeological excavation and survey has found no mosque that can be shown to be earlier. In the first half of the eighth century, mosques suddenly abound (Johns 1999).[7] New mosques of this date continue to be discovered (Almagro and Jiménez 2000; Walmsley 2003). The earliest palace is perhaps that at Kūfa, which is attributed on the weakest of historical grounds to Ziyād b. Abī Suf-yān in 50/670, although there is not a shard of archaeological evidence to support that attribution. Kūfa was first excavated seventy years ago, but since then no earlier palace has yet been found. Soon after the Kūfa palace was built, there was a boom in palace construction throughout Bilād al-Shām. Indeed, new examples from the first half of the eighth century of both the urban governor's palace (*dār al-imāra*) and the lux-ury rural villa (*qaṣr*) are found so frequently that it is difficult to keep up to date.[8] The question to be answered, therefore, is not why procla-mations of Islam are absent, but why the media that carry such procla-mations after 72/691–2 are so rare in the preceding period.

The answer, I suggest, is that the polity that found itself ruling the conquests was a loose confederation of Arab tribes, not a hegemonic state. It might be argued that the rulers of the Arab polity, based as it was upon Arab kinship, required no legitimization for their rule beyond the fact of conquest. But that would be to ignore the testimony of Ara-bic poetry that from the time of 'Uthmān, if not of 'Umar, the Arab leader claimed to rule as "the deputy of God" (*khalīfat Allāh*; Crone and Hinds 1986, 30–42). Well into the Marwanid period and beyond, poetry remained the primary medium through which the rulers of Islam pro-claimed the ideological basis of their rule, but only from the eleventh century were legitimatory verses inscribed on palaces. Archaeology has to date furnished no evidence for the ideological basis of the early cali-phate because there was not yet any state to commission the coins, docu-ments, and inscriptions through which such declarations could be made. Only during and immediately after the Second Civil War (680–92) did a series of significant advances in the process of state formation lead to the adoption of material culture as the medium for a "new rhetoric of rule."[9] We shall examine shortly the material evidence for the nature of

Marwānid state formation, but first we need to focus more closely upon the caliphate of Muʿāwiya.

Muʿāwiya b. Abī Sufyān, the first Umayyad ruler in Syria (661–80), figures largely in both the Islamic literary tradition and the non-Islamic sources (Hinds 1991; Hawting 1986, 24–45). He also stands out in the archaeological record as the first Muslim ruler whose name appears on coins (figure 5.4; see Walker 1941, 1:25–26; Album 1992, 178; Album and Goodwin 2002, 15 and plates 17.245–6, 18.269; Foss 2002, 360 and n. 28), documents,[10] and monumental inscriptions (figure 5.5).[11] (After Muʿāwiya, the name of the ruler again disappears from these media until ʿAbd al-Malik[12]). In a recent article, Clive Foss argued that Muʿāwiya governed a "highly organized and bureaucratic" realm and that, because "a sophisticated system of administration and taxation employs coinage," the Arab-Byzantine bronze types with bilingual inscriptions and mint marks, and a few rare gold coins, all of which were assigned to ʿAbd al-Malik by Michael Bates (figure 5.6), must in fact have been minted in Syria under Muʿāwiya (Foss 2002, 356–57). Although it is now increasingly likely that the Muslims did mint coins in Syria during the reign of Muʿāwiya, just as they did in Iraq, the case is being made, and will have to be proven, upon purely numismatic grounds.[13] Fortunately for Foss, it does not depend upon demonstrating the sophistication of Muʿāwiya's administrative and fiscal apparatus—because that he fails to do.

Foss assumes that the clear evidence in the papyri from Nessana in the Naqab (Palestine) for the continuity of preconquest administrative institutions at the local level in the 670s implies that Muʿāwiya governed through a sophisticated central administration and bureaucracy (Foss 2002, 356–57). This is the view of a Byzantinist, seeing through the eyes of an ʿAbbāsid historian. In fact, the Nessana papyri tell a very different story, in two episodes, one set before, and one after, the accession of ʿAbd al-Malik.

The "abrupt demands"—the phrase is Foss's own—made in the years 674–77 by the Arab governor of Gaza to the villagers of Nessana were not for taxes to be paid in money but for *rizq* (Greek *rouzikon*), the "food allowance" paid in kind to local Arab troops.[14] The rizq, consisting of equal numbers of units of wheat and oil, was payable in advance, usually at periods of two months. But the amounts varied widely from a maximum of 310 to a minimum of 90 *modii* of wheat and *sextarii* of oil. This, as the editor points out, is clear evidence that these were not regular taxes collected as part of a uniform and centralized fiscal system

Figure 5.4 Drachm of Muʿāwiya, Dārābjird, circa 54–55/674 (Shamma Collection 7481, after Album and Goodwin 2002, plate 17.245). Obverse field: typical late Arab-Sasanian bust with name of Muʿāwiya *amīr al-muʾmi-nīn* (in Middle Persian). Obverse margin: *bism Allāh*. Reverse field: typical Arab-Sasanian fire altar with attendants; mint (abbreviation) and date in Middle Persian, that is, frozen year 43 (circa 54–55/674). Reverse margin: plain.

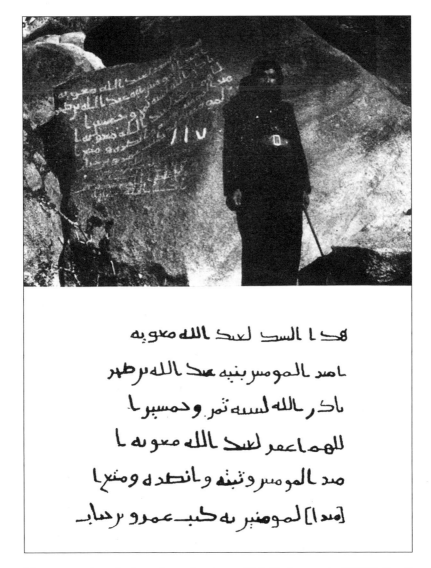

Figure 5.5 Inscriptions from the dam of Muʿāwiya, east of Ṭāʾif, Saudi Arabia (after Miles 1948, plate 18A and fig. 1). The inscription in the name of Muʿāwiya is uppermost; beneath it is an undated graffito, assigned to the late first or early second century, invoking "the peace of God and His blessing" for three generations of the same family, al-Ḥakam, his son Muḥammad, and his grandson ʿAbd Allāh.

Figure 5.6 Drachm of ʿAbd al-Malik ibn ʿAbd Allāh, Zubayrid governor of Bīshāpūr, 66/685–6 (Shamma Collection 7496, after Album and Goodwin 2002, plate 11.152). Obverse field: typical late Arab-Sasanian bust with name of ʿAbd al-Malik ibn ʿAbd Allāh (in Middle Persian). Obverse margin: / *bism Allāh / Muḥammad rasūl / Allāh*. Reverse field: typical Arab-Sasanian fire altar with attendants; mint (abbreviation) and date in Middle Persian, that is, 66/685–6. Reverse margin: pellet at 7h30.

but "irregular requisitions demanded as needed" (Kraemer 1958, 178). There is no suggestion that any of these demands originated in a central administration at Damascus or anywhere except in Gaza. The rizq was delivered not to fiscal officers, but directly to individual representatives of the Arab tribes. These irregular requisitions were not a heavy burden on the villagers. An account of the rizq requisitioned from Nessana in one complete year (indiction IX, possibly 680-1), when converted into money for accounting purposes, amounted to 86⁴⁄₅ *solidi*, a modest sum compared with the 1,444²⁄₃ solidi paid by the village as annual taxes in the mid-sixth century (Kraemer 1958, 199-201, no. 69; cf. 119-25, no. 39).

All this changed under ʿAbd al-Malik. The first evidence of intervention by the central administration in the affairs of the Naqab comes in a Greek daybook that records the names of individual Arab soldiers against their duties or the payments made to them. For each entry, the name of the authorizer is also noted, including the *amīr al-muʾminīn* ʿAbd al-Malik, and his brother ʿAbd al-ʿAzīz, the governor of Egypt (Kraemer 1958, 290-99, no. 92).[15] From the same time comes the first evidence that Nessana was now fully integrated into the administrative structure of the whole military province (*jund*) of Filasṭīn, in the form of an order for two laborers and two camels to perform unspecified public service on the road between Caesarea and Scythopolis, two hundred kilometers from the village (Kraemer 1958, 209-11, no. 74). The first evidence for a cadastral survey of Nessana's lands dates from the 680s.[16] And a register of households liable for the poll tax (*epikefalion*), dated circa 687-9, provides the first evidence for a census of the population (Kraemer 1958, 215-21, no. 76). Demands for payment of the poll tax (Kraemer 1958, 202-3, no. 70) and receipts for payment of both the poll tax and the land tax (*dēmosia*) also first occur at this time (Kraemer 1958, 153-55, no. 55 and 172-74, no. 59). The annual poll tax paid by Nessana may be calculated at 1,044 solidi (Kraemer 1958, 219); with the land tax, this would have amounted to a far heavier burden than the irregular tribute in kind levied in the 670s. So onerous were the new taxes that four or more villages, including Nessana, planned to send a joint delegation to the governor in Gaza to protest and to seek remission (Kraemer 1958, 212-14, no. 75).[17]

The evidence from Nessana matches the far more extensive testimony of the Egyptian papyri and the varied evidence—including that of Islamic sources—for northern Mesopotamia: A centralized administrative and fiscal apparatus is absent under Muʿāwiya and is first introduced under ʿAbd al-Malik and his successors.[18] A contrast between the two reigns is also drawn by non-Muslim authors, who howl in protest at the administrative and fiscal reforms instituted by ʿAbd al-Malik.[19] The reign of Muʿāwiya, in comparison, they remembered as a golden age, when the Arabs exacted only the tribute (Syriac *madattā*) and allowed the conquered population "to remain in whatever faith they wished"; "justice flourished . . . and there was great peace in the regions under his control; he allowed everyone to live as they wanted"; harvests were plentiful, and trade prospered (Brock 1987, 61; Hoyland 1997, 194–200, 263 n. 14; Robinson 2000, 47).

And yet, although Muʿāwiya did not govern by means of a sophisticated and centralized administration, he did attempt to found his own monarchy. The following much quoted passage from the *Maronite Chronicle* may have been written by a near contemporary of these events:

> Many Arabs gathered at Jerusalem and made Muʿāwiya king . . . In July of the same year the emirs and many Arabs gathered and gave their allegiance to Muʿāwiya. Then an order went out that he should be proclaimed king in all the villages and cities of his dominion and that they should make acclamations and invocations to him. He also minted gold and silver, but it was not accepted because it had no cross on it. Furthermore, Muʿāwiya did not wear a crown like other kings in the world. He placed his throne in Damascus and refused to go to the seat of Muḥammad. (Palmer, Brock, and Hoyland 1993, 31–32; Hoyland 1997, 136–39)

As we have seen, it was Muʿāwiya who introduced his name or the title *amīr al-muʾminīn* on coins, documents, and monumental inscriptions—clear evidence of his royal pretensions. He also built or repaired public buildings, including the mosque on the Temple Mount in Jerusalem,[20] a church in Edessa,[21] a bathhouse in Palestine, and a dam (or two) near Ṭāʾif. Significantly, the non-Islamic sources suggest that he was a ruler not just to the Arabs, and that he arbitrated in disputes between his non-Muslim subjects (Palmer, Brock, and Hoyland 1993, 30–31; Adomnan 1965, 192–94). But, although the evidence for his rule is distributed from Egypt to Iraq and from the Ḥijāz to northern Syria, it was in Jerusalem and Damascus that he based his kingdom, and he is reported to have "favoured the people of the West over those of the East, since the former had submitted to him."[22] The surviving evidence is admittedly sparse and patchy, but it suggests that Muʿāwiya attempted to found his monarchy in Syria upon the material trappings of kingship rather than upon the business of government. He sought to look like a king, rather than to build solid administrative foundations for his kingdom. Again, all this was to change under ʿAbd al-Malik.

The Greek daybook that shows the *amīr al-muʾminīn* ʿAbd al-Malik assigning duties and authorizing the pay of Arab soldiers stationed in the Naqab dates from the year of his accession, 66/685, or immediately thereafter.[23] The other Nessana papyri that attest to the increasing intervention of the central administration in the affairs of Nessana all belong to the early years of his reign. This dating is highly significant for it establishes, on archaeological evidence, that ʿAbd al-Malik's administrative reforms in Syria and Egypt were initiated immediately upon his accession.

That ʿAbd al-Malik's fiscal reforms date from as early as 66/685 offers a new perspective on the debate over the date of the Dome of the Rock. It had always been assumed that the dating clause at the end of the mosaic inscription on the outer façade of the octagonal arcade recorded the completion of the building: "There built this dome the servant of God ʿAb[d al-Malik, commander] of the believers in the year seventy-two, may God accept it from him and be pleased with him. Amen. Lord of the Worlds, to God belongs praise." Until, that is, Sheila Blair (1992) argued forcibly that the date referred to the building's inception and should be regarded as the *terminus a quo* for its construction. The testimony of the Nessana papyri significantly weakens her initial objection that the Dome of the Rock could not have been built in a period "not conducive to financing major construction" (Blair 1992, 62).[24] Her principal arguments—epigraphic, numismatic, and artisanal—are entirely circumstantial and may, or may not, be right. It is the historical case that is decisive.

A persistent report has it that ʿAbd al-Malik built the Dome of the Rock as part of his struggle with ʿAbd Allāh b. al-Zubayr. The latter had taken control of Mecca and, during the *ḥajj*, "used to catalogue the vices of the Marwānid family, and to summon [the people] to pay homage to him." ʿAbd al-Malik therefore forbade the Arabs of Syria from performing the pilgrimage and built the Dome of the Rock "in order to divert their attention from the ḥajj [to Mecca]." Before beginning construction, ʿAbd al-Malik consulted widely in order to draw away the sting of the inevitable criticism from Ibn al-Zubayr. Nonetheless, the rebel added the Dome of the Rock to his list of charges against ʿAbd al-Malik, claiming that he had "transferred the *ṭawāf* [ritual circumambulation] from the House of God [in Mecca] to the *qibla* of the Children of Israel." The fullest and most circumstantial account, from which I have quoted here, is based upon the testimony of, among others, Muḥammad b. al-Sāʾib, whose father was a supporter of Ibn al-Zubayr and died fighting alongside his brother, Muṣʿab b. al-Zubayr, against ʿAbd al-Malik (Elad 1992).[25]

In 1950, Shlomo Dov Goitein argued that this report should be rejected as anti–Umayyad Shīʿite propaganda, and most recent historians of the Dome of the Rock have accepted his view (Goitein 1950, 1966; Rabbat 1989, 1993). Undoubtedly, the report is anti-Umayyad propaganda. Indeed, the harshest criticism of ʿAbd al-Malik is put into the mouth of Ibn al-Zubayr. There is good reason, therefore, to distrust the charge that ʿAbd al-Malik was seeking to supplant Mecca with Jerusalem. However, since Amikam Elad published the fullest and most circumstantial version of the report yet known, together with a new study of the historiographical and historical circumstances, it has become increasingly difficult to dismiss the whole episode as fiction. In particular, it is becoming increasingly clear that the context in which the foundation of Dome of the Rock must be seen is the ideological contest between ʿAbd al-Malik and his opponents during the civil war.[26] Moreover, if Blair were right, then the propagandists would be extraordinarily incompetent, for, by moving the date of the inception of the Dome of the Rock back to 69/688–9, to the height of the civil war, when Mecca was securely in the hands of Ibn al-Zubayr, the propagandists would have provided ʿAbd al-Malik with the perfect excuse for his actions—that Ibn al-Zubayr prevented pilgrimage to Mecca—an excuse that, by all accounts, he used.[27] Whereas, had the propagandists left the date of construction unchanged, so that ʿAbd al-Malik began to build what they claimed to be a counter-Kaʿba only after his victory over the rebels in Iraq and a few months before he regained control of Mecca and defeated and killed Ibn al-Zubayr, then there would have been no mitigation for his diverting the ḥajj to Jerusalem.

For the moment, therefore, I shall carry on believing that the Dome of the Rock was completed in 72/691–2. If so, ʿAbd al-Malik began the formation of his state with administrative and fiscal reforms, and, some three years later, proceeded to build the Dome of the Rock. This was only part of a far more ambitious project that in time included the development of the entire Ḥaram al-Sharīf, including the Aqṣā mosque, a number of minor structures, its walls, and its gates; the foundation of the palatial complex to the south; and the construction of a network of roads leading to Jerusalem. Whether or not ʿAbd al-Malik intended Jerusalem to replace Mecca as the destination of the ḥajj, the redevelopment of the city on such an ambitious scale clearly issued a challenge to the lord of Mecca, his opponent Ibn al-Zubayr. What makes this interpretation so attractive is that the rebels had already begun to use material culture as a weapon for ideological conflict.

In 66/685-6, the year after ʿAbd al-Malik's accession (Ramaḍān 65/ April–May 685), the Zubayrid governor of Bīshāpūr, ʿAbd al-Malik b. ʿAbd Allāh (b. ʿĀmir), issued a silver drachm (figure 5.6) that bore the so-called "short" *shahāda-bism Allāh Muḥammad rasūl Allāh* ("In the name of God, Muḥammad is the messenger of God"). The issue was repeated in 67/686-7 (Walker 1941, 1:96–97; Gaube 1973, 62; Album and Goodwin 2002, 25, plate 11.151–55). In 69/688-9, another rebel, Qaṭarī b. al-Fujāʾa, had control of Bīshāpūr and there struck a drachm bearing the Khārijite slogan *bism Allāh lā ḥukma illā li-llāh* ("In the name of God, judgment belongs to God alone"), and his own name and titles in Middle Persian — "the Servant of God, Katari, Commander of the Believers" (Walker 1941, 1:112–13; Album and Goodwin 2002, 30, plates 3.32–34, 13.193–95, 18.265–66, 22.320). In 72/691-2, the Zubayrid governor of Sīstān, ʿAbd al-ʿAzīz b. ʿAbd Allāh, struck a unique drachm with a version of the "long" *shahāda* in Middle Persian (figure 5.7; see Mochiri 1981; Sears 1989; Ilisch 1992; Album and Goodwin 2002, 27). No Umayyad coin had previously borne any religious declaration except the *basmala*, but the first gold and silver coins struck in Syria by ʿAbd al-Malik, and the first silver issues by his governors in Iraq, all carried one version or other of the shahāda (see Treadwell 1999, 243–45 and table 3; Album and Goodwin 2002, 27–28). It seems highly probable, therefore, that the Marwānids learned from their opponents to use the coinage in this way (Hoyland 1997, 550–53, 694–95, following Crone and Hinds 1986, 25–26).

We shall come back shortly to the Marwānid coinage, but first it is necessary to return briefly to the Dome of the Rock. The inscriptions on the outer and inner façades of the octagonal arcade, dated as we have seen to 72/691-2, contain the earliest securely datable occurrence of passages that also appear in the Qurʾān. This is not the place for a detailed discussion of the implications of these inscriptions for the debate over the date at which the text of the Qurʾān began to crystallize. Suffice it to say that both those who favor a date before 72/691-2 and those who argue that the text was only fixed later have cited the inscriptions of the Dome of the Rock in their support (Whelan 1998).

Attention has tended to focus on the inscription on the inner façade of the octagon, which is principally concerned with defining the position of Jesus within the Islamic scheme. In the context of Marwānid state

Figure 5.7 Drachm of ʿAbd al-ʿAzīz ibn ʿAbd Allāh, the Zubayrid governor of Sīstān, Sijistān, 72/691–2 (after Mochiri 1981, plate 1). Obverse field: typical late Arab-Sasanian bust with Middle Persian inscriptions (left) "May his glory increase"; (right) "ʿAbd al-ʿAzīz ibn ʿAbd Allāh ibn Āmir." Obverse margin:–? / *bism Allāh* / *al-ʿazīz* ("/ In the name of God / the glorious"). Reverse field: Middle Persian inscription on five lines, "Seventy-two / One God, except He / no other god exists / Muḥammad [is] the messenger of God" (cf. Arabic "There is no god but God alone, Muḥammad is the messenger of God"). Reverse margin: plain.

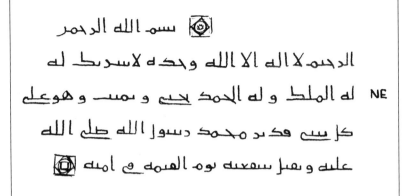

Figure 5.8 Transcription of part of the mosaic inscription from the outer octagonal arcade in the Dome of the Rock, northeast side (after Kessler 1970, 9). For photographs of the same inscription, see Nuseibeh and Grabar (1996, 98–99, mislabeled "Southeast").

formation, it is the inscription on the outer façade that is of greater interest. Here, it is the figure of Muḥammad that dominates. The inscription consists of four unitarian or anti-trinitarian verses, punctuated by five invocations to Muḥammad. The invocation on the northeast side particularly attracts attention (figure 5.8): "Muḥammad is the messenger of God. May God bless him and accept his intercession on the day of the resurrection on behalf of his [His?] community" (*Muḥammad rasūl Allāh ṣallā Allāh ʿalayhi wa-taqabbala shaf[ā] ʿatahu yawm al-qiy[ā]ma fī ummatihi*). It calls upon God to accept the intercession of Muḥammad for the Muslims on the Day of Judgment. The idea is not Qurʾānic, for nowhere in the Qurʾān does Muḥammad appear as an intercessor.[28] What is more, the idea of Muḥammad as intercessor does not fit comfortably with the Umayyad conception of the caliphate, according to which the most direct path to salvation led through the caliph (Crone and Hinds 1986, 27–42). After this appearance in the Dome of the Rock, Muḥammad does not again appear in the role of intercessor for some 150 years. This particular venture was an experiment that failed. Nor was it the only one.

For five to seven years after 72/691–2, ʿAbd al-Malik in Damascus and his governors in Iraq introduced an extraordinary series of images on their coinage, including the "standing caliph" (figure 5.9), the "caliph orans" (figure 5.10), and the "*miḥrāb* and *ʿanāza*" (figure 5.11). Such a variety of images over such a short period demonstrates that this was a phase of intense experimentation, which came to an abrupt end when all representational imagery was dropped from the coinage, and the purely epigraphic dinar was introduced in 77/696–7 (figure 5.12), followed by the dirham in 79/698–9. The meaning of these images has been much discussed and is beyond the scope of this essay (see Jamil 1999; Tread-well 1999, forthcoming). What matters here is the experiment, its failure and abandonment, and then the prodigious success of the epigraphic coinage that was to be the model for Islamic coinage for the next half millennium.

The evidence of the Dome of the Rock and of the coinage confirms what we might expect—that the process of articulating public declarations of the religious basis of the Marwānid state was not without difficulties. Unlike the Byzantine emperor, who could draw upon more than half a millennium's experience of bending material culture to the service of the state, ʿAbd al-Malik was a complete beginner. The ideological basis was already there, and al-Farazdaq and other poets show themselves to be masters at its manipulation, but poetry was more equivocal than lapidary and numismatic inscriptions; it had a more limited audience and did not circulate as widely as did the coinage among the population at large.

During the civil war, two Zubayrid governors had already attempted to use the medium of coinage to claim that Muḥammad fought on their side. After their victory, the Marwānids used all available state media to broadcast their counterclaim to the Prophet. But, in giving such new prominence to Muḥammad, the Marwānids forged new weapons for their opponents—not only for those who claimed descent from Muḥammad but, ultimately, also for those who sought to interpose the figure of the Prophet between the caliph and God (Crone and Hinds 1986, 33). We can only speculate why ʿAbd al-Malik allowed Muḥammad to appear in the role of intercessor in the Dome of the Rock, but in doing so he weakened his own claim to be the best path to salvation. We can only guess what forces caused ʿAbd al-Malik to drop his own image and titles from the coinage in favor of religious inscriptions that proclaimed the centrality of Muḥammad and omitted all mention of the caliph, but— purely numismatic considerations aside—it is difficult not to see this as an ideological compromise that was forced upon him. Nor do we know what pressures led his son, Sulaymān—of all names!—to turn his back on Jerusalem and build his new capital at Ramla, but his abandonment

Figure 5.9 "Standing caliph" dinar with transformed cross-on-steps reverse, presumably struck at Damascus, and produced each year from 74/
693–4 to 77/696–7 (Ashmolean purchase, Peus. 24.3.71, lot. 1029, after Album and Goodwin 2002, plate 45.705). Obverse: normal standing caliph
figure, surrounded by *bism Allāh lā ilāha illā Allāh waḥdahu Muḥammad
rasūl Allāh* ("In the name of God, there is no god but God alone. Muḥammad is the messenger of God"). Reverse: transformed cross-on-steps, surrounded by *bism Allāh ḍuriba hādhāal-dīnār sana sabʿ wa-sabʿīn* ("In the
name of God, this dinar was struck in the year seventy-seven").

Figure 5.10 "Caliph orans" drachm, Baṣra 75/694–5 (Bibliothèque Nationale 1969.75, after Treadwell 1999, 266, B1). Obverse field: typical late Arab-
Sasanian bust with the name of Bishr ibn Marwān (in Middle Persian). Obverse margin: legend in quarters 1–3, AN? (in Middle Persian) / *bism Allāh
Muḥammad / rasūl Allāh*. Reverse field: within three beaded circles, three
standing figures. The large central figure, flanked by two attendants, has
traditionally been identified as the "caliph orans," but more probably represents the Marwānid *khaṭīb*, either the caliph ʿAbd al-Malik or his brother
Bishr, delivering the Friday *khuṭba* with both hands raised. Mint name and
date (in Middle Persian): Baṣra, 75.

Figure 5.11 "Miḥrāb and ʿanaza" drachm, no mint or date, but probably struck in Damascus in the mid-70s A H (sold Sotheby's July 12, 1993, no. 167, after Treadwell 1999, 269). Obverse field: within two dotted circles, right facing bust flanked by standard Middle Persian inscriptions, "May his glory increase / *Khusraw.*" The bust is an extensively modified version of the Sasanian prototype; note, in particular, the cap, the visible arms, and the sheathed sword held in his right hand. Obverse margin: *bism Allāh lā ilāha illā Allāh waḥdahu Muḥammad rasūl Allāh* ("In the name of God, there is no god but God alone. Muḥammad is the messenger of God"). Reverse field: within three dotted circles, two columns supporting a ribbed arch (the "miḥrāb"), framing a spear (the ʿanaza), and flanked by inscriptions: (left) *amīr al-muʾminīn* ("the commander of the believers"); (right) *khalīfat Allāh* ("the caliph of God"); (flanking spear) *naṣara Allāh* ("May God aid [him]") or *naṣr Allāh* ("the victory of God"). Treadwell (forthcoming) argues convincingly that the arch on the columns of the reverse should be seen as a *sacrum*, not as a miḥrāb. Reverse margin: Middle Persian inscription, perhaps *AF[D]*: "praise."

Figure 5.12 Epigraphic dinar, anonymous ('Abd al-Malik), Damascus, 77/ 696–7. Obverse field: *lā ilāha illā Allāh waḥdahu lā sharīka lahu* ("There is no god but God alone. He has no associate"). Obverse margin: *Muḥammad rasūl Allāh alladhīarsala rasūlaha bi-l-hudāwa-dīni l-ḥaqqi li-yuẓiraha 'alāal-dīni kullihi* ("Muḥammad is the messenger of God whom He sent with guidance and the religion of truth that He might make it prevail over all religion"; Qur'ān 9.33). Reverse field: *Allāh aḥad Allāh al-ṣamad lam yalid wa-lam yūlad wa-lam yakun lahu kufuwan aḥad* ("God is one. God the eternal. He did not beget and was not begotten"; Qur'ān 112). Reverse margin: *bism Allāh ḍuriba hādhā al-dīnār sana sab' wa-sab'īn* ("In the name of God this dinar was struck in the year seventy-seven").

of the city in which his father and brother had invested such energy and wealth was a clear victory for Mecca in her ongoing struggle with Jerusalem for dominance over the new sacred geography of Islam.

The shortage of archaeological evidence for the religion of Islam during the first seventy years of the hijra is not surprising. Only with the formation of the state, which produced the media that preserved the evidence for the religion, does archaeology begin to be able to contribute to what is essentially a historical, and above all historiographical, debate. This is unlikely to change. With every year that passes without new material evidence being found for the emergence of Islam before 70/690, despite the intensification of archaeological fieldwork, the more likely it becomes that such evidence simply does not exist. This absence of evidence is frustrating, but it cannot be used to argue that a cult bearing the essential characteristics of Islam had not already emerged — on that, the testimony of non-Muslim authors is clear (Hoyland 1997, 548–49). It is particularly frustrating that there has been no archaeological investigation of the Arabian environment traditionally associated with the life of the Prophet and the early development of Islam. Nor will there be. The Mosque of the Ḥaram at Mecca and the Mosque of the Prophet at Medina have been razed to the ground and completely rebuilt in such a manner as to deny any possibility of archaeological excavation, even were it to be permitted. Outside the precincts of the two holy mosques, archaeological investigation of sites in Saudi Arabia that might yield evidence for the nature of religion in the sixth and seventh centuries is actively discouraged. Historians cannot expect any *deus ex cavea*.

Notes

This chapter was originally published in a slightly different form in the *Journal of the Economic and Social History of the Orient* 46 (4): 411–36. Copyright © 2003 by Brill Academic Publishers. Reprinted by permission.

    1. See also Nevo and Koren (1990), and Nevo (1994, 1991). For a critique, see Foss (1995). The publication of Nevo's *Crossroads to Islam* was halted by his death in February 1992 but was published in 2003 by Prometheus Books. Unlike his interpretation of the excavations at Sde Boqer, Nevo's epigraphic studies demand to be taken seriously.

    2. The first part of Noth's *Habilitationsschrift, Quellenkritische Studien zu Themen, Formen und Tendenzen frühislamischer Geschichtsüberlieferung, Themen und Formen*, was published by the Department of Oriental Studies at the University of Bonn in 1973 and was read and cited with approval by Cook, Crone, Hawting, and

Wansbrough. Although the second part, on *Tendenzen*, was never published, a revised English edition subsequently appeared as Noth and Conrad (1994).

3. For an up-to-date and wide-ranging introduction to the controversy, see Berg (2003).

4. See Crone and Cook (1977, 23 and n. 26) and Crone (1987, 198, n. 131). For a balanced discussion of the question, see Hoyland (1997, 560–73).

5. For the Dome of the Rock inscriptions, see van Berchem (1920–27, 2:223–55), Kessler (1970), Grabar (1996, 184–86, figs. 42–49), and Nuseibeh and Grabar (1996, 78–96). Later in this chapter, I discuss the argument that the date of 72/691–2 records the foundation of the Dome of the Rock, not its completion.

6. An analysis of early Arabic poetry, one of the few Muslim sources that can be shown to be contemporary with the events to which it refers, leads to the same conclusion.

7. What little material evidence there is regards Kūfa and Jerusalem. At Kūfa, the reentrant angle between the *qibla* wall of the mosque and the outer wall of the governor's palace (*dār al-imāra*) are said "to be one piece of work." This has never been satisfactorily documented and, in any case, the palace cannot be securely dated, although it is generally ascribed on historical grounds to Ziyād b. Abī Sufyān in 50/670. In a long-awaited study, Julian Raby will argue that the earliest traces of the Aqṣā mosque—Robert Hamilton's Aqṣā I—are earlier than ʿAbd al-Malik, and should be attributed to Muʿāwiya (early 40s/660s). There does seem to have been a mosque on the Temple Mount by circa 639, but the evidence is all literary, as I discuss later in this chapter. Only a relative sequence can be established for the archaeological remains of the Aqṣā, and the argument for absolute dating is again purely historical.

8. A probable *dār al-imāra* has been located, but not yet excavated, next to the Umayyad mosque in Jerash (see Walmsley 2003, 18). An Umayyad *qaṣr* with extraordinary wall paintings has come to light two kilometers south of Bālis (Syria); see Leisten (2002, 1999–2000).

9. For the nature of the Arab polity and the crucial role of the Second Civil War in the formation of the Marwānid state, see Robinson (2000). He writes of "a very loose tributary state," "the Arab kinship state," "the nascent Islamic state," and I too have elsewhere referred to "the early Islamic state," but the seminar that we convened on "ʿAbd al-Malik b. Marwān and the Marwānids" at the Oriental Institute, Oxford, in Hilary Term 2003, has persuaded us that the term must be used with greater precision.

10. A single protocol bearing the ruler's name in Greek and Arabic—*abdella Mouaouia amiralmoumnin* / ʿabd Allāh Muʿāwiya amīr al-muʾminīn (Grohmann 1960, 6–13). That Muʿāwiya's name appears only on this protocol, and never in the text of the papyri, indicates how limited central influence was upon the provincial administration of Egypt.

11. A Greek inscription dated 42/662–3 records the restoration of the baths at Ḥammet Gader (Palestine) by the governor (*symboulos*) ʿAbd Allāh b. Abī Hāshim "in the days of the servant of God Muʿāwiya, the commander of the believers"—*abdalla Maavia amēra almoumenēn* (Green and Tsafrir 1982, 94–96). An Arabic inscription dated 58/678 records the construction of a dam near Ṭaʾif (Arabia) "on behalf of the servant of God Muʿāwiya, the commander of the believers . . . O God, forgive the servant of God Muʿāwiya, the commander of the believers, strengthen

him and help him, and let the faithful profit by him" (Miles 1948, 237, 241, plate 18A, also 239, n. 18, for a possible third inscription of Muʿāwiya).

12. An Arab-Sasanian drachm bears on the reverse margin the legend in Persian "Year one of Yazīd," that is, Yazīd I b. Muʿāwiya, 61/681 (Mochiri 1982). A silk *ṭirāz* inscription in the name of *[ʿAbd] Allāh Marwān amīr al-muʾ[min]īn* has been attributed to Marwān I (64/684–65/685) by Day (1952). It is more probably in the name of Marwān II (127/744–132/750), as was originally thought by Grohmann (1967–71, 2:81).

13. See Morrisson (1992), Treadwell (2000), Foss (2002, 360–64), Album and Goodwin (2002, 99–107) and Oddy (2003). In addition to the numismatic evidence, see the famous passage in the *Maronite Chronicle* (quoted in this chapter) and the discussion of this passage in Hoyland (1997, 136–38).

14. See Kraemer (1958, 175–87, 190–95, nos. 60–63, 67–6; no. 64, on pages 188–90, is not from Nessana).

15. There is nothing to connect the daybook with Nessana, and the editor suggests that it may have been "compiled in another fort town in the Naqab and thrown away by the commandant or an adjutant while passing through Nessana."

16. Kraemer (1958, 168–71, no. 58): "the land survey of the Saracens" (*geōmetria tōn Sarakēnōn*).

17. The letter bears no date but is postconquest.

18. For Egypt, see Morimoto (1981) and the relevant sections in Simonsen (1988); for northern Mesopotamia, see Robinson (2000).

19. See the *Zuqnin Chronicle*, pseudo-Methodius, and pseudo–John the Less, all conveniently in Robinson (2000, 45–48). See the discussion of all these in Hoyland (1997, 263–67, 267–70, 409–14).

20. Anastasius of Sinai, apparently writing at the time of construction of the Dome of the Rock (circa 691) witnessed demons clearing the "Capitol" for the Muslims "thirty years ago," that is, circa 661 (Flusin 1992, 25–26). In the 670s, the pilgrim Arculf saw a "house of prayer" (*orationis domus*) built by the Saracens on the site of the temple (Adomnan 1965, 186). *The Jewish Apocalypse on the Umayyads* prophesies that Muʿāwiya will "restore the walls of the Temple" (Levi 1914). The tenth-century Muslim author Abū Naṣr al-Muṭahhar b. al-Muṭahhar al-Maqdisī, also reports that Muʿāwiya restored the temple and adds that it was there that the Muslims swore the oath of allegiance to him (al-Maqdisī 1899–1919, 4:87; trans. 82). There was apparently a mosque (Georgian *midzgitha*, from Arabic *masjid*) on the Temple Mount before the death of the Patriarch Sophronius (circa 639; Flusin 1992, 19–22). See the discussion of these sources in Hoyland (1997, 61–65, 101, 219–23, 316–17). There is no published archaeological evidence for or against the suggestion that Muʿāwiya may have begun the palatial complex to the south of the Temple Mount (Hoyland 1997, 222–23).

21. See the sources cited in Hoyland (1997, 646, n. 96) and in Robinson (2000, 41 and n. 47).

22. See the sources cited in Hoyland (1997, 644 and n. 76).

23. The account was written after indiction XII. During the reign of ʿAbd al-Malik, indiction XIII corresponds to either 684–5 or 699–700. If the *Assoun* in line 15 is to be identified with Ḥasan b. Mālik b. Baḥdal — see Kraemer (1958, 298 n. 14[c] and n. 23) — who governed Filasṭīn in 680–3, then the year in which it was written must be 685.

24. That 'Abd al-Malik was not short of ready cash is also suggested by the tribute he is said to have agreed to pay Constantine IV in 685 (see Hoyland 1997, 647, n. 102). But such a hemorrhage of gold to Byzantium might rather strengthen Blair's point.

25. The quotations are from 53 (trans. 34) and 54 (trans. 35), with full references to the primary sources and secondary literature.

26. Elad (1992, 49–51): "Before the fall of the Umayyads it was already claimed that 'Abd al-Malik had 'destroyed the Sacred House of God and revived the way of the foolish [Jews?], then he gave the Rock a form like that of the Place [of Ibrāhīm], [and] to it the rough Arabs of Syria go on pilgrimage.'"

27. See also the theological justifications that al-Yaʿqūbī puts into 'Abd al-Malik's mouth and the discussion of them by Elad (1992, 43–44).

28. See Hamza (2002, 124–49) for a detailed discussion of the early history of the Prophet as intercessor.

Bibliography

Adomnan. 1965. "De locis sanctis." In *Itinera et alia geographica*, ed. L. Bieler, 175–234. Corpus Christianorum Series Latina, 175. Turnhout: Brepols.

Album, Stephen. 1992. "An Arab–Sasanian Dirham Hoard from the Year 72 Hijri." *Studia Iranica* 21:161–95.

Album, Stephen, and Tony Goodwin. 2002. *The Pre-Reform Coinage of the Early Islamic Period*. Sylloge of Islamic Coins in the Ashmolean, 1. Oxford: Ashmolean Museum.

Almagro, Antonio, and Pedro Jiménez. 2000. "The Umayyad Mosque of the Citadel of Amman." *Annual of the Department of Antiquities of Jordan* 44:459–76.

van Berchem, Max. 1920–27. *Matériaux pour un corpus inscriptionum Arabicarum. Deuxième partie: Syrie du sud.* 3 vols. Mémoires publiés par les membres de l'Institut français d'archéologie orientale du Caire, 43–5. Cairo: Institut français d'archéologie orientale du Caire.

Berg, Herbert, ed. 2003. *Method and Theory in the Study of Islamic Origins*. Islamic History and Civilization Studies and Texts, 49. Leiden, Netherlands, and Boston: Brill.

Blair, Sheila. 1992. "What Is the Date of the Dome of the Rock?" In *Bayt al-Maqdis: 'Abd al-Malik's Jerusalem*, ed. J. Raby and J. Johns, 59–87. Oxford Studies in Islamic Art, 9:1. Oxford: Oxford University Press.

Brock, Sebastian P. 1987. "North Mesopotamia in the Late Seventh Century: Book XV of John Bar Penkāyē's *Rīš Mellē*." *Jerusalem Studies in Arabic and Islam* 9:51–75.

Crone, Patricia. 1987. *Meccan Trade and the Rise of Islam*. Cambridge: Cambridge University Press.

Crone, Patricia, and Michael A. Cook. 1977. *Hagarism: The Making of the Islamic World*. Cambridge: Cambridge University Press.

Crone, Patricia, and Martin Hinds. 1986. *God's Caliph: Religious Authority in the First Centuries of Islam*. Cambridge: Cambridge University Press.

Day, Florence E. 1952. "The Ṭirāz Silk of Marwān." In *Archaeologica Orientalia in Memoriam Ernst Herzfeld*, ed. G. C. Miles, 39–61. Locust Valley, N.Y.: J. J. Augustin.

Elad, Amikam. 1992. "Why did ʿAbd al-Malik Build the Dome of the Rock? A Reexamination of the Muslim Sources." In *Bayt al-Maqdis: ʿAbd al-Malik's Jerusalem*, ed. J. Raby and J. Johns, 33–58. Oxford Studies in Islamic Art, 9:1. Oxford: Oxford University Press.

Flusin, Bernard. 1992. "L'Esplanade du Temple à l'arrivée Arabes, d'après deux récits byzantins." In *Bayt al-Maqdis: ʿAbd al-Malik's Jerusalem*, ed. J. Raby and J. Johns, 17–32. Oxford Studies in Islamic Art, 9:1. Oxford: Oxford University Press.

Foss, Clive. 1995. "The Near Eastern Countryside in Late Antiquity: a Review Article." In *The Roman and Byzantine Near East: Some Recent Archaeological Research*, ed. J. H. Humphrey, 213–34. Journal of Roman Archaeology Supplementary Series, 14. Ann Arbor, Mich.: Journal of Roman Archaeology.

———. 2002. "A Syrian Coinage of Muʿawiya." *Revue numismatique*, 353–65.

Gaube, Heinz. 1973. *Arabosasanidische Numismatik*. Handbücher der mittelasiatischen Numismatik, Bd. 2. Braunschweig: Klinkhardt and Biermann.

Goitein, Shlomo D. 1950. "The Historical Background of the Erection of the Dome of the Rock." *Journal of the American Oriental Society* 70:104–8.

———. 1966. "The Sanctity of Jerusalem and Palestine in Early Islam." In *Studies in Islamic History and Institutions*, 135–48. Leiden, Netherlands: Brill.

Grabar, Oleg. 1996. *The Shape of the Holy: Early Islamic Jerusalem*. Princeton, N.J.: Princeton University Press.

Green, Judith, and Yoram Tsafrir. 1982. "Greek Inscriptions from Ḥammat Gader: A Poem by the Empress Eudocia and Two Building Inscriptions." *Israel Exploration Journal* 32:77–96.

Grohmann, Adolf. 1960. "Zum Papyrus-protokoll in früharabischer Zeit." *Jahrbuch der Österreichischen Byzantinischen Gesellschaft* 9:1–19.

———. 1967–71. *Arabische Paläographie*. Vienna: Österreichische Akademie der Wissenschaften.

Hamza, Feras. 2002. "To Hell and Back: a Study of the Concepts of Hell and Intercession in Early Islam." PhD diss., University of Oxford.

el-Hawary, Hassan M. 1930. "The Most Ancient Islamic Monument Known Dated A.H. 31 (AD 652)." *Journal of the Royal Asiatic Society*, 321–33.

Hawting, Gerald R. 1986. *The First Dynasty of Islam: The Umayyad Caliphate AD 661–750*. Revised ed., London and Sydney: Croom Helm, 2000.

Hinds, Martin. 1991. "Muʿāwiya I." In *The Encyclopaedia of Islam*, vol. 7, ed. H. A. R. Gibb et al., 263–68. Leiden, Netherlands: Brill.

Hoyland, Robert. 1997. *Seeing Islam as Others Saw It: A Survey and Evaluation of Christian, Jewish, and Zoroastrian Writings on Islam*. Studies in Late Antiquity and Early Islam 13. Princeton, N.J.: Darwin.

Humphreys, R. Stephen. 1991. *Islamic History: A Framework for Inquiry*. Revised ed. London and New York: I. B. Tauris.

Ilisch, Lutz. 1992. "Review of the First Volume of American Journal of Numismatics." *Der Islam* 69:381–82.

Jamil, Nadia M. 1999. "Caliph and Quṭb. Poetry as a Source for Interpreting the Transformation of the Byzantine Cross on Steps on Umayyad Coinage." In *Bayt al-Maqdis: Jerusalem and Early Islam*, ed. J. Johns, 11–57. Oxford Studies in Islamic Art, 9:2. Oxford: Oxford University Press.

Johns, Jeremy. 1999. "The 'House of the Prophet' and the Concept of the Mosque." In *Bayt al-Maqdis: Jerusalem and Early Islam*, ed. J. Johns, 59–112. Oxford Studies in Islamic Art, IX.2. Oxford: Oxford University Press.

Kessler, Christel. 1970. "'Abd al-Malik's Inscription in the Dome of the Rock: A Reconsideration." *Journal of the Royal Asiatic Society*, 2–14.

Koren, Judith, and Yehuda D. Nevo. 1991. "Methodological Approaches to Islamic Studies." *Der Islam* 68:87–107.

Kraemer, Caspar J. 1958. *Excavations at Nessana*, vol. 3, *Non-literary Papyri*. Princeton, N.J.: Princeton University Press.

Leisten, Thomas. 1999–2000. "II. Balis. Preliminary Report on the Campaigns 1996 & 1998." *Berytus* 44:35–57.

———. 2002. "The Umayyad Complex at Balis." Paper delivered to Symposium on the Archaeology of the Islamic Period, Museum für Islamische Kunst, Berlin, November 16–18, 2002.

Levi, Israel. 1914. "Une apocalypse judéo-arabe." *Revue des Études Juives* 67:178–79.

al-Maqdisī, Abū Naṣr al-Muṭahhar b. al-Muṭahhar. 1899–1919. *Kitāb al-bad' wa-l-ta'rīkh*. Ed. and trans. C. Huart. 6 vols. Paris: Leroux.

Miles, George C. 1948. "Early Islamic Inscriptions near Ṭā'if in the Ḥijāz." *Journal of Near Eastern Studies* 7:236–42.

Mochiri, Malek I. 1981. "A Pahlavi Forerunner of the Umayyad Reformed Coinage." *Journal of the Royal Asiatic Society*, 168–72.

———. 1982. "A Sasanian-Style Coin of Yazīd b. Mu'āwiya." *Journal of the Royal Asiatic Society*, 137–41.

Morimoto, Kosei. 1981. *The Fiscal Administration of Egypt in the Early Islamic Period*. Kyoto: Dohosha.

Morrisson, Cécile. 1992. "Le monnayage omeyyade et l'histoire administrative et économique de la Syrie." In *La Syrie de Byzance à l'Islam: VIIe–VIIIe siècles*. Actes du Colloque International Lyon, Maison de l'Orient Méditerranéen, Paris, Institut du Wonde Arabe, September, 11–15, 1990, ed. P. Cañivet and J. P. Rey-Coquais, 309–18. Damascus: Institut Français de Damas.

Nevo, Yehuda D. 1991. *Pagans and Herders: A Re-examination of the Negev Run-off Cultivation Systems in the Byzantine and Early Arab Periods.* Midreshet Ben-Gurion Negev: IPS Ltd.

———. 1994. "Towards a Prehistory of Islam." *Jerusalem Studies in Arabic and Islam* 17:108–41.

Nevo, Yehuda D., Zemira Cohen, and Dalia Heftman. 1993. *Ancient Arabic Inscriptions from the Negev.* Midreshet Ben-Gurion Negev: IPS Ltd.

Nevo, Yehuda D., and Judith Koren. 1990. "The Origins of the Muslim Description of the Jahili Meccan Sanctuary." *Journal of Near Eastern Studies* 49:23–44.

———. 2003. *Crossroads to Islam: The Origins of the Arab Religion and the Arab State.* Amherst: Prometheus Books.

Noth, Albrecht. 1973. *Habilitationsschrift, Quellenkritische Studien zu Themen, Formen und Tendenzen frühislamischer Geschichtsüberlieferung, vol. 1, Themen und Formen.* Bonner orientalistische Studien, neue Serie, Bd. 25. Bonn: Selbstverlag des Orientalischen Seminars der Universität.

Noth, Albrecht, and Lawrence I. Conrad. 1994. *The Early Arabic Historical Tradition: a Source-Critical Study.* Trans. Michael Bonner. Studies in Late Antiquity and Early Islam 3. Princeton, N.J.: Darwin Press.

Nuseibeh, Saïd, and Oleg Grabar. 1996. *The Dome of the Rock.* London: Thames and Hudson.

Oddy, Andrew. 2003. "The Christian Coinage of Early Muslim Syria." *ARAM* 15:185–96.

Palmer, Andrew N., Sebastian P. Brock, and Robert Hoyland. 1993. *The Seventh Century in the West-Syrian Chronicles.* Liverpool: Liverpool University Press.

Rabbat, Nasser. 1989. "The Meaning of the Umayyad Dome of the Rock." *Muqarnas* 6:12–21.

———. 1993. "The Dome of The Rock Revisited: Some Remarks on al-Wasiti's Accounts." *Muqarnas* 10:67–75.

Robinson, Chase F. 2000. *Empire and Elites after the Muslim Conquest: The Transformation of Northern Mesopotamia.* Cambridge Studies in Islamic Civilization. Cambridge: Cambridge University Press.

Safar, Fuad. 1945. *Wasit: The Sixth Season's Excavations.* Baghdad: Directorate General of Antiquities.

Sears, Stewart D. 1989. "A Hybrid Imitation of Early Muslim Coinage Struck in Sijistan by Abū Bardhāʿa." *American Journal of Numismatics* 1:137–69.

Simonsen, Jørgen B. 1988. *Studies in the Genesis and Early Development of the Caliphal Taxation System.* Copenhagen: Akademisk Forlag.

Treadwell, W. Luke. 1999. "The 'Orans' Drachms of Bishr ibn Marwān and the Figural Coinage of the Early Marwānids." In *Bayt al-Maqdis: Jerusalem and Early Islam*, ed. J. Johns, 223–70. Oxford Studies in Islamic Art, 9:2. Oxford: Oxford University Press.

———. 2000. "The Chronology of the Pre-Reform Copper Coinage of Early Islamic Syria." *Supplement to the Oriental Numismatic Society Newsletter* 162: 1–14.

———. Forthcoming. "'Miḥrāb and 'Anaza' or 'Spear in Sacrum' — A Reconsideration of the Iconography of an Early Marwānid Silver Drachm."

Walker, John. 1941. *A Catalogue of the Muhammadan Coins in the British Museum*, vol. 1, *Arab-Sasanian Coins*. London: British Museum.

Walmsley, Alan. 2003. "Searching for Islamic Jerash." Report on the 2002 field season of the Danish-Jordanian Islamic Jerash Project. Copenhagen: Islamic Art and Archaeology, Carsten Niebuhr Institute, University of Copenhagen. Circulated typescript.

Whelan, Estelle. 1998. "Forgotten Witness: Evidence for the Early Codification of the Qur'ān." *Journal of the American Oriental Society* 118:1–14.

6

In the Beginning Was the Word
Excavating the Relations between History and Archaeology in South Asia

THOMAS TRAUTMANN AND CARLA M. SINOPOLI

The study of the historic past, through material evidence and texts, was an integral component of colonial practice in India under British rule and remains a highly visible governmental and public focus in contemporary South Asia. In this chapter, we present an overview of the development of knowledge and research on ancient India, beginning with the formation of the Asiatic Society at Calcutta in 1784 and the institutionalization of archaeology as an entity in itself with the creation, in 1861, of the Archaeological Survey of India. We then trace this development into the postcolonial period, examining how archaeology and ancient history are practiced and conceptualized today, through four case studies that explore the existing state of, and potential for, productive partnerships between historians and archaeologists. The first case considers the contrasting instances of early state formation, the Indus Valley civilization, where archaeological knowledge dominates, and the Mauryan empire, where textual knowledge overpowers the limited material remains. We turn next to the topic of Indo-European language spread, to consider how, and if, linguists, historians, and archaeologists can contribute to understandings of this process. Our third example explores recent archaeological and historical research on the expansion and organization of early Buddhism, and our final example surveys productive interdisciplinary research on the Vijayanagara empire of South India.

One of the problems of this bird's-eye view of more than two centuries of scholarship is that the terms of the relation—history and archaeology—are not stable through time and do not acquire their current identities as separate disciplines until quite late, long after the starting point of the period under discussion. We take it that archaeology and history as disciplines direct themselves to the same ultimate object, the elucidation of the human past, but differ in the more immediate objects upon which they work to achieve that end: texts in the case of history, and material remains for archaeology. Throughout this discussion, then, we will be examining the relation of texts and material culture as objects of study in colonial and postcolonial South Asia, as stand-ins for disciplinary history and archaeology, which did not exist as such at the beginning of our period. A second problem arises from this very distinction between material culture and texts, since all texts require a material platform, and some of them, such as inscriptions, coin legends, and graffiti, appear on the durable objects of material culture that are the special province of the archaeologist's expert knowledge. These amphibious sources seem to belong both to archaeology and to history, making it impossible to draw a line between the disciplines that is hard and fast. A third problem is that "history" stands both for the ultimate object of both disciplines and for the disciplinary history of today that is distinct from disciplinary archaeology, and it will be necessary to keep this distinction in mind when using the word. Thus, "prehistory" is a period of history into which disciplinary history cannot penetrate because it lacks texts, and over which archaeology reigns, therefore, in solitary splendor.

The Asiatic Society

The impulse to recover the historic past of South Asia became strong as the British merchant presence in small toeholds along the coast evolved into a colonial state ruling the vast agrarian interior. To a degree this urge to recover the past was a part of making India legible, in James Scott's sense (Scott 1998), and it is above all in the study of land tenures that the historical imperatives were embedded into the workings of the colonial state. But in the "history of civilization" sense, the recovery of the South Asian past was located, not in the state itself, but in the learned societies formed at the colonial capitals, beginning with the Asiatic Society, founded at Calcutta in 1784, which was a model for the other two, the Bombay Literary Society (1804) and the Literary Society of Madras (1812). These were voluntary associations, not part of the government, and they pursued many topics of study that did not spring from the practical reason of the colonial government. But they were closely intertwined with the colonial administration; their membership, at the beginning, was almost wholly of East India Company employees, and the overall purpose of making India legible tinges all their productions, merging colonial and scientific motives and making it impossible to distinguish between them.

The Asiatic Society in turn was modeled upon the Royal Society, as an all-purpose learned society, whose scope was broadly defined by Sir William Jones in his opening address as president:

> If now it be asked, what are the intended objects of the inquiries . . . limits, we answer, MAN and NATURE; whatever is performed by the one, or produced by the other. Human knowledge has been elegantly analysed according to the three great faculties of the mind, *memory*, *reason*, and *imagination*, which we constantly find employed in arranging and retaining, comparing and distinguishing, combining and diversifying, the ideas, which we receive through our senses, or acquire by reflection; hence the three main branches of learning are *history*, *science*, and *art*; the first comprehends either an account of natural productions, or the genuine records of empires and states; the second embraces the whole circle of pure and mixed mathematicks, together with ethicks and law, as far as they depend on the reasoning faculty; and the third includes all the beauties of imagery and the charms of invention, displayed in modulated language, or represented by colour, figure, or sound. (Jones 1788a)

In keeping with these wide boundaries we find in the first volume of the society's journal, the *Asiatic Researches*, papers on the pangolin and the madhuka tree, the manner of distilling and the manner of extracting the essence of roses, several articles on astronomy, and one called "Hints on Friction in Mechanics." But the overwhelming number of them are concerned with elucidating the South Asian past. Among these are the famous papers by Jones, establishing a system of romanization for Asian languages ("On the Orthography of Asiatic Words"), comparing Hinduism with the religions of ancient Greece and Rome ("On the Gods of Greece, Italy, and India"), and the first three of the anniversary discourses, including the famous "Third Anniversary Discourse, on the Hindus," in which he adumbrates a historical kinship between Sanskrit, Greek, Latin, Gothic, and Old Persian, an early conceptualization of the Indo-European language family (Jones 1788b, 1788c, 1788e). Apart from the papers by Jones, a surprisingly large number — six — deal with inscriptions, which tells us that the special privilege of inscriptions as sources for historic South Asia began very early in the colonial period. These articles are supplied with transcriptions, some of them lavishly presented in engravings. Illustrations include what amount to archaeological drawings of the inscribed stone pillar of Buddal, translated by Charles Wilkins ("An Inscription on a Pillar near Buddal," Wilkins 1788), and a carefully executed drawing of the Delhi-Topra pillar of Ashoka, here called the "Staff of Firuz Shah" and said to be "partly in a character yet unknown" (Jones 1788d). The decipherment of the Brahmi script of the Ashokan pillars would be one of the great accomplishments of the Asiatic Society—fully as important as the better-known decipherments of Egyptian hieroglyphics and Mesopotamian cuneiform—under James Prinsep in 1837–38 (Kejariwal 1988, 162–220).

Examining this and other early volumes of the *Asiatic Researches*, one finds that although they are meant to admit human and natural objects of all kinds, texts and material culture are not represented equally, and their relations are structured in a certain way. Material culture is represented, but only in very few articles and always in close association with the texts of inscriptions or ancient manuscripts, and as their context. There are a couple of structuring principles that account for this embeddedness of material culture within textual studies.

In the first place, the subordination of material culture to text has to do with the terms of the new type of Orientalism that was formed at Calcutta and for which the productions of the Asiatic Society became famous in Europe, to the point of fomenting a kind of Indomania that provoked the repeated pirating of *Asiatic Researches* in Europe and its translation into languages of the Continent. The new Orientalism of Calcutta distinguished itself from the histories and travel writers of the past, extending all the way back to the ancient Greeks, whose authority derived from having directly seen something—autopsy—the authority that comes from being able to say, "I was there." The new Orientalism claimed a superior authority based on knowledge of Oriental languages, by which one did not merely see the outer person but had access to the mind and intentionality of the Asian, the inner person (Trautmann 1997, 30–37). Ultimately the authority of this kind of Orientalist scholarship derives from a text in Sanskrit or some other Asian language. The strong focus on mastery of Sanskrit and other South Asian languages as sources for authoritative scholarly work created the conditions under which material culture could emerge only in relation to texts, and in the service of further elucidating them.

The other reason for this structure of subordination for the material remains of the South Asian past has to do with the traditional history of India itself. The many long texts called *Puranas*—whose very name means something like "Antiquities"—are vast syntheses of mythology and historical traditions of past ages composed in the early centuries of the Common Era. These, together with the great epics (the *Mahabharata* and the *Ramayana*), give a version of the past in South Asia that contains much genuine history and much that is not. As the historian Romila Thapar (1966, 28) observes, had the Puranas been the only source available, "the basis for discussion of the beginnings of Indian history would have been limited," and the picture of the South Asian past was greatly changed by the discoveries of philology (the Indo-European context of the Vedas) and archaeology (the Indus civilization).

British Orientalists of the early colonial period had sought out the Puranas. As we have seen, Jones said that history, science, and art corresponded to the mental faculties of memory, reason, and imagination, and even before he arrived in India, the Puranas had been identified as the locus of the national memory of the Indian people, and therefore of the history of India. Radhakantha Sharma had composed an abstract of history from the Puranas in Sanskrit (called *Puranarthaprakasa*) at the request of one of the British Orientalists, Halhed, even before Jones's arrival (Rocher 1983). But disappointment with the Puranas set in quickly, because of the meager quality and quantity of credible history that could be extracted from them, and the large proportion of myth. The reaction was complex, because Jones, notably, found in the Puranas a genuine historical memory of an event he regarded as indubitably true, the flood of Noah, a belief that is memorialized on a scene sculpted on the base of the statue of Jones that may still be seen in St. Paul's Cathedral, London. But Puranic history purported to go back long before Adam and Eve, and, although "civil history" began very early in India, the record of it was very unreliable. Thus, the Jonesean program for the historical study of India, stated in the "Third Anniversary Discourse," sets out from this sense of disappointment that the Puranas do not deliver the national memory of India in the form of a reliable history, and sets up a recovery operation. As the history of the Indians is "a cloud of fables, we seem to possess only four general means of satisfying our curiosity concerning it," namely, (1) languages and letters; (2) philosophy and religion; (3) the "actual remains" of sculpture and architecture; and (4) sciences and arts. To recuperate the defects of the Indian national memory, then, Orientalist study follows these various paths, which include, under the third head, the study of material remains of human making. But the development of the conceptualization remains stunted and confined within the more fundamental commitment to language study as the route to the inwardness of Indian civilization.

The conception of these early British Orientalists was contained within the relatively short chronology of biblical time for human history, which effectively begins in 4004 BC with the creation, or even more recently following the flood of Noah, and they uniformly rejected the astronomically long time cycles of human history in the Puranic texts. In the conception of the British Orientalists, there were texts all the way back to the beginning of human history, more or less, whether of the Bible, of Greek and Latin, or of Sanskrit, all of them sources for knowledge of the primitive state of the human race. The omnicompetence of the text was broken by the Time Revolution of the 1860s, and the discovery of human remains in association with long extinct forms of animal life. The word "prehistory," introduced into English in 1851 (Daniel 1962), comes into use to denote that longer past into which texts do not reach, and within which the study of material culture comes into its own for the first time (Trautmann 1992).

Alexander Cunningham and the Institutionalization of Archaeology in Colonial India

The formalization of archaeology as a distinct and official focus of the colonial government occurred in 1861, when viceroy Lord Canning approved the formation of the Archaeological Survey of India (ASI). The decision to create the survey was due in no small part to the efforts of Alexander Cunningham, who was appointed its first director. In a memorandum to Canning, Cunningham had argued that "a careful and systematic investigation of all of the existing monuments of ancient India" was a moral obligation of the colonial government (Cunningham 1866, iii). This was not a new idea for Cunningham; he had made the same case eighteen years earlier in a letter published in the *Journal of the Royal Asiatic Society* (Cunningham 1843). By the time he wrote his 1861 memo, however, he had a much more focused vision for his survey: It would "follow the footsteps of the Chinese pilgrim Hwen Thsang (Xuan-zang),[1] who, in the seventh century of our era, traversed India from west to east and back again for the purpose of visiting all the famous sites of Buddhist history and tradition" (Cunningham 1866, iv). In this section, we provide a brief summary of Cunningham's contributions to the development and institutionalization of Indian archaeology, and consider why the historic period, and particularly early Buddhism, came to be defined as the primary objective of archaeological research in the first six decades of the ASI.

Alexander Cunningham first arrived in India in June 1833 as a nineteen-year-old second lieutenant in the Bengal Engineers. Excluding brief returns to England in 1860 and 1866, he remained in India for more than sixty years, retiring from government service in 1885 (Imam 1966, 3). From his early years in military service, Cunningham developed an avid interest in the antiquities of South Asia. In this, he was one of a large community of colonial officers who pursued Orientalist interests and published on language, numismatics, and antiquarian research. Cunningham was unusual, however, in his early and continuing passion for archaeological fieldwork. His focus on material remains was coupled with a distrust, which he shared with many of his peers, of the use of Puranic texts for the reconstruction of ancient Indian history. Nonetheless, he explicitly acknowledged the necessity of textual study to archaeological knowledge (Chakrabarti 1988, 59), was trained in Sanskrit, and was a friend and collaborator of James Prinsep (Cunningham 1866, v–xviii). He published his first paper, on coins, in 1834, at the age of twenty, and in that same year conducted excavations into a stupa at Sarnath. Over two and a half decades of military service, Cunningham's surveying missions to Kashmir, Tibet, Burma, and other regions inevitably included an emphasis on archaeological remains, including monuments, coins, and inscriptions. By the time he sent his 1861 memorandum to Lord Canning, he had published numerous archaeological reports and was widely acknowledged as the subcontinent's foremost expert in archaeology.

As noted, Cunningham envisioned the mission of the Archaeological Survey as identifying the major Buddhist centers described in the newly available chronicles of Chinese pilgrims. His interest in early Buddhism was shared by many of his contemporaries in both Europe and India. In part, this may have derived from the disdain of the historical value of the Sanskrit Puranic literary sources that had begun with Jones. But it also grew out of a discovery about India's past that was as exciting in its way as the recognition of the antiquity of the Indus Valley sites would be in the 1920s.

At the start of the nineteenth century, western scholars knew little about Buddhism, and the history of South Asian civilization was understood as the story of Hinduism (Imam 1966, 35).[2] Buddhism was no longer being practiced in India and was not recognized as indigenous to the region, nor was it believed to have been historically important in South Asia. This view changed dramatically in the mid-nineteenth century. Prinsep's decipherment of Brahmi and the reading of the Ashokan inscriptions were critical in this, opening up a vast new period in Indian history and new resources with which to explore it. At the same time, large numbers of Buddhist monastic texts, in Sanskrit and in Tibetan, were being accumulated by officials such as Brian Hodgson, stationed at the Court of Nepal (Lopez 1995, 3). Hodgson sent 147 manuscripts to Eugène Burnouf in Paris, and these became the source for his mammoth 1844 *Introduction à l'histoire du Buddhism indien.* For Cunningham and others, additional interest was fueled by the translations of two Chinese pilgrim accounts: by the fifth-century pilgrim Fa-Hsien (published 1836) and the seventh-century traveler Xuanzang (published by M. Julien in three vols. from 1853–1858). These pilgrims provided a geography of Buddhist South Asia, describing the sacred places they visited and their associations with the life of the Buddha and providing some information on the contemporary kingdoms in which they were located. Here were texts that a field researcher like Cunningham could trust and use. As Cunningham (1866, 84–85) enthusiastically wrote: "It is almost impossible to exaggerate the importance of these travels for the light which they throw upon early Indian history; and for the illustration of the Buddhist antiquities of India, it is not too much to say that they are quite invaluable."

Under Cunningham, the primary focus of the ASI (initially consisting of Cunningham and two assistants) was to locate and document the many sites listed in the pilgrims' texts. He spent as many as six months per year in the field carrying out this work, and the remainder of the year preparing publications. While Cunningham was aware of the many megalithic sites being documented in the peninsula (and speculated about their relation to Buddhist stupas; Cunningham 1866, xxx–xxxi), and though he recorded many Hindu temples, the documentation of the broadest range of archaeological remains was not part of his initial vision for the ASI. Instead, this was a focused archaeology guided by primary literary sources. The role of archaeology was to confirm the texts — through identifying sites, monuments, and other features described by Fa-Hsien and Xuanzang.

Cunningham's work within the new disciplinary sphere of archaeology solidified the relationship between material and textual evidence in South Asia that had begun under Jones and his successors, and that, to a considerable extent, continues until the present. That is, various kinds of written records provided a frame through which the archaeological data could be understood and, importantly, placed in a temporal framework. The archaeological evidence (primarily architecture and sculpture) served to provide illustrative materials for this history, lending a tangible substantiation to historically attested events and locales.

The contributions to Indian archaeology made by Cunningham, his assistants, and (to a lesser extent) his immediate successors were enormous. They described and mapped hundreds of sites, including most of the major Buddhist monuments of India. And, guided by inscriptional evidence and other written sources, Cunningham and his successors extended the chronology of Indian architectural and other remains to "Hindu" and "Muslim" periods,' defining a series of chronological divisions spanning from around 1000 BC to AD 1750 (Chakrabarti 1988, 72–73).

However, like his contemporaries in Europe and elsewhere (see Moreland 2001), Cunningham's archaeology was limited and limiting by today's standards. It remained dependent on the written word to provide the main outline for the past. It was impossible for Cunningham and his contemporaries to conceive of a prehistoric civilization in South Asia or to incorporate archaeological evidence that lay outside the constructed historical framework. Thus, Cunningham first conducted excavations at Harappa in 1853 and 1856 (Imam 1966, 33), and other archaeologists visited the site repeatedly over the next half-century; however, it took some seventy years before a later ASI director general, Sir John Marshall, was able to assign this problematic site a Bronze Age date, after recognizing its associations with "historic" Mesopotamia (Lahiri 2002).

In addition, under Cunningham, and largely continuing into the present, the primary emphasis of fieldwork at historic sites has been on documenting religious architecture and recovering sculptures, coins, and precious materials. More mundane artifacts such as ceramics, stone tools, non-elite households, and so forth, which could inform on aspects of the past that are often difficult to elicit from texts, were seldom collected or described. In such a framework, where the material was seen as a source of illustrations to describe a known past rather than as primary evidence for the production of historical knowledge, the potential contributions of archaeology were profoundly constrained.

Following Cunningham's retirement in 1885, the ASI continued for five years under the direction of James Burgess, and then was restructured several times—first decentralized and placed under local governments, then divided into five regional divisions, or "circles," and finally recentralized under John Marshall in 1902. Nonetheless, two broad themes persisted throughout, and indeed well beyond, these various reorganizations. The first was the official commitment to archaeology as a necessary and an important governmental role. This is as true in postcolonial South Asia as it was in the colonial period. Today, India, Pakistan, and Bangladesh all have government-funded national departments of archaeology (there are also now regional and state or provincial de-

partments of archaeology, as well as a number of universities and research institutes that teach and conduct archaeological research). And
in India in particular, archaeology, like ancient history, is highly visible
and has come to play an increasingly prominent role in ongoing debates
about religion, identity, and future directions of the Indian nation state.
Second, the intellectual framework that Cunningham and his contemporaries established for the role of archaeology in the study of Indian
history has also persisted. Much historic-period archaeology in South
Asia remains focused on the illustrative use of monuments, sculpture,
and elite productions to adorn the pages of history texts.

Archaeology and History in South Asia: Four Cases

We turn now to four case studies that trace the interplay of archaeology
and history in contemporary South Asia. Our aim is both to historically contextualize research on these topics—the Indus civilization and
Mauryan empire, Indo-European language expansion, early Buddhism,
and the Vijayanagara empire—and to explore the successes and rich
potential for a more creative merger of the written and the material in
their study.

The Indus Civilization and the Mauryan Empire

The Indus civilization and the Mauryan empire are examples at the ex-
tremes of relations between archaeological and historical, or material-
cultural and textual, approaches, partly because of the nature of the
remains left by each, partly because of the historical circumstances of
the ways in which they were first approached in the colonial period.
The Harappan, or Indus, civilization (figure 6.1) was formally taken up
by colonial archaeology when engineers of the Lahore-Multan railway
began removing bricks from ancient mounds as ballast to fill in the low
places. Scholarship on the empire of the Mauryans, on the other hand,
commenced with the study of texts, beginning with the Greek writings
on ancient India, including especially the book on India of Megasthenes,
ambassador to Chandragupta Maurya, and the decipherment of the inscriptions of Chandragupta's grandson, Ashoka.

The Indus Civilization. The earliest published accounts of the conspicuous mounds at Harappa come from Charles Masson, a deserter from
the East India Company army who passed through the region in 1829.

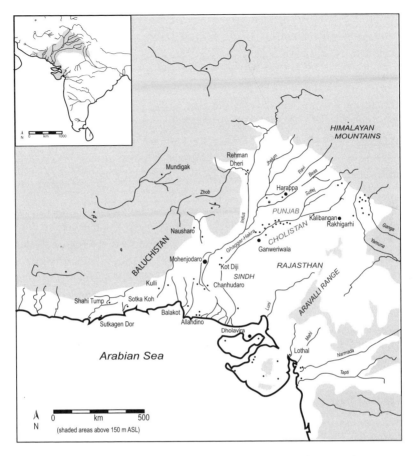

Figure 6.1   The Indus Valley civilization: major sites and geographic extent

Subsequent visitors included Lieutenant Alexander Burnes, who saw the site when he traveled the Indus River in 1831, and Alexander Cunningham in 1853 and 1856 (Possehl 1999, 44–49). Cunningham revisited the site in 1875 and, distressed by the damage that had been caused by the railway construction since his previous visit, conducted some small excavations (Cunningham 1875). Among the artifacts he reported was a seal inscribed with an unknown script. Two additional seals were recovered at Harappa in succeeding decades, and two more were found in ASI excavations in 1922 at the newly discovered site of Mohenjo-Daro, nearly six hundred kilometers south of Harappa. By then, archaeologists realized they had discovered something important—massive urban sites with sophisticated architecture, broad streets, distinctive ceramic and other artifacts (with *no* iron), and writing in an unknown script. In 1924, nearly a century after Masson's initial visit to Harappa, Sir John Marshall published an announcement in the *Illustrated London News*. Describing remains from Harappa and Mohenjo-Daro, Marshall requested assistance in determining the age of this previously unknown pre-Mauryan Indian civilization. Within two weeks, letters from Mesopotamian specialists A. H. Sayce (1924) and C. J. Gadd and Sidney Smith (1924) reported that similar seals had been recovered in several third-millennium BC Mesopotamian sites, including Susa and Ur. The chronological mystery was solved.

The recognition of an ancient Bronze Age civilization in South Asia radically changed the direction of Indian archaeology. The archaeology of Buddhist sites and the Mauryan period, previously the region's earliest "civilization," which had been the priority of the ASI since its inception, was displaced by an enthusiastic focus on the Indus civilization, an exclusively archaeological domain. The emphasis on Indus research continued throughout the colonial period and into postcolonial times. After 1947, Pakistani scholars continued excavations at Harappa, Mohenjo-Daro, and several other sites that had been discovered in the intervening decades. M. Rafique Mughal's important survey in Cholistan in the 1970s resulted in the discovery of more than four hundred additional sites, including the large and still unexcavated urban site Ganweriwala Thar (Mughal 1997). In India, access to the known Indus sites was lost to Pakistan due to the partition of British India at Independence, and archaeologists began a period of intensive exploration within the Republic of India that continues today. The shift to prehistoric research, in the greater Indus region and elsewhere in the subcontinent, has contributed to dramatic growth in our knowledge of the region's deep past. However, there has been a concomitant negative effect, in the decline in archaeology of historic periods. Indeed, in 1999 archaeologist M. K. Dhavalikar (1999, xii) wrote: "the most neglected aspect of Indian archaeology is the archaeology of the historic period." This is a marked change indeed from the archaeological mission defined by Alexander Cunningham.

For the Indus civilization, the results of the many archaeological field projects of the last eighty years have been astounding. Today, more than two thousand sites with Indus materials have been identified, spreading from Oman to Gujarat, making this the most geographically extensive of the famous Bronze Age civilizations. And unlike historical periods, where the focus has been almost entirely on urban centers, the majority of Indus sites were small villages and hamlets, and in several regions, we have at least a basic understanding of site distributions and regional infrastructure. In addition, three more large urban centers have been added to Harappa and Mohenjo-Daro: Ganweriwala Thar in Pakistan and Dholavira and Rakhigarhi in India (see Kenoyer 1998; Possehl 1999). The application of modern excavation and dating techniques have given us a more than five-thousand-year sequence from the appearance of agricultural communities in Baluchistan in the seventh millennium BC up to and beyond the abandonment of the large urban centers at the start of the second millennium BC.

Although thousands of seals and inscribed artifacts have been recovered, the Indus script remains undeciphered. Unlike Egypt or Mesopotamia, this remains a civilization inaccessible to historians. Also setting the Indus apart from its Bronze Age contemporaries is the absence of an ongoing historical tradition. The earliest city-states of Mesopotamia (in the late Uruk period), where writing was also limited, were succeeded by millennia of literate state societies that produced a literature and a tradition of statecraft accessible to both Mesopotamians and later scholars. The continuities in Egypt were, if anything, more extraordinary. These continuities are, of course, not unproblematic, as they risk naive reading of later "known" state forms onto earlier societies that may have been quite differently organized. However, they nonetheless provide an invaluable starting point for research. In the Indus case, while the descendants of urban dwellers and technological practices did not entirely disappear, the cities their ancestors had inhabited did. Indus script and the information it recorded also were no longer remembered.

Indus archaeologists have learned a tremendous amount about economy, settlement, trade, and social organization. What we lack are the historical particularities that can make the past seem so much more tangible: the names of kings, the tales of gods and heroes (which seem to be depicted on small stone and faience tablets but are difficult to interpret), legal codes and agreements, and records of economic transactions. Indus scholars continue to debate many important questions: about Indus religion and ideology, linguistic affiliations, and the nature of Indus political organization. Opinions on the latter range widely, from a network of city-states (e.g., Kenoyer 1997, 1998), to a unified empire (Ratnagar 1991), to even a prestate tribal confederation (Possehl 1998). Within the Indus literature, there remains the sense that there are many open questions, which will be resolved only through the acquisition of more and better archaeological evidence.

Until very recently, few comparable self-conscious debates have appeared in the scholarly literature on the Mauryan state, and the limited historical sources have been largely accepted as unproblematic. Yet, in terms of sheer quantity, our data on the Indus civilization are far greater and more diverse than our evidence for the Mauryans. The differences in interpretations and in the faith we place in them may lie in the fact that it has been easier for scholars to accept the ambiguities and partial nature of the archaeological record, particularly when unsupported by text, than it has been to accept the partial evidence of the written word unsupported by significant material evidence.

The Mauryan Empire. In contrast to the Indus civilization, where the study of material culture dominates in the absence of an agreed decipherment of the writing system, in the study of the Mauryan empire, the texts overwhelm the material remains, excepting only the magnificent stone pillars of Ashoka (about 272–235 BC), on which his texts were inscribed.

One of those stone pillars, as we have already noted, was published in the very first volume of the *Asiatic Researches*, but its Ashokan inscription could not be read at that time, as it could not in the times of Sultan Firuz Shah when it was brought to Delhi. It would be several decades after its first publication that James Prinsep and his team, working with the bilingual coins of Indo-Greek rulers of the Panjab, inscribed in Greek and Brahmi scripts on opposite sides, would decipher the Brahmi and restore Ashoka's voice (Kejariwal 1988, chap. 5). Ashoka's inscriptions became the premier source for the recovered knowledge of the Mauryan empire. The other main source was the Greek account of India by Megasthenes, the ambassador of Seleucus to Chandragupta Maurya. Jones had long since identified the Sandrokottos of the Greek texts with Chandragupta Maurya, which served as a valuable point of location for Indian history within the ancient history known to Europeans, putting him in the time of Alexander, fourth century BC (Jones 1807a).

These two sources, the *Indika* of Megasthenes and the inscriptions of Ashoka, were objects of intense investigation and scholarly publication. Megasthenes' account of India was no longer extant, but extensive fragments survived in quotations or paraphrases by later writers, especially Arrian. Schwanbeck collected and published the fragments systematically in 1846 and M'Crindle produced English translations of these and other Greek sources on ancient Indian history that made these materials widely available (Megasthenes 1846, 1860). They are still in use.

The Ashokan inscriptions, inscribed on rock faces and pillars in many parts of the Indian subcontinent and beyond, one of them as far west as Kandahar, were elaborately published in the series, *Corpus Inscriptionum Indicarum*, as its first volume, including ink estampages, transliterated texts, synoptic texts where multiple copies exist, and translations, with extensive historical and linguistic notes (Hultzsch 1969). Bloch's French version of this material is a valuable linguistic analysis, also with synoptic texts and discussion of variants (Bloch 1950).

The Puranas make note of the Mauryans but say little of them except their names and that they are "mostly Shudras and unrighteous" (Pargiter 1962). The Ashokan inscriptions and Megasthenes' account, together with Buddhist stories of Ashoka, especially those in the Pali Chronicles of Sri Lanka, threw a flood of light on an empire and a period that was obscure and created a rush of excitement about a hitherto little-known India in which Buddhism was prominent and India was politically unified by a very able line of rulers. The Ashokan inscriptions were and remain especially appealing, for a couple of reasons. The texts, though in the third person as a matter of royal style, are evidently the words of the emperor himself (or his speech writers) and give us an access to this individual as to no other figure of Indian history at so early a date. And Ashoka himself is interesting as someone who, because of regrets about the unmerited suffering he had caused through expansionist warfare in eastern India, turned toward Buddhism, vegetarianism, and pacifism. The interest in Ashoka grew with the rise of Gandhian nonviolent nationalism in the twentieth century.

The text of Megasthenes is also of great interest, but it has many problems of interpretation and is, as we have said, fragmentary. A third text, spectacular in its own way, is a work of statecraft, the *Arthashastra* of Kautilya, who is often identified with Chanakya, learned and devious minister of Chandragupta Maurya as known from a cycle of story texts. The *Arthashastra* is often used as if it were a primary source for Mauryan history, but it is very much later than the Mauryan period in its present form and was probably compiled in the second century AD (Trautmann 1971).

In the study of the Mauryan empire, the physical remains have been overshadowed by the texts, which remain the principal focus of attention. This is partly because remains that can be definitely dated to the Mauryan period are few, except for the rock faces and stone pillars on which the Ashokan inscriptions are written. The pillars themselves attract study; massive monoliths, over fifty tons in weight, with elaborately carved capitals and a mirror-like polish to their surface, moved great distances with immense labor from the quarry sites (recently documented by Jayaswal 1998) to their present locations, they proclaim themselves as monuments of empire. Excavations in Patna in the early twentieth century revealed the wooden palisade of the Mauryan capital, Pataliputra, but the greater part of it is inaccessible because there is a crowded modern city built on top of it (Waddell 1903; Spooner 1913). That excavation apart, the Mauryan empire is notable for the virtual absence of an archaeology of settlements, and few material remains can be definitively dated to the Mauryan period. This is not because such remains do not exist, but because current archaeological chronologies, based on long-lived ceramic wares, do not yet provide the resolution necessary to pinpoint the relatively brief (by archaeological standards) one-and-a-half–century Mauryan period in sites with much longer occupational histories. Apart from the very palpable and durable rock faces and pillars of Ashoka's inscriptions, the huge, powerful Mauryan empire, which had diplomatic relations with the Hellenistic successor states of Alexander, the Seleucids of Syria, and the Ptolemies of Egypt, left a physical imprint that is surprisingly slight as far as we know, and the enterprise of recovering its history has been nearly wholly a matter of studying texts.

Indo-Europeans and South Asians

Sir William Jones posited a relation of siblingship among Sanskrit, Latin, Greek, Gothic, Celtic, and Old Persian, and their descent from a more ancient language "now perhaps lost" (Jones 1788c). This grouping of languages substantially outlines the language family now called Indo-European, and the inferred ancestral language now called Proto-Indo-European. This larger framing for the historical location of Sanskrit was without precedent, in terms both of existing European ideas and of Indian ones, and was contradictory of the brahmins' idea of eternal Sanskrit. But there was more. Jones identified Iran as the central point from which these sibling languages and other ancient languages had dispersed, because it was the only center from which straight lines could be drawn to the locations of the languages without any two of the lines crossing. It pleased Jones that this logic placed the point of origin of ancient languages and the nations speaking them in the near neighborhood of the Plain of Shinar in the Bible, whence the dispersal of nations commenced after God had put an end to the building of the Tower of Babel by confusing the languages of the people (Jones 1807b). The consequence, that Sanskrit-speaking adherents of the Vedic religion were immigrants to India from without, was also an entirely new and revolutionary view of India's deep history, though the central point of Indo-European dispersal migrated soon enough to Central Asia and other contenders for the Indo-European homeland.

The acquisition of knowledge of Sanskrit by European scholars had been critical to the first formulation of the concept of the Indo-European language family, and it led directly to the creation of a science of comparative philology, of which Franz Bopp was the first master. His pamphlet of 1816 was the first of a flood of new scholarship on historical linguistics, and his comparative grammar of Indo-European of 1833 (translated into English in 1845–53) was recognized as the standard work on the subject, now, finally, put on a sound scientific footing (Bopp 1816, 1833, 1845–53). In consequence, this aspect of the reconstruction of the South Asian past fell under the control of a technical science that rested on texts alone, and on highly complex manipulations of those texts at that. Moreover, the publication and modern study, in Europe and in India, of the text of the Vedas, which had been a kind of Holy Grail pursued by the early Orientalists of British India, deepened the reliance on texts for the question of the origins of Indian civilization. An archaeology of Indo-European dispersal was slow to take shape, and when it did, it was troubled by a variety of forces, among them the racial politics that attached to the topic.

Archaeology directed itself to discerning the material imprint of the migrations implied by the linguist's *Stammbaum* of Indo-European, and to the physical remains of supposed speakers of ancient Indo-European languages. The growth of a "race science" (Stepan 1982) in nineteenth-century Europe marked the end of the hegemony of linguistics over the study of the Indo-European languages and their speakers and the emergence of a strongly biologized concept of race, presided over by the anthropology of bodily measurement (e.g., Topinard 1885). Archaeologists played various roles in these developments, sometimes in tandem with the linguists, sometimes independent of them and in opposition to them. The rise and defeat in World War II of the Nazi doctrine, which had used a highly racialized version of the Indo-European idea, interpreted in terms of a pure, white Nordic race and homeland for the original speakers of Indo-European languages, rendered much of the scholarship associated with this topic suspect. V. Gordon Childe's archaeology of Indo-European, titled *The Aryans*, published before the war, for example, was not reissued after it (Childe 1926).

Both the philology and the archaeology of Indo-European as a whole was essentially centered in Europe and directed itself to European concerns, above all to the deep history of the European people. While India played a critical role in the discovery of the Indo-European language family and in comparative philology, the focus upon Europe is perhaps a reason why the study of Indo-European as a whole has never taken root in Indian universities, though the study of the Indian branch of the Indo-European language family (Indo-Aryan languages — Sanskrit and its relatives) is highly developed. Nevertheless, the interpretation of India's past is deeply affected by the Indo-European idea.

By the second half of the nineteenth century, linguistic study in India had established that the languages of India fall into three distinct language families, the Indo-Aryan branch of the Indo-European family, the Dravidian family, and the Austroasiatic family (Kolarian or Munda language in the older literature). This finding about the ancient linguistic components of Indian civilization was read in a highly racialized way, leading to the creation of a racial theory of Indian civilization that became the master narrative of Indian history. In this master narrative, Indian civilization was formed by the clash of two races — the invading, light-skinned, Sanskrit-speaking, civilized Aryans and the indigenous, dark, savage Dravidians — and the formation of the caste system as the central institution of Indian civilization (Trautmann 1997, chap. 7). This colonial formation, achieved through new readings of Vedic texts, has proven remarkably durable.

The discovery of the Indus civilization posed the problem of its relation to the testimony of the Vedic texts, a problem with material remains and undecipherable texts on the one side, and texts with little material context on the other. Practically all Western scholars, and many in India, hold that whether or not Aryan invaders destroyed the Indus civilization, as Wheeler suggested ("Indra stands accused"; Wheeler 1953), the Vedic Indians migrated into India *from without* and *after* the time of the Indus civilization. But there are many scholars in India who have identified the Vedic texts with the Indus civilization material remains and attempted to read the latter through the former. And there has always been a large number of Indian scholars who regard the people of the Vedic texts to be autochthonous to India, an idea which has been much developed recently, with the implication that India is the homeland of the Indo-European languages, the central point from which they have spread. These issues are highly contentious in India just now, and they have a political charge to them that is increasingly evident and makes it increasingly difficult to do good scholarly work on the question (see, e.g., Witzel and Farmer 2000; Bryant 2001).

The writings of Colin Renfrew on the archaeology of Indo-European offered unintended support to these developments (Renfrew 1987). Renfrew's purpose was to shake archaeology free from the consensus of the linguists about the timing and spread of the Indo-European languages, and to show the effects of a "wave of advance" model for the spread of Indo-European speakers and their agrarian frontier across Europe. This model was very slow-moving, so that the spread into Europe had to begin thousands of years earlier than the previous consensus provided for, based on the first datable appearance of Indo-European names and words in the historical record of the ancient Near East. It was a kind of declaration of independence of archaeology from linguistics, throwing over what Renfrew interpreted as too great a subservience. The whole exercise was mainly focused on Europe, and India appeared in the book largely as a detail that did not affect the main point, to the degree that Renfrew offered two quite different versions of how Indo-European may have gotten to India from without, namely, by military invasion at the *end* of the Indus civilization or by *creating* the Indus civilization, between which he did not think it necessary to choose. This theory seems to have reached its half-life and is now decaying at a rapid rate (Yoffee 1990). It has served to make more pointed the problems of coordinating the textual and the material-cultural record without contributing notably to their solution.

Prospects for a greater collaboration of archaeology and history, and of integrating the interpretation of material and textual remains in respect to the Vedic Aryans and their relation to the Indus civilization, are dimmed by methodological estrangement and hyperpoliticization of scholarship in India at this moment. And it must be said that the earliest Vedic texts offer little for which we might expect to find a material consequence that is decisive. The one telling feature is the use of the horse and the horse-drawn chariot that is markedly a part of warrior and royal culture, complete with horsey names for warriors, such as Brihadashva ("possessor of a great horse"), of the kind found also among other Indo-European speakers in the ancient Near East and in Iran, and largely absent from peasant culture, which uses oxen for plowing and draft. This pattern, so typical of India—though of course the chariot eventually becomes obsolete and remains only in the temple car used in religious festivals—does seem traceable in the archaeological record, and does seem to confirm an arrival after 2000 BC (Meadow and Patel

1997), from without, of the Vedic Aryans. But it is in the study of the early Vedic period that the challenges of finding a productive collaboration between archaeology and history continue to be at their most difficult.

Early Buddhism

By the early twentieth century, the outlines of Buddhist history and doctrines had been sketched out and numerous Buddhist sites had been identified (figure 6.2). From the inception of western scholarship on Buddhism, a pronounced division appeared. On one side were scholars focused on translating and interpreting ancient monastic texts. On the other were the archaeologists and epigraphers, who documented monasteries and religious monuments and recorded the numerous inscriptions placed on them by donors and pilgrims. The study of monastic texts came under the purview of the academic discipline of Buddhist studies, and scholars studying the material remains of early Buddhism came to be located in art history departments or in departments of ancient history. Communication among these various specialists was minimal at best.

Recent developments in Buddhist studies, archaeology, and ancient history have contributed to the emergence of new perspectives for the study of early Buddhism. Within Buddhist studies, Gregory Schopen and others have criticized approaches that focus overmuch on sacred principles and philosophical discourses presented in the monastic texts (Schopen 1997; Lopez 1995). They call instead for greater emphasis on *religious practice*—understanding what Buddhist monks and laity actually did. Schopen in particular has argued that the study of practice cannot be accomplished from proscriptive texts alone but requires the incorporation of material evidence, specifically archaeological and epigraphical data.

Within archaeology and ancient history, a comparable critique has emerged, as a number of scholars (e.g., Coningham 1995, 1998; Dehejia 1992, 1997; Morrison 1995b; Ray 1986, 1994, 2003; Thapar 1992, 1997; Willis 1992) have sought to move beyond the largely chronological and descriptive focus of past research to consider a range of behavioral and cultural questions. In their work, and particularly in the writings of historian Himanshu Ray (1986, 1994, 2003), the emphasis has shifted from the monasteries to the social, political, and economic contexts in which early Buddhism expanded and flourished. Recently, field archaeologists have taken up this call and have undertaken archaeological surveys that

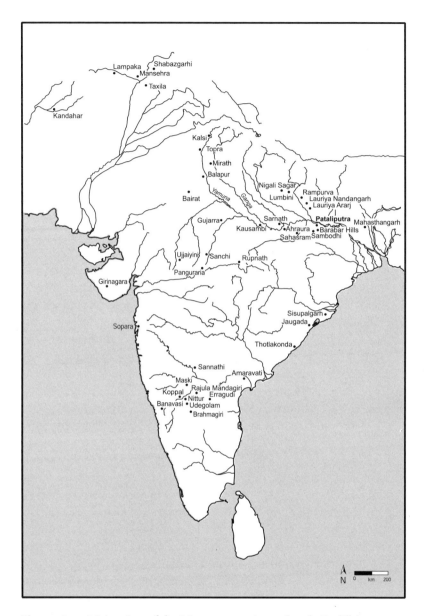

Figure 6.2   Major sites of the Mauryan empire and early Buddhist centers

look beyond monastic walls to the broader social and physical environments of early Buddhist communities. Such projects include Julia Shaw's extensive village-to-village survey in a 750 square-kilometer area around Sanchi (Shaw 2000; Shaw and Sutcliffe 2001) and a more intensive, smaller scale survey conducted by Lars Fogelin around the small monastic center of Thotlakonda in Andhra Pradesh (Fogelin forthcoming a, b, c).

Thus, we see a broadening of perspectives and research questions within the various disciplines that study early Buddhism, creating the possibility for increasing dialogue *between* them on a range of subjects. Here, we limit our discussion to one topic for which the use of archaeology and textual sources has forced a reevaluation of accepted knowledge: the study of Buddhist mortuary behavior.

Buddhist Religious Practice: Death and Burial. The Buddhist stupa is believed to have originated from hemispherical mounds built to contain the cremated remains of the Buddha and his disciples.[4] The earliest extant stupas are significantly later, dating no earlier than the third century BC (Coningham 2001), and had a number of additional features: The hemispherical dome was elevated on a cylindrical drum, topped by a finial, and in some cases surrounded by circumambulatory paths enclosed by elaborate sculpted railings and gateways. Stupas were erected to house the relics of the Buddha and to mark sites important in his life. Stupas were found in virtually all Buddhist monasteries, where they were settings for worship as well as for pilgrimage.

Based on readings of a tenth-century monastic text, Buddhist scholars have long argued that stupa worship was the exclusive focus of the Buddhist laity (who, unlike monks, needed this physical presence to help them focus their minds on the Buddha), forbidden to members of monastic communities. Schopen has criticized this view, combining a reexamination of the text and several other documents with archaeological data from a number of sites. In particular, he has focused on the large numbers of small stupas that archaeologists have described clustering around the central stupas at sites such as Bedsa, Bharhut, Sanchi, Taxila, Ratnagiri, and others (all early sites of the late centuries BC to the early centuries AD; Schopen 1987, 1989, 1991b, 1991c, 1995). Several of these small stupas have been excavated and shown to contain burnt human bone, ash, and mortuary offerings; some at Ratnagiri contained brief texts addressing matters of death and rebirth (Schopen 1987). The placement of these small stupas is generally haphazard, a result of a gradual filling in of available space around the central stupa over decades or generations. At the site of Bodh-Gaya, documented by Cunningham, there were thousands of these small stupas superimposed in at least four strata, totaling more than twenty feet deep.

While Cunningham and other archaeologists reported these small stupas, there was no attempt in the archaeological literature to explain their presence. Schopen has convincingly argued that they contain the remains of the monastic dead and that their distribution suggests an effort to place the remains of deceased monks as near as possible to those of the Buddha. This emphasis on proximity suggests that these early monks believed that Buddha's relics were more than mere symbols for the laity; they were instead understood as the presence of the "living Buddha," and proximity to them could confer spiritual benefits after death. Thus, Schopen argued, the dominant views of a vast discontinuity between monks and laity must be discarded. The result is a better interpretation of the texts, of the archaeological evidence, and of early Buddhist religious practice.

All the mortuary features discussed by Schopen lie within monastery complexes, close to its central stupa. A recent archaeological survey project near the Thotlakonda monastery in coastal Andhra Pradesh has provided evidence for a complex mortuary landscape *outside* a monastery. Thotlakonda sits on a hilltop overlooking the Bay of Bengal. In a systematic survey of an approximately ten square-kilometer area surrounding Thotlakonda, archaeologist Lars Fogelin (forthcoming a, b, c) has identified more than three hundred small stone cairns on the Thotlakonda hill, and observed at least a hundred more on the face of the adjacent hill in view of the monastery. These are small mounds, one to three meters in diameter, constructed of unmodified, locally available stones. None has yet been excavated, though multiple lines of evidence indicate that they are contemporary with the monastery. Fogelin has interpreted these mounds as mortuary features, containing the remains of individuals who were ineligible or unable to be buried within the monastery complex. Though stupa-like, they lack several of the essential elements of stupas (e.g., the drum and finial). At this point, there is insufficient evidence to determine whether these were lesser monks or laity, but their form, large number, and placement outside the monastery suggest the latter.

We see then a second tier of what Schopen (1987) has termed "burial *ad sanctos.*" The remains of monks were placed proximate to relics in the monastery's main stupa, while the remains of other individuals were

placed in proximity to, or in view of, the monastery. These latter burials receive no mention in monastic texts and are evidence of a form of
religious practice that further blurs the lines between monks and laity
and points to an extension of Buddhist practice in interaction with, but
outside, monastic control.

The archaeological data described above provide evidence *about*
Buddhist practice that contemporary scholars can read and interpret.
Perhaps more important, they also demonstrate that the physical, material constructions built by early Buddhists, and the sensory and emo-
tional experiences that they fostered, were important constitutive elements of the religion. Being a Buddhist did not entail the intellect alone;
the Buddhist monk and lay worshipper also engaged with the physical
world — in pilgrimage, circumambulation, donation and consumption
of a range of goods, and the disposal of the dead. Thus, the archaeological data need not serve only to illustrate Buddhist practice; they also
provide evidence of the material contexts through which Buddhism was
constituted and experienced.

Vijayanagara. Robert Sewell certainly exaggerated when he titled his
1900 book *Vijayanagara: A Forgotten Empire*. However, it was true that
the South Indian Vijayanagara empire (figure 6.3) had received far less
scholarly attention than the earlier Chola empire in the south or the Mu-
ghals in the north. Colonel Colin Mackenzie prepared the first archaeological map of the deserted Vijayanagara capital in 1800, and the ASI
conducted documentation and conservation work at the site in the first
decades of the twentieth century (Michell 1985). On the history side, a
number of studies of Vijayanagara appeared in the early twentieth century, most containing photographs of the spectacular remains of the
imperial capital (e.g., Saletore 1934; Dutt 1925; Heras 1931; Mahalingam
1940). Nonetheless, while not forgotten, Vijayanagara historiography remained far from the intellectual center of scholarship on precolonial
India. This changed in the late 1970s.

The renewed interest in Vijayanagara came from both archaeology
and history. The late 1970s and early 1980s saw the beginnings of
three new archaeological projects at the empire's first, eponymous, capital. The city, home to at least a quarter-million inhabitants, had been
abruptly abandoned in 1565, following a major military defeat. It was
never significantly reoccupied, leading to extraordinary preservation of
monuments and surface features; the walled core of the city covers an
area of some 25 square kilometers, and its fortified hinterland is esti-

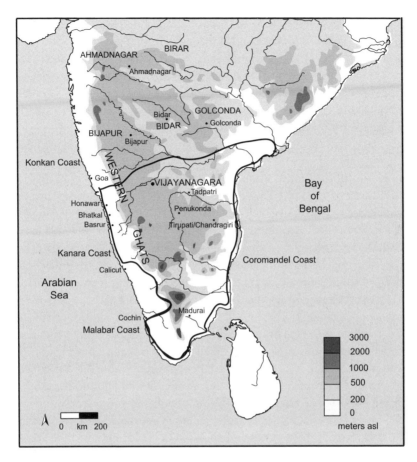

Figure 6.3   The Vijayanagara empire

mated at circa 450 square kilometers. The three archaeological projects included excavation projects by the ASI and the Karnataka Department of Archaeology and Museums, and a surface documentation project (the Vijayanagara Research Project), under anthropological archaeologist John Fritz and architectural historian George Michell. On the historical side, Burton Stein's 1980 work, *Peasant State and Society in Medieval South India*, was a catalyst for renewed interest in the later precolonial history of South India. In his book, Stein elaborated a radical new model for the medieval South Asian state, which he derived from the writings of the Africanist cultural anthropologist Aidan Southall: the segmentary state. Stein's controversial work fueled an outburst of new and sophisticated historical research by his supporters and detractors and elevated Southern India and Vijayanagara from a marginal position in theoretical discussions of the Indian state to center stage. The archaeologists working on Vijayanagara came together with Stein, as well as a number of other historians, art historians, epigraphers, and others, in a conference held in Heidelberg in 1983 (Dallapiccola 1985), beginning a period of long-term dialogue and collaboration.

The recent research on Vijayanagara thus differs from the cases discussed above in several respects and provides a valuable illustration of how fruitful collaboration can be fostered among scholars from diverse disciplinary traditions. This has involved, first, the explicit emphasis on collaboration and active dialogue, rather than merely the use of data derived from other disciplines. Second, Fritz, Michell, M. S. Nagaraja Rao,[5] and Stein all recognized that large-scale interdisciplinary research required a long-term commitment (the Vijayanagara Research Project has been running for more than twenty years) and a large team of scholars. They successfully attracted a number of younger scholars to pursue research on a range of Vijayanagara-related topics.[6] In addition, much of the research undertaken over the last few decades has been structured by explicit theoretical concerns, many of which require both historical and material sources to be adequately addressed. These include efforts to explore Vijayanagara political economy, theoretical models of the South Asian state, and the constitution of political and sacred authority at Vijayanagara. Considering only the latter, we can cite archaeological work by Fritz (1986; Fritz and Michell 1989), exploring how the Vijayanagara urban plan mapped royal authority onto a sacred landscape associated with events of the Ramayana epic, and in so doing helped to constitute that authority; and Phillip Wagoner's (1993, 1996) research, which merges evidence from architecture, sculpture, costume, royal titles, and literary works to understand the construction of kingship and political dynamics between Vijayanagara and its northern neighbors, the Deccani Sultanates.

On the archaeological side, the Vijayanagara work has contributed important methodological as well as theoretical advancements to South Asian historic period archaeology, and the results have been published in more than fifteen monographs to date, with several more in press or preparation.[7] Methodologically, work by Fritz and team in the Vijayanagara urban core and by Kathleen Morrison and Sinopoli in the Vijayanagara hinterland, while not neglecting monumental elite architecture, has brought attention to the remains of non-elites through careful documentation of the full array of surface remains (Fritz, Michell, Nagaraja Rao 1985; Fritz and Morrison forthcoming) and domestic artifacts (Sinopoli 1993). Morrison and Sinopoli's Vijayanagara Metropolitan Survey, conducted from 1987 to 1997 (see Sinopoli and Morrison forthcoming; Morrison 1995a), documented more than seven hundred archaeological sites. Included are rural settlements, sacred architecture and sculptures, fortifications, agricultural features, and craft production sites. Taken together these permit the first understandings of the economic infrastructure of this enormous imperial city and of the lives of the laborers who generated it. This emphasis on non-elite activities and remains is a radical departure for historic period archaeology in India, which as noted above has traditionally been focused on monuments and elite productions, and is one with enormous potential.

Texts and Objects

The colonial establishment of modern programs of archaeology and history in South Asia and the nature of the historical record of its past have had a number of consequences for the interactions between them. Because of the long, rich record of the South Asian past—both the textual record, which extends back to at least 1400 BC (the Vedas) and, potentially a millennium or so further (the undeciphered Indus seals), and the material record of monumental architecture and settlements, ceramics, craft production, coins, and stone inscriptions—a focus upon the archaeology and history of South Asia in the periods from which textual records are available was inevitable and led to a long collaboration between history and archaeology. At the same time, the place of the material record was defined at the outset in the Jonesean vision that guided the work of the Asiatic Society, and the rationale that led to the institution of the Archaeological Survey of India, as one means of several by which to supplement and make good the deficiencies of the Puranas and epics as repositories of the historical memory of the Indians. This has meant that the material record largely subserves programs of study that derive from the study of texts. It has also meant that while the material record has been interpreted in light of ideas coming from the study of texts, the reverse is rarely the case. The hierarchization of text over material record is evident at the very moment when archaeology in South Asia achieves public definition, by the creation of the Archaeological Survey of India, on Cunningham's program of archaeological study of the sites mentioned in the texts of the Chinese Buddhist pilgrims. That the collection, study, and publication of inscriptions has been one of the responsibilities of the ASI through the office of the chief epigrapher for India further epitomizes the linkage.

A second generalization that we can make is that archaeology has been especially centralized, governmentally instituted, and top-down in its relation to the people of South Asia. Archaeology as such was virtually the monopoly of the central government agency and its branches until Independence. Archaeology in South Asia did not crystallize out of the informal archaeology of enthusiastic amateur South Asians but was created by elite foreigners, at the capital, by an act of state. Developments of archaeological method and program in Europe reached India late and often imperfectly. Archaeology had still not been inserted into universities of British India when Independence came, and the last British-Indian director of the ASI, Mortimer Wheeler, took the first steps in training a young generation of archaeologists to do so. A much improved and thickened connection of archaeology and its public followed Independence and the work of archaeologists such as H. D. Sankalia.

One of the notable effects of the colonial structure of archaeology and the slow movement of ideas toward British India from the metropole was the lateness with which prehistoric archaeology developed as an institutional component of archaeology in South Asia. Individual officers such as T. J. Newbold (1843, 1852), Robert Bruce Foote (1866, 1914, 1916), and Meadows Taylor (1862) had documented prehistoric sites in peninsular India (particularly megaliths and ash mounds), but the formal focus of the ASI was firmly in historic periods. It is in practicing archaeology without texts that archaeology has developed its powers most fully. In South Asia, the primary focus was on the historic period from the beginning, when scholars like Jones believed that the beginning of Indian civilization was but a short time after the dispersal of peoples following the biblical flood, a mere ten generations after the creation of Adam and Eve. In short, at the beginning of the colonial period, and in the minds of the colonizers, the historic period of Indian history was the whole of Indian history, and there was no period before texts. Even after the Time Revolution had upset the short biblical chronology for human history, and prehistory had been created as a term and as an idea of a space in human history into which texts did not reach, it was a long time coming to colonial South Asian archaeology. When it did, the form it took was the Indus civilization, prehistoric in the technical sense of having no currently readable texts.

The Indus civilization may have been created as a concept in 1924 on the pages of the *Illustrated London News* (Marshall 1924). From then on, it was the grand site at which South Asian archaeology developed its powers, and it remains so after the partition of British India, and of the Indus civilization itself, between India and Pakistan. The qualitative effects of this development have been very positive. The sophistication of archaeological methodologies has improved dramatically in prehistoric sites and is today as good as anywhere in the world in every way — methods of absolute dating, scientific analysis of all kinds, and excavation practices. Paradoxically, it is at the *historic* sites that methods have not kept pace with change and remain more or less as they were at Independence, which is to say, the methods of Wheeler. Thus, excavators do not screen, do not generally save plant and animal remains, and often do not save ceramics. There is still a sense that the texts tell us, however imperfectly, the truth about the past, and that the archaeology serves to provide illustrations for what is known from the texts.

The study of early Buddhism best illustrates the effects of overvaluing the text in South Asia. Through the work of Schopen (1987, 1988–89; 1991a), we see that Buddhism as an object in history has been identified with the *doctrine* delivered in authoritative texts, and not the *practices* of Buddhist monks, nuns, and laypeople. As a result, archaeology could contribute to the history of Buddhism by extending and illustrating the testimony of the texts but could not controvert them or cause them to be read differently. Thus, the archaeology of burial sites near monasteries could not shake the scholarly consensus that the memorialization of the dead was not a practice of monks but of the laity, a popular practice. Schopen's campaign to give the archaeological record a weight equivalent to that of the texts and to reinterpret the texts in the light of archaeological evidence is a clear example of the new knowledge that can come from more equal partnerships between history and archaeology, and of the knowledge that has been blocked by a hypervaluation of text over material culture, and of doctrine over practice.

The privilege of the text in the investigation of the South Asian past derives from an idea that is expressed by the early Orientalists of British India, about the texts giving access to the inward meaning of the South Asian past, against the authority of sight, which delivers only the outward and material side of South Asia. The privileging of the texts by Orientalists, tinged though it was with Protestant Christian ideas of the inner and the outer, spirit and matter, coincided considerably with the views of the pandits and munshis who taught them Sanskrit, Persian, and Hindustani. And it remains very much in evidence today.

We have been emphasizing the distortions that have come from an overvaluation of texts. Nevertheless, the accomplishments of history and archaeology in South Asia have been substantial and even revolutionary. To return to the sentiment of Romila Thapar, leading historian of ancient India, who is a good example in her own work for giving archaeological results their due weight and synthesizing textual and material evidence in historical writing, without the work of the scholars of the past two centuries, who completely rewrote the history of India by means of philology and archaeology, we would still be dependent upon the Puranas for our understanding of the South Asian past. The gains have been immense.

Moreover, it remains the case that the opportunities for fruitful cooperation of archaeology and history in South Asia are excellent. In the case of Vijayanagara, conditions seem optimal. They are less promising for the Mauryan empire, for reasons we have recited (e.g., a capital city buried under a living city) and for others we have not. The period of Mauryan greatness was quite short, and in the degree to which textual study focuses on political history, its tempo was quick. At present, our archaeological chronologies, with divisions of many centuries, are too broad to capture the Mauryan moment. It is likely that archaeologists can obtain better temporal resolution through greater attention to the subtleties of changes in ceramics and other artifacts, and by an enlarged suite of absolute dates. This would allow us a broader view of social and economic conditions and relations during the period in which the Mauryans claimed political hegemony. However, it remains an open question how, or if, we will be able to link the archaeological picture to the Mauryan dynastic sequence or political history. In the degree to which historians broaden their field of vision from the political history of the Mauryan throne and the administrative apparatus of the state, and get into its economic arrangements and everyday life, the difficulty declines and the possibilities for fruitful collaboration rise.

In the end, we are optimistic about the potential for improved collaboration between archaeology and history in the South Asian context. Reaching that potential will require change in both disciplines and a rethinking of fundamental assumptions about material and written evidence. It also will require new kinds of interactions among scholars from different disciplines that extend beyond merely mining each other's data for illustrations or supports, to active, ongoing interdisciplinary collaborations such as we see in the Vijayanagara case. In addition, archaeologists studying historic periods must bring the same rigor to field techniques, data recovery, and analysis that is applied to prehistory and should, like historians, pay greater attention to the potentials of the archaeological record as an independent source of evidence on the past. Within history, diligent use of archaeological, as well as inscriptional, evidence can allow scholars to move beyond rulers and dynasties to examine social, economic, and ideological conditions and processes, and to explore how people actually lived and behaved alongside the ideals and prescriptions presented in sacred texts. We have seen the beginnings of this process in the works of historians such as Schopen, Thapar, and Ray, and also in writings by Champakalakshmi (1994, 1995, 1996), Gurukkal (1995), and Parasher-Sen (1993a, 1993b; Parasher 1994), among others. The grounds for optimism are considerable indeed.

Notes

This chapter was originally published in a slightly different form in the *Journal of the Economic and Social History of the Orient* 45 (4): 492–523. Copyright © 2002 by Brill Academic Publishers. Reprinted by permission.

1. Also transliterated as Hsuan-tsang, Yuan Chwang, Hiuen Tsang, and other forms (Wriggins 1996, xviii).

2. "Prehistoric" archaeological sites such as ash mounds and megaliths had already been identified, but these were not considered part of the main narrative of Indian civilization by text-focused Orientalists.

3. The definitions of Buddhist, Hindu, and Muslim architectural and historical periods was, of course, a vast oversimplification, and a dangerous one that continues to play out today in South Asia, giving primacy to religious identity as the major variable in South Asian history and denying the complexity of historical South Asia's religious, ethnic, political, and social landscapes.

4. Conventional dates for the Buddha have been 563–483 BC, though these have recently been called into question by scholars who suggest that he may have lived as much as a century later.

5. Nagaraja Rao was director of Karnataka Archaeology in the late 1970s and early 1980s, and later director general of the ASI from 1985–1987.

6. Included among this group are Kathleen Morrison, C. S. Patil, Carla Sinopoli, Anila Verghese, Phillip Wagoner, and others, who have published extensively on Vijayanagara and who all became involved with the Vijayanagara Research Project as graduate students.

7. Fritz, Michell, and Nagaraja Rao (1985); Dallapiccola, Fritz, Michell, and Rajasekhara 1992; Michell 1990, 1992, 2002; Sinopoli 1993, 2003; Morrison 1995a; Patil and Patil 1995, 1997; Davison-Jenkins 1997; Verghese 1995, 2000; Dallapiccola and Verghese 1998; Tobert 2000; Mack 2002.

Bibliography

Bloch, Jules. 1950. *Les Inscriptions d'Asoka.* Paris: Les Belles Lettres.

Bopp, Franz. 1816. *Über das Conjugationssystem der Sanskrit Sprache in Vergleichung mit jenem der grieschischen, persischen und germanischen Sprache.* Frankfurt: Andreäischen Buchhandlung.

———. 1833. *Vergleichende Grammatik des Sanskrit, Zend, Grieschichen, Lateinischen, Litauischen, Gothischen und Deutschen.* Berlin: F. Dummler.

———. 1845–53. *A Comparative Grammar of the Sanskrit, Zend, Greek, Latin, Lithuanian, Gothic, German and Slavonic Languages.* Trans. Lieut. Eastwick. Ed. H. H. Wilson. London: Madden and Malcolm.

Bryant, Edwin. 2001. *The Quest for the Origins of Vedic Culture: The Indo-Aryan Migration Debate.* Oxford: Oxford University Press.

Chakrabarti, Dilip K. 1988. *A History of Indian Archaeology from the Beginning to 1947.* New Delhi: Munshiram Manoharlal.

Champakalakshmi, R. 1994. "Urban Processes in Early Medieval Tamil Nadu." In *The City in Indian History,* ed. I. Banga, 47–68. New Delhi: Manohar.

———. 1995. "States and Economy: South India, circa AD 400–1300." In *Recent Perspectives of Early Indian History,* ed. R. Thapar, 266–308. Bombay: Popular Prakashan.

———. 1996. *Trade, Ideology and Urbanization: South India 300 BC to AD 1300.* Delhi: Oxford University Press.

Childe, V. Gordon. 1926. *The Aryans: A Study of Indo-European Origins.* New York: A. A. Knopf.

Coningham, Robin. 1995. "Monks, Caves and Kings: A Reassessment of the Nature of Early Buddhism in Sri Lanka." *World Archaeology* 27:222–42.

———. 1998. "Buddhism 'Rematerialized' and the Archaeology of Gautama Buddha." *Cambridge Archaeological Journal* 8:121–26.

———. 2001. "The Archaeology of Buddhism." In *Archaeology and World Religion,* ed. T. Insoll, 61–95. London: Routledge.

Cunningham, Alexander. 1843. "An Account of the Discovery of the Ruins of the Buddhist City of Samkassa." *Journal of the Royal Asiatic Society of Great Britain and Ireland* 14:241–49.

———. 1866. *Four Reports Made During the Years 1862-63-64.* 2 vols. Archaeological Survey of India. Repr., Delhi: Indological Book House, 1972.

———. 1875. "Harappa." *Archaeological Survey of India: Report from the Years 1872-3,* 105–8. Calcutta: Archaeological Survey of India.

Dallapiccola, Anna L., ed. 1985. *Vijayanagara: City and Empire.* 2 vols. Weisbaden, Germany: Franz Steiner Verlag.

Dallapiccola, Anna L., John M. Fritz, George Michell, and S. Rajasekhara. 1992. *The Ramachandra Temple at Vijayanagara*. New Delhi: Manohar.

Dallapiccola, Anna L., and Anila Verghese. 1998. *Sculpture at Vijayanagara: Iconography and Style*. New Delhi: Manohar.

Daniel, Glyn. 1962. *The Idea of Prehistory*. Baltimore: Penguin Books.

Davison-Jenkins, Dominic J. 1997. *The Irrigation and Water Supply Systems of Vijayanagara*. New Delhi: Manohar.

Dehejia, Vidya. 1992. "Collective and Popular Bases of Early Buddhist Patronage: Sacred Monuments, 100 BC–AD 250." In *The Powers of Art: Patronage in Indian Culture*, ed. B. S. Miller, 35–45. Delhi: Oxford University Press.

———. 1997. *Discourse in Early Buddhist Art: Visual Narratives of India*. New Delhi: Munshiram Manoharlal.

Dhavalikar, M. K. 1999. *Historical Archaeology of India*. Delhi: Books and Books.

Dutt, B. B. 1925. *Town Planning in Ancient India*. Calcutta: Thacker, Spink, and Co.

Fogelin, Lars. Forthcoming a. "Early Buddhism in Coastal Andhra: Sacred Architecture, Sacred Landscapes." In *Archaeology as History*, ed. H. P. Ray and C. M. Sinopoli. Delhi: Pragati Publications.

———. Forthcoming b. "Recent Research at the Buddhist Monastery of Thotlakonda." In *South Asian Archaeology 2001*, ed. C. Jarrige. Paris: Editions Recherche sur les Civilisations.

———. Forthcoming c. "The Mortuary Landscape of Thotlakonda." In *Buddhism in Andra: Papers in Commemoration of Dr. Hanumantha Rao*, ed. A. Parasher-Sen. New Delhi: Bharatiya Kala Prakashan.

Foote, Robert Bruce. 1866. "On the Occurrence of Stone Implements in Laterite Formations in Various Parts of the Madras and North Arcot Districts." *Madras Journal of Literature and Science* (3rd series) 2:1–42.

———. 1914. *Indian Prehistoric and Protohistoric Antiquities—Catalogue Raissone*. Madras, India: Government Press.

———. 1916. *Indian Prehistoric and Protohistoric Antiquities—Notes on Their Ages and Distribution*. Madras, India: Government Press.

Fritz, John M. 1986. "Vijayanagara: Authority and Meaning of a South Indian Imperial Capital." *American Anthropologist* 88:44–55.

Fritz, John M., and George A. Michell. 1989. "Interpreting the Plan of a Medieval Hindu Capital: Vijayanagara." *World Archaeology* 19:105–29.

Fritz, John M., George A. Michell, and M. S. Nagaraja Rao. 1985. *The Royal Center at Vijayanagara: Preliminary Report*. Tucson: University of Arizona Press.

Fritz, John M., and Kathleen D. Morrison. Forthcoming. *Archaeological Inventory of the Royal Center of Vijayanagara*. 2 vols. New Delhi: Manohar.

Gadd, C. J., and Sidney Smith. 1924. "The New Links between Indian and Babylonian Civilizations." *Illustrated London News*, October 4, 614–16.

Gurukkal, Rajan. 1995. "The Beginnings of the Historic Period: The Tamil South." In *Recent Perspectives of Early Indian History*, ed. R. Thapar, 237–65. Bombay: Popular Prakashan.

Heras, H. 1931. "Seven Days at Vijayanagara." *Journal of Indian History* 9:103–18.

Hultzsch, Eugen. 1969. *Inscriptions of Ashoka*. Vol. 1 of Corpus Inscriptionum Indicarum. New ed. Delhi: Indological Book House.

Imam, Abu. 1966. *Sir Alexander Cunningham and the Beginnings of Indian Archaeology*. Dacca: Asiatic Society of Pakistan.

Jayaswal, Vidula. 1998. *From Stone Quarry to Sculpturing Workshop: A Report on Archaeological Investigations around Chunar, Varanasi, and Sarnath*. Delhi: Agam Kala Prakashan.

Jones, William. 1788a. "A Discourse on the Institution of a Society, for Inquiring into the History, Civil and Natural, the Antiquities, Arts, Sciences, and Literature, of Asia." *Asiatic Researches* 1:ix–xvi.

———. 1788b. "A Dissertation on the Orthography of Asiatick Words in Roman Letters." *Asiatic Researches* 1:1–56.

———. 1788c. "On the Gods of Greece, Italy, and India." *Asiatic Researches* 1:221–75.

———. 1788d. "Inscriptions on the Staff of Firuz Shah, Translated from the Sanscrit, as Explained by Radhacanta Sarman." *Asiatic Researches* 1:379–82.

———. 1788e. "The Third Anniversary Discourse, on the Hindus." *Asiatic Researches* 1:415–31.

———. 1807a. "On the Chronology of the Hindus." *The Works of Sir William Jones* 4:1–46. London: John Stockdale and John Walker.

———. 1807b. "The Ninth Anniversary Discourse, on the Origin and Families of Nations." *The Works of Sir William Jones* 3:24–29. London: John Stockdale and John Walker.

Kejariwal, O. P. 1988. *The Asiatic Society of Bengal and the Discovery of India's Past 1784–1838*. Delhi: Oxford University Press.

Kenoyer, Jonathan Mark. 1997. "Early City-states in South Asia: Comparing the Harappan Phase and Early Historic Period." In *The Archaeology of City-States: Cross-Cultural Approaches*, ed. D. S. Nichols and T. H. Charlton, 51–70. Washington, D.C.: Smithsonian Institution Press.

———. 1998. *Ancient Cities of the Indus Valley Civilization*. Oxford: Oxford University Press.

Lahiri, Nayanjot. 2002. "Archival Perspective on the Discovery of the Indus Civilization." Paper presented at Archaeology as History conference, New Delhi, March 2002.

Lopez, Donald S., Jr. 1995. "Introduction." In *Curators of the Buddha: The Study of Buddhism under Colonialism*, ed. D. S. Lopez Jr., 1–29. Chicago: University of Chicago Press.

Mack, Alexandra. 2002. *Spiritual Journey, Imperial City: Pilgrimage to the Temples of Vijayanagara*. New Delhi: Vedams.

Mahalingam, T. V. 1940. *Administration and Social Life under Vijayanagar*. Repr., Madras: University of Madras Press, 1975.

Marshall, John. 1924. "First Light on a Long-Forgotten Civilization." *Illustrated London News*, September 20, 528–32, 548.

Meadow, Richard, and Ajita Patel. 1997. "A Comment on 'Horse Remains from Surkotada' by Sándor Bökönyi." *South Asian Studies* 13:308–15.

Megasthenes. 1846. *Megasthenis Indica: Fragmenta Collegit, Commentationem et Indices addidit E. A. Schwanbeck*. Repr., Amsterdam: A.M.S., 1960.

———. 1960. *Ancient India as Described by Megasthenes and Arrian*. 2nd rev. Trans. J. W. McCrindle. Ed. R. C. Majumdar. Calcutta: Chuckervertty, Chatterjee.

Michell, George. 1985. "A Never Forgotten City." In *Vijayanagara: City and Empire*, ed. A. L. Dallapiccola, 196–207. Wiesbaden, Germany: Franz Steiner Verlag.

———. 1990. *Vijayanagara: Architectural Inventory of the Urban Core*. 2 vols. Mysore, India: Directorate of Archaeology and Museums.

———. 1992. *The Vijayanagara Courtly Style*. New Delhi: Manohar.

———. 2002. *Vijayanagara: Architectural Inventory of the Sacred Center*. New Delhi: Manohar.

Moreland, John. 2001. *Archaeology and Text*. London: Duckworth.

Morrison, Kathleen. 1995a. *Fields of Victory: Vijayanagara and the Course of Intensification*. Berkeley: Archaeological Research Facility, University of California.

———. 1995b. "Trade, Urbanism, and Agricultural Expansion: Buddhist Monastic Institutions and the State in Early Historic Western Deccan." *World Archaeology* 27:203–21.

Mughal, Mohammad Rafique. 1997. *Ancient Cholistan: Archaeology and Architecture*. Rawalpindi, Pakistan: Ferozsons.

Newbold, T. J. 1843. "On Some Ancient Mounds of Scorious Ash in Southern India." *Journal of the Royal Asiatic Society of Great Britain and Ireland* 7:129–36.

———. 1852. "Ancient Sepulchres of the Panduvarama Dewal in South India." *Journal of the Royal Asiatic Society of Great Britain and Ireland* 13:90–95.

Parasher, Aloka. 1994. "Social Structure and Economy of Settlements in the Central Deccan (200 BC–200 AD)." In *The City in Indian History*, ed. I. Banga, 19–46. New Delhi: Manohar.

Parasher-Sen, Aloka. 1993a. "Culture and Civilization: The Beginnings." In *Social and Economic History of Early Deccan: Some Interpretations*, ed. A. Parasher-Sen, 66–114. New Delhi: Manohar.

———. 1993b. "Introduction—Problems of Interpretations." In *Social and Economic History of Early Deccan: Some Interpretations*, ed. A. Parasher-Sen, 1–65. New Delhi: Manohar.

Pargiter, F. E. 1962. *The Purana Text of the Dynasties of the Kali Age.* 2nd ed. Varanasi, India: Chowkhamba Sanskrit Series Office.

Patil, C. S., and V. C. Patil. 1995. *Inscriptions at Vijayanagara (Hampi).* Mysore, India: Directorate of Archaeology and Museums.

———. 1997. *Inscriptions of Bellary District.* Mysore, India: Directorate of Archaeology and Museums.

Possehl, Gregory L. 1998. "Sociocultural Complexity without the State: The Indus Civilization." In *Archaic States,* ed. G. M. Feinman and J. Marcus, 261–92. Santa Fe, N.Mex.: School of American Research Press.

———. 1999. *Indus Age: The Beginnings.* Delhi: Oxford and IBH Publishing.

Ratnagar, Shereen. 1991. *Enquiries into the Political Organization of Harappan Society.* Pune, India: Ravis Publishers.

Ray, Himanshu P. 1986. *Monasteries and Guild: Commerce under the Satavahanas.* Delhi: Oxford University Press.

———. 1994. *The Winds of Change: Buddhism and the Maritime Links of Early South Asia.* Delhi: Oxford University Press.

———. 2003. *Archaeology of Seafaring in Ancient South Asia.* Cambridge: Cambridge University Press.

Renfrew, Colin. 1987. *Archaeology and Language: The Puzzle of Indo-European Origins.* London: Penguin Books.

Rocher, Rosanne. 1983. *Orientalism, Poetry and the Millennium: The Checkered Life of Nathanial Brassey Halhed 1751–1830.* Delhi: Motilal Banarsidass.

Saletore, Bhasker A. 1934. *Social and Political Life in the Vijayanagara Empire.* Madras, India: B. G. Paul and Co.

Sayce, A. H. 1924. "Remarkable Discoveries in India." *Illustrated London News,* September 27, 526.

Schopen, Gregory. 1987. "Burial *Ad Sanctos* and the Physical Presence of the Buddha in Early Indian Buddhism: A Study in the Archaeology of Religion." *Religion* 17:193–225.

———. 1988–89. "On Monks, Nuns, and Vulgar Practices: The Introduction of the Image Cult into Indian Buddhism." *Artibus Asiae* 49:152–68.

———. 1989. "The *Stupa* Cult and the Extant Pali *Vinaya.*" *Journal of the Pali Text Society* 13:83–100.

———. 1991a. "Archaeology and Protestant Presuppositions in the Study of Indian Buddhism." *History of Religions* 31:1–23.

———. 1991b. "Monks and the Relic Cult in the *Mahaparinibbana-sutta*: An Old Understanding in Regard to Monastic Buddhism." In *From Benares to Beijing: Essays on Buddhism and Chinese Religion,* ed. K. Shinohara and G. Schopen, 187–201. Oakville, Ontario: Mosaic Press.

———. 1991c. "An Old Inscription from Amaravati and the Cult of the Local Monastic Dead in Indian Buddhist Monasteries." *Journal of the International Association of Buddhist Studies* 14:281–329.

———. 1995. "Monastic Law Meets the Real World: A Monk's Continuing Right to Inherit Family Property in Classical India." *History of Religions* 35:101–23.

———. 1997. *Bones, Stones, and Buddhist Monks: Collected Papers on the Archaeology, Epigraphy, and Texts of Monastic Buddhism in India.* Honolulu: University of Hawaii Press.

Scott, James C. 1998. *Seeing like a State: How Certain Schemes to Improve the Human Condition Have Failed.* New Haven, Conn.: Yale University Press.

Sewell, Robert. 1900. *A Forgotten Empire (Vijayanagar): A Contribution to the History of India.* London: S. Sonnenschein and Co.

Shaw, Julia. 2000. "Sanchi and Its Archaeological Landscape: Buddhist Monasteries, Settlements and Irrigation Works in Central India." *Antiquity* 74:775–76.

Shaw, Julia, and John Sutcliffe. 2001. "Ancient Irrigation Works in the Sanchi Area: An Archaeological and Hydrological Investigation." *South Asian Studies* 17:55–75.

Sinopoli, Carla M. 1993. *Pots and Palaces: The Archaeological Ceramics of the Nobleman's Quarter of Vijayanagara.* New Delhi: Manohar.

———. 2003. *The Political Economy of Craft Production: Crafting Empire in South India, AD 1350–1650.* Cambridge: Cambridge University Press.

Sinopoli, Carla M., and Kathleen D. Morrison. Forthcoming. The Regional Landscapes of the Imperial City of Vijayanagara: Report on the Vijayanagara Metropolitan Survey Project. In *South Asian Archaeology 1999*, ed. K. R. van Kooij and E. Raven. Groningen: Egbert Forsten Publishing.

Spooner, D. B. 1913. "Mr. Ratan Tata's Excavations at Pataliputra." *Annual Report of the Archaeological Survey of India 1912–13*, 53–86. Calcutta: Archaeological Survey of India.

Stein, Burton. 1980. *Peasant State and Society in Medieval South India.* Delhi: Oxford University Press.

Stepan, Nancy 1982. *The Idea of Race in Science: Great Britain 1800–1960.* London: Macmillan.

Taylor, Meadows. 1862. "Description of Cairns, Cromlechs, Kistvens and Other Celtic, Druidical or Scythian Monuments in Dekhan." *Transactions of the Royal Irish Academy, Antiquities* 24:329–62.

Thapar, Romila. 1961. *Asoka and the Decline of the Mauryas.* Oxford: Oxford University Press.

———. 1966. *A History of India.* Vol. 1. Harmondsworth: Penguin.

———. 1992. "Patronage and Community." In *The Powers of Art: Patronage in Indian Culture*, ed. B. S. Miller, 19–34. Delhi: Oxford University Press.

———. 1997. *Asoka and the Decline of the Mauryas*. 2nd ed. Delhi: Oxford University Press.

Tobert, Natalie. 2000. *Anegondi: Architectural Ethnography of a Royal Village*. Delhi: Manohar.

Topinard, Paul. 1885. *Éléments d'anthropologie générale*. Paris: Adrien Delahaye et Émile Lecrosier.

Trautmann, Thomas R. 1971. *Kautilya and the Arthasastra*. Leiden, Netherlands: Brill.

———. 1992. "The Revolution in Ethnological Rime." *Man*, n.s. 27:379–97.

———. 1997. *Aryans and British India*. Berkeley: University of California Press.

Verghese, Anila. 1995. *Religious Traditions at Vijayanagara*. New Delhi: Manohar.

———. 2000. *Archaeology, Art and Religion: New Perspectives on Vijayanagara*. Delhi: Oxford University Press.

Waddell, L. A. 1903. *Report on the Excavations at Patilaputra (Patna)*. Calcutta: Bengal Secretariat Press.

Wagoner, Phillip B. 1993. *Tidings of the King: A Translation and Ethnohistorical Analysis of the Rayāvācakamu*. Honolulu: University of Hawaii Press.

———. 1996. "'Sultan among Hindu Kings': Dress, Titles, and the Islamicization of Hindu Culture at Vijayanagara." *Journal of Asian Studies* 55:851–80.

Wheeler, R. E. M. 1953. *The Indus Civilization*. Supplementary vol., Cambridge History of India. Cambridge: Cambridge University Press.

Wilkins, Charles. 1788. "An Inscription on a Pillar near Buddal." *Asiatic Researches* 1:131–41, with remarks by Sir William Jones, 142–44.

Willis, Janice D. 1992. "Female Patronage in Indian Buddhism." In *The Powers of Art: Patronage in Indian Culture*, ed. B. S. Miller, 46–53. Delhi: Oxford University Press.

Witzel, Michael, and Steve Farmer. 2000. "Horseplay in Harappa: The Indus Valley Decipherment Hoax." *Frontline*, October 13.

Wriggins, Sally Hovey. 1996. *Xuanzang: A Buddhist Pilgrim on the Silk Road*. Boulder, Colo.: Westview Press.

Yoffee, Norman. 1990. "Before Babel: A Review Article." *Proceedings of the Prehistoric Society* 56:299–313.

7

Jinan in the First Millennium BC
Archaeology and History

LI MIN

The discipline of historiography, that is, briefly, the accounts of how historians understand the past, has dominated the interpretation of archaeological data in China (Falkenhausen 1993). Often, however, historical texts are themselves archaeological artifacts, aspects of material culture (Barker 1995, 2), and their provenances and contexts must be analyzed in the manner of other artifacts. Of course, the methods of analysis of the various classes of archaeological data require appropriate procedures, and different kinds of data can reflect quite different aspects of social phenomena (Yan Wenming 1999, 10).

For example, it is nearly a truism that archaeological data often allow insight into the "people without history" (after Wolf 1982), that is, people who are laconically represented or underrepresented in historical documents or who were forcibly supplied with their history by imperial governments or colonizers. Furthermore, archaeologists typically reconstruct long-term patterns of change, especially in mundane activities, at a rhythm that is undetectable to contemporaneous observers. It is no wonder that archaeologists, including myself, often appeal to Braudel's formulation of the *longue durée*. In this sense, to archaeologists, texts seem to supply the persons, events, and policies at a different scale than they themselves consider in the analysis of ecology and material culture. Of course, texts can be used simply to "periodize" time (as in this chapter) and to link trends in artifactual change with political events. Although broad movements of economies, social structures, and political institutions can and must be studied using both texts and archaeological data (Snodgrass 1991, 62), in some cases people represent themselves and their world differently in documents than in architecture or in mortuary practices, and this inconsistent picture must itself be the subject of research because it has the potential for revealing the underlying values of the society in question.

According to the archaeologist Barker (1995, 1), following Braudel, "long-term" history includes the history of cognitive structures or mentalities, in particular how religious and ideological systems attempted to bind societies together. These topics, normal subjects of historical research, are relatively novel in archaeological investigations as archaeologists turn from matters of demography, environment, and social and political transformations in order to assess "the hearts and minds of past societies as symbolized in the changing components of material culture," as one archaeologist put it (Bintliff 1991, 19). The topics include the short-term and contingent as well as long-term structures (Hodder 1999, 130), and "agents" (Snodgrass 1991), people who belong to various organizations simultaneously and therefore must negotiate their identities as conditions of social life and practical interests change (Sahlins 1985).

In this chapter, I review and synthesize recent archaeological work in the attempt to present an archaeological history of the region of Jinan in the first millennium BC. The analysis of settlement patterns, burial practices, and occasional inscriptions and transmitted texts reveals the gradual integration of the Jinan region first into centralized regional states and networks of interregional trade, then into the encompassing political and economic structures of the Qin and Han empires. The transition from the Late Bronze Age to the Iron Age included the development of commerce, urbanism, and centralizing political structures, which in turn affected local lifestyle. A description of landscapes, both natural and cultural, and the basic prehistoric and early historic terms and periods used to describe the region, provide context for understanding settlement patterns in the first millennium BC and for examining changes in social and political structure, specifically how major technological and economic systems, such as the introduction of iron technology and monetary systems, were represented in local communities over time. Further, an analysis of the changing patterns of burial ritual illuminates the effect of various political structures on status and belief systems, roughly, and on the structures and emotions of residents of the region (McGuire 1992, 203).

Regional Landscape and History

The study region, Jinan, the land south of the Ji River, is part of Shandong Province in eastern China. In this study, the region is defined by the modern Yellow River, which followed the channel of the historical Ji

River, as its northwestern boundary, the Long Wall of Qi as its southern boundary, and Mount Changbai as its eastern limit (figures 7.1 and 7.2).

The local landscape is characterized by two major types of terrain—the steeply rising slopes of the Tai mountain range in the south and a strip of alluvial plain in the north. Iron and copper ore were mined at the northern foothills of Mount Tai. Mount Tai, as a prominent site for a mountain cult, has been incorporated in the cosmology of imperial China over the last two millennia and was the scene of numerous royal pilgrimages (Chavannes 1910; Wilkinson 2000).

The limestone formation of the mountain range intercepts the flow of underground water, creating many natural springs in the northern plain, making it fertile agricultural land for wheat, millet, and other crops. Meandering waterways crosscut the plain and empty into the Yellow River and the Bohai Gulf. Located in the center of the plain, Jinan is the regional political and industrial center. An east-west trade route served as the backbone of the alluvial plain, along which major regional centers have been located from antiquity to the present (Hou Renzhi 1979). To its east, it reached the industrial city of Zibo, built over the ruins of Linzi, the metropolitan center of the Qi state, in the late first millennium BC. To its west, it reached the central plain. Dozens of inscriptions left by travelers and diplomats on a first-century stone shrine along the road at Xiaotangshan (XTS) reveal the importance of this route in antiquity (Chavannes 1913, vol. 1; Luo Zhewen 1961; Yu Zhonghang 1983).

The climatic condition of the study region was characterized by a gradual transition from a warm, subtropical climate in the second millennium BC to the cooler, temperate climate of northern China today. The turning point was at the beginning of the first millennium, as seen in the southern migration of local fauna, such as elephants and rhinos (Zou Yilin 1997, 16–17). The social implication of this climatic change has not been studied extensively, but the effect on long-term change in agriculture is inevitable.

Archaeological work in Jinan has an extraordinary antiquity. Field-based academic inquiries began in the fifth century AD, when the historical geographer Li Daoyuan investigated the ruins of Han towns and monuments and described them in their association with the natural landscape and river channels (Fu Ssu-nien et al. 1934; Luo Xunzhang 1993). In the centuries to follow, scholars have made vigorous efforts in recording local history and cultural relics from the perspectives of historiography, classics, and antiquarianism (Ning Yintang 1994).

At the beginning of the twentieth century, Chavannes (1910, 1913) in-

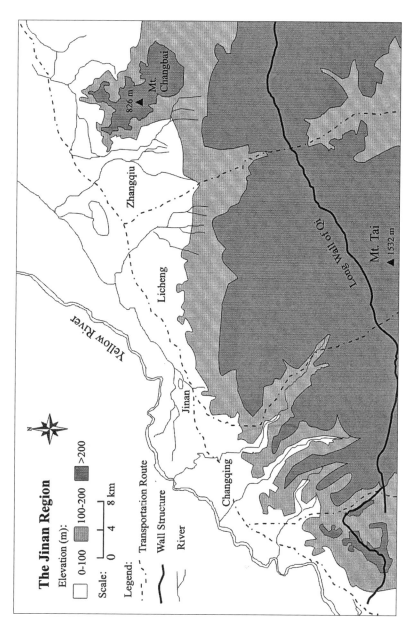

Figure 7.1 Map of the Jinan region

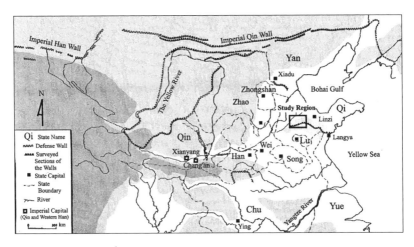

Figure 7.2 Jinan in the historical landscape of ancient China in the late first millennium BC. (This is a composite map of the Warring States, Qin, and Western Han periods; base map adapted from Ye Xiaoyan 1987, 42.)

vestigated Han monuments in Jinan and the religious landscape associated with the imperial cult of Mount Tai. In the following decades, Wu Chin-ting (1930) investigated the Han remains at Pingling (DPLC), and Li Chi excavated the prehistoric and the Bronze Age remains at Chengziyai (CTY). In an effort to bridge material culture with historiography, Li Chi argued that the "black pottery culture" at Chengziyai represents the indigenous foundation for Chinese civilization, and the upper layer deposit represents the Bronze Age successors of this indigenous culture (Fu Ssu-nien et al. 1934). At the time when archaeologists and historians had offered incompatible paths for the origin of Chinese civilization, one preoccupied with a Near Eastern diffusion model, the other concerned with the sage kings and their legendary regimes, Li Chi's proposal led to new directions in studying the question (Chen Xingcan 1997).

Works by generations of archaeologists after the pioneering effort at Chengziyai have revealed that the regional society had deep roots in prehistory. The first permanent settlements were founded in the seventh millennium BC in the plain area (Wang Sili 1957; SPIA 1998). By the third millennium BC, settlements and burials indicate social differentiation and the emergence of walled communities with a number of traits that led to the development of more complex society in China (Fu Ssu-nien et al. 1934; Pearson 1981, 1996–97; Yan Wenming 1997). The political structure associated with these communities has been characterized as "chiefdoms" (Underhill 1993; Liu 1996). Local polities, represented by the walled towns such as Chengziyai, continued to flourish in the early Bronze Age until their political prominence was eventually over-shadowed by rising centers with elite regalia bearing Shang symbolism, first at Daxinzhuang (DXZ) and later at Xingfuhe (XFH), believed to be Shang colonies (Chang 1986, 371; Bagley 1999, 221). After the collapse of the Shang hegemony in the late second millennium BC, the region was inhabited by several lineage-based local polities, which may have main-tained tributary obligations to the Zhou court or, more likely, to its re-gional representatives, such as the states of Qi to the east and Lu to the south. The poem "Greater East" in *Shijing*, an anthology of contempo-rary poetry, presents a poetic recollection of the antagonism between the local population and the Zhou elite along the trade route at the time (Waley 1937).

As the Zhou hegemony declined after the seventh century BC, feudal states competed for dominance during the Eastern Zhou period, which is conventionally subdivided into the Spring and Autumn period and the Warring States period. Historical narratives commonly emphasize broad social and political developments characterized by the rise of a more rationalized and centralized political structure at the expense of kinship ties and aristocratic order underlying elite lineages and branch lineages (Falkenhausen 1999, 451). By encouraging trade, mining, and craft industry, the state of Qi emerged as a dominant economic power in eastern China. Eventually, the states of Qi and Lu annexed the small polities in this area, and Jinan became the frontier region for intensive military and economic interaction for Qi and its rivals.

In 221 BC, Qin unified the empire and the Jinan region became part of the Qi commandery under the direct control of the Qin govern-ment. The Qin government imposed the standardization of measure-ment, currency, and writing system. To reinforce Qin's control of the new territories, the First Emperor of Qin initiated the construction of imperial highways running through the region, connecting the capital to the eastern regions. He further attempted to foster an imperial cos-mology through the imperial pilgrimages to Mount Tai. Underlying the decisive event of Qin unification in 221 BC were processes of change within crucial aspects of social life, which included the emergence of centralized government, the growth of urban life, the formation of a monetary system, and the transition to iron technology. These transfor-mations set the stage for rapid changes to unfold in the late first millen-nium BC (Hsü 1965).

The enormous amount of labor investment demanded for these grand projects and the harsh legalist governance employed by Qin led to widespread resentment from the populace. Soon the empire was overthrown by peasant rebellions, and the Western Han empire emerged from the aftermath of the Qin collapse in 206 BC (compare Kern 2000). To reinforce imperial control, the Han court created a dual administrative system by strategically placing kingdoms governed by members of the royal lineage amidst commanderies governed by appointed administrators. Jinan was part of the Qi kingdom, the most powerful in these semiautonomous states.

The kings reinforced their political autonomy through their independent operations of mining, minting, iron working, and salt production, which posed threats to imperial revenue and sovereignty. The imperial court responded by dividing large kingdoms into smaller ones, carving land out of kingdoms, and removing the right of succession from the royal lineage members. The Jinan region became part of Jinan kingdom and Jibei kingdom, both carved out of the Qi kingdom and ruled by two junior lineages of the Qi royal house.

Tension between the imperial court of Han and the kingdoms eventually led to the Rebellion of the Seven Kingdoms in 154 BC, when the kingdoms of Jinan and Jibei rebelled unsuccessfully against imperial Han government with their coastal allies. In the following decades, the imperial government transferred the administrative and military authority from the kings to the officials of the commanderies appointed by the central government. The imperial control further reinforced its regional economy by imposing a state monopoly on the production of currency, salt, and iron after 118 BC. The handicraft agency, *gongguan*, and iron monopoly agency, *tieguan*, under direct control from the central government, were established in Jinan and in Tai'an in Shandong as well as in major economic centers in Henan and Sichuan (Wang 1982, 85).

The imperial government suppressed the private production and commercialism that had flourished since the Warring States period.[1] Local industry became a source for imperial revenue for wars of expansion and ambitious projects. In the late first century BC, the empire gradually weakened as a result of ruinously expensive wars and corruption. During the final decades of the millennium, widespread natural disasters swept through the region and central plain, which intensified the existing social tensions and set the stage for change (An Zuozhang 1993, 57–59). Responding to the opportunities derived from the crisis, tyrant Wang Mang, a native of Jinan, seized the throne in AD 9 and ended the Western Han. At the end of the millennium, the population density of the region was roughly at 87.5 persons per square kilometer, which made it one of the most populated regions in the Han Empire (Lao Kan 1935, 217).

Settlement Patterns in the Western Zhou Period

Information from the Zhangqiu survey and from the excavations at Wangfuzhuang (WFZ), Ningjiabu (NJB), DXZ, Wangtuiguanzhuang (WTGZ), and Xiangrentai (XRT) shed light on the local life at the turn of the millennium (see figure 7.3; Sun Bo 1999; Ren Xianghong, Li Yuting, and Wang Jianguo 1993; Ning Yintang 1994, 38; Ren Xianghong and Cui Dayong 1998; Liu Yanchang and Ning Yintang 1996; Cui Dayong and Ren Xianghong 1998; Xu Ji 1995). The presence of storage facilities, permanent house structures, wells, and burials in settlement sites suggests that residents of Jinan led a settled agricultural life. The presence of polished stone molds for bronze casting and kilns in the settlement sites indicates bronze casting and pottery production. Artifacts representing domestic life and food production activities, such as sickles, awls, pendants, and food vessels, found on house floor F4 at XRT indicate that craft and subsistence production were carried out at the community level without strong signs of specialization.

Data from house floors at XRT and pit features at NJB suggest that daily activities were primarily carried out with implements made of polished stone, shell, antler, and bone. At both sites, bronze was reserved for artifacts associated with hunting activities and warfare, such as arrowheads and knives. The presence of an inscribed bronze tripod bearing the name of a polity tentatively identified as *Guo*, which may come from a destroyed elite burial at Muotianling (MTL), suggests the presence of political and ritual authority within the region (Chang Xingzhao and Ning Yintang 1989, 71).

Settlement Patterns in the Spring and Autumn Period

The most imposing landmark in the region was the Long Wall of Qi. Our knowledge of this structure increased significantly after the completion of the first full-coverage, systematic survey of the wall remains in 1997, undertaken by a heroic team consisting of senior citizens led by the late Lu Zongyuan (Lu Zongyuan 1998). The extensive publication by this volunteer group of avocational archaeologists offered detailed informa-

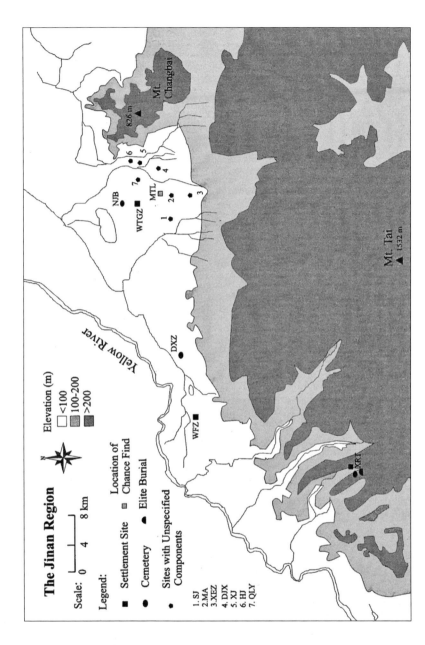

Figure 7.3 Distribution of sites from the Western Zhou period

tion on the distribution, construction methods, preservation condition, and associated features for this monumental structure, such as smoke signal towers, passes, and fortifications for stationing troops.

The wall meanders from Guangli (GL) at the western end of the region eastward and reaches the western shore of the Yellow Sea beyond the regional boundary (figure 7.4), stretching over a distance of 618.9 kilometers at its full length (Lu Zongyuan 1998, 30). A third of the wall is located in the region, of which 75 percent has visible surface remains. The body of the wall is about six meters wide and is primarily constructed of stone. Different methods and raw materials were employed, depending on local resources.

The remains of the Long Wall of Qi are dated on the basis of textual references to the wall from inscriptions on bronze vessels and in historical texts from the first millennium BC (Wang Xiantang 1979). Inscriptions on the Biao Qiang set of bronze chime bells discovered at Jincun, Luoyang, in 1930 mentioned the invasion of the *Changcheng* ("the Long Wall") and its nearby towns by an army from the state of Jin in the "twenty-second year" (Li 1985, 34). Similar historical instances took place in 555 BC and 404 BC, leaving space for scholars to debate the exact match between the inscription and the historical reference (Wang Xiantang 1979, 198; Li 1985, 34; Ren Xianghong 1998, 32). In either case, it is clear that this section of the wall mentioned in the inscription, located in the western part of the study region, had been completed by the time of invasion, and it did witness military confrontations in the mid-first millennium BC. Historical accounts suggested that the eastern sections were gradually added on later to defend against the northern expansion of the southern states from the Yangtze River basin, such as Chu and Yue, and the wall was finally completed in the late fourth century BC (Wang Xiantang 1979, 199).

The construction of the Long Wall by the end of this period represents archaeological evidence of territorial control of the region by a powerful political authority lying beyond the regional boundary. Like the Roman walls, the purpose of the wall was probably both military and financial (Collingwood and Myres 1936). With the Ji River (modern Yellow River) serving as the northern barrier and the wall and mountain range as the southern one, the heartland of the Qi state was protected from its hostile neighbors, such as Yan, Lu, Jin, Chu, and Yue (Wang Xiantang 1979, 194). The financial aspect is implied in the inscribed Qi standard measurement containers bearing the term *guan* ("pass") found at Lingshanwei (LSW) in the eastern end of the wall in 1857, presum-

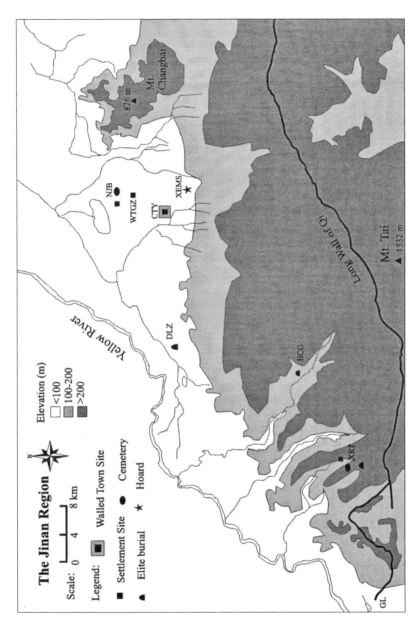

Figure 7.4 Distribution of sites from the Spring and Autumn period

ably used for taxation purposes in the period following the completion of the wall (Wang Xiantang 1979, 194; Li 1985, 133).

Town life, represented by the combination of a rammed-earth town wall, kiln production, and a rich inventory of artifacts associated with domestic life and craft production, flourished at the site of CTY, which was built over the site of a prehistoric town that once flourished in the third and second millennia BC (Fu Ssu-nien et al. 1934). The Eastern Zhou settlement associated with the upper layer deposit was enclosed by a rammed-earth wall, which measures approximately four hundred meters on each side and was dated to the Spring and Autumn Period (Zhang Xuehai 1993, 2). No contemporaneous burials have been found in the walled town; they may lie outside the town wall, away from the community.

Settlement sites at WTGZ, XRT, and NJB represent smaller communities in the region (Liu Yanchang and Ning Yintang 1996; Cui Dayong and Ren Xianghong 1998; Ren Xianghong and Cui Dayong 1998; Ren Xianghong 1998). In addition to residential remains, excavations at XRT also produced the lineage cemetery for the ruling house of the Si polity. Isolated elite burials have been reported at Dianliuzhuang (DLZ) and Beicaogou (BCG; Sun Jingming 1998, 21; Zhu Huo 1973, 64; Ren Xianghong, Li Yuting, and Wang Jianguo 1993, 48–79). Artifacts of polished stone, bone, antler, and shell dominate the tool assemblage at CTY, XRT, and NJB. These materials were probably manufactured locally with native resources. For instance, Fu Ssu-nien and others (1934) reported that the lithic tools at CTY were primarily fashioned from raw material from Mount Tai. A fragment of ceramic mold for casting a bronze artifact with an ornate intertwining design presents evidence for metal working at the XRT polity. The great diversity of the nonmetal tools, in contrast to the general absence of metal tools and their molds, indicates that metal was not widely used in subsistence production, despite claims based on occasional finds of metal tools (Wang Sili 1957; Yu Zhonghang 1979).

Bronze was primarily used for weapons and ritual instruments. Bronze weapons, such as knives and arrowheads, were reported in the upper layer deposit at CTY (Fu Ssu-nien et al. 1934). A hoard of bronze ritual items unearthed on the northern slope of a hill at Xiao'emeishan (XEMS) is characterized as a ritual deposit (Chang Xingzhao and Ning Yintang 1989). The hoard produced at least eighty bronze items, including chime bells of various types, *gui*-shaped plaques, and *bi*-shaped disks, all forms of ritual implements. One bronze chime measures 0.75

meters in height. Based on the extraordinarily large size of the instrument and the symbolic significance of the artifacts, Chang Xingzhao and Ning Yintang (1989) argue that elite patronage was involved in the ritual deposit.

Settlement data from the Spring and Autumn Period reveal that subsistence production in local communities was primarily carried out with a virtually Neolithic tool assemblage with limited use of metal. A basic division between town life and rural life created by the town walls is observed. However, the nature of this distinction and the mechanism of social control are not fully understood. Signs of territorial control, represented by the construction of the large defense wall, indicate the imposition of centralized control by the end of this period. The labor force mobilized for such massive construction and the impact it had on the local society are questions to be further explored.

Settlement Patterns in the Warring States Period

Residential remains, consisting of features such as houses, kilns, wells, and storage pits, have been excavated in the Warring States component at NJB and DXZ (Ren Xianghong, Li Yuting, and Wang Jianguo 1993, 48–79; Xu Ji 1995). Cemeteries have been excavated at Nülangshan (NLS; Li Yuexun 1993a, 1993b), Wuyingshan (WYS; Liu Guifang 1954; Jin Lu'an 1980), WTGZ (Liu Yanchang and Ning Yintang 1996, 43), Gaozhuang-cun (GZC; CXEC 1992, 420). Isolated elite burials have been reported at Zuojiawa (ZJW; Liu Shanyi and Wang Huiming 1995), Qianfoshan (QFS; Li Xiaofeng and Yin Peiyang 1991), Tianqiao (TQ; Yu Zhonghang 1997), and Gangxin (GX; Luo Xunzhang 1980) (see figure 7.5).

The presence of kilns, coins, and potter's tools at NJB and DPLC indicates a close association of monetary exchange and craft production. Among these sites, DPLC had the most categories of material dealing with long-distance trade, state control, and craft production during the contemporary period. The presence of coin molds for casting coins indicates efforts for facilitating taxation and market exchange. The combination of these functions at DPLC suggests that it emerged as a center for craft production and trade in the Warring States period.

Signs of state administrative control of production and exchange are evident from pottery bearing seals of state agencies. A volume measurement container found at DXZ in 1939 has the stamp of *shi* ("market"), which stands for the state market-control agency and indicates that the state of Qi was imposing a standard measurement system on the region

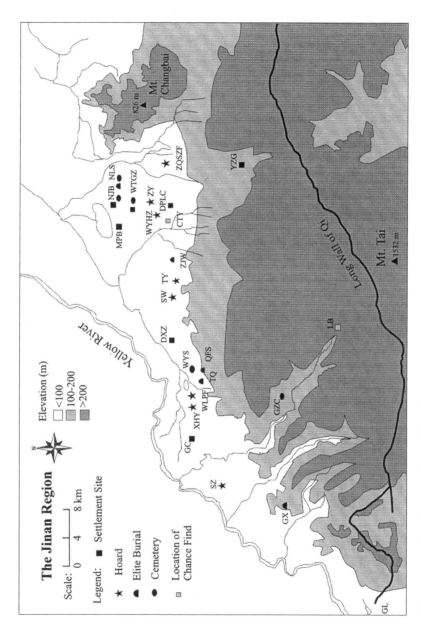

Figure 7.5 Distribution of sites from the Warring States period

(Yu Zhonghang 1997; Qiu Xigui 1980). Numerous potsherds from *dou* stemmed plates collected at Mapengbei (MBP) and DPLC were stamped with seals bearing place names and the terms *li* ("block"), and *lizheng* ("block supervisor"; Liu Boqin and Sun Liang 1995, 308; Zheng Tongxiu and Yuan Ming 1997).

According to historical accounts, li, a community of up to one hundred households, was the basic administrative unit for controlling the populace by the time of regional states and empires in the first millennium BC (Tu Cheng-sheng 1990, 110). Organized by residential rather than kinship affiliations, these community blocks formed the basic unit for providing taxation, corvée labor, and military service (Tu Cheng-sheng 1990, 104–26). In case of violation of law, all members of the community, particularly the lizheng, would shoulder the legal responsibilities. Some of these community units were potters' communities, which specialized in pottery production (Qiu Xigui 1980. 288). According to contemporaneous regulations, only state-registered craftsmen, who had a tax obligation to the state, could formally engage in commerce and craft production (Li 1985, 470). The presence of pottery stamped with seals identifying the municipal affiliation of the craftsmen and their supervisors at MPB and DPLC indicates that the local communities had been involved in state-controlled production or traded in pottery vessels from state-controlled manufacture.

Currency is a new category of archaeology data of this period, indicating an important development in taxation and trade. Coin hoards have been found at Sunzhuang (SZ), Xiheyai (XHY), Wulipaifang (WLPF), Shenwu (SW), Tangye (TY), Wangyahouzhuang (WYHZ), Zaoyuan (ZY; Zhu Huo 1972), and Zhangqiushizhengfu (ZQSZF; Ning Yintang 1994, 137). Fragments of coins have also been reported at CTY, NJB, and DPLC (Fu Ssu-nien et al. 1934, 89; Ren Xianghong, Li Yuting, and Wang Jianguo 1993; Zheng Tongxiu and Yuan Ming 1997).

The inventory of the bronze coins found at the settlement sites and hoards suggest that the local community maintained extensive trade connections with major Qi cities to the east and the state of Yan and its adjacent areas north of Jinan. Most coins were issued by the state of Qi, including several types of inscribed large knife coins and three types of round coins. Names of several Qi cities were represented on the coins, such as Jimo, Ju, and Anyang (Zheng Tongxiu and Yuan Ming 1997, 159; Zhu Huo 1984, 105; Li 1985, 391). Information from these hoards reveals that Qi state currency played a dominant role in the local economy during the late Warring States period. Comparison between spatial distribution of Qi coins and textual description of Qi territory has revealed that Qi currency was centrally manufactured in the Qi heartland and rarely circulated beyond the Qi state boundary (Yu Zhonghang 1996a). Further, Zhu Huo (1984) has demonstrated that the spatial pattern of coin hoards roughly coincides with the major trade routes in historical accounts.

Small knife coins from the TY hoard and a fragment of a small knife coin found at CTY were probably made locally because the ceramic molds for this type of coin have been reported from DPLC and other parts of Shandong (Song Baichuan 1991; Zheng Tongxiu and Yuan Ming 1997, 159; Yu Zhonghang and Song Baichuan 1998, 382). Except for a stylistic distinction in its inscription, these small knife coins are virtually indistinguishable from the arch-backed small knife coins minted in the state of Yan (Zhu Huo 1984, 149–55; Li 1985, 389). The circulation of these small knife coins in the Qi-Yan border region and Zhongshan territory is indicated by their presence in large money hoards unearthed at Xiaojialou (XJL) in Cangzhou and at Dongchengnancun (DCNC) in Lingshou (TCACR 1973; Gao Yingmin 1982). This indicates that the regional economy was once part of a large monetary network encompassing the Yan, Zhongshan, and Qi territory by the mid–Warring States period (Sun Jingming 1991). The absence of inscribed bronze cowries and stamped gold plate, which were circulating in large volumes south of the region, indicates minimal monetary transaction with the southern economy dominated by the state of Chu (Kong Fanyin 1982; Zhu Huo 1984, 211, 317; Li 1985, 393).

Finally, the discovery of two bronze weapons commissioned by historical figures enables us to make a possible link between archaeological remains and specific historical events. A fragment of a bronze spearhead bearing the inscription *Yanwang Zhi* ("King Zhi of Yan") has been unearthed at Liubu (LB) with unspecified provenance (Yu Zhonghang 1996b, 124). A bronze *ge*-halberd commissioned by the same king for his royal guard was also found in scrap metal collected from the Jinan area (Yu Zhonghang 1996b, 124–25). Using historical documents and the spatial distribution of weapons made by this very person, scholars have convincingly demonstrated that these weapons were left in the Qi territory during the military expedition between 284 and 279 BC under King Zhi of Yan (Zhang Zhenze 1973, 244; Shi Yongshi 1982; Yu Zhonghang 1996b). This presents direct evidence of intensive military confrontation that the local society had witnessed in the late Warring States period and adds a political dimension to the economic interaction represented by the distribution of currency.

Settlement Patterns in the Qin and Western Han Period

Two large walled towns emerged during this period, indicating more intensive urban development. In the western part of the plain area, Ren Xianghong (1997) reported a large walled-town site at Luchengwa (LCW; figure 7.6), submerged under heavy sedimentation from the Yellow River. It features a relatively square layout with a north-south orientation. The rammed-earth wall measures approximately two kilometers on each side. Although Han architecture remains have been found in the bottom of modern wells within the enclosed area, few artifacts remain on the surface because of sedimentation. Ren Xianghong (1997, 12) located the remains of a large specialized workshop for manufacture of roof tiles and wall bricks at Chujicun (CJC), immediately north of the walled town. A large number of Han burials have been reported in the current river channel of the Nadashahe River south of the town wall.

In the eastern part of the plain, data from several surface collections at the walled town site of DPLC have been reported (Wu Chinting 1930; Ning Yintang 1994; Zheng Tongxiu and Yuan Ming 1997). The site also has a square-shaped layout with a north-south orientation. The rammed-earth wall measures 1.9 kilometers on each side. The width of the wall measures twenty-four meters at top and forty meters at the base. The remaining sections of the wall still stand one to five meters high. Archaeological reconnaissance in 1975 reported a large volume of Han remains and identified traces of gates and roads (Zheng Tongxiu and Yuan Ming 1997, 154).

Surface survey reported areas of craft production for iron, currency, and pottery. Iron workshops are recorded in the southwest quarter of the city and outside the city wall, indicated by a concentration of charcoal, ash, iron ore, and debris from iron smelting spread over an area of two hundred meters on each side (Yang Huiqing and Shi Bensan 1955; ZXEC 1992, 535; Zheng Tongxiu and Yuan Ming 1997, 154, 181). A pottery production area with a concentration of kilns was reported north of the iron production area (Ning Yintang 1994, 80; Zheng Tongxiu and Yuan Ming 1997, 154). Fragments of soapstone molds for several types of *banliang* and *wuzhu* coins were also recorded in the city (figure 7.7; Wu Chin-ting 1930, 480; Zheng Tongxiu and Yuan Ming 1997, 167). The

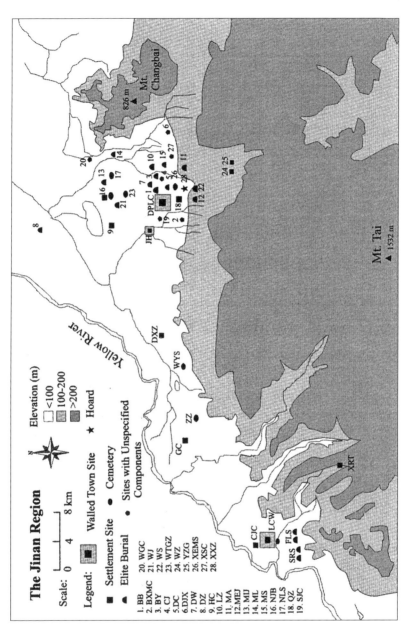

The Jinan Region

Scale: 0   4   8 km

Legend:
■ Settlement Site   ● Cemetery
▲ Elite Burial   • Sites with Unspecified Components

Elevation (m)
□ <100
▨ 100–200
▨ >200
★ Hoard

■ Walled Town Site

1. BB
2. BXMC
3. BY
4. CJ
5. DC
6. DJX
7. DW
8. DZ
9. HC
10. LZ
11. MA
12. MEJ
13. MIJ
14. ML
15. MS
16. NJB
17. NLS
18. QZ
19. SJC
20. WGC
21. WJ
22. WS
23. WTGZ
24. WZ
25. YZG
26. XEMS
27. XSC
28. XXZ

Yellow River

Mt. Changbai ▲ 826 m

Mt. Tai ▲ 1532 m

Figure 7.6 Distribution of sites from the Qin and Western Han period

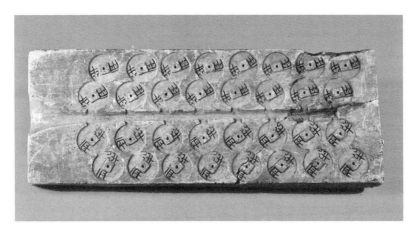

Figure 7.7 Han soapstone mold for banliang coin, from Pingling (DPLC). Photograph courtesy of Zheng Tongxiu, Shandong Provincial Institute of Archaeology.

variety of coins represented by the molds indicates that the local mint was engaged in production of currency for an extended period.

Architectural remains and a full range of artifacts associated with urban life were reported from the DPLC survey. Architectural remains include stone column bases, earthenware sewage pipes, roof tiles, decorated bricks, and roof ends decorated with various motifs or inscriptions of auspicious phrases: *qianqiu wansui* ("forever glorious") and *wansui fugui* ("forever conspicuous"; figure 7.8). In the northwestern area of the town, locally known as *dianjidi* ("palatial foundation"), the presence of a rammed-earth foundation, possibly for a large palatial structure, has been reported. Artifacts associated with this area include large quantities of decorated floor bricks, roof tiles, and column bases.

Ceramics include various types of pottery vessels for food preparation and consumption, spindle whorls, toy figurines, and fragments of molds for stack-casting iron hoes. Besides soapstone coin molds, stone artifacts also include mortars and grinding stones. Bronze artifacts include fittings for the sunshades on chariots, belt hooks, mirrors, seals, coins, and arrowheads with iron stems (Ning Yintang 1994, 81; Zheng Tongxiu and Yuan Ming 1997, 163–65). Iron artifacts were found in great abundance. They include cast-iron molds for casting iron implements and a wide variety of finished iron implements for craft production, agriculture, warfare, transportation, and domestic life (figure 7.9; Zheng

Figure 7.8 Han roof tile bearing the inscription "wansui fugui," from Pingling (DPLC) site. Photograph courtesy of Zheng Tongxiu, Shandong Provincial Institute of Archaeology.

Tongxiu and Yuan Ming 1997, 169–81; Ning Yintang 1994, 80). The wide range of agricultural activities associated with iron implements, such as plowing, weeding, and harvesting, suggests that iron had been used in the full range of subsistence production.

Metallurgical analysis shows that a variety of iron-working techniques had been employed in the iron artifacts from DPLC, including forging, quench-hardening, heat treatment, and decarbonization, which produced high-grade steel and durable malleable cast iron (Zheng Tongxiu and Yuan Ming 1997, 181). The techniques employed, particularly the use of blast furnaces, ceramic stacked-up molds, and cast-iron molds for iron casting, clearly indicate mass production of metal implements. The presence of malleable cast iron at DPLC, which involved a lengthy heat treatment up to 1,000 degrees (C) for improving the mechanical properties of cast iron, indicates that the technology for the manufacture of inexpensive and durable iron products had been adopted in the local workshops (Wagner 1993, 338). The use of blast furnaces for iron cast-

Figure 7.9 Han iron mold for casting plow, from Pingling (DPLC) site. Photograph courtesy of Zheng Tongxiu, Shandong Provincial Institute of Archaeology.

ing and sophisticated heat-treatment techniques placed high demand on the wood supply, implying a new pattern for the interaction between the local economy and the regional environment.

Some iron artifacts from DPLC have cast inscriptions (Zheng Tongxiu and Yuan Ming 1997, 183). A single-character inscription possibly representing a family name for the owner of a privately operated iron workshop is found on a set of cast-iron molds for casting plowshares and on four finished plowshares. A cast-iron mold for casting iron hammers bears a two-character inscription, *Tai'er* ("Tai 2"), which combines the initial for the government-operated iron workshop in the Taishan commandery south of the region with a serial number (figure 7.10). The introduction of finished cast-iron molds from another state workshop to the local production is a sign of a higher level of specialization in the large network of state-controlled craft production.

Evidence for monetary exchange, elaborate elite residences, and craft production represents vibrant urban life at regional centers. Elite burial mounds are distributed in the hinterland of the two walled towns, indicating the political prominence of these centers. Mass production of iron agricultural implements at regional centers indicates closer economic integration between these urban centers and their hinterland. The presence of iron products bearing the initial of the imperial monopoly agency indicates that the imperial state was once engaged in production and distribution of iron items in Jinan and its adjacent regions. The

Figure 7.10   Han cast-iron hammer mold bearing the inscription "Tai'er," from Pingling (DPLC) site. Photograph courtesy of Zheng Tongxiu, Shandong Provincial Institute of Archaeology.

diversity of bronze and iron artifacts at DPLC and NJB, as well as the virtual absence of polished stone tools at these sites, suggests metal was used in most aspects of daily life at the basic level of local society.

A smaller Han settlement site with a rammed-earth wall has been reported at Juhe (JH) (Fu Ssu-nien et al. 1934). The remains of other Han walled settlements were also identified at Gucheng (GC), Huicun (HC), and Wenzu (WZ; Ning Yintang 1994, 44). These small town sites, however, have not been investigated archaeologically. Little information is known for other sites. Molds for the banliang coins of the early Western Han as well as weapons have been reported at Yeizhangou (YZG; ZXEC 1992, 537). In addition, stone molds for casting the small banliang coins were reported in Zhangqiu without specific locality (Yu Zhonghang and Song Baichuan 1998, 386).

A coin hoard containing Qin-style banliang round coins and Qi round coins has been reported at Xixingzhuang (XXZ) (Ning Yintang

1994, 137). This hoard is the only Qin remains among the available data. The apparent decline of hoarding activities in the Qin-Han period may be the result of a decline of social unrest in the region under the imperial governance. Nevertheless, the XXZ hoard reveals that the standardization of currency in Qin as a key transition in the monetary system of ancient China was not rigidly implemented locally, as coins from both Qi and imperial Qin were present in the hoard (Ning Yintang 1994, 137).

The presence of coin production at DPLC and sites beyond the regional center, such as YZG along the trade route going through the mountainous area, suggests that more communities were involved in monetary exchange as the monetary economy increased in intensity. Historical accounts suggest that the local production of coinage flourished until 113 BC, when the imperial mint at Shanglinyuan, the imperial park, was given the monopoly to mint wuzhu coins (He Chuanfen 1998). Therefore, economic powers at the regional and local level might have been involved in the local production of banliang coins (circa 221 to 118 BC) and some types of wuzhu (first issued in 118 BC). The presence of molds for two versions of banliang coins with significant difference in their sizes and two types of wuzhu coins with stylistic differences in inscriptions indicates that the local mints were coping with various imperial monetary reforms in the historical accounts for achieving a national standard (Peng Xinwei 1958). Local production of imperial currency suggests that the local economy was closely integrated into the imperial economy through trade and taxation.

Historically, iron production went through a similar transition from local operation to imperial monopoly in 118 BC. As both the family name of a private owner and the initial of the imperial workshop have been found on cast-iron molds from DPLC, clearly both have been involved in the production at different times. Archaeologically, it is difficult to identify who controlled the coin production and to what extent the local authority was involved in the iron production at a specific time. Further, it is not clear if changes in national economic policies were uniformly implemented locally as described in most Chinese histories.

Mortuary Patterns

Mortuary patterns emphasize the changing nature of ritual expression in burials as well as the markers of wealth, status, and political authority. The strong tendency for certain types of vessels to appear in grave goods as a set expresses certain views of the afterlife (Chang 1973). The function and, in some cases, the symbolic meaning of artifact types can be known from historical sources, especially in categories of food vessels. A significant shift in the pattern of the ritual assemblage can indicate the transformation of concepts about the passage to the afterlife.[2]

Vessel types are grouped in three general categories by function: food vessels, beverage vessels, and washing vessels. Food vessels were used for preparation, storage, and presentation of cereal, meat, and vegetable dishes. For instance, the *ding* and li tripods were used for stewing and serving meat, the *yan* and *zeng* steamers for steaming grain, dou for serving meat and vegetable dishes, and *dui, zhou, fu,* and gui for serving cereal food. Beverage vessels were used for storing and serving water and wine, which include the *bei* cups, the *hu* and *lei* bottle-like containers, and the *weng* urns. Hand-washing vessels include the *yi* ewers for pouring water and the *pan* basins for receiving water. They were used in the hand-washing ritual associated with dining, which involves two persons to assist the wash (Ma Chengyuan 1988, 272; Sun Ji 1991, 259).

Some vessel types were perceived to embody greater symbolic significance than others. According to the textual account and bronze inscriptions, the ding tripod was the most important vessel type for feasting and offering sacrifices in ancestor ritual (Ma Chengyuan 1988, 84). These activities served to consolidate political authority and kinship solidarity. These vessels and the codified food-serving practices associated with them were among prominent status markers in the burial ritual of Zhou elites, particularly *lieding*, a set of ding tripods of different sizes forming a series in grave furnishings (Li 1985, 461).

Although this study uses the presence of ritual bronze vessels as a defining attribute of elite status, status markers were not restricted to it. Historical accounts from the late first millennium BC offer a fragmented recollection of the Zhou institutions for the representation of rank hierarchy with appropriate ritual assemblage, nested coffins, and other symbolism. For instance, the sovereign ruler was given nine ding tripods and eight gui cereal food containers as a ritual set. Aristocrats of lower ranks, such as *qingdaifu* (ministers) and *yuanshi* (knights), used the same ritual assemblage with a descending number of vessels in each vessel type. The presence of both textual and archaeological sources enables inference about the social hierarchy observed in burial analysis (Pearson et al. 1989). Since the exact correlation between each rank and the ritual assemblage associated with it varies from text to text (Li 1985, 462; Li Yuexun 1993b, 146), I primarily use textual information to identify relative status differentiation among elites without linking them to specific ranks in various textual accounts. I discriminate, more crudely than might be desired, between elites and commoners based on the presence or absence of ritual assemblages in tombs, although there were certainly many gradations between royal princes and tenant farmers.

The Western Zhou Period

Inscribed bronzes from different graves (M1, M2, and M3) identify XRT as the lineage cemetery for the ruling lineage of the Si polity (Ren Xianghong 1998, 30). A basic set of ding tripods as cooking and serving vessels for meat and vegetables, and fu or gui as a serving vessel for cereal food, form the basis of the grave goods assemblage in elite burials. Remains of fish and chicken were found in the bronze ding tripod and cereal food was found in the fu. The inscriptions on the fu suggest that Zhao, an elite person of the ruling lineage at the Si polity, made it for his mother, presumably the deceased, as a container for cereal food.

The deceased were all buried in two layers of nested coffins. Based on his observation of the bronze collection gathered from the damaged M1, Ren Xianghong (1998, 29) suggests that it probably had a set of five ding and four gui. M2 and M3 both have a rank-defining set of two ding and two fu from the excavation. These indicate that the deceased at XRT belonged to two different ranks in the Zhou hierarchy. The inscription on the bronze vessel indicates that the elite status associated with the deceased derived from a direct kinship affiliation with the ruling lineage of the local polity.

Among the commoners from NJB and DXZ (Ren Xianghong, Li Yuting, and Wang Jianguo 1993; Xu Ji 1995), a ritual assemblage is not visible due to the small sample. Collectively, activities of food stewing (represented by li tripods), meat and vegetable serving (dou stemmed plates), cereal food serving (bo bowls and gui cereal food containers), and food storage (guan jars) are represented. Despite difference in material, many vessel types are shared by elites and commoners, such as li, dou, gui, and guan, indicating a similarity in the basic food vessel assemblage. The ding tripods, however, appear to be exclusive to elite persons. No metal objects were associated with the commoners.

The Spring and Autumn Period

Three elite burials (M4, M5, and M6) have been excavated at the XRT cemetery, which was continuously used by the same lineage from the

Western Zhou period (Ren Xianghong 1998). Grave goods from an elite burial have been reported at BCG (Zhu Huo 1973, 64; Li 1985, 143). A commoners' cemetery excavated at NJB was spatially clustered in two groups, which probably represent two lineages (Ren Xianghong, Li Yuting, and Wang Jianguo 1993).

At the XRT cemetery, three elite ranks were represented. The deceased in M6, a male elite, was furnished with a rank-defining set of nine ding tripods and eight gui cereal food containers among a display of bronze vessels. The lieding set indicates that the deceased was given the highest status for the local area in the idealized Zhou hierarchy. The deceased in M5, a female elite, was furnished with a rank-defining set of three ding tripods and two dui cereal food containers. A rank-defining set of five ding and four gui was reported from M4. The status difference among these burials is further expressed through the number of nested coffins. For instance, while M6 used four layers of nested coffins, M4 and M5 had only two. The elite status for the deceased at BCG is expressed through a basic set of one bronze ding tripod and one gui.

At NJB, a ritual assemblage of pottery vessels containing one li, one guan, one *yu* (food container), and two dou is repeatedly represented in grave goods. This set represents the basic activities of food preparation, presentation, and storage. These vessel types were also frequently represented in contemporaneous elite burials. These vessels, particularly the tripods, were often used for ancestral ritual and communal feasting for the lineage. It could be argued that the fabric of kinship cohesion was strongly emphasized among the local lineages at NJB in the passage to afterlife. On the other hand, the ding tripod, cereal food containers (gui, dui, zhou), and the vessel set for the hand-washing ritual, including pan basin and yi ewer, appear to be exclusive to elites. These vessel types indicate a metropolitan lifestyle associated with elaborate dining and related rituals.

Political authority is characterized by the categories of items exclusive to the elite. In addition to bronze vessels, the two deceased in M5 and M6 at XRT were furnished with chariots, ritual jades, weapons, and musical instruments (Cui Dayong and Ren Xianghong 1998, 14–24). These indicate that coercive force and a command of ritual knowledge were emphasized as attributes that define elite status (Chang 1983). These were further emphasized by the fact that metal was used exclusively for artifacts associated with these functions.

No direct evidence of control from a higher level of political authority can be found in the contemporary grave goods, such as official title or rank that would attribute the deceased to social identities associated with a larger political hierarchy. Instead, the rank expression at burial XRT-M6, with the nine-lieding set, suggests the highest level of authority was the local political structure. Because M4, M5, and M6 at XRT were all members of the same lineage, which had been using the cemetery since the late Western Zhou period, it is clear that local political authority at XRT was lineage based and had remained stable for an extended period of several centuries.

The inscriptions on bronze vessels from XRT and BCG suggest active elite interaction with political powers lying beyond the region. The inscription on a bronze gui from the BCG burial indicates that the cereal food container was commissioned by Bodafu, a member of the ruling lineage of the Lu state, for his youngest daughter Jian as her dowry, wishing her a life of "perpetual longevity" (Zhu Huo 1973, 64). Inscribed dowry bronzes made by Bodafu for his two elder daughters, Jiang and Yu, had been discovered previously (Li 1985, 143). Similarly, the inscription on a bronze pan basin from XRT-M5 reveals that the washing basin was commissioned by Dian, a member of the ruling lineage of the Si polity, for a female elite, presumably the deceased, married in from a Jiang lineage (Fang Hui and Cui Dayong 1998, 23). Fang Hui (1998, 62) argues that the elite female probably came from the state of Qi, which was ruled by the Jiang lineage until 391 BC, which indicates that marriage alliances among elite lineages were an important form of interregional interaction in this period.

In contrast to the elite burials, a minimum expression of wealth and status difference can be observed in the two clusters of commoners' burials at NJB. Among all sixteen burials, the majority used one coffin and only one used two. Hair accessories made of bone are the only personal ornaments associated with the deceased. No metal goods have been found in association with commoners at NJB.

The Warring States Period

Excavations of elite burials of the Warring States period have been reported at NLS-M1 and GX, ZJW, QFS, and TQ (Liu Shanyi and Wang Huiming 1995; Li Yuexun 1993b; Li Xiaofeng 1991; Li Xiaofeng and Yin Peiyang 1991; Luo Xunzhang 1980). Each elite burial suffered loss of information to some extent. For instance, both NLS-M1 and GX were looted in antiquity. The grave goods in a storage chamber in NLS-M1 were plundered in the Han period. For GX, only the grave goods in a storage pit survived. Commoners' burials have been reported at NJB, NLS, WYS, and WTGZ (Ren Xianghong, Li Yuting, and Wang Jianguo 1993; Liu Yanchang and Ning Yintang 1996; Liu Guifang 1954).

Looting and deterioration of organic material, such as lacquerware, made it difficult to pinpoint exactly which types of vessels were present in the original assemblage of the elite burials. However, when we compare the vessel types of the elite with the intact miniature vessel set associated with the five female retainers at NLS-M1, a basic set for elite life (consisting of ding, dou, hu, pan, yi, and zhou) starts to emerge. These vessels represent activities of food serving and the hand-washing ritual associated with dining, showing a continuum of the lifestyle associated with the elite in the Spring and Autumn period.

The general assemblage of vessel types for commoners' burials closely resembles that of the elite burials, such as the serving vessels for meat and vegetables of ding and dou, serving vessels for cereal food of dui and zhou, general food storage vessels of guan, and hand-washing vessels of pan and yi. The similarity in food vessel types used by elite and commoners indicates a continuum in lifestyle from elite to at least some commoners. For instance, the new additions to the inventory of commoners' pottery vessels, such as ding, zhou, dui, pan, and yi, all have their bronze counterparts in the elite burials of the contemporary period and the earlier period. This shift may indicate an emulation of a metropolitan lifestyle associated with the elite life in Zhou centers, which is characterized by elaborate dining with feasting vessels and hand-washing rituals associated with dining.

Evidence revealed in elite burials of the Warring States period collectively suggests the presence of a more complex political structure with greater status differentiation, increasing occupational specialization, and uneven distribution of wealth. The extraordinary size and the nature of artifacts in the GX burial represent the presence of paramount leadership within the region. The GX burial once had a rammed-earth mound of 6.8 meters in height and 60 meters in diameter. Under the mound, the grave pit measures 46.8 meters in length and 34.8 meters in width at ground level and 7.5 meters in depth. The sheer scale of this burial mound rivals the mausoleums of the contemporaneous Qi kings located in the hinterland of Linzi (Luo Xunzhang 1997; Yu Zhonghang 1999).

Among a small number of artifacts that survived the plunder, including bronze ritual vessels, a crossbow belt, and chariot accessories, a set of bronze fittings for a ceremonial "conference tent" stands out as a distinctive status marker for the deceased. The conference tent was described as *weiwo* in contemporaneous textual accounts, which was used by rulers on occasions of meeting, military campaign, and religious ceremony (Luo Xunzhang 1980, 331). Although it is impossible to speculate on the full spectrum of political power from the surviving grave goods, this special item suggests the deceased was attributed with a central position in decision making.

The deceased at NLS-M1 held a rank of high nobility defined by a set of five lieding tripods. The burial pit measures 13 meters long, 12.6 meters wide, and 3.3 meters deep, which is significantly smaller than the GX burial. The deceased, an elderly male, was buried in three nested coffins furnished with bronze ritual vessels, weapons, chariot accessories, ritual jades, musical instruments, and personal ornaments (Li Yuexun 1993b, 146). A dismembered sacrificial human offering and five female retainers in individually furnished burials were found associated with the main chamber. The occupation of the deceased as a military specialist was redundantly emphasized with a large quantity of weapons placed in the burial. Archaeologists have speculated that the deceased was a renowned Qi general, after whom the county was named (Li Yuexun 1993b).

The elite burials at ZJW, TQ, and QFS represent those with modest status, as no more than three bronze ding tripods have been reported in each burial. Both ZJW and QFS have bronze weapons, representing military affiliation. QFS burials also have a collection of 136 small arch-backed knife coins, similar to the molds found at DPLC and in the ZY hoard. The deceased at TQ was probably a low-ranked elite involved in the administration of taxation and trade, indicated by the presence of a standard measurement container stamped with the seal of a state market-control agency. Evidence for administrative control of exchange from TQ and QFS reveals that some sector of the local population was engaged in state-regulated commercial transaction at such a frequency that they considered the new economic order applicable to the realm of afterlife.

Among the commoners' burials of the Warring States period, personal belongings other than pottery vessels include weapons, clothing accessories, and implements of daily life. In general, commoners' grave goods increased in quantity and variety in comparison with previous periods. Over a fifth of burials had weapons, including bronze and iron weapons, and soft metal imitations. The fact that weapons, real or imitation, were repeatedly emphasized and redundantly displayed in burials of both elite and commoners suggests that weapons were no longer exclusive to elites. Non-elites not only had access but also advertised their military achievements because war was an important source of social mobility. Further, half the burials included metal items. Evidence of iron in forms of agricultural implements and weapons has been found in burials of both elites and commoners. These indicate the extended access to metal by the local population.

The Western Han Period

Commoners' burials of the Western Han period have been excavated at WYS (JCM 1972), NJB (Ren Xianghong, Li Yuting, and Wang Jianguo 1993), WTGZ (Liu Yanchang and Ning Yintang 1996), and NLS (Li Yue-xun 1993a). These burials were modest in size, normally two to three meters in length. The majority of furnished Han commoners' graves contained either a guan storage jar or hu bottle for food and beverage. The consistency of this convention in cemeteries spanning over two centuries suggests a high level of homogeneity in the death ritual among the commoners. The use of these two forms of vessels seems to represent the most basic need of an individual, rather than a family, in the passage to afterlife.

Tomb M1 at Shuangrushan (SRS) of the early first century BC remains the only Western Han elite burial that has been extensively reported (Ren Xianghong and Cui Dayong 1997). The grave pit of SRS-M1 was dug into the peak of a small hill and had a ramp approximately 60 meters long (Ren Xianghong 1997). The rammed-earth mound over M1 was 12 meters high and 65 meters long on each side of its square base. Its chamber is 25 meters long, 24.3 meters wide, and 22 meters deep. The construction would have required enormous labor investment, indicating that supreme power, status, and wealth was attributed to the deceased, who was buried in five nested coffins. Expressions of political authority and status include a rank-defining set of nine bronze ding tripods. Other expressions of status and wealth include ritual jade disks, a jade mask, a set of jade body plugs, jade ornaments, chariots, wagons, and bronze and iron weapons.

A broad range of vessel types, including ding, hu, *fang* (wine container), pan, *jian* (deep basin), *pen* (basin), and guan for the storage and serving of food and wine were featured. In addition, a large quantity of lacquer food containers has been reported. Due to deterioration of lacquerware, vessel types are unspecified. Ritual vessel types used by the elite of the previous period, such as bronze ding tripods, were still important symbols of elite power, which suggests that kinship cohesion was strongly emphasized as an important source of power in burial ritual.

Bronze currency and gold were represented in SRS-M1. The presence of twenty gold ingots inscribed with the titles *wang* ("king"), Qi, and *Qiwang* ("the king of Qi") suggests an emphasis on this new form of wealth used for elite transaction. The kingdom of Qi refers to the powerful semiautonomous state governed by the lineage of Prince Liu Fei. Bronze *wuzhu* coins were also found. The occurrence of inscribed gold ingots, bronze currency, and the burial itself reveals the presence of three sources of political power at the national (Han), macroregional (Qi kingdom), and local level, which were ultimately defined and consolidated by the kinship ties of the Han royal lineage.

Based on historical account, Ren Xianghong (1997, 14) identifies the deceased as the last king of the Jibei kingdom, who was forced to commit suicide by the imperial court after the failed Rebellion of the Seven Kingdoms in 87 BC. The capital of the Jibei kingdom was the city of Lucheng, which was the site of Luchengwa described previously. One burial mound of similar scale has been reported at SRS and another pair at Fulushan (FLS) close by, which probably buried other kings and their spouses. Recent excavation of a dozen storage pits for grave offerings surrounding a large elite burial mound at Luozhuang (LZ) near DPLC produced horse chariots, chime bell sets, ritual bronze vessels, gold pieces, and lacquerware inscribed by the royal house of the Qi kingdom, suggesting that the burial probably belonged to a ruler of DPLC, once a major city of the Qi kingdom and the capital of the Jinan kingdom. These burials at SRS, FLS, and LZ represent remains of the highest level of regional authority in the early decades of the Han empire, which contested rigorously with the power of the imperial government that is less visible archaeologically at a regional scale.

In commoners' burials, personal items included iron daggers, bronze coins, bronze seals, carved bone ornaments, bronze belt hooks, and bronze mirrors. Metal objects were found in more than half of the commoners' burials. Unlike the previous period, bronze coins were associated with both elites and commoners, and a significant portion of commoners placed money in burials, even those of children.

In general, the local grave goods assemblage of the Western Han period is characterized by a wide gap between elites and commoners in regard to wealth and social activities. Elaborate vessel types for feasting became exclusive to the elite. This indicates that some aspects of social life were deployed by the elites in their passage to the afterlife, whereas this was not the case for commoners. On the other hand, a continuum in the representation of imperial coins is observed for both elite and commoners' burials.

Toward an Integrated History

A comparative examination of patterns of change in local political structure, settlements, economy, and technology, and in changes in burial ritual allows us to infer how people in Jinan responded to their new circumstances during the first millennium BC. During the first half of the millennium, low frequency of bronze agricultural implements and the absence of casting molds for them in archaeological sites indicate limited use of metal tools in subsistence production. The use of metal (bronze) was first reserved for warfare and ritual artifacts, such as arrowheads, knives, and ritual items. The prominence of nonmetallic implements in settlements of the Western Zhou and the Spring and Autumn periods, such as TY and XRT, suggests a continuum of a Neolithic tool assemblage in local life during the late Bronze Age. In the representation of technology in burial ritual, bronze was exclusive to elite burials. Metal objects were not featured in any commoners' burials. This is consistent with the low frequency of metal artifacts associated with subsistence production in settlement data.

Inscriptions on bronze vessels from contemporary burials indicate that political authority in these communities was characterized by local elite lineages with limited territorial claim. For instance, the XRT cemetery was continuously used by the ruling elites of the Si polity for over two centuries, but the political influence of Si did not reach beyond the vicinity of the XRT area. The local elite interacted with their counterparts in other regions through marriage alliances, as elite women from the states of Lu and possibly Qi married into the local communities (as stated in the bronze inscriptions from elite burials at BCG and XRT). These two superpowers may have extended their political influence over the regional society indirectly through these informal alliances.

The intensity of elite interaction is represented by conformity to the general rules of symbolism in the Zhou political sphere. The elites at XRT carried various ranks in the Zhou hierarchy as indicated by the lieding sets found in their burials, which included the status of a sovereign ruler at XRT-M6. This represents a local manifestation of the ranked and kinship-based Zhou political structure. The elite status expressed in local burials, such as in the case of XRT-M6, suggests a high level of local autonomy and no signs of subordination to any greater political authority. This evidence indicates that the local elite ignored or denied the relationship of dominance and subordination, if it existed in reality, through their burial rituals.

In furnishing their graves, both elite and commoners stressed the continuity of the fabric of kinship solidarity into the afterlife by placing food and vessels for sacrifice and feasting in burials. At NJB, consistent representation of a vessel set in two clusters of burials, possibly representing two lineages, indicates a strong shared tradition in regard to the passage to the afterlife among members of these two corporate groups. While elites used all the vessel types found in commoners' graves, they used additional vessel types, such as the ding tripod and the vessel set for hand-washing rituals, which represented a metropolitan lifestyle of the Zhou elite. Categories of objects exclusive to elite burials, such as weapons, musical instruments, ritual bronze vessels, and chariots, indicate that authority was defined by coercive power, ritual knowledge, and kinship solidarity.

After the mid-first millennium BC, significant change took place in the settlement data. The construction of a regional wall in the late Spring and Autumn period indicates restrictive access to the region and the emergence of regional powers at either side of the wall capable of engaging in military competition at an immense scale. Many social implications associated with this dramatic change came to be archaeologically observable during the Warring States period, when the transformation of economic and political structure took place within the local society. The presence of currency, state-issued standard measurement containers, and pottery manufactured under state control in different parts of the region suggests that the local economy was being increasingly incorporated into a larger, centrally managed economic structure, and many aspects of local life were affected by and engaged in it. The emergence of territorial and administrative control by a centralized authority as seen, even today, in the fragments of a monumental wall, stands as a testimony of Qi purposiveness, which presaged the construction of the defense walls in the neighboring states and of the Great Wall(s) on the northern frontier by the Qin-Han empires of the late first millennium BC (or earlier, see Di Cosmo 1999, 2002).

The concentration of pottery production, coinage, and other signs of market exchange at the site of DPLC indicates the growth of urban life in the region. The growing importance of the plains may have been stimulated by the increasing scale of the economy and political control, since all major sites and coin hoards are located along the route of transportation connecting the central plain and the heartland of Qi territory (Zhu Huo 1972).

The pattern of interregional interaction shifted from marriage alliances and shared symbolism to evidence of direct administrative control and intensified economic interaction. The inventory of currency found locally suggests intensive economic interaction with the northern and eastern regions associated with the states of Yan and Qi. This exchange became an underlying force for increasing economic integration that operated side by side with increasing militarism. Therefore, the invasion of Yan King Zhi in the early third century BC, which has left inscribed weapons in the region, could not have been independent of the economic interrelations, since the two regions were already using a common currency in the preceding centuries. Similarly, the increasing economic integration in the form of monetary exchange preceded the political unification of Qin and the Qin policy of standardizing currency in 221 BC.

Presence of artifacts used in state-regulated trade in elite burials, such as coins found in the QFS burial site and the standard measurement container at TQ, probably represents a perceived extension of state-defined economic order in the representation of the afterlife. Despite their prominence in hoards and settlement finds, the large knife coins from the state of Qi were absent in contemporaneous burials, and the pattern is consistent across the Qi territory (Zhang Guangming 1991). Yu Jiafang (1990, 1991) postulates that the state may have set a high face value for this currency, which was primarily used for taxation; people chose not to carry it across boundaries beyond which the state power was perceived to be ineffective. As a result, the large Qi knife coin was found neither beyond the Qi border nor in the realm of the afterlife. The inconsistency in frequency of currency found in hoards and in burials suggests that the majority of the local population did not perceive this new form of wealth as negotiable in the afterlife. Neither did they recognize that the economic order defined by the centralized authority continued to be effective in the afterlife. On the other hand, the small knife coins, as common currency with full metal value, were traded across multiple state boundaries and occasionally placed in burials.

Information from elite burials offers a glimpse of the paramount political authority in the region, represented by the sheer scale of the burial construction and symbolic significance of the artifacts found in the elite burial at GX. A shift from a ranked status within a lineage-based polity to an elite of specialized occupation as well as ranked status is also evident. For instance, military power was emphasized with a display of weapons at NLS-M1. The representation of a high but not sovereign status with a lieding tripod indicates subordination to higher authority within or beyond the regional border. Localized, lineage-based political authority at XRT, which characterized the traditional political structure in the region, ceased to exist after the mid-first millennium BC.

The expression of militarism among the local population, represented by weapons in both commoners' and elite burials, is consistent with the pattern of military confrontation observed in the settlement pattern and historical record. Vessel types once exclusive to the elite were found in the commoners' assemblage. This continuum in lifestyle suggests the emulation of a metropolitan lifestyle by the commoners. In addition, a general increase of wealth in commoners' burials and the disproportional distribution of this wealth suggest a high social mobility for this period, which may be based on military achievement.

The use of bronze expanded from the ritual and military spheres to the realm of trade and personal ornamentation for commoners. Bronze objects were no longer exclusive to elite burials, indicating increasing access to products of specialized manufacture among the local population. However, the presence of metal currency in several settlement sites and hoards indicates expanded metal use in local life. The widespread signs of metal currency, as well as the local production of it, indicate not only an increasing intensity in economic interaction, but also a shift in the way that the economy was controlled and organized.

Iron first appeared in the region during this period primarily as agricultural implements and weapons. The presence of iron in both elite and commoner burials indicates that the new metal was made accessible to the public. It is difficult to estimate the extent that metal implements were used in subsistence economy from settlement data, but the decrease of Neolithic tool assemblage in contemporaneous archaeological context is clearly notable.

In general, settlement and burial data both demonstrate that as centralized control of territorial states intensified in the context of intense interstate competition, a series of significant changes took place in people's relationships with each other and with the local landscape. Local people were mobilized for military campaigns, and new technologies were actively promoted to increase their performance in warfare and production.

The last two centuries witnessed the emergence of imperial involvement in the most rudimentary levels of local life. In the mountains, the regional defense structures, such as walls and garrisons, were deserted, unlike those in the northern frontier of the empire, which were connected and expanded (Ye Xiaoyan 1987; Di Cosmo 2002). When we look slightly beyond the ruins of the Long Wall to the peak of the Tai mountain range, the remains of imperial pilgrimages represent the transformation of the mountain from a military frontier into a religious landscape promoting an imperial cosmology.

Signs of full-blown urban life and monetary economy were evident. Two large walled-town sites, specialized workshops for craft production, and elite burial mounds are located along a transportation route. This is consistent with the macroregional pattern, where state workshops were incorporated into imperial road networks to facilitate control (Hsü 1980). The level of specialization in craft production at DPLC indicates that a sizable portion of the local population was involved in mining, logging, smelting, casting, and transportation. Further, supplying local iron production with mass-produced molds from another state workshop in the adjacent region, which is a frequent practice among Han iron workshops, was probably a centrally coordinated strategy for increasing efficiency in production (Li Jinghua 1997). These indicate that regional economics was increasingly integrated into a centrally managed imperial economy that cut across regional boundaries.

Major trends in technology include increased mass production of iron agricultural and craft tools with methods such as combination molds for casting a large number of products simultaneously, blast furnaces for cast iron, and various methods of heat treatment for improving the physical property of cast-iron products. Productivity was further enhanced by the increase in scale and specialization of workshops. Iron agricultural implements, as well as iron weapons, were found in relative abundance in regional centers, such as DPLC, as well as in rural communities, such as NJB. They include plowing, weeding, and harvesting tools, indicating that iron technology had successfully replaced nonmetal implements in essential aspects of subsistence production. Consistent with the pattern of mass production and redistribution in settlement data, metal objects of mass production, such as bronze mirrors, belt hooks, and coins, increased in commoners' burials, indicating that products of specialized manufacture became accessible to the commoners, and items obtained from exchange and craft production, rather than produced by a household, became an essential part of daily life.

For elite burials at SRS, elaborate vessels for feasting and sacrifice were redundantly displayed, often with inscribed royal titles, emphasizing the kinship solidarity of the royal lineage. The basis of elite kinship as a source of political authority shifted from membership in localized elite lineage at XRT to membership in the royal lineage at SRS, suggesting an increasing centralization in political organization. The claim of sovereign status with the rank-defining set of nine ding tripods and the enormous construction effort at SRS expressed a high level of political autonomy at the regional level in the realm of imperial order. In addition, sheer wealth, in the form of gold ingots for elite transaction, had emerged as a distinctive expression of elite power.

In contrast, commoners' burials show a significant shift from the metropolitan lifestyle; they did not emulate the elite lifestyle in their burial ritual. The frequency of burials containing weapons declined dramatically as did the inventory of grave goods. Absent from commoners' grave goods are ding tripods and vessels associated with elaborate dining. These indicate a shift away from the representation of lineage solidarity and the high social mobility associated with militarism that we observed during the preceding period.

Despite the homogenous expression of lifestyle, objects representing state-regulated transactions, such as bronze coins and seals, became evident in commoners' burials. Since coins ultimately depended on the authority of the ruler, increasing use of currency in market transactions brought the local life closer to the state-controlled economic network (Lewis 1999, 33). The use of coins in burials indicates that the economic order defined by the centralized authority became incorporated into the representation of the afterlife. The emphasis on money in burials probably represents the ritual acknowledgement of money as an important asset of "daily life" in the world after death, indicating a local response to the increasing reliance on currency in the domains of taxation and salary in the society of imperial order (Peng Xinwei 1958, 70). For instance, in the imperial Han tax system, the commoners were taxed at a rate of ¹⁄₁₅ of their harvest. In addition, every adult (between age fifteen and sixty) was taxed 120 coins (An Zuozhang 1993, 26). The practice of using money as grave goods seems to represent the perceived continuity of the state-regulated economy into the afterlife.

Using both archaeological and historical sources, Tu Cheng-sheng

(1990) and Lewis (1990) argue that the action of the ruling elite to maximize resources directly at their disposal for interregional competition was the underlying force for increasing centralization. As the intensity of competition shifted from ritualized chariot elite combat to large-scale, infantry-based warfare, the ruling elite gave land to peasants, who were attached to the aristocrats as members of cadet lineages, in exchange for their military service. The expansion of military duty from aristocrats to rural peasantry culminated in universal military service and a "complete identification of the people with the army" (Lewis 1990, 94). In this process, the traditional structure of lineage-based authority was deliberately undermined by new means of economic and political control aimed at building a direct connection between the state rulers and their subjects. In a nutshell, interregional competition for dominance and hegemony was the underlying force for the reorganization of political structure and economy, which brought intended and unintended consequences to society, such as the emergence of a new small-landholding peasantry class as providers of military recruits, corvée labor, and agricultural surplus to the centralized state.

These sociopolitical changes, as well as the new demands and opportunities emerging from them, altered considerably the fabric of local life. The change in land tenure offers valuable insight to understanding the process of technological and economic change. Despite the central place that metal (bronze) held in symbolizing political authority in the first half of the millennium, metal was not widely used in subsistence production until the rise of the centralized state and iron production after the mid-first millennium BC, which marks a final breakaway from the Neolithic mode of production. The relative cheapness of iron and its greater hardness have been offered as explanation for its replacement of bronze. However, these properties were the result of technological innovations for mass production and quality control, which neither came with the introduction of iron technology nor emerged spontaneously with long-term experience of iron handling (Wagner 1993, 409).

What were the social forces underlying the attempts to overcome the technological obstacles for mass production of metal objects, such as items for personal consumption, exchange, and subsistence production, as seen in DPLC? A plausible interpretation lies in the changing social conditions deriving from changes in social structure, which promoted elite-sponsored mass production of currency and agricultural implements as well as the active adoption of these specialized manufactured items by commoners for exchange and subsistence production.

The creation of a small-landholding peasantry class as a result of centralized control of the populace encouraged the adoption of technological innovations in agriculture, as the commoners were allowed partial access to their own produce (Hsü 1980). The centralized state, on the other hand, encouraged agricultural production, and in turn received taxes to finance its capital projects and wars of expansion (Bray 1979–1980, 5).

As a result, metal objects for daily consumption, which came in both iron and bronze, were mass produced in workshops operated by the state or merchants and were increasingly used among local people. The sequence of local trends observed from archaeological remains, particularly the decline of local lineage-based polities, emergence of large-scale defense projects that required massive mobilization of labor, and evidence for administrative control, high social mobility, and militarism, seems to support this interpretation. Economic controls were increasingly visible as commoners gained access to and then became dependent upon metal agricultural tools and currency. The increasing emphasis on currency in commoners' burial rituals indicates that producers had access to at least part of their agricultural produce and could store their value as money to increase their economic choices and fulfill their tax obligations. It further shows that the state-defined economic order had been incorporated into the worldview of the local people.

This archaeological study of Jinan in the first millennium BC has portrayed a local history as depicted by local people in the remnants of their lives and times as the region underwent transitions from local autonomy to the establishment of imperial control. Over a period of centuries, the decline of localized, lineage-based political authority, which characterized the local political structure before the mid-first millennium BC, was followed by an increase in the centralized control of territory, exchange, and production, and to some extent the subsistence economy. As Jinan entered into a larger political network, one observes in the material culture the increasing use of weaponry and militarism and more opportunities for social mobility due to the interregional nature of social interactions, especially in conflicts and commerce.

The landscape itself became altered through the monumental defensive walls, imposing burial mounds, workshops, and imperial towns along transportation routes. The mountain ranges became sites for the state defensive system, then for royal pilgrimage. The gradual introduction of metal as currency (compare Weber 1964; Wertime and Muhly 1980) marked the transition from prestige-goods economies and exchange among elites to market transactions (Barnes 1993, 149). The increasing use of iron tools in subsistence production and the state control associated with their production led to increasing integration between the local centers and their rural hinterland since the tools were mass produced in blast furnaces employing a dependent labor force and a system of distribution (Wagner 1993, 409).

The strong emphasis on kinship solidarity tended to resist inroads into social change. Throughout the millennium, the fabric of kinship was symbolically extended to the afterlife, as we see in the use of food vessels for communal feasting and ancestral rituals, particularly in elite burials. From the polities controlled by the Si ruling lineage to kingdoms controlled by members of the Han royal lineage, political authority was never fully imposed on the kinship network despite the shift toward centralized control in ways that the local people and economy were organized.

Against the deeply entrenched structures of kinship solidarity, changes in perceptions and values, such as were associated with the rise and decline of militarism and social mobility, can be observed in burial rituals. Greater variability and elaboration in tombs was expressed among commoners when the local society first became involved in regional (not simply local) networks. In contrast, less variability was observed among commoners following the increase of mass-produced objects in the imperial period, indicating a change toward representation of a homogenous lifestyle among commoners, a centrally imposed order in the perceptions about the afterlife. The strong emphasis on kinship solidarity among members of the royal lineage, however, suggests a different rate of change among elite. There was a tension within the political system, apparently, in which leaders attempted to use kinship ties among themselves to reinforce central power, while recognizing that kinship ties on lower social levels could be an obstacle for the implementation of centralized governance. The archaeological data show how—at least in some aspects—Jinan's entry into the Chinese imperial structures profoundly affected the lives of local persons and landscapes. The archaeologically derived social history complements the political narratives in the texts by revealing some of the most basic dimensions of human life.

Notes

This chapter was originally published in a slightly different form in the *Journal of the Economic and Social History of the Orient* 46 (1): 88–126. Copyright © 2003 by Brill Academic Publishers. Reprinted by permission.

1. The philosophical debates underlying this policy change have been covered by Nylan (1999, 2001). See also Lionel Jensen's *Manufacturing Confucianism* (1997). Policies adopted in "Confucian ideology" are those defended by "legalists" and opposed by *ru* in *Debates on Salt and Iron*; see, for example, Martin Powers 1991.

2. For imaginations of the afterlife in ancient China, see Michael Loewe (1982), Poo (1998), and Yü Ying-shih (1987).

Bibliography

An Zuozhang. 1993. *Shandong tongshi: Qin-Han juan* [A Comprehensive History of Shandong: Qin-Han]. Jinan: Shandong People's Publishing House.

Bagley, Robert. 1999. "Shang Archaeology." In *The Cambridge History of Ancient China: From the Origins of Civilization to 221 BC*, ed. M. Loewe and E. L. Shaughnessy, 124–31. Cambridge: Cambridge University Press.

Barker, Graeme. 1995. *A Mediterranean Valley: Landscape Archaeology and Annales History in the Biferno Valley*. London: Leicester University Press.

Barnes, Gina L. 1993. *China, Korea, and Japan: The Rise of Civilization in East Asia*. London: Thames and Hudson.

Bintliff, John. 1991. "The Contribution of an Annaliste/Structural History Approach to Archaeology." In *The Annales School and Archaeology*, ed. J. Bintliff, 1–33. Leicester, UK: Leicester University Press.

Braudel, Fernand. 1972. *The Mediterranean and the Mediterranean World in the Age of Philip II*. Vol 1. Trans. Sian Reynolds. New York: Harper and Row.

———. 1973. *The Mediterranean and the Mediterranean World in the Age of Philip II*. Vol 2. Trans. Sian Reynolds. New York: Harper and Row.

Bray, Francesca. 1979–1980. "Agricultural Technology and Agrarian Change in Han China." *Early China* 5:3–13.

Chang, Kwang-chih. 1973. "Food and Food Vessels in Ancient China." *Transactions of the New York Academy of Sciences* 35:495–520.

———. 1983. *Art, Myth, and Ritual: The Path to Political Authority in Ancient China*. Cambridge, Mass.: Harvard University Press.

———. 1986. *The Archaeology of Ancient China*. 4th ed. New Haven, Conn.: Yale University Press.

Chang Xingzhao and Ning Yintang. 1989. "Shandong Zhangqiu chutu qingtongqi xuyao jiantan xiangguan wenti" [A Brief Overview of Bronzes Excavated in Zhangqiu, Shandong, with a Discussion on Related Questions]. *Wenwu* 6:66–72.

Chavannes, E. 1910. *Le T'ai Chan: Essai de Monographie d'un Culte Chinois*. Paris: Ernest Leroux.

———. 1913. *Mission Archaéologigue dans la Chine Septentrionale*. 13 vols. Paris: Imprimerie Nationale.

Chen Xingcan. 1997. *Zhongguo Shiqian Kaogu Xueshi Yanjiu 1895–1949* [History of Prehistoric Archaeology in China, 1895–1949]. Beijing: Sanlian Shudian.

Collingwood, R. G., and J. Myres. 1936. *Roman Britain and the English Settlements.* Oxford: Oxford University Press.

Cui Dayong and Ren Xianghong. 1998. "Shandong Changqingxian Xianrentai Zhou-dai mudi" [A Zhou-Dynasty Cemetery at the Xianrentai Site in Changqing County, Shandong]. *Kaogu* 9:11–25.

CXEC [*Changqing Xianzhi* Editorial Committee]. 1992. *Changqing Xianzhi* [The County Gazetteer of Changqing]. Jinan: Jinan Publishing House.

Di Cosmo, Nicola. 1999. "The Northern Frontier in Pre-Imperial China." In *The Cambridge History of Ancient China: From the Origins of Civilization to 221 BC,* ed. M. Loewe and E. L. Shaughnessy, 885–966. Cambridge: Cambridge University Press.

———. 2002. *Ancient China and its Enemies: The Rise of Nomadic Power in East Asian History.* Cambridge: Cambridge University Press.

von Falkenhausen, Lothar. 1993. "On the Historiographical Orientation of Chinese Archaeology." *Antiquity* 67 (257): 839–49.

———. 1999. "The Waning of the Bronze Age: Material Culture and Social Developments, 770–481 BC." In *The Cambridge History of Ancient China: From the Origins of Civilization to 221 BC,* ed. M. Loewe and E. L. Shaughnessy, 450–544. Cambridge: Cambridge University Press.

Fang Hui. 1998. "Sigong Dian pan ming kaoshi" [A Study of the Inscription on the Bronze *Pan* Basin by Gong Dian of Si]. *Wenwu* 9:62–63.

Fang Hui and Cui Dayong. 1998. "Changqing Xianrentai wuhaomu fajue jianbao" [A Preliminary Report on the Excavation of Tomb Number Five at the Xianrentai Site in Changqing]. *Wenwu* 9:18–30.

Fu Ssu-nien, Li Chi, Tung Tso-pin, Liang Ssu-yung, Wu Chin-ting, Kuo Pao-chun, and Liu Yu-hsia. 1934. *Cheng-tzu-yai* [Chengziyai: The Black Pottery Culture Site at Longshanzhen in Lichengxian, Shandong Province]. Nanjing: Institute of History and Philology, Academia Sinica.

Gao Yingmin. 1982. "Hebei Lingshouxian chutu Zhanguo qianbi" [Warring States Coins Discovered in Lingshou County, Hebei]. In *Kaogu*, vol. 2, ed. Kaoguxue Jikan, 83–92. Beijing: Chinese Social Science Press.

He Chuanfen. 1998. "Hanchu Shandong de zhuqianye ji xiangguan wenti yanjiu" [On the Coinage Industry in Shandong during the Early Han Period]. *Zhongguo Qianbi* 2:24–28.

Hodder, Ian. 1991. *Reading the Past.* 2nd ed. Cambridge: Cambridge University Press.

———. 1999. *The Archaeological Process: An Introduction.* Malden, Mass.: Blackwell.

Hou Renzhi. 1979. "Ziboshi zhuyao chengshi de qiyuan yu fazhan" [The Origin and

Development of the Major Towns in Zibo City]. In *Lishi Dili Xue de Lilun yu Shi-jian*, ed. Hou Renzhi, 336–88. Shanghai: Shanghai People's Press.

Hsü, Cho-yün. 1965. *Ancient China in Transition: An Analysis of Social Mobility, 722–222 BC*. Stanford, Calif.: Stanford University Press.

———. 1980. *Han Agriculture: The Formation of Early Chinese Agrarian Economy, 206 BC–AD 220*. Seattle: University of Washington Press.

JCM [Jinan City Museum]. 1972. "Shitan Jinan Wuyingshan chutude Xihan yuewu, zaiji, yanyin taoyong" [Tentative Discussion of the Western Han Dancing/Sing-ing, Acrobatic, and Feasting Effigies Unearthed at Wuyingshan, Jinan]. *Wenwu* 5:19–24.

Jensen, Lionel M. 1997. *Manufacturing Confucianism: Chinese Traditions and Univer-sal Civilization*. Durham: Duke University Press.

Jin Lu'an. 1980. "Jinan Wuyingshan faxian taoguanzang" [An Urn Burial found at Wuyingshan in Jinan]. *Wenwu* 12:92.

Kern, Martin. 2000. *The Stele Inscriptions of Ch'in Shih-huang: Text and Ritual in Early Chinese Imperial Representation*. New Haven, Conn.: American Oriental Society.

Kong Fanyin. 1982. "Qufu Dongdachengcun faxian yipi yibiqian" [A Hoard of In-scribed Bronze Cowry Found at Dongdachengcun in Qufu]. *Wenwu* 3:92.

Lao Kan. 1935. "Liang Han junguo mianji zhi guji ji koushu cengjian zhi tuice" [Population and Geography in the Two Han Dynasties]. *Guoli Zhongyang Yan-jiuyuan Lishi Yuyan Yanjiusuo Jikan* 5 (2): 215–40.

Lewis, Mark Edward. 1990. *Sanctioned Violence in Early China*. Albany: State Uni-versity of New York Press.

———. 1999. *Writing and Authority in Early China*. Albany: State University of New York Press.

Li, Xueqin. 1985. *Eastern Zhou and Qin Civilizations*. Trans. K. C. Chang. New Haven, Conn.: Yale University Press.

Li Jinghua. 1997. "Dui Chang'ancheng yezhu yizhi de jianbao tan jidian yijian" [Some Comments on the Report of Foundry Remains at Chang'an]. *Huaxia Kaogu* 4:86–88.

Li Xiaofeng. 1991. "Jinan Chaiyoujichang chutu de Ming daohuo" [A *Ming* Knife Coin Excavated at the Jinan Diesel Engine Factory]. In supplement to *Shandong Jinrong Yanjiu*, ed. Pang Yuqin, Song Baichuan, and He Chuanfen, 104–10. Jinan: Shandong Society of Finance and Institute of Finance for Shandong Branch of People's Bank of China.

Li Xiaofeng and Yin Peiyang. 1991. "Jinan Qianfoshan Zhanguo mu" [A Warring States Tomb at Qianfoshan in Jinan]. *Kaogu* 9:813–17.

Li Yuexun. 1993a. "Zhangqiu Nülangshan Zhanguo Handai mudi fajue baogao" [Report on the Excavation of the Warring States and Han Cemetery at the Nülang-shan Site in Zhangqiu]. In *Jiqing Gaoji Gonglu Zhangqiu Gongduan Kaogu Fajue Baogaoji*, ed. Shandong Institute of Archaeology, 150–78. Jinan: Qilu Publishing House.

———. 1993b. "Zhangqiu Xiuhui Nülangshan yihao Zhangguo damu fajue baogao" [Report on the Excavation of Tomb Number One of the Warring States Period at the Nülangshan Site in Xiuhui, Zhangqiu]. In *Jiqing Gaoji Gonglu Zhangqiu Gongduan Kaogu Fajue Baogaoji*, Shandong Institute of Archaeology, 115–49. Jinan: Qilu Publishing House.

Liu, Li. 1996. "Settlement Patterns, Chiefdom Variability, and the Development of Early States in North China." *Journal of Anthropological Archaeology* 15:237–88.

Liu Boqin and Sun Liang. 1995. "Shandong Zhangqiu Mapengbei yizhi diaocha jian-bao" [Report of the Survey of the Mapengbei Site in Zhangqiu, Jinan]. *Kaogu* 4:305–11.

Liu Guifang. 1954. "Shandongsheng wenguanhui zai Jinan shijiao qinglila wuzuo Zhangguo shidai muzang" [Five Warring States Period Tombs Excavated by the Shandong Provincial Committee for Administration of Cultural Resources]. *Wenwu Cankao Ziliao* 7:156.

Liu Shanyi and Wang Huiming. 1995. "Shandong Jinanshi Zuojiawa chutu Zhanguo qingtongqi" [Bronze Vessels of the Warring States Period Discovered at Zuojiawa in Jinan, Shandong]. *Kaogu* 3:209–13, 225.

Liu Yanchang and Ning Yintang. 1996. "Shandong Zhangqiushi Wangtuiguanzhuang yizhi fajue baogao" [Report on the Excavation at the Wangtuiguanzhuang Site in Zhangqiu City, Shandong]. *Huaxia Kaogu* 4:27–51.

Loewe, Michael. 1982. *Chinese Ideas of Life and Death: Faith, Myth and Reason in the Han Period (202 BC–AD 220)*. London: G. Allen & Unwin.

Lu Zongyuan, ed. 1998. *Qi Changcheng* [The Long Wall of Qi]. Jinan: Shandong Friendship Press.

Luo Xunzhang. 1980. "Shandong Changqing Gangxin Zhanguo mu" [The Warring State Tomb at Gangxin in Changqing, Shandong]. *Kaogu* 4:325–32.

———. 1993. "Zhangqiu Longshanzhen fujin de shuidao gucheng ji xiangguan wenti" [River Channels and Ancient Towns near the Town of Longshan in Zhang-qiu]. In *Jinian Chengziyai Yizhi Fajue Liushi Zhounian Guoji Xueshu Taolunhui Wenji*, ed. Zhang Xuehai and Wang Shuming, 305–13. Jinan: Qilu Publishing House.

———. 1997. "Tian-Qi wangling chutan" [A Preliminary Study of the Mausoleums of Qi Kings of the Tian Lineage]. In *Zhongguo Kaogu Xuehui Dijiuci Nianhui Lunwenji*, Archaeological Society of China, 251–62. Beijing: Wenwu Publishing House.

Luo Zhewen. 1961. "Xiaotangshan Guoshimu shici" [The Stone Offering Shrine of Guo's Tomb at Xiaotangshan]. *Wenwu* 4–5:44–51.

Ma Chengyuan, ed. 1988. *Zhongguo qingtongqi* [Chinese Bronzes]. Shanghai: Shanghai Guji Publishing House.

McGuire, Randall H. 1992. *A Marxist Archaeology*. San Diego: Academic Press.

Ning Yintang. 1994. *Zhangqiu Wenwu Huikao* [Cultural Relics of Zhangqiu]. Jinan: Jinan Publishing House.

Nylan, Michael. 1999. "A Problematic Model: The Han 'Orthodox Synthesis,' Then and Now." In *Imagining Boundaries: Changing Confucian Doctrines, Texts, and Hermeneutics*, ed. Kai-wing Chow, On-cho Ng, and John B. Henderson, 17–56. Albany: State University of New York Press.

———. 2001. *The Five "Confucian" Classics*. New Haven, Conn.: Yale University Press.

Pearson, Richard. 1981. "Social Complexity in Chinese Coastal Neolithic Sites." *Science* 213:1078–86.

———. 1996–97. "Ritual Vessel Sets and their Spatial Arrangements in the Hsi-hsiahou and Ta-wen-k'ou Neolithic Sites, Shan-tung." In *Ancient Chinese and Southeast Asian Bronze Age Cultures*. 2 vols., ed. F. D. Bulbeck, 641–52. Taipei: SMC.

Pearson, Richard J., Jong-wook Lee, Wonyoung Koh, and Anne Underhill. 1989. "Social Ranking in the Kingdom of Old Silla Korea: Analysis of Burials." *Journal of Anthropological Archaeology* 8(1): 1–50.

Peng Xinwei. 1958. *Zhongguo Huobishi* [The Monetary History of China]. Shanghai: Shanghai People's Publishing House.

Poo, Mu-chou. 1998. *In Search of Personal Welfare: A View of Ancient Chinese Religion*. Albany: State University of New York Press.

Powers, Martin Joseph. 1991. *Art and Political Expression in Early China*. New Haven, Conn.: Yale University Press.

Qiu Xigui. 1980. "Zhanguo wenzizhong de 'shi'" [The Chinese Character for "Market" in the Warring States Period]. *Kaogu Xuebao* 3:285–96.

Ren Xianghong. 1997. "Shuangrushan yihao Hanmu muzhu kaolüe" [A Study on the Identity of the Deceased in the Han Tomb No. 1 at Shuangrushan]. *Kaogu* 3:10–15.

———. 1998. "Shandong Changqing Xianrentai Zhoudai mudi ji xiangguan wenti chutan" [A Preliminary Study of the Zhou Cemetery at the Xianrentai Site in Changqing, Shandong and Related Questions]. *Kaogu* 9:26–35.

Ren Xianghong and Cui Dayong. 1997. "Shandong Changqingxian Shuangrushan yihao Hanmu fajue jianbao" [Preliminary Report on the Excavation of Han Tomb No. 1 at the Shuangrushan Site in Changqing County, Shandong]. *Kaogu* 3:1–9, 26.

———. 1998. "Shandong Changqingxian Xianrentai yizhi fajue jianbao" [Report on the Excavation at the Xianrentai Site in Changqing County, Shandong]. *Kaogu* 9:1–10.

Ren Xianghong, Li Yuting, and Wang Jianguo. 1993. "Zhangqiu Ningjiabu yizhi fajue baogao" [Report on the Excavation of the Ningjiabu Site in Zhangqiu]. In *Jiqing Gaoji Gonglu Zhangqiu Gongduan Kaogu Fajue Baogaoji*, ed. Shandong Institute of Archaeology, 1–114. Jinan: Qilu Publishing House.

Sahlins, Marshall. 1985. *Islands of History*. Chicago: University of Chicago Press.

Shi Yongshi. 1982. "Yan Xiadu di 23 hao yizhi chutu yipi tongge" [The Bronze *ge*-halberds Excavated at Site No.23 in Xiadu of Yan]. *Wenwu* 8:42–50.

Snodgrass, Anthony. 1991. "Structural History and Classical Archaeology." In *The Annales School and Archaeology*, ed. J. Bintliff, 57–72. Leicester, UK: Leicester University Press.

Song Baichuan. 1991. "Qi mingdao shulüe" [On the *ming* Knife Coin of Qi]. In Supplement to *Shandong Jinrong Yanjiu*, ed. Pang Yuqin, Song Baichuan, and He Chuanfen, 117–26. Jinan: Shandong Society of Finance and Institute of Finance for Shandong Branch of People's Bank of China.

SPIA. Shandong Provincial Institute of Archaeology. 1998. "Shandong faxian baqiannianqian juzhi juluo" [A Settlement Site from 8,000 BC Excavated in Shandong]. *Zhongguo Wenwubao* No.6, Jan. 21.

Sun Bo. 1999. Personal Communication.

Sun Ji. 1991. *Handai Wuzhi Wenhua Ziliao Tushuo* [An Illustrated Catalogue of Han Material Culture]. Beijing: Wenwu Publishing House.

Sun Jingming. 1991. "Shilun huan Bohai diqu kaoguxue wenhua de daobi" [On Knife Coins from Archaeological Cultures of the Bohai Rim]. In Supplement to *Shandong Jinrong Yanjiu*, ed. Pang Yuqin, Song Baichuan, and He Chuanfen, 62–73. Jinan: Shandong Society of Finance and Institute of Finance for Shandong Branch of People's Bank of China.

———. 1998. "Qi, Lu huobi wenhua bijiao yanjiu" [A comparative study of the monetary systems of Qi and Lu]. *Zhongguo Qianbi* 2:19–23, 47.

TCACR. Tianjin City Administration of Cultural Resources. 1973. "Hebei Cangxian Xiaojialou chutu de daobi" [Knife Coins Excavated at the Xiaojialou Site in Cangxian, Hebei]. *Kaogu* 1:35–41.

Tu Cheng-sheng. 1990. *Bianhuqimin: Chuantong Zhengzhi Shehui Jiegou zhi Xingcheng* [State Registered Peasantry: The Formation of the 'Traditional Sociopolitical Structure']. Taipei: Lien-ching.

Underhill, A. 1993. "Variation in Settlements during the Longshan Period of Northern China." *Asian Perspectives* 33 (2): 197–228.

Wagner, Donald B. 1993. *Iron and Steel in Ancient China*. Leiden, Netherlands: Brill.

Waley, Arthur, trans. 1937. *The Book of Songs: The Ancient Chinese Classic of Poetry*. London: G. Allen & Unwin.

Wang, Zhongshu. 1982. *Han Civilization*. Trans. K. C. Chang. New Haven, Conn.: Yale University Press.

Wang Shougong. 1995. "Lubei diqu zaoqi xinshiqi wenhua de faxian yu renshi" [The Discovery and Understanding of the Early Neolithic Remains in Northern Shandong]. *Huaxia Kaogu* 2:41–54.

Wang Sili. 1957. "Dui Daxinzhuang caiji de xiaoxing qingtong ju de yijian" [Comments on a Small Bronze Saw Collected from the Daxinzhuang Site]. *Wenwu* 12:60.

Wang Xiantang. 1979. "Shandong Zhoudai de Qi changcheng" [The Zhou-dynasty Long Wall of Qi in Shandong]. *Shehui Kexue Zhanxian* 4:193–203.

Weber, Max. 1964. *The Religion of China*. Trans. Hans H. Gerth. New York: Free Press.

Wertime, T. A., and J. D. Muhly, eds. 1980. *The Coming of the Age of Iron*. New Haven, Conn.: Yale University Press.

Wilkinson, E. P. 2000. *Chinese History: A Manual*. Cambridge, Mass.: Harvard University Asia Center for the Harvard-Yenching Institute.

Wolf, Eric. 1982. *Europe and the People without History*. Berkeley: University of California Press.

Wu Chin-ting. 1930. "Pingling fanggu ji" [Description of an Archaeological Trip to Pingling]. *Guoli Zhongyang Yanjiuyuan Lishi Yuyan yanjiusuo jikan* 1 (4): 471–88.

Xu Ji. 1995. 1984 nian qiu Jinan Daxinzhuang yizhi shijue shuyao [Preliminary Report on the Excavation at the Daxinzhuang Site in Jinan during the Fall of 1984]. *Wenwu* 6:12–27.

XZEC. *Xiuhui Zhenzhi* Editorial Committee. 1999. *Xiuhui Zhenzhi* [The municipal history of Xiuhui]. Draft.

Yan Wenming. 1997. "Longshan shidai chengzhi de chubu yanjiu" [A Preliminary Study of Walled Towns of the Longshan Period]. *Zhongguo Kaoguxue yu Lishixue ji Zhenghe Yanjiu*, 235–56. Taipei: Academia Sinica.

———. 1999. "Yi kaoguxue wei jichu quanfangwei yanjiu gudai wenming" [An Archaeologically Based, Integrated Approach to the Study of Ancient Civilizations]. *Gudai Wenming Yanjiu Tongxun* 1:9–12.

Yang Huiqing and Shi Bensan. 1955. "Shandong shifan xueyuan lishixi tongxue fu Dongpinglingcheng jinxing kaogu shixi" [Fieldwork at the Site of Dongpinglingcheng for the Students from the Department of History at Shandong Normal College]. *Kaogu Tongxun* 4:64–65.

Ye Xiaoyan. 1987. "Zhongguo zaoqi changcheng de tansuo yu cunyi" [An Investigation of Long Walls in Early China]. *Wenwu* 7:41–48.

Yu Jiafang. 1990. Personal Communication.

———. 1991. "Qi daobi yuanyuan zaikao" [A Reinvestigation of the Origin of Qi Knife Coins]. In Supplement to *Shandong Jinrong Yanjiu*, ed. Pang Yuqin, Song

Baichuan, and He Chuanfen, 41–49. Jinan: Shandong Society of Finance and Institute of Finance for Shandong Branch of People's Bank of China.

Yü Ying-Shih. 1987. "O Soul, Come Back!" A Study in the Changing Conceptions of
the Soul and Afterlife in Pre-Buddhist China. *Harvard Journal of Asiatic Studies*
47 (2): 363–95.

Yu Zhonghang. 1979. "Jinanshi faxian qingtong lihua" [A Bronze Ploughshare Found
in Jinan]. *Wenwu* 12:36.

———. 1983. "Yuanfeng liunian Yang Jinglüe deng fengshi Gaoli timingkao" [A
Study of the Inscription by the Imperial Embassy to Korea led by Liang Jinglue
in the Sixth Year of Yuanfeng Reign]. *Wenwu* 9:87–88.

———. 1996a. "Lun Qiguo qianfan" [On Coin Molds of the State of Qi]. *Zhongguo
Qianbi* 2:3–6.

———. 1996b. "Yanwang Zhi bingqin yu Zhaowang faqi" [Weapons of King Zhi of
Yan and the Invasion of Qi by the King of Zhao]. *Gugong wenwu yuekan* 154:124–
29.

———. 1997. "Shandong Jinanshi Tianqiao Zhanguomu de qingli" [The Excavation of a Warring States Tomb at the Tianqiao Site in Jinan, Shandong]. *Wenwu*
8:78–79.

———. 1999. Personal communication.

Yu Zhonghang and Song Baichuan. 1998. "Shandong suojian Xian-Qin Xihan qianfan yanjiu" [A Study of Coin Molds from the Pre-Qin and Western Han Periods
Found in Shandong]. In *Liu Dunyuan Xiansheng Jinian Wenji*, ed. Department
of Archaeology, Shandong University, 377–97. Jinan: Shandong University Press.

Zhang Guangming. 1991. "Qi daobi buxun wenti tanlüe" [A Preliminary Study on
the Absence of Qi Knife Coins in Burials]. In Supplement to *Shandong Jinrong
Yanjiu*, ed. Pang Yuqin, Song Baichuan, and He Chuanfen, 50–59. Jinan: Shang-
dong Society of Finance and Institute of Finance for Shandong Branch of People's
Bank of China.

Zhang Xuehai. 1993. "Qianyan" [Preface]. In *Jinian Chengziyai Yizhi Fajue Liushi
Zhounian Guoji Xueshu Taolunhui Wenji*, ed. Zhang Xuehai and Wang Shuming,
1–3. Jinan: Qilu Publishing House.

Zhang Zhenze. 1973. "Yanwang Zhi ge kaoshi" [Notes on the *ge*-halberd of King Zhi
of Yan]. *Kaogu* 4:244–46.

Zheng Tongxiu and Yuan Ming. 1997. "Shandong Zhangqiushi Han Dongpingling
gucheng yizhi diaocha" [The Reconnaissance at the Han City Site of Dongpingling in Zhangqiu City, Shandong]. In *Kaoguxue Jikan*, vol. 11, ed. Wang Zhongshu, 154–86. Beijing: Chinese Encyclopedia Press.

Zhu Huo. 1972. "Cong Shandong chutu de Qi bi kan Qiguo de shangye he jiaotong"
[A Study of Trade and the Transportation Network in the State of Qi Based on
the Distribution Pattern of Qi Currency]. *Wenwu* 5:55–59.

————. 1973. "Shandong Licheng chutu Lu Bodafu ying Jiji gui" [A Bronze *gui* for the Dowry of the Youngest Daughter of Lu Bodafu Discovered in Licheng, Shandong]. *Wenwu* 1:64.

————. 1984. *Guqian xintan* [A New Study of Numismatics]. Jinan: Qilu Publishing House.

Zou Yilin, ed. 1997. *Huang-Hua-Hai Pingyuan Lishi Dili* [The Historical Geography of the Huang-Huai-Hai Plain]. Hefei: Anhui Education Press.

ZXEC. *Zhangqiu Xianzhi* Editorial Committee. 1992. *Zhangqiu Xianzhi* [The County Gazetteer of Zhangqiu]. Jinan: Jinan Publishing House.

8

On the Use of Archaeology and History in Island Southeast Asia

PETER V. LAPE

The relationship between material and textual data sources in investigating past human cultures has long been an explicit concern for scholars. Since archaeologists are typically more likely than historians to collect and interpret both kinds of data in their raw forms, they have also been the source of most of the scholarship on the relationship between the two kinds of data. The use of archaeological and documentary data in Island Southeast Asia has had its own particular trajectory of scholarship. This history of scholarship has been defined, as in other regions, by the nature of archaeological sites and their accessibility to certain restricted groups of archaeologists, as well as the sources and availability of textual sources. This chapter is a review of these region-specific disciplinary paths, a description of the unique nature of textual and material evidence related to Island Southeast Asia, and a contextualization of the historical archaeology of the region in global scholarship.

Documents and Material Remains: Where Are We Now?

Archaeologists and historians have used a combination of documents and material remains to investigate and interpret the past since the beginnings of the disciplines. While these two types of data require different research methods, some scholars have developed the required skills to work with both. More typically, however, historians and archaeologists have relied on each other to do the initial data recovery and interpretation, and have worked with secondary sources for areas outside their particular disciplinary boundaries. The increasing specialization in academic scholarship has had the effect of further limiting the crossing of disciplinary boundaries. Few scholars who identify themselves as "archaeologists" can be found working in archives, and even fewer "historians" can be found excavating archaeological sites.

The development of "anthropological" archaeology in the United States and Europe has also contributed to this disciplinary split. While Classical archaeology is rooted in art history, and typically requires its practitioners to be well versed in the documentary record of the Classical world, anthropological archaeology began with a specific focus on the prehistory of nonliterate groups. The explicitly scientific and generalizing orientation of the New Archaeology of the 1960s largely rejected the "culture history" of earlier archaeology in favor of the investigation of cultural processes (Flannery 1972; Trigger 1989). One effect of this has been to both demand more time for training in natural scientific methods and de-emphasize the usefulness of written documents, with their specific and temporally narrow cultural data.

However, a cross current in anthropological archaeology was the simultaneous development of historical archaeology. While this subdiscipline has been subjected to varying definitions and restrictions by its self-identified practitioners (Andrén 1998; Schuyler 1978), most historical archaeologists see themselves as archaeologists first, who also use the texts written by or about the people whose past they are studying. The subdiscipline of historical archaeology (which can be viewed as a mosaic of other more specialized traditions, such as medieval archaeology, culture contact archaeology, colonial archaeology, etc.) has also had internal divisions that mirror those in anthropological archaeology, such as between an emphasis on culture history and process, science, postmodernism, and so forth (M. Hall 2000; Kirch and Sahlins 1992; Knapp 1992; Leone and Potter 1988; Lightfoot 1995; Orser 1996; Rogers and Wilson 1993; Schuyler 1988; South 1977).

Anthropological archaeology today incorporates all these historical trends, as well as some new attempts to move past their theoretical limitations. Both older culture history and more recent culture process orientations continue to be represented in the literature (with culture history perhaps more common in American historical archaeology and cultural resource management research). Some have called for a holistic approach that incorporates both particularistic studies and cross-cultural generalizing ones (Trigger 1984, 1989). Archaeologists have looked to historians who are sympathetic to generalizing approaches (such as those in the *Annales* school) for models of incorporating particularistic textual data into variable temporal scales typical of archaeological research (Bintliff 1991; Knapp 1992; Last 1995). Unfortunately, much of this attempt to integrate archaeology and history would appear to relegate archaeology solely to the *longue durée*, ignoring the potential relevance of archaeological data to shorter terms, or even events. However, they have highlighted the potential of long-term culture history to provide general conclusions that are applicable cross-culturally.

These myriad influences and cross currents, along with broader debates in the humanities and social sciences, have all influenced the ways scholars have used texts and material remains in combination. These influences have been analyzed extensively in other publications, some with book-length treatments, and I will not attempt to review them all here (Andrén 1998; Beaudry, Cook, and Mrozowski 1991; Bintliff 1991; Boyd, Erwin, and Hendrickson 2000; Faubion 1993; Kepecs 1997; Kirch and Sahlins 1992; Leone and Potter 1988; Lightfoot 1995; Schuyler 1978; Schuyler 1988; Trigger 1989; Young 1988). Another topic of concern that I will not attempt to review closely is the role of oral history, tradition, and myth in combination with archaeology (Kus 1997; McBride and Rudden 2000). However, I will discuss some currents of debate that appear to be most salient for the discussion of the use of texts and material remains in Island Southeast Asia. These include assigning the appropriate interpretive "weight" to each body of data and different strategies for combining the disparate data obtained from texts and material remains to create interpretations that transcend the individual limitations of each kind of data.

Assigning Interpretive Weight, Transcending Tyranny

The famous epitaph that historical archaeology is an expensive way to find out what we already know about the past sums up one critique of archaeological studies of periods from which we have written texts. Historical archaeologists typically see this statement as an example of a pervasive "tyranny of the text" in academic and popular culture (Champion 1990; Thurston 1997). They echo an earlier call by New Archaeologists for archaeology to free itself from misleading conclusions derived from culturally constructed history (Binford 1962; Clarke 1973). This view holds that western academic culture (which is populated by individuals who gain their authority and status largely from reading and writing texts) places too much emphasis on writing, and not enough on material objects. Euro-American culture in general often confuses writing for truth. In this view, we do not "already know" everything even if we have extensive texts, and archaeological data can provide an alternate point of view (Kirch and Sahlins 1992; Leone and Potter 1988). This alternate point of view has the potential, for example, to give a historical voice to those people traditionally missing from the documentary record: the colonized, the poor, the less educated, the illiterate, and "those of little note" (Ferguson 1992; Scott 1994). Archaeological data can therefore fill gaps in our knowledge, somehow making historical studies more "complete."

If we accept that archaeological data have a valuable contribution to make, we are still left with the problem of how to weigh these different types of evidence, particularly when they appear contradictory. On one side, some historical archaeologists (echoing both Binford and Foucault) claim that written sources, particularly those from colonial contexts, are ideologically tainted, and the archaeology of material culture provides the only portal to a nonideological "truth" (Rubertone 1989; Trouillot 1995). Others use textual data to construct hypotheses that can then be "tested" against archaeological data. This method allows for contradictions to be highlighted, which can often provide insights into the cultural production of texts. However, debate continues on how methodologically separated the two lines of evidence actually are in constructing "hypotheses" and "tests." Some types of data, such as inscriptions, actually fall between; they are both texts and artifacts, and require the use of both historical and archaeological methods (Morrison and Lycett 1997). Methodological separation is an important part of source criticism and remains an area of concern (Andrén 1998; Feinman 1997; Kowalewski 1997).

Beyond Artifacts and Texts

Although the process of assigning the appropriate weight and methodological status to textual versus material evidence remains unclear, what is clear is that the two kinds of evidence used together can provide more interpretive power than either used alone. For example, while archaeologists and historians worked separately on the problem of Danish state formation (AD 800–1050), they came up with different conclusions regarding the chronology and spatial extent of political integration. Thurston's study (1997) unified these previously contradictory models in a way that showed both to be "true"; discrepancies between the data mirrored actual conflicts during this period of social transformation to statehood. Others have used texts and materials to extend the dynamics of the "historical" period into the artificially static "prehistoric" past through analogy (Deagan 1988; Kolb 1997; Lightfoot 1995). This line of thinking is an important component of so-called "holistic," or interpretive, archaeology, which seeks to reintroduce culture history into archaeology, and at the same time introduce the longue durée into history, while incorporating theoretical or comparative perspectives.

The common themes linking much recent scholarship in historical archaeology, including that discussed above, are discussions of ways to move beyond the "tyranny of texts" and master narratives about the past, which are seen as lacking interpretive power to explain the incredible diversity of human responses to historical situations. For example, some archaeologists have called for a new historical archaeology that looks "back from the edge" (Funari, Jones, and Hall 1999). Among the many things that this means is the idea that it is possible to transcend the disciplinary oddities of American archaeology, such as those mentioned above, and consider local histories as framing narratives on an equal basis with European histories. For example, local histories need not be "about" the rise of capitalism and world systems, or the age of exploration, but rather can be seen as driven by local motives and situations, influenced in varying degrees by world events filtered through local actors. This approach can be seen as part of a larger movement to decentralize historical scholarship (Clarke and Torrence 2000; Cusick 1998b; Gosden 1999; Orser 1994; Rowlands 1998; Schmidt and Patterson 1995). A running theme in this movement is an attempt to shift control of the production of archaeological knowledge to local or indigenous people, and by doing so, make archaeological knowledge relevant to those people (Layton 1989; Miller 1980; Moser 1995).

History and Archaeology in Island Southeast Asia

Documentary and material data have long been used jointly to investigate Island Southeast Asia's past (Island Southeast Asia is considered here to include the nations of Indonesia, the Philippines, Singapore, insular Malaysia, and East Timor; see figure 8.1). Sir Thomas Raffles (1817), for example, used epigraphic references and descriptions of ancient monuments to create his *History of Java* in the early nineteenth century. Raffles' work inspired a new interest in the antiquity of the monumental architecture of Java and the excavation of several temple complexes and translation of their inscriptions. This work was done almost exclusively by European colonial scholars and administrators, and throughout the Dutch colonial period, history and archaeology in Indonesia were characterized by a colonialist perspective, which empha-

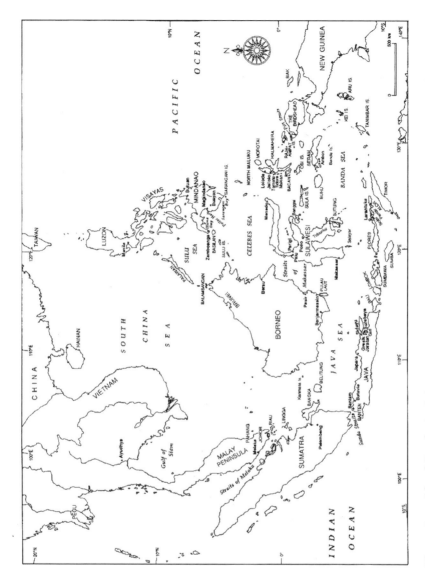

Figure 8.1 Island Southeast Asia

sized foreign "civilizing" influence (in this case primarily from India and the Arab world), and de-emphasized indigenous ingenuity (Tanudirjo 1995; Trigger 1989, 110–47). The colonialist approach was also evident in studies relying primarily on documentary data, despite the fact that some of the documents were evidently written by Indonesians (Schrieke 1960; Wisseman Christie 1995).

Historical and archaeological scholarship on Island Southeast Asia has also been influenced by western preconceptions about islands as isolated geographic spaces. While the "myth of the primitive isolate" (Terrell 1998) has not dominated scholarship to the degree it has in Oceana, it still shows up, particularly in eastern Indonesia, despite overwhelming evidence that these islands were a zone of particularly intensive cross-cultural interaction (Lape 2004).

A representative example of the changing uses of documents and material data to investigate the past in Island Southeast Asia is the evolving theories of the rise of "kingdoms" and other forms of complex polities. Archaeologists currently see the development of social complexity in the region, such as the development of chiefdoms and early states, as linked to the growing importance of maritime trade and resulting cultural influences and contacts from the outside world, primarily China and India after 500 BC (Wisseman Christie 1995). The earliest surviving written documents that describe Island Southeast Asia date to this period and include both texts written by "foreign" observers from China and India, and, later, "indigenous" texts, the earliest surviving examples being stone inscriptions. These texts definitively describe Island Southeast Asia as a zone of cross-cultural interaction (Lape 2003). As early as AD0, these documents strongly suggest that there were communities in Island Southeast Asia that were regularly visited by traders from distant places (Ray 1989; Rockhill 1915). Archaeologically, there is also definitive evidence of this interaction, including trade goods from mainland Asia and the subcontinent, and similarities in art and architectural styles, particularly with Hindu-Buddhist temple styles replicated in western Indonesia (Glover 1990).

While much historical and archaeological research in Island Southeast Asia has followed theoretical trends developed in other regions, there are some examples where the regional data has inspired theory building. One example is the ongoing debate on "Indianization." The traditional view has been that state formation in Indonesia required the import of people and ideas from India (Coedès 1968). Other theorists, such as van Leur (1967), proposed the then radical theory that Indonesians took an active role in the process of state formation, although even he still believed that the one-way transmission of ideas from India to Indonesia was an essential catalyst. More recently, and as more data from both India and Indonesia became available, some theorists have proposed a two-way exchange of ideas, technology, and personnel (Wolters 1999). Kulke (1990) proposes a "convergence hypothesis" that uses new data on state development in the Bay of Bengal region of India, which had the most direct contact with Island Southeast Asia during the early stages of state formation. Kulke uses precise dating of architectural style shifts in both regions to demonstrate that states developed in both regions at about the same time, and that influences on architecture traveled in both directions. This theoretical shift, from a focus on outside "civilizations" to internal forces as the source of cultural innovation, is mirrored in theoretical shifts away from acculturation in general culture contact theory in other parts of the world (Cusick 1998a). Features of this shift include a focus on the two-way transfer of ideas, influences and technologies in culture contact situations, an increased concern with the specific mechanisms of information transfer, and a focus on local uses and meanings of foreign ideas and material objects. This theoretical shift provides an interesting comparison with the situation in North American archaeology. It seems that internal innovation was emphasized in regions like Indonesia that gained independence from colonial powers in the 1940s, before it became fashionable in North America, where Native American societies continue to exist in a colonial situation (MacKnight 1986; Wisseman Christie 1995).

There are several examples of innovative uses of documents and material remains in the region. Laura Junker also has combined documentary and archaeological sources in her studies of social complexity and trade in the Philippines from the tenth to the seventeenth century (Junker 1993, 1994, 1996, 1998, 1999). In her work, Chinese, Arab, and Spanish texts and Malay oral traditions provide disparate narratives about the nature of foreigner interactions and political developments. These are compared with a relatively large set of archaeological data from the same period regarding local and long-distance trade and social organization at a variety of spatial scales. Contradictions between texts serve to both expose biases and illuminate the context of their production, and ultimately to provide an analytical portal to generate questions for the archaeological data. The result is a rich description of Philippine political development that allows for anthropologists to compare Philippine chiefdoms with other chiefdomlike societies without succumbing to the overhomogenization that often results from attempts at broad comparison (Junker 1998, 292), while also adding to regional culture history and informing other studies (Bacus 1999; Skowronek 1998).

In Indonesia also, a few historical archaeology projects have contributed to both regional and global anthropological theory. Bulbeck and Caldwell have used Bugis texts in conjunction with archaeological settlement and mortuary data to investigate shifts to chiefdoms as a result of Bugis colonization of the Luwu region of South Sulawesi (Bulbeck 1992; Bulbeck and Prasetyo 2000; Caldwell 1995). In this case, Caldwell's analysis of Bugis texts provided a starting point for Bulbeck's archaeological research, which also incorporated consideration of oral history, myth, and ethnographic analogy. While not clearly methodologically separate from textual analysis, the archaeological questions derive from and in some cases depart from historical analysis. For example, while Bugis texts and mythology suggest that their colonization of Luwu was a transformative "event" that revolutionized the region politically, archaeological data suggest that the Bugis brought nothing new to the region, which had long been involved in long-distance trade. By rereading the texts and myths (such as *La Galigo*) against the new archaeological data, Bulbeck concludes that the originating force behind the texts and myths was the need to define Bugis status, which required promulgating heroic stories of Bugis political and economic prowess (Bulbeck and Prasetyo 2000).

In some parts of Island Southeast Asia, archaeologists continue to search for material expression of the complex polities described primarily in texts by foreigners such as the Chinese. In the Philippines, Junker (1994, 250–52) concludes that the discrepancy between Chinese descriptions of elaborate and wealthy "kingdoms" in Tanjay and archaeological remains of somewhat more modest settlements results from exaggeration of the scale of polities by the ruling elite. In western Indonesia, where this discrepancy also apparently exists, archaeologists have generally accepted the textual and epigraphical data at face value and have looked for alternate explanations to explain the discrepancies, with the result that considerable theoretical progress has been made (though real data remain somewhat scarce). For example, much work has been done on developing locally appropriate models for state development (Edwards McKinnon 1984; K. R. Hall 1985; Wisseman Christie 1995; Wolters 1974), and on postdepositional and landscape factors that might reduce the archaeological visibility of certain sites (Allen 1991). Others have questioned the role of cities and urbanism as a necessary feature of states in Island Southeast Asia. Miksic (1999, 2000), for example, suggests that dense settlement characteristic of urban areas may not have been possible in the humid tropics until technological solutions were found for problems with water supply and waterborne diseases.

The study of the processes by which Islam became the dominant religion in much of Island Southeast Asia provides a somewhat different perspective (Lape forthcoming). While it is clear that the foundations of the Islamic belief system originated in regions far removed from Island Southeast Asia, Muslim identity and practice in the region was seen as locally distinctive by the earliest foreign observers. Unlike traditional views of early state development, the growing presence of Islamic thought and practice in Island Southeast Asia has always been described, at least by outside observers, as partly a local invention, with a continuous influence of non-Islamic indigenous belief systems. Even the earliest texts describing Muslim practice in Island Southeast Asia tended to emphasize its difference from Muslim practice in the Middle East. Early Arab visitors to the region were often appalled by unorthodoxies (Tibbetts 1979), while early European visitors, who may have been looking for excuses to engage in trade with Southeast Asians in an anti-Islam political climate in Europe, were less judgmental but equally curious about different practices (Pires and Rodrigues 1944; Reid 1993a). This descriptive pattern is continued in western academic analyses (Bowen 1989; Feener 1998; Geertz 1960; Hooker 1983; Milner 1983; Ricklefs 1993, 1979) and may reflect an attempt by western scholars to differentiate Southeast Asian "liberal Islam" from the threatening fundamentalist forces in the Middle East.

Many studies by historians and cultural anthropologists have brought into focus the different ways individual actors strategically utilized and manipulated available religious dogma, including fundamentalist Islam, Hindu-Buddhist thought, ancestor worship, and animism (Anderson 1990; Geertz 1960). Most western academic historians of Island Southeast Asian Islam depict history in terms of these kinds of processes. Johns (1995), for example, has reevaluated the role of the Sufi mystic, particularly in spreading a text-centered religion like Islam through the largely nonliterate world of thirteenth- through seventeenth-century Island Southeast Asia. In the framework of culture contact theory, this concern with local difference could be seen as innovative. However, as studies of the history of Islam in Island Southeast Asia have been almost entirely dependent on documentary evidence, this concern can be attributed to the reflection of biases inherent to the data. Some researchers have worked to transcend these biases by critically analyzing local texts within local contexts through lenses of local politics and history or relationships to the diversity of Muslim practice in other places (Feener 1998; Hooker 1983; Johns 1995).

The power of archaeological data to provide an alternative line of evidence that is independent of documents produced during the politically charged interaction between Islam and Christianity in the early modern era has not yet been fully realized. It may have a significant role in the future. Archaeological data has been used to interpret the Islamization process in other parts of the Muslim world (for example, Insoll 1996, 1999). The relatively few archaeological studies that address Islamization in Island Southeast Asia suggest that the history of the process is considerably more complex than can be inferred from the written record. My own research on the role of Islam in eastern Indonesia provides an example of the ways in which archaeological data used in conjunction with texts can provide key insights into these cultural processes.

Case Study: Foreign Trade and Islam in the Banda Islands

My research has centered on questions of cross-cultural interaction in eastern Indonesia during the tenth through seventeenth centuries. This case study concerns the relationship between foreign trade and settlement patterns in the Banda Islands (see figure 8.2). These eleven islands were once the world's sole source of nutmeg and mace and were visited by long-distance maritime traders from insular and mainland Asia and the Middle East for at least two millennia. Muslim traders brought ideas as well as trade goods, and by the mid-fifteenth century, many Bandanese considered themselves Muslims. In the sixteenth and seventeenth centuries, the islands became the site of some of the fiercest struggles for trade and colonial dominance in the early modern era. The Banda Islanders first encountered Europeans in 1512, with the arrival of the first Portuguese trading ships. Just over a century later in 1621, the Bandas were irrevocably changed when Dutch East India Company (VOC) forces, aided by Japanese mercenaries, massacred, enslaved, or banished some 90 percent of Banda's population. Dutch farmers and their Asian slaves subsequently repopulated the islands, the first footholds in what became the Dutch colonial empire in the East Indies (Hanna 1978; Loth 1995a, 1995b, 1998; Masselman 1963; van der Chijs 1886).

In this case, research was directed toward questioning received wisdom about "foreign" influence in Banda, in particular the Islamization

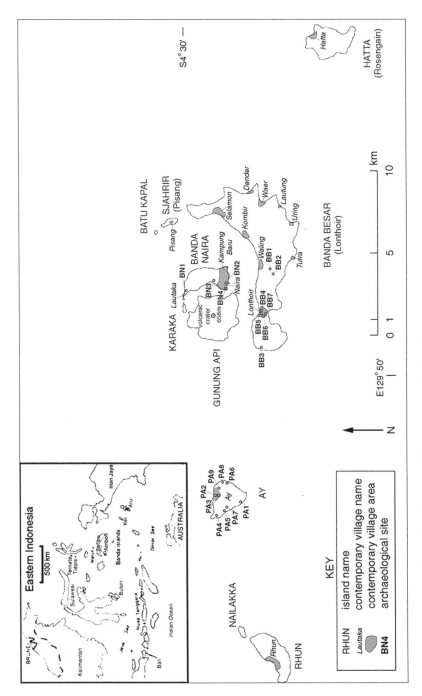

Figure 8.2 The Banda Archipelago, Maluku Province, Indonesia

process. I used a combination of archaeological and textual data to establish a chronology of changing long-distance trade patterns and to map the locations of foreign trade ports. The combined data were used to analyze how Bandanese society changed as foreign trade volume and intensity increased, particularly during the fourteenth through seventeenth centuries leading up to the Dutch colonial conquest. Combining the data also provided insight into the cultural production of those texts and maps, and added the dimension of those who were not recorded in written history. Banda archipelago settlement patterns are an aspect of Bandanese society that can be investigated using both textual and archaeological data, and that can also illuminate other social changes to investigate in subsequent studies, such as those at the household or village level. These results have been described in detail in other publications (Lape 2000a, 2000b, 2000c, 2002, 2003) but will be briefly reviewed here.

Textual Data

Textual data available for this research included a variety of descriptions, maps, and images of the islands recorded by foreigners, including Chinese, Javanese, Arab, and various European travelers and traders. Maps were a particularly useful set of data, although only maps drawn by European visitors after 1512 were located in archives. The motivations behind the making of maps were (and still are) multiple and sometimes conflicting. In many cases, maps were made to help future travelers find their way. For traders, the names and locations of principal market or trading towns were crucial. However, maps also served political purposes, and for these reasons the information on maps may have been deliberately misleading. For example, trading companies may have hidden the location of potentially profitable trading locations to gain an advantage over competitors (Harley and Woodward 1987; Suarez 1999; Zandvliet 1998). As these companies were entangled in national interests, they may have altered the geographic location of places to bring them under their political realm to conform to existing treaties. Treaties made with native groups may have also influenced map making. Groups or settlements that refused to sign over monopoly privileges may have been excluded from maps to make it seem as though there was unanimous consent for such treaties (for other colonial situations, see Fisher and Johnston 1993; Galloway 1995; Stahl 2001). Areas that resisted foreign control or allied with an enemy may have been shown as empty,

devoid of settlement, in some cases simply because a mapmaker was denied access to them (Trouillot 1995; Winer 1995).

Other unintentional errors creep into the texts written on maps. The
transcription of unfamiliar languages into European phonology may
have meant that places with unpronounceable names (for Europeans)
were altered. Because maps of Banda were often made after rather short
visits to the islands, misunderstandings, incomplete knowledge, and
confusions may have altered the place names we now see on old maps.
Places in Banda probably had multiple names in the past, as they do
today, including sacred names and names for everyday use. Language
change on Banda itself, stimulated by the increasing numbers of foreigners who settled there, may have altered place names over time. The
fact that Europeans gained information through nonindigenous inter-
mediaries such as Turks, Malays, or Javanese, all of whom spoke different languages than the native Bandanese, probably altered the toponyms
that have been recorded on maps (*Description* 1598; *Tweede* 1601; Valentijn 1724; Wall 1928).

There are dozens of potential biases that could have altered maps
from a "true" representation of the physical space of Banda. However,
these biases do not simply make the maps less accurate. Geographers
and historians have successfully deconstructed maps and teased out new
insights into the "social world in which [they] were produced" (Harley
1992, 232). Historical archaeologists have similarly used maps as one set
of documentary data to cast against other kinds of data as a sort of test
or comparison (such as M. Hall 2000; Winer 1995). By contextualizing
and comparing maps of late precolonial Banda with other maps and
the documentary and archaeological record, we can better understand
the mindset of European visitors to Banda, and the cultural process at
work there. What mapmakers saw and how they conceived of the geographic space of Banda was, in part, determinant of the cultural encoun-
ters among the various European and Asian groups present in Banda.
When compared against the archaeological record, many biases can be
exposed, and their power as data considerably enhanced.

In the course of archival research, I located fifteen different maps depicting the pre- and early colonial Banda Islands with settlement-level
detail, dating from 1570–1680. These were located in a wide variety of
private collections, archives, and published sources and are discussed in
detail in other publications (Lape 2000b, 2002). Five of those maps are
discussed here to illustrate their use in conjunction with archaeological
data. The first appearance of Banda on surviving world maps dates to

an anonymous *mappamundi* of 1457, which was probably informed by the account of Nicoló de'Conti, who claimed to have visited the islands (Suarez 1999, 79). Another early map showing Banda is the *Rodrigues Map*, which was probably copied from an Asian-drawn map used by the first Portuguese expedition to the islands in 1512 (Cortesão and Mota 1987, pl. 22; Lape 2000b, 84–85; Nakamura 1963, 28–32; Sollewijn Gelpke 1995); however, neither of these maps shows individual settlements. The earliest map to do that in detail is the *van Neck Map*, which was first published in 1601, immediately after the Dutch expedition commanded by Cornelius van Neck returned to Holland from Banda and the East Indies. This particular map was probably the first detailed map of the Banda Islands published in Europe, and it became extremely influential on subsequent mapmaking and European ideas about the configuration of the islands.

Archaeological Data

In 1997–98, I conducted archaeological survey and excavations at various late precolonial sites on three of the Banda Islands, aimed at locating settlements, determining their occupation chronology, and describing settlement level features, such as exotic trade-good presence, settlement-wide foodways, and architectural features, particularly fortifications. Research objectives were to collect chronological data on settlement pattern changes and to investigate whether individual settlements were distinctive in terms of material markers of behavior and settlement history in the five centuries leading up to the conquest of the islands by VOC forces in 1621. Archaeological survey, excavation, and most artifact analysis were conducted during two field seasons. A full-coverage settlement analysis was not attempted (compare Fish and Kowalewski 1990), given the short time frame available and conditions that made systematic site survey impossible.

Rapid sediment deposition from the Gunung Api volcano has buried signs of older settlements with a thick layer of volcanic tephra, making sites difficult or impossible to see during pedestrian survey. The islands are generally covered in either dense vegetation or currently occupied settlements. Many of the late precolonial settlements very likely were reoccupied after the colonial conquest in 1621 and evolved into the currently occupied towns. In response to these limitations, I attempted various strategies to locate a reasonably large sample of different settlement locales dating to the late precolonial era. A total of twenty sites (defined as places of archaeological interest) were discovered by these means and subjected to test excavations, with the objective of identifying those sites with late precolonial period remains (figure 8.3). Six sites had such remains, but due to time constraints, only four of those were excavated extensively (BN1, BN2, BN4, and PA2). One additional site, PA1, was also excavated extensively but it dated to an earlier period (c. 1200 BC). Pedestrian survey was most productive on the outer island of Pulau Ay on land cleared for agriculture. In currently occupied towns, sites were located through nonsystematic subsurface testing in areas where we could obtain local permission and which had reasonable security, such as the walled garden areas of Dutch colonial houses (sites PA2, PA3 and BB4, BB5 and BB6). Some sites were discovered because shoreline erosion had revealed older deposits in wave-cut banks (such as site BN1). Site BN4, formerly on the sixteenth-century shoreline, is now some eighty meters inland, inside the walls of the former VOC governor's house, and was located through subsurface testing, guided by a series of eighteenth- and nineteenth-century colonial period maps that documented shoreline progradation on southern Banda Naira. A limited experiment allowing local oral historians to guide site selection on Banda Besar was not archaeologically productive, although local informants often directed us to surface remains on Pulau Ay.

Cultural deposits were primarily midden deposits, composed of ceramics, metal, and faunal remains. Sites on Banda Naira and Banda Besar were clearly stratified due to the regular deposition of culturally sterile volcanic tephra. In some cases, these tephra lenses could be linked to historically recorded volcanic eruption episodes. Excavation strategy was oriented to obtaining chronological data using small (1×1 and 2×2 meter) isolated block units, for a total of 4–11 square meters of excavated area per site. Test pits were used to identify site boundaries, and units were interspersed evenly across the site area, subject to the limitations of current use and geography of the sites. Generally, the built environment and intrasite structure remains poorly understood, though evidence for stone structures was encountered in some cases (see Lape 2000b). As is apparent, the archaeological data collected should not be considered a representative sampling of human use of the islands over time and space, and it is likely that conclusions about individual site use will change as larger areas are tested. However, the sites that were tested archaeologically do provide information about dates of occupation and abandonment, changes in settlement area, trade goods, and foodways that allow at least a preliminary view of settlement patterning. Strata were dated

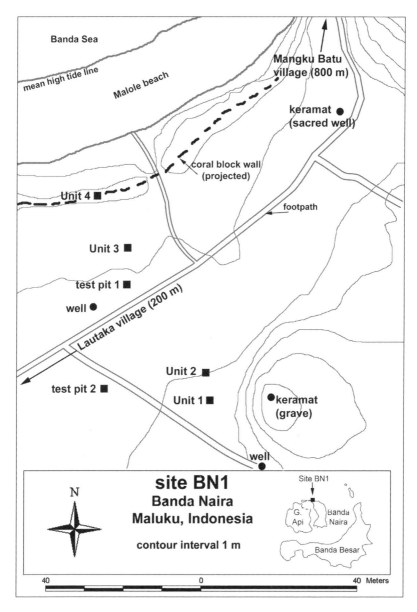

Figure 8.3   Plan of Site BN1, Banda Naira, at Maluku, Indonesia

with a series of radiocarbon dates and cross-checked with dateable Chinese ceramic tradeware assemblages.

Synthesizing Different Lines of Evidence

In several cases, the archaeological data showed areas of human settlement on the landscape that mapmakers did not depict on their maps. These "unmapped" settlements had some characteristic features. They were typically located in sections of the coastline that had poor boat access, particularly for large ships. They were exposed to prevailing winds and waves, were cut off from deep water by barrier reefs, or were situated on elevated terraces with steep drop-offs or cliffs leading down to the shore. These "forgotten" settlements were often out of sight of the central protected bay between Banda Naira, Banda Besar, and Gunung Api Islands. In addition to these common geographic features, some of these unmapped settlements (and one settlement that was mapped) also showed archaeological evidence of non-Islamic occupation. While all but one of the "mapped" settlements lacked remains of pig in their faunal assemblages and were typically first occupied beginning in the eleventh and twelfth centuries, unmapped settlements often had a longer occupation chronology (dating to the fifth century or earlier) and had substantial amounts of pig bones in precolonial contexts (although there is some variation, pig is generally not eaten by Muslims; see Insoll 1999; Reid 1993b, 1995). My interpretation of this pattern was that non-Islamic settlements in Banda were either invisible to European chroniclers or intentionally not recorded. European chronicles suggest that European traders had more contact and trade relationships with Muslim-oriented settlements in Banda, despite the prevailing opposition to Islam that characterized the European colonial project in the East Indies.

A specific example of this pattern involves two settlements located on the island of Banda Naira, on the north and south ends of the island. In textual sources, the two settlements are both identified in the earliest European maps and descriptions of the islands, dating to the late sixteenth century. While the earliest descriptions of the two settlements suggest that they were of equivalent size and prominence in trade, by 1615 the northern settlement appeared to be declining in physical size and was less frequently noted by foreign chroniclers. The northern settlement (known by various similar names such as Labbetacca), is protected by a barrier reef and completely disappears in postconquest (post-

1621) maps, while the southern settlement (originally known as Nera, a name that later described the entire island) is located inside the protected Banda Bay; it became the new colonial center and is today the largest town and administrative center of the islands.

Five square meters of archaeological site BN1, which appears to be the remains of Labbetacca, were excavated at various parts of the site (see figure 8.3). These excavations produced a faunal assemblage dominated by pig bones, distinctive earthenware pottery with incised decoration, remains of Chinese ceramics dating to the tenth century and possibly as early as the fifth century AD, and evidence of human cremation burials. A portion of the site was bounded by the remains of a coral block wall parallel to the shoreline that would have been at least two meters high and thirty to forty meters long during the fourteenth through sixteenth centuries. The earliest occupation dated to the fifth century, with evidence of abandonment by the mid-seventeenth century. The site is currently used as an agricultural field.

Two archaeological sites were located on the presumed locale of the settlement of Nera (BN2 and BN4), and a total of fifteen square meters were excavated from the two sites. The earliest occupation levels dated to the twelfth century, and the precolonial faunal assemblage was dominated by fish and completely lacked pig. These sites also lacked the distinctive decorated earthenware of site BN1, and no human remains were found. Site BN2 also had a coral block wall parallel to the shoreline.

Following the synthesis of the archaeological and documentary evidence, the questions remained: What roles did apparently non-Islamic settlements such as Labbetacca play in the nutmeg trade economy and the Bandanese resistance to European colonial objectives? Why were they established earlier, in less accessible sections of the coast, and why did they disappear by the mid-seventeenth century?

My approach to answering these questions was to revisit the archival record to search for additional clues about divisions in Bandanese society that may have followed religious or ethnic lines. These clues were not apparent to me on the first reading of the texts. While some texts described factional splits and battles between different villages in Banda, the factions were described as political rather than religious. Labbetacca and Nera were members of rival factions according to early Dutch chronicles. One description from the early seventeenth century describes a violent battle between the settlements and their allies (*Tweede* 1601, 32). However, a close reading of personal names and titles of village leaders, for example, revealed that so-called political divisions closely followed lines of religious identity that European chroniclers may not have been aware of, and that religion, ethnicity, and politics were not necessarily separate categories for the Bandanese (Lape 2002, forthcoming).

A deeper reading of this text and others that describe the two settlements reveals other clues. The names and political titles of men from Labbetacca recorded on Dutch treaty documents revealed that typical Bandanese Muslim political titles (such as Imam and Syabandar) were not used in Labbetacca. Other clues in regional oral traditions suggest also that Labbetacca was the more ancient center of political power, perhaps associated with pre-Islamic belief systems (Lape 2000b, 286–97).

In this case, textual and archaeological data were given equal interpretive weight and used in concert to generate hypotheses that were tested against each other. While limited and subject to considerable bias, when used together these data sets allowed for insights beyond what either could provide alone. In particular, archaeological patterns suggested a second reading of the texts, which in turn showed evidence for cultural processes that the original recorders of the text may not have noticed. It appears that internal divisions of Bandanese society followed religious lines, which overlaid geographic and historical lines. This suggests that Islamization in Banda was not all-encompassing and instantaneous, but affected different settlements at different times. As discussed in other publications (Lape 2000a, 2000b, 2000c, forthcoming), sixteenth- and early seventeenth-century documents also suggest that this uneven Islamization process caused significant conflict within Bandanese society, and that European colonizers were able to use these internal divisions to their advantage in the colonial conquest. The colonial conquest, in this interpretation, was not a simple matter of Dutch military force overwhelming an inferior Bandanese resistance, but rather was the result of the long-term processes of Bandanese factionalization that had its origins in changing economic forces and the geography of belief.

Future Directions

Despite the potential suggested by these examples, Island Southeast Asia continues to lag behind other regions in both the quantity of archaeological studies and the integration of those studies into global theoretical concerns. Scholars have long called for improvements in this arena and have demonstrated the clear need for more archaeological data (Bellwood 1997; Hutterer 1982; MacKnight 1986; Tanudirjo 1995). However, political unrest, bureaucratic obstacles to foreign research permission, lack of funding and institutional support for indigenous archaeologists, and lack of open exchange of theories and data among scholars in different disciplines have continued to limit the amount and the usefulness of historical archaeological research in the region. While it could be argued that historians have not been subject to these constraints, since their source data is located in accessible archives in Southeast Asian capital cities or in Europe, it is likely that some documentary sources are as yet untapped by historians in Asia with relevance to Island Southeast Asia. Oral history similarly has been underutilized, as both historians and archaeologists have struggled with its shifting and subjective meanings (Bowen 1989).

This review of historical archaeology in Island Southeast Asia, while not exhaustive, still suggests considerable potential for new ways of combining textual and material data in the study of the past. Because Island Southeast Asia has been a cultural crossroads for so long, most of the region has been a part of the historical record of other places for more than a millennium, even if it lacked an indigenous written record in some earlier periods. Unlike the situation in North America, where early textual descriptions are almost universally from the point of view of European colonists, historic texts in Island Southeast Asia are written from a wide variety of cultural points of view and time periods, allowing for comparative analyses. Island Southeast Asia has not had as sharp an artificial disciplinary boundary between historic and prehistoric archaeology as North America has had, and a greater proportion of archaeologists have straddled these periods. Finally, while there have been some abuses of the direct historical method and analogy, in general archaeologists have been careful to explicitly separate different lines of evidence in their analyses. The results, particularly in recent work in the region, have been advances in methods of combining multiple data sets that should see wider application, both in Island Southeast Asia and in other places.

Note

This chapter was originally published in a slightly different form in the *Journal of the Economic and Social History of the Orient* 45 (4): 468–91. Copyright © 2002 by Brill Academic Publishers. Reprinted by permission.

Bibliography

Allen, Jane. 1991. "Trade and Site Distribution in Early Historic–Period Kedah: Geo-archaeological, Historic, and Locational Evidence." *Bulletin of the Indo-Pacific Prehistory Association* 10:307–19.

Anderson, Benedict R. O. 1990. *Language and Power: Exploring Political Cultures in Indonesia*. Ithaca, N.Y.: Cornell University Press.

Andrén, Anders. 1998. *Between Artifacts and Texts: Historical Archaeology in Global Perspective*. New York: Plenum.

Bacus, Elisabeth. 1999. "Prestige and Potency: Political Economies of Protohistoric Visayan Polities." In *Complex Polities in the Ancient Tropical World*, ed. E. Bacus and L. J. Lucero, 67–87. Washington, D.C.: American Anthropological Association.

Beaudry, Mary C., Lauren J. Cook, and Stephen A. Mrozowski. 1991. "Artifacts and Active Voices: Material Culture as Social Discourse." In *The Archaeology of Inequality*, ed. R. McGuire and R. Paynter, 150–91. London: Basil Blackwell.

Bellwood, Peter. 1997. *Prehistory of the Indo-Malaysian Archipelago*. Honolulu: University of Hawaii Press.

Binford, Lewis. 1962. "Archaeology as Anthropology." *American Antiquity* 28:217–25.

Bintliff, J. 1991. *The Annales School and Archaeology*. Leicester, UK: Leicester University Press.

Bowen, John R. 1989. "Narrative Form and Political Incorporation: Changing Uses of History in Aceh, Indonesia." *Society for Comparative Study of Society and History* 31:671–93.

Boyd, Matthew, John C. Erwin, and Mitch Hendrickson. 2000. *The Entangled Past: Integrating History and Archaeology*. Calgary: The Archaeological Association of the University of Calgary.

Bulbeck, David F. 1992. "A Tale of Two Kingdoms: The Historical Archaeology of Gowa and Tallok, South Sulawesi, Indonesia." PhD diss., The Australian National University, Canberra.

Bulbeck, F. David, and Bagyo Prasetyo. 2000. "Two Millennia of Socio-cultural Development in Luwu, South Sulawesi, Indonesia." *World Archaeology* 32:121–37.

Caldwell, Ian. 1995. "Power, State and Society among the Pre-Islamic Bugis." *Bijdragen tot de Taal- Land- en Volkenkunde* 151:394–421.

Champion, T. C. 1990. "Medieval Archaeology and the Tyranny of the Historical Record." In *From the Baltic to the Black Sea: Studies in Medieval Archaeology*, ed. D. Austin and L. Alcock, 79–95. London: Unwin Hyman.

van der Chijs, J. A. 1886. *De Vestiging van het Nederlandische Gezag over de Banda-Eilanden (1599–1621)*. Batavia: Albrecht and Co.

Clarke, Anne, and Robin Torrence. 2000. *The Archaeology of Difference: Negotiating Cross-Cultural Engagements in Oceania*. New York: Routledge.

Clarke, David. 1973. "Archaeology: The Loss of Innocence." *Antiquity* 47:6–18.

Coedès, Georges. 1968. *The Indianized States of Southeast Asia*. Ed. W. F. Vella. Trans. S. B. Cowing. Honolulu: East-West Center Press.

Cortesão, Armando, and Avelino Teixeira da Mota. 1987. *Portugaliae Monumenta Cartographica*. Lisboa: Imprensa Nacional–Casa da Moeda.

Cusick, James G. 1998a. "Historiography of Acculturation: An Evaluation of Concepts and their Application in Archaeology." In *Studies in Culture Contact: Interaction, Culture Change and Archaeology*, ed. J. G. Cusick, 126–45. Occasional Paper No. 25. Carbondale: Center for Archaeological Investigations, Southern Illinois University.

————. 1998b. *Studies in Culture Contact: Interaction, Culture Change and Archaeology*, Occasional Paper No. 25. Carbondale: Center for Archaeological Investigations, Southern Illinois University.

Deagan, Kathleen. 1988. "Neither History nor Prehistory: The Questions that Count in Historical Archaeology." *Historical Archaeology* 22:7–12.

Description. 1598. *The Description of a Voyage Made by Certain Ships of Holland into the East Indies, with their Adventutres and Successe, April 1595–Aug 1597*. Translated from the Dutch by William Phillip. London.

Edwards McKinnon, E. 1984. "Kota Cina: Its Context and Meaning in the Trade of Southeast Asia in the Twelfth to Fourteenth Centuries." PhD diss., Cornell University.

Faubion, James D. 1993. "History in Anthropology." *Annual Review of Anthropology* 22:35–54.

Feener, R. Michael. 1998. "A Re-examination of the Place of al-Hallaj in the Development of Southeast Asian Islam." *Bijdragen tot de Taal- Land- en Volkenkunde* 571–92.

Feinman, Gary. 1997. "Thoughts on New Approaches to Combining the Archaeological and Historical Records." *Journal of Archaeological Method and Theory* 4:367–77.

Ferguson, Leland G. 1992. *Uncommon Ground: Archaeology and Early African America, 1650–1800*. Washington, D.C.: Smithsonian Institution Press.

Fish, Suzanne K., and Stephen A. Kowalewski. 1990. *The Archaeology of Regions: A Case for Full-Coverage Survey*. Washington, D.C.: Smithsonian Institution Press.

Fisher, Robin, and Hugh Johnston. 1993. *From Maps to Metaphors: The Pacific World of George Vancouver*. Vancouver: University of British Columbia Press.

Flannery, Kent. 1972. "Culture History vs. Culture Process: A Debate in American Archaeology." In *Contemporary Archaeology*, ed. M. Leone, 119–21. Carbondale: Southern Illinois University Press.

Funari, Pedro Paulo A., Sian Jones, and Martin Hall. 1999. *Historical Archaeology: Back from the Edge*. New York: Routledge.

Galloway, Patricia Kay. 1995. *Choctaw Genesis, 1500–1700*. Lincoln: University of Nebraska Press.

Geertz, Clifford. 1960. *The Religion of Java*. New York: The Free Press of Glencoe.

Glover, Ian C. 1990. *Early Trade between India and South-East Asia: A Link in the Development of a World Trading System*. Occasional Paper No. 16. Hull, UK: Centre for East Asian Studies, University of Hull.

Gosden, Chris. 1999. *Anthropology and Archaeology: A Changing Relationship*. New York: Routledge.

Hall, Kenneth R. 1985. *Maritime Trade and State Development in Early Southeast Asia*. Honolulu: University of Hawaii Press.

Hall, Martin. 2000. *Archaeology and the Modern World: Colonial Transcripts in South Africa and the Chesapeake*. New York: Routledge.

Hanna, Willard Anderson. 1978. *Indonesian Banda: Colonialism and its Aftermath in the Nutmeg Islands*. Philadelphia: Institute for the Study of Human Issues.

Harley, J. B. 1992. "Deconstructing the Map." In *Writing Worlds: Discourse, Texts, and Metaphors in the Representation of Landscape*, ed. T. J. Barnes and J. S. Duncan, 231–47. London: Routledge.

Harley, J. B., and David Woodward. 1987. *Cartography in Prehistoric, Ancient, and Medieval Europe and the Mediterranean*. Vol. 1. Chicago: University of Chicago Press.

Hooker, M. B. 1983. *Islam in South East Asia*. Leiden, Netherlands: Brill.

Hutterer, Karl. 1982. "Early Southeast Asia: Old Wine in New Skins?—A Review Article." *Journal of Asian Studies* 61:559–70.

Insoll, Timothy. 1996. *Islam, Archaeology and History: Gao Region (Mali) ca. AD 900–1250*. Oxford: Tempvs Reparatvm.

———. 1999. *The Archaeology of Islam*. Oxford: Blackwell.

Johns, Anthony H. 1995. "Sufism in Southeast Asia: Reflections and Reconsiderations." *Journal of Southeast Asian Studies* 26:169–83.

Junker, Laura. 1993. "Craft Goods Specialization and Prestige Goods Exchange in Philippine Chiefdoms of the Fifteenth and Sixteenth Centuries." *Asian Perspectives* 32:1–35.

———. 1994. "Trade Competition, Conflict, and Political Transformations in Sixth- to Sixteenth-Century Philippine Chiefdoms." *Asian Perspectives* 33:229–59.

———. 1996. "Hunter-Gatherer Landscapes and Lowland Trade in the Prehispanic Philippines." *World Archaeology* 27:389–410.

———. 1998. "Integrating History and Archaeology in the Study of Contact Period Philippine Chiefdoms." *International Journal of Historical Archaeology* 2:291–320.

————. 1999. *Raiding, Trading, and Feasting: The Political Economy of Philippine Chiefdoms.* Honolulu: University of Hawaii Press.

Kepecs, Susan. 1997. "Introduction to New Approaches to Combining the Archaeological and Historical Records." *Journal of Archaeological Method and Theory* 4:193–98.

Kirch, Patrick V., and Marshall Sahlins. 1992. *Anahulu: The Anthropology of History in the Kingdom of Hawaii.* Vol. 2, *The Archaeology of History.* Chicago: University of Chicago Press.

Knapp, A. Bernard. 1992. *Archaeology, Annales, and Ethnohistory.* Cambridge: Cambridge University Press.

Kolb, Michael. 1997. "Labor Mobilization, Ethnohistory and the Archaeology of Community in Hawai'i." *Journal of Archaeological Method and Theory* 4:265–86.

Kowalewski, Stephen. 1997. "A Spatial Method for Integrating Data of Different Types." *Journal of Archaeological Method and Theory* 4:287–306.

Kulke, H. 1990. "Indian Colonies, Indianization or Cultural Convergence? Reflections on the Changing Image of India's Role in South-East Asia." In *Onderzoek in Zuidoost-Azie: Agenda's voor de Jaren Negentig,* ed. H. S. Nordholt, 8–32. Leiden, Netherlands: Rijksuniversiteit te leiden, Vakgroep Talen en Culturen van Zuidoost-Azie en Oceanie.

Kus, Susan. 1997. "Archaeologists as Anthropologists: Much Ado about Something after All?" *Journal of Archaeological Method and Theory* 4:199–214.

Lape, Peter V. 2000a. "Contact and Colonialism in the Banda Islands, Maluku, Indonesia." *Bulletin of the Indo-Pacific Prehistory Association* 20:48–55.

————. 2000b. "Contact and Conflict in the Banda Islands, Eastern Indonesia, 11th–17th Centuries." PhD diss., Brown University.

————. 2000c. "Political Dynamics and Religious Change in the Late Pre-colonial Banda Islands, Eastern Indonesia." *World Archaeology* 32 (1): 138–55.

————. 2002. "Historic Maps and Archaeology as a Means of Understanding Late Pre-colonial Settlement in the Banda Islands, Indonesia." *Asian Perspectives* 41 (1): 43–70.

————. 2003. "Theoretical Insights from Studies of Culture Contact in Eastern Indonesia." *Archaeology in Oceania* 38:102–9.

————. 2004. "The Isolation Metaphor in Island Archaeology." In *The Archaeology of Insularity: Examining the Past in Island Environments,* ed. S. Fitzpatrick, 295–98. New York: Greenwood Press.

————. Forthcoming. "Archaeology of Islam in Island Southeast Asia." *Antiquity.*

Last, Jonathan. 1995. "The Nature of History." In *Interpreting Archaeology: Finding Meaning in the Past,* ed. I. Hodder et al., 141–57. New York: Routledge.

Layton, Robert. 1989. *Conflict in the Archaeology of Living Traditions.* New York: Routledge.

Leone, Mark, and Parker Potter. 1988. *The Recovery of Meaning: Historical Archaeology in the Eastern United States*. Washington, D.C.: Smithsonian Institution Press.

van Leur, J. C. 1967. *Indonesian Trade and Society: Essays in Asian Social and Economic History*. The Hague: W. van Hoeve.

Lightfoot, Kent. 1995. "Culture Contact Studies: Redefining the Relationship between Prehistoric and Historical Archaeology." *American Antiquity* 60:199–217.

Loth, Vincent. 1995a. "Armed Incidents and Unpaid Bills: Anglo-Dutch Rivalry in the Banda Islands in the Seventeenth Century." *Modern Asian Studies* 29:705–40.

———. 1995b. "Pioneers and Perkeniers: The Banda Islands in the 17th Century." *Cakalele* 6:13–35.

———. 1998. "Fragrant Gold and Food Provision: Resource Management and Agriculture in Seventeenth Century Banda." In *Old World Places, New World Problems: Exploring Issues of Resource Management in Eastern Indonesia*, ed. S. Pannell and F. V. Benda-Beckmann, 66–93. Canberra: Australian National University.

MacKnight, C. C. 1986. "Changing Perspectives in Island Southeast Asia." In *Southeast Asia in the 9th to 14th Centuries*, ed. D. G. Marr and A. C. Milner, 215–27. Singapore: Institute of Southeast Asian Studies.

Masselman, George. 1963. *The Cradle of Colonialism*. New Haven, Conn.: Yale University Press.

McBride, Terry, and Beth Rudden. 2000. "Where are All the Myths? Native American Oral Traditions and their Place in Archaeological Inference." In *The Entangled Past: Integrating History and Archaeology*, ed. M. Boyd, J. C. Erwin, and M. Hendrickson, 330–35. Calgary: The Archaeological Association of the University of Calgary.

Miksic, John. 1999. "Water, Urbanization and Disease in Ancient Indonesia." In *Complex Polities in the Ancient Tropical World*, ed. E. Bacus and L. J. Lucero, 167–84. Washington, D.C.: American Anthropological Association.

———. 2000. "Heterogenetic Cities in Premodern Southeast Asia." *World Archaeology* 32:106–20.

Miller, Daniel. 1980. "Archaeology and Development." *Current Anthropology* 21:709–26.

Milner, Anthony C. 1983. "Islam and the Muslim State." In *Islam in South East Asia*, ed. M. B. Hooker, 23–49. Leiden, Netherlands: Brill.

Morrison, Kathleen, and Mark Lycett. 1997. "Inscriptions as Artifacts: Precolonial South India and the Analysis of Texts." *Journal of Archaeological Method and Theory* 4:215–38.

Moser, Stephanie. 1995. "The 'Aboriginalization' of Australian Archaeology." In *Theory in Archaeology: A World Perspective*, ed. P. J. Ucko, 150–77. London: Routledge.

Nakamura, Hiroshi. 1963. *East Asia in Old Maps*. Honolulu: East-West Center Press.

Orser, Charles. 1994. "Towards a Global Historical Archaeology: An Example from Brazil." *Historical Archaeology* 28:5–22.

———. 1996. *A Historical Archaeology of the Modern World*. New York: Plenum Press.

Pires, Tomé, and Francisco Rodrigues. 1944. *The Suma Oriental of Tomé Pires, An Account of the East, from the Red Sea to Japan, Written in Malacca and India in 1512–1515, and the Book of Francisco Rodrigues, Rutter of a Voyage in the Red Sea, Nautical Rules, Almanack and Maps, Written and Drawn in the East before 1515*. Translated by A. Cortesão. London: The Hakluyt Society.

Raffles, Thomas Stamford. 1817. *The History of Java*. London: Black, Parbury, and Allen.

Ray, Himanshu Prabha. 1989. "Early Maritime Contacts between South and Southeast Asia." *Journal of South East Asian Studies* 20:42–54.

Reid, Anthony. 1993a. "Islamization and Christianization in Southeast Asia: The Critical Phase, 1550–1650." In *Southeast Asia in the Early Modern Era: Trade, Power, and Belief*, ed. A. Reid, 151–79. Ithaca, N.Y.: Cornell University Press.

———. 1993b. *Southeast Asia in the Early Modern Era: Trade, Power, and Belief*. Ithaca, N.Y.: Cornell University Press.

———. 1995. "Continuity and Change in the Austronesian Transition to Islam and Christianity." In *The Austronesians: Historical and Comparative Perspectives*, ed. P. Bellwood, J. Fox, and D. Tryon, 314–31. Canberra: Australian National University.

Ricklefs, Merle C. 1979. "Six Centuries of Islamization in Java." In *Conversion to Islam*, ed. N. Levtzion, 100–128. New York: Holmes and Meier.

———. 1993. *A History of Modern Indonesia Since c. 1300*. London: Macmillan.

Rockhill, W. W. 1915. "Notes on the Relations and Trade of China with the Eastern Archipelago and the Coast of the Indian Ocean during the Fourteenth Century, Part II." *T'oung Pao* 26:61–626.

Rogers, J. Daniel, and Samuel M. Wilson. 1993. *Ethnohistory and Archaeology: Approaches to Postcontact Change in the Americas*. New York: Plenum Press.

Rowlands, Michael. 1998. "The Archaeology of Colonialism." In *Social Transformations in Archaeology: Global and Local Perspectives*, ed. K. Kristiansen and M. Rowlands, 327–33. New York: Routledge.

Rubertone, Patricia. 1989. "Archaeology, Colonialism and 17th Century Native America: Towards an Alternative Explanation." In *Conflict in the Archaeology of Living Traditions*, ed. R. Layton, 32–45. New York: Routledge.

Schmidt, Peter, and Thomas Patterson. 1995. *Making Alternative Histories: The Practice of Archaeology and History in Non-Western Settings*. Santa Fe, N.Mex.: School of American Research.

Schrieke, Bertram Johannes Otto. 1960. *Indonesian Sociological Studies: Selected Writings*. Bandung, Indonesia: Summur Bandung.

Schuyler, Robert. 1978. *Historical Archaeology: A Guide to Substantive and Theoretical Contributions*. Farmingdale, N.Y.: Baywood Publishing.

———. 1988. "Archaeological Remains, Documents and Anthropology: A Call for a New Culture History." *Historical Archaeology* 22:36–44.

Scott, Elizabeth M. 1994. *Those of Little Note: Gender, Race, and Class in Historical Archaeology*. Tucson: University of Arizona Press.

Skowronek, Russell K. 1998. "The Spanish Philippines: Archaeological Perspectives on Colonial Economics and Society." *International Journal of Historical Archaeology* 2:45–71.

Sollewijn Gelpke, J. H. F. 1995. "Alfonso de Albuquerque's Pre-Portuguese 'Javanese' Map, Partially Reconstructed from Francisco Rodrigues' Book." *Bijdragen tot de Taal- Land- en Volkenkunde* 151:76–99.

South, Stanley. 1977. *Method and Theory in Historical Archaeology*. New York: Academic Press.

Stahl, Ann Brower. 2001. *Making History in Banda: Anthropological Visions of Africa's Past*. New York: Cambridge University Press.

Suarez, Thomas. 1999. *Early Mapping of Southeast Asia*. Hong Kong: Periplus Editions.

Tanudirjo, Daud A. 1995. "Theoretical Trends in Indonesian Archaeology." In *Theory in Archaeology: A World Perspective*, ed. P. J. Ucko, 61–75. London: Routledge.

Terrell, John E. 1998. "30,000 Years of Culture Contact in the Southwest Pacific." In *Studies in Culture Contact: Interaction, Culture Change and Archaeology*, ed. J. G. Cusik, 191–219. Occasional Paper No. 25. Carbondale: Center for Archaeological Investigations, Southern Illinois University.

Thurston, Tina. 1997. "Historians, Prehistorians, and the Tyranny of the Historical Record: Danish State Formation through Documents and Archaeological Data." *Journal of Archaeological Method and Theory* 4:239–64.

Tibbetts, Gerald R. 1979. *A Study of the Arabic Texts Containing Material on South-East Asia*. The Royal Asiatic Society Oriental Translation Fund. Leiden and London: E. J. Brill.

Trigger, Bruce. 1984. "Archaeology at the Crossroads: What's New?" *Annual Review of Anthropology* 13:275–300.

———. 1989. *A History of Archaeological Thought*. Cambridge: Cambridge University Press.

Trouillot, Michel-Rolph. 1995. *Silencing the Past: Power and the Production of History*. Boston: Beacon Press.

Tweede. 1601. *Het Tvveede Boeck, journael oft dagh-register, inhoudende een warachtich verhael ende historische vertellinghe vande reyse, gedaen door de acht schepen van Amstelredamme, gheseylt inden maent martij 1598. onder 'tbeleydt vanden Admirael Iacob Cornelisz. Neck, ende Wybrant van VVarvvijck als vice-admirael. . . . Met . . . een vocabulaer van hare woorden.* Middelburg, Netherlands: Barent Langhenes.

Valentijn, François. 1724. *Oud en Nieuw Oost-Indien, Vervattende een naaukeurige en uitvoerige verhandelinge van Nederlands mogentheyd in die gewestenk, benevens eene wydluftige beschryvinge der Moluccos.* 5 vols. Dordrecht, Netherlands: J. van Braam.

van de Wall, Victor Ido. 1928. *De Nederlandsche Oudheden in de Molukken.* 'S-Gravenhage: Martinus Nijhoff.

Winer, Margot. 1995. "The Painted, Poetic Landscape: Reading Power in Nineteenth-Century Textual and Visual Representations of the Eastern Cape Frontier." *Kroeber Anthropological Society Papers* 79:74–109.

Wisseman Christie, Jan. 1995. "State Formation in Early Maritime Southeast Asia: A Consideration of the Theories and the Data." *Bijdragen tot de Taal- Land- en Volkenkunde* 151:235–88.

Wolters, O. W. 1974. *Early Indonesian Commerce: A Study of the Origins of Srivijaya.* Ithaca, N.Y.: Cornell University Press.

———. 1999. *History, Culture, and Region in Southeast Asian Perspectives.* Ithaca, N.Y.: Southeast Asia Program Publications, Cornell University.

Young, T. C. 1988. "Since Herodotus, Has History been a Valid Concept?" *American Antiquity* 53:7–12.

Zandvliet, Kees. 1998. *Mapping for Money: Maps, Plans and Topographic Paintings and their Role in the Dutch Overseas Expansion during the 16th and 17th Centuries.* Amsterdam: Batavian Lion International.

9

Textualized Places, Pre-Angkorian Khmers, and Historicized Archaeology

MIRIAM T. STARK

Archaeologists' growing commitment to studying the historical period has generated rich insights globally (e.g., Andrén 1998; Funari 1999; Orser 1996); this turn has also identified methodological challenges. Understanding the relationship between documentary and archaeological sources has been among the most persistent of these challenges (e.g., Feinman 1997; Kepecs 1997; Stark and Allen 1998). Chapters in this volume use case studies across the Old World to offer original contributions and explore significant, if sometimes intractable issues. Kohl (chapter 10) directly asks whether archaeological and written sources are qualitatively distinct or complementary. Acknowledging that most documentary sources are also archaeological in origin, I examine this relationship between archaeological and historical sources by tacking between my region of specialty in Southeast Asia (Cambodia and the pre-Angkorian Khmer) and chapters in this volume. Let us first turn to Cambodia in the first millennium A D and the origins of the Khmer people.

Cambodia's Origins and the Khok Thlok Story

It is the year A D 68. Preah Thaong, a brahmin from the east, reaches the Mekong delta by water. Standing at the prow of his ship, he sees the island of Khok Thlok; at its shore is a beautiful woman serpent princess named Nagi Somā. She sees the intruder, assembles her army, and defends the island against Preah Thaong through pitched battle. Preah Thaong conquers her, they fall in love, and their marriage ceremony is held in her father's subterranean *nāga* kingdom. After they are wed, Somā's father (the *nāga* king) "drinks the waters" that cover this land, and creates a land he calls Kambuja. The descendants of this kingdom's residents are the modern-day Khmers who live in the kingdom of Cambodia.

Cambodians teach this amalgamated version of the origin story to their children today. This Khok Thlok, Preah Thaong, or Kaundinya story appears in Cambodian schoolbooks, and King Preah Thaong and his queen, Somā, are also described in post-fourteenth-century Cambodian royal annals (Gaudes 1993, 335–38). Cambodian brides and grooms reenact this story in each traditional Khmer wedding because wedding rituals symbolize the marriage of Preah Thaong and his beloved Nagi Somā (Gaudes 1977; Lewitz 1973). Deeply entrenched in Cambodian ideology, the Preah Thaong story is integral to understanding the origins of the Khmer people.

The Preah Thaong story is not only encoded in texts and reenacted in ritual. It is also closely associated with a particular place: the settlement of Angkor Borei, in Cambodia's Mekong delta. One of Angkor Borei's administrative districts today is called Khok Thlok; the Preah Thaong reservoir sits in the community's center, south of a Buddhist pagoda. Below the contemporary community of Angkor Borei lies a three-hundred-hectare archaeological site, bounded by remnants of a four-meter-tall earthen and brick wall. Within the wall's enclosed area, grazing areas for livestock contain piles of collapsed brick architecture and their accompanying moats and ponds. This Khmer oral tradition has been textualized and materialized through centuries of ritual practice and through the association of a physical place with the original Khok Thlok.

Cambodia's Origins and External Documentary Evidence

Southeast Asian scholars have long acknowledged the profound influence of South Asia on first millennium AD populations throughout the region (e.g., Coedès 1968; Christie 1995; Groslier 1966; Jacques 1979; Kulke 1986; Mabbett 1997; Wheatley 1983; Wolters 1999). As Trautmann and Sinopoli (chapter 6) indicate, the early historic period in South Asia witnessed the emergence of mature states like the Mauryas and the Kushanas across much of north India and Tamil kingdoms in the south (see also Abraham 2003; Smith 2001). Southeast Asia was a valuable source of raw materials for South Asian polities, particularly its tin sources and its gold (Basa 1998, 409). The coastal regions and inland river valleys of Southeast Asia's South China Sea proved fertile ground for the diffusion of Indic ideology. Whether by accident, through intent, or a combination of both, Hindu and Buddhist beliefs traveled to Southeast Asia with South Asian merchants and missionaries perhaps as early as the late first millennium BC (Bellina 1999, 2003; Ray 1989, 1994). Brick masonry Indic shrines; Vaishnavite, Saivite, and Buddhist stone sculptures; and inscriptions with indigenous Indian *brāhmī* scripts compose the first millennium landscape of Southeast Asia's coasts and river valleys. Despite this rich record of interaction or "Indianization" (see Mabbett 1997 for recent review), no substantial South Asian documentary corpus has been found that describes Southeast Asia and its people during this time. The majority of external documentation instead lies in Chinese dynastic histories.

The first documentary evidence for Southeast Asia in Chinese chronicles occurs during the Han dynasty (Ishizawa 1995, 11–13; Wheatley 1983, 152) during its often unsuccessful attempts to conquer the land of the southern barbarians. In the latter part of the later Han period (c. AD 25–220), international maritime trade was conducted between China, south India, and ultimately Rome through the South China Sea. Southeast Asia became a transshipment zone for Chinese merchants, who brought gold and silk to coastal polities along the South China Sea to trade for South Asian gems and pearls (Ishizawa 1995, 12). The recovery of several sewn-plank and lashed-lug boat remains, which the Chinese called *kunlun bo* (Manguin 1993, 261) and that date to the mid-first millennium AD (e.g., Manguin 1996), suggest that Southeast Asians played an important role in this international trade network.

Maintaining open routes through Southeast Asia required China either to conquer or to establish political linkages with Southeast Asian polities. The most abundant Chinese documentary evidence for diplomatic missions in the first millennium AD dates to the second through sixth centuries (Wheatley 1983, 153). The Chinese consistently describe one Southeast Asian polity as "Funan," and mention of these polities is found in multiple sources (review in Ishizawa 1995, 13). Emissaries Kang-tai and Zhuying visited Funan in AD 228 and reported the following:

> The people of Funan are malicious and cunning. They abduct and make slaves of inhabitants of neighboring towns who do not pay them homage. As merchandise they have gold, silver, and silks . . . The inhabitants of Funan make rings and bracelets of gold, and plates of silver. They cut down trees to make their dwellings. The king lives in a storied pavilion. They make their city walls of wooden palisades . . . The people also live in raised dwellings" (translation in Coedès 1968, 58; from Pelliot 1903, 261).

Early Chinese contact with Southeast Asian populations was essentially economic in nature (Jacques 1995, 38). For more than a millennium, the Chinese formalized tributary trade relationships throughout areas of Southeast Asia that they could not conquer; this broad area ranged from central Vietnam and the Philippines to the Mekong delta (see also Junker 1998, 302–5). From the third through the seventh centuries, Chinese emissaries were dispatched to Funan at least twenty-six times (Ishizawa 1995, 17). Southeast Asian tribute to the Chinese court included (but was not limited to) gold, silver, copper, tin, aromatic tropical wood, ivory, kingfishers and parakeets, sugar cane, pomegranates and oranges, and bananas (Wheatley 1983, 111). To the Chinese, this protourban polity was a kingdom (Wolters 1999, 109); to some historians, a chiefdom (Wheatley 1983, 119–98); and to others, an early state (Hall 1982, 1985; Vickery 1998). The Chinese recorded an oral tradition of the origins of Funan in third- through tenth-century Chinese dynastic histories (Hall 1982; Jacques 1979; Pelliot 1903). It is nearly identical to the Khok Thlok story that Cambodians recount and reenact today.

For decades, historians and archaeologists have sought the geographic location of Khok Thlok, and more than a dozen scholars have suggested competing locations for Funan (e.g., Colless 1972–73; Loofs-Wissowa 1968–69; Vickery 1998, 45; Wheatley 1983, 148). Yet the locations of this polity's inland capitals remain a mystery, despite concerted efforts to match Chinese toponyms with the Mekong delta's landscape. Angkor Borei also produced the earliest dated Khmer inscription in Cambodia (K. 600), which dates to AD 611, or Çaka year 533. It also contained an area called Khok Thlok.

Cambodia's Origins and Indigenous Evidence

In the Çaka year 533, on the thirteenth day of the lunar crossing of Māgha, lunar house of Pusya, the balance was at the horizon. The *Poñ Uy* made these gifts to *Kpoñ Kamratān Añ*: working or field personnel (4 males, 2 females, and one male infant), 60 head of bovines (cattle?), 2 buffaloes, 10 goats, 40 coconut trees, and 2 rice fields at the place of Ampon. Working personnel given by *Jam Añ* to *Vrah Kamratān Mahāganapati*: five male working personnel, 4 women working personnel, and a child, 20 head of cattle, two women specialists to serve the ceremonial specialist, to record sacred days and to make ritual offerings of flowers and incense to the god. (K. 600, north face; from Coedès 1942, 22–23).[1]

The received knowledge of early Cambodia during the first half of the first millennium AD derives primarily from Chinese documentary accounts (described previously) and secondarily from a corpus of indigenous inscriptions. Because these inscriptions predate the establishment of Angkor in AD 802, they are described as pre-Angkorian in age. Many examples of pre-Angkorian indigenous writing, in the form of inscribed stone stelae, have been recovered from sites across southern Cambodia and date as early as the seventh century AD. Some inscriptions have also been recovered from Vietnam's portion of the Mekong delta and from areas of central and northwestern Cambodia (Jacob 1979, 425; Vickery 1998, 97). The few scholars who have studied these pre-Angkorian inscriptions systematically have found evidence for social, political, and religious organization, for measurement systems, and for the natural and artificial environment in which these seventh- and eighth-century Cambodians lived (see, for example, Jacob 1979; Jacques 1979, 1995; Vickery 1998; Wolters 1979).

These pre-Angkorian inscriptions often contained two sections. The first section, or prologue, was commonly Sanskrit. It contained praise for the deity for whom the monument was dedicated and for the current ruler, explained the purpose of the brick structure in which it was found, named the donor of this structure, and listed the date of the dedication. The second section, in Khmer script, listed the date, deity, and donor; it also detailed the nature and precise content of the donations. This section also commonly included a malediction that warned of punishment to any who dared violate the building or its contents (see Vickery 1998, 98). Laudatory, reverent, fiscal, and punitive, these inscriptions provide the earliest internal documentary data from the ancient Khmers.

The seventh- and eighth-century Khmer inscriptions are rife with descriptions of elites, from royalty to local cult leaders. At least seven kings and one queen are listed in the inscriptions, as are seventeen other individuals whose titles suggest the status of king or chief (Vickery 1998, 177–89). Several terms for nonroyal elite officials appear in many inscriptions (Vickery 1998, 190–205). Yet the real power behind these titles remains unclear. Joffe (chapter 3) explores the disjunction between historical and archaeological evidence for the tenth- and ninth-century BC Levantine Iron Age: The former reconstructs large and powerful states, while the latter suggests a series of small and fragile polities. Similarly, Johns (chapter 5) questions the existence of a unified Islamic state during its first seventy years, when scant archaeological evidence suggests centralization and hegemony. Southeast Asian archaeology lags behind Near Eastern archaeology by many decades. Yet increased research on pre-Angkorian Cambodia holds potential to overturn conventional histories of unified kingdoms and large-scale military conquests. Elites in each of the competing polities across the ancient Khmer landscape elevated their material and ideological standing through erecting monuments inscribed with their acts, but we privilege such documentary evidence over the archaeological record at our own peril.

The earliest dated Khmer inscription (K. 557 and 600) was erected in the year A D 611 and later curated at the Buddhist temple of Wat Chruoy in the community of Angkor Borei (Coedès 1942, 21–23). Recovered in 1935 by French scholar Henri Mauger, only two of this sandstone stele's inscribed four sides were intact. Its Sanskrit and Khmer inscriptions list offerings to the local gods (perhaps female [Vickery 1998, 151–55]). Viewed in isolation, as its original translator Georges Coedès (1942, 21) dismissively noted, this inscription contains only lists of servants, land, and domestic animals. Yet analyzed as part of a corpus of seventh- and eighth-century inscriptions from southern Cambodia, these indigenous documents provide hypotheses regarding the sociopolitical organization and economy for this period. As previous historians (particularly Coedès 1968, 68; Vickery 1998, 45) have noted, one strong candidate for this ancient polity's capital is the archaeological site of Angkor Borei.

Cambodia's Origins and Archaeological Evidence

Angkor Borei is thus an archaeological site, a textualized origin story, and perhaps the center of a first millennium complex polity. During its early first-millennium A D occupation, this settlement was part of a regional economic, political, and social system that stretched across the Mekong delta and perhaps across the Gulf of Siam. Angkor Borei (figure 9.1) was part of early Southeast Asia (following Smith and Watson 1979) during a time when Hinduism and Buddhism first swept eastward from the Indian subcontinent, maritime trade routes between Rome and China traversed the South China Sea, and complex polities emerged along the coasts and river valleys of mainland Southeast Asia. While the Cambodians view Angkor Borei as the cradle of Khmer civilization, scholars view the site as integral to understanding early state formation between around 500 BC and AD 500. Despite its rich potential and until recently, however, most archaeologists have left this early historic period to art historians to decipher.

The Lower Mekong Archaeological Project has undertaken field investigations at Angkor Borei since 1996 (e.g., Stark 2001; Stark and Sovath 2001; Stark et al. 1999). Research examines the origins of state for-

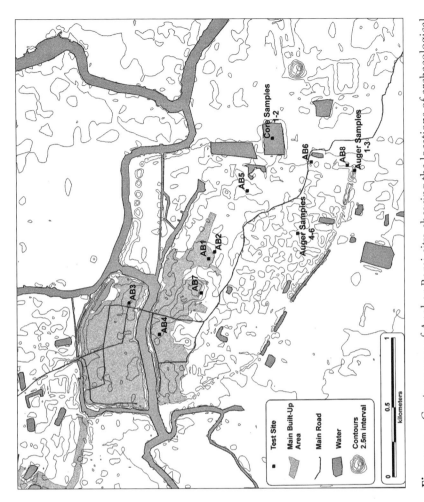

Figure 9.1 Contour map of Angkor Borei city, showing the locations of archaeological field investigations.

mation in the Mekong delta, where third- and sixth-century Chinese emissaries described the kingdom of Funan (Hall 1982, 1985). Louis Malleret's (1959, 1960, 1962) pathbreaking research during World War II on the possible Funan port site of Oc Eo, in southern Vietnam, produced physical evidence of Indian and Roman contact, including Indian seals, jewelry, and coins associated with Antoninus Pius (AD 152) and Marcus Aurelius. For more than twenty years, Vietnamese archaeologists have identified and tested more than seventy-nine "Oc Eo" culture sites (e.g., Ha Van Tan 1986). Yet no archaeological work had been done on Cambodia's side of the delta since Captain Lunet de Lajonquière completed his survey of historic sites in Cambodia a century ago (Lunet de Lajonquière 1902).

Lower Mekong Archaeological Project members combine archaeological excavations, paleoenvironmental research, and geoarchaeological techniques to reconstruct the occupational history of Angkor Borei and the canal system that linked this center to a network of contemporary settlements (Bishop et al. 2003; Sanderson et al. 2003). Work thus far has established an occupational history that begins in the fourth century BC, more than five hundred years before the Chinese first described Funan, and that has continued without interruption to the present day.

These archaeological approaches illuminate locational, economic, and ecological aspects of this ancient Mekong delta polity. Examination of documentary sources is equally important to understanding the polity that the Chinese visited and with whom they established political alliances through the mid-first millennium AD. Documentary data have been translated and analyzed by several generations of scholars. Exogenous sources consist primarily of Chinese dynastic annals, translated by Pelliot (1903), Wheatley (1983), and Ishizawa (1995). Indigenous sources, which include both Sanskrit and Khmer inscriptions, have been the subject of interest for nearly as long and continue to undergo reanalysis (e.g., Coedès 1968, 40–42; 55–62; Vickery 1998).

Research at Angkor Borei falls within the realm of historical archaeology, because it involves the material culture of literate societies (Andrén 1998; Funari 1999, 57; Funari, Jones, and Hall 1999, 7; cf. Orser 1996). Integrating archaeological and documentary sources on Angkor Borei, and on the early historic period Mekong delta more generally, remains difficult for methodological reasons that archaeologists have debated (e.g., Andrén 1998; Feinman 1997; Kepecs 1997; Leone and Potter 1998). Research in the Mekong delta and more generally on early Southeast Asia provides a comparative context for discussing issues raised in this volume's chapters. Doing so provides a framework for examining the complicated relationship of archaeology and history, which involves both methodological and conceptual issues. Because my background lies in Asian archaeology, the bulk of my comments focus on the South, East, and Southeast Asia chapters in this volume (i.e., chapters 6–8).

Methodological Concerns and Chapters in This Volume

One of the most salient methodological issues concerns the tyranny of the historical record (e.g., Johnson 1999, 27). A second issue focuses on the relative importance of documentary versus archaeological data to interpret different points in the ancient past. I will, finally, discuss how chapters in this volume inform on the relative importance or value of indigenous documentary data versus exogenous data. Although some of the chapters did not discuss these topics explicitly, their content exemplifies some of the issues.

Alexander H. Joffe (chapter 3) notes scholars' "historicist" tendency to privilege documentary data over archaeological data. Archaeologists working across the Old World have also confronted this problem in Africa (e.g., Stahl 2001), South Asia (e.g., Morrison and Lycett 1997), and Southeast Asia (Allard 1998; Allen 1998; Junker 1998; Lape 2001; Stark 1998; Welch 1998). This volume reveals how a reliance on documentary records, often without sufficient source-side criticism, characterizes research on the Mauryan empire (Trautmann and Sinopoli, chapter 6), sixteenth-century Indonesia (Lape, chapter 8), and work on the first millennium BC in the Levant (Joffe, chapter 3).

Such historicist approaches characterize much current scholarship in the field, either through a "philological" approach (following Andrén 1998, 113–20) in which archaeology is undertaken to recover new texts, or through an approach intended to provide background information that facilitates textual analysis. Archaeology has played a subordinate role to history in the scholarship of ancient Mesopotamia, to the detriment of the field. Perhaps one explanation for this imbalance lies in the sheer quantity of indigenous documentation for historic Mesopotamia: seventeen thousand tablets were recovered from Nippur, and thirty thousand tablets from the site of Tello (Zettler, chapter 4). In such circumstances, it is no surprise that archaeology has sometimes been viewed primarily as a retrieval system for documentary data, and as a strategy for enriching textual reconstructions.

The Indian case that Trautmann and Sinopoli describe, in which eighteenth- and nineteenth-century colonial scholarship used epigraphy and philology rather than archaeology to understand the past, also characterizes Southeast Asian countries formerly under French, British, and Dutch colonial control (Wang Gungwu 1986, xii). This European colonial tradition that subordinated archaeological work to confirming claims made on historical evidence also left huge gaps in our knowledge of critical junctures in history, like how the Mauryan empire (India) stimulated the eastward spread of Buddhism. A similar pattern characterizes mainland Southeast Asia, where a virtual black hole exists for the period around 500 BC to AD 500 (Stark and Allen 1998, 165–66).

Ideally, archaeological and documentary data should complement each other to enrich reconstruction and identify contradictions in the data sources (Funari, Jones, and Hall 1999). Pioneering work of this sort has been done on the Shang period in China (e.g., Chang 1983; Keightley 1983) and has stimulated subsequent archaeological research programs. Research on the port town of Berenike, so ably reported in this volume by Wendrich and colleagues, also offers an excellent example of complementarity, despite the methodological limitations the authors describe. Their botanical analysis was particularly useful, since few textual sources discussed the range of foods and organic raw materials that would have circulated in the Mediterranean–Indian Ocean basin trade network. Some evidence, like the recovery of rice and Job's tears, might support economic models in which foreign traders (including South Asians) lived in these international trading ports. While such a scenario has been proposed for coastal polities in Island Southeast Asia during this period (e.g., Allen 1998; Bronson 1977), preservation conditions do not permit the recovery of supporting botanical evidence in the Southeast Asian tropics.

Gauging the relative importance of documentary versus archaeological data at different points in the past is a second methodological concern raised in this volume's chapters. For the late prehistoric period, and for societies whose writing systems we still do not understand, like the Indus civilization, documentary data may provide an important source of analogies (Andrén 1998, 121–24). But the relationship is more complex at points in the historic sequence when either indigenous documents do not yet exist (leaving the burden of explanation to outsiders' descriptions) or they have a very restricted informational content. The earliest indigenous inscriptions in the Mekong delta, for example, are dedicatory stelae placed in or near brick monuments that were religious in function (some perhaps mortuary, and others local cult shrines). These inscriptions yield information on dynastic genealogies and political structure (Vickery 1998) but remain largely silent on place names and economic organization.

Turning to the Indus civilization, Trautmann and Sinopoli contend that scholars have been less critical of partial or limited documentary evidence that is unsupported by archaeological evidence than the opposite. When writing and literacy become established in a particular society, does the archaeological record recede in importance? Can documentary evidence in the absence of archaeological data be sufficient to establish claims of statehood (following Johns, chapter 5)? Peter Lape's analysis of early colonial organization in eastern Indonesia (chapter 8) illustrates how archaeological data illuminates and challenges reconstructions based primarily on documentary data. His identification of a range of settlements ignored by colonial cartographers underscores the incompleteness of documentary information, and the need to use multiple lines of evidence to study these phenomena. In Li Min's case study of Jinan (China), archaeological information complements the documentary sources and also enables us to study local-level developments within a much larger polity (chapter 7).

Chapters in this volume explore alternative ways to define the relationship between documentary and archaeological data. Andrén (1998, 148) wonders whether texts are superior to artifacts at expressing certain ideas, or vice versa. But perhaps complementarity, rather than ranking or even concordance, is the best possible result of merging archaeological and documentary data. Li Min's comparison of the spatial distribution of Qi coins against textual records produces insights regarding the nature of the local economy. Likewise, comparison of historical accounts with the archaeological distribution of inscribed bronze weaponry yields information on the nature of military confrontation.

My final methodological concern centers on the relative value of indigenous documentary data versus exogenous data. One might argue that indigenous sources are more valuable than exogenous sources, since the latter are written with specific (and often colonialist) audiences in mind. Yet literacy comes to many of the world's regions from the outside first, and the earliest indigenous writing often employs outsiders' writing systems and even vocabulary. In pre-Angkorian Cambodia, inscribed stelae generally include both Sanskrit and Khmer inscriptions, and the content of each inscription varies (Vickery 1998, 95–96).

This volume's chapters have relied on many forms of indigenous documentary data, from inscriptions on stelae (in Iron Age southern

Levant and in the Ashokan edicts in South Asia); inscribed bronze tripods, chime bells, measurement containers, weapons, iron artifacts, and
stamped pottery (Jinan in eastern China); inscribed seals (Indus Valley);
stamp seals, cylinder seals, and tablets (southern Levant); coins, papyri,
tombstones, and travelers' graffiti (Syria and Palestine region); to customs archives and contracts (Berenike). Exogenous sources are also
varied, including dynastic annals (Jinan) and official histories (southern
Levant), travelers' accounts (Berenike, Banda Islands of Indonesia), and
maps (Banda Islands). These various sources inform differently, and to
different degrees, on the kinds of questions that interest archaeologists.
In some cases, archaeologists find entire populations that documentary
sources exclude from their records. Lape's identification of Banda settlements excluded from sixteenth-century Dutch maps is one case in point,
while the exclusion of transhumant populations in northern Mesopotamia from the Ebla texts (Zettler, chapter 4) is another. Oral traditions
can serve as another important indigenous documentary source, at least
in early Southeast Asia (Wang Gungwu 1979, 4), but analytical tools for
using oral traditions remain poorly developed.

Despite repeated calls for source-side criticism (e.g., Johnson 1999,
30; Stahl 1993), most historical archaeologists do not engage in the kind
of analysis necessary to make these documents truly useful. Little evidence exists for source-side criticism in Chinese historical archaeology;
if such exists, archaeologists of China rarely discuss it (but see Allard
1998, 323–27). In chapter 4, Zettler contends that a lack of source-side
criticism characterizes both archaeologists who use documentary data
(e.g., the mistranslation of the Curse of Akkad) and historians who rely
exclusively on misleading documents (e.g., studies of fish consumption
in southern Mesopotamia during the Assyrian and Old Babylonian periods). Johns's systematic analysis of documentary evidence for the origins of the Islamic state (chapter 5) effectively demonstrates the need to
interrogate historical sources as closely as we do archaeological sources.

Archaeologists and historians need to engage more aggressively in
source-side criticism in each direction, and to collaborate more closely
and frequently. Historians of early Southeast Asia also recognize this
need (e.g., Brown 1996; Christie 1979; Jacques 1979; Wang Gungwu 1986;
Wheatley 1983; Wolters 1999), since the early historic period contains
scant (and predominantly exogenous) documentary data and also establishes the foundation for Classical states that emerge across the region
some seven hundred years later. Yet close collaborative research is still
rare, and holistic strategies must be generated to overcome these prob-

lems. The Sumerian Agricultural Group structure that Zettler describes might serve as a useful precedent.

Writing, Power, and Identity

Despite the geographic, temporal, and thematic diversity of this volume's chapters, some conceptual issues resonate throughout the collection that focus on the relationship between writing, power, and identity. The first concerns social and political impacts of the development of writing. Writing was a technological innovation with deep ramifications (Joffe, chapter 3, and Zettler, chapter 4). Throughout much of early Southeast Asia, organizational changes coincide with the earliest written records (e.g., Stark 1998; Welch 1998, 222). Writing, as an innovation, was particularly transformative when enterprising individuals and groups were able to restrict access to knowledge required to participate in literate culture (Andrén 1998, 147).

The development and control of writing conferred ritual and social power to individual elites. Writing and monumental constructions are, of course, closely linked: Writing inscribes power, monumentality radiates power, and inscribed monuments institutionalize power. In early state societies like pre-Angkorian Cambodia, royalty, nonroyal officials, and elites inscribed records of their economic largesse and religious commitment on and around the earliest architectural monuments in the region (Vickery 1998). In ancient China, Shang and Zhou literate elites worked directly with the kings as diviners and archivists (Chang 1980; Keightley 1978). Activities like prognostication imbued them with authority that derives from restricted access to knowledge of the written word (e.g., Keightley 1994), and diviners whose names are preserved in Shang inscriptions may well have included chieftains from polities that the Shang conquered (Lewis 1999, 15). Writing was used for similar ends in ancient Cambodia: Jayavarman II inscribed himself as Cambodia's first universal monarch (or *cakravartin*) in AD 802. Subsequent generations erected inscribed stelae in their brick and (later) sandstone monuments that traced direct ancestry back to this king to legitimize their rule.

That writing was linked to economic power is clear across much of the Old World. Yet religious and economic power merged in the indigenous documentary traditions of Egypt and in Mesopotamia (Zettler, chapter 4): In both cases, temple economies controlled substantial wealth. In this light especially, our continued inability to translate the Harap-

pan texts (Trautmann and Sinopoli, chapter 6) is a handicap in efforts
to understand the growth and nature of Indus civilization.

The act of writing also conferred social power and created social
identity. Societies inscribed themselves on their social and political landscapes through outsiders' descriptions and through indigenous texts.
The earliest indigenous writing in the lower Mekong basin was derived
from a Sanskrit alphabet and appears first in the early seventh century AD; its appearance coincides with the first descriptions of ethnically Khmer populations. Joffe's chapter illustrates the indigenous use of
documentary data to inscribe a large scale of social identity in the process that he calls "ethnicization."

From the Delta Outward

Decades of scholarship by dedicated Khmer epigraphers and historians have been, and continue to be, essential to reconstructing the early
history of the Mekong delta. So, too, is systematic archaeological research that not only identifies and recovers "new" inscriptions for the
epigraphers, but also provides information on the ancient economic and
regional political organization. Historians have repeatedly called for archaeological research in the region (e.g., Wheatley 1983, 124), including
the memorable plea that "the answer . . . will be provided by the trowel"
(Christie 1979, 287). In studies of early Southeast Asia, archaeologists
and historians must work together more closely if for no other reason
than mutual need. But beyond that need is a synergy that can be produced only through collaboration.

Oral history, exogenous accounts, and indigenous texts are all as
integral to studying emergent state formation in the Mekong delta as
is archaeological information; pre-Angkorian research is thus subject
to the same methodological issues seen globally in historical archaeology. In many parts of the world, efforts to distinguish documentary
sources from archaeological sources are ultimately problematic: cuneiform tablets, Mayan stelae, Ashokan edicts, and Islamic coins are simultaneously documentary and archaeological data sources. Chapters in
this volume have incorporated these various documentary forms, sometimes in concert with the archaeological record, and sometimes in contrast. Compared with the deep traditions of Chinese (Li Min, chapter 7), Indian (Trautmann and Sinopoli, chapter 6), and Mesopotamian
scholarship (Zettler, chapter 4), archaeological and historical research
in the Mekong delta is in its infancy. This volume's substantive and in-

sightful chapters illustrate the great potential inherent in merging documentary and archaeological sources, and offer suggestions for methodological approaches. Their contributions not only identify areas for future research, but also provide valuable guidelines for future studies in lesser-known regions across Asia.

Notes

My thanks are extended to Norman Yoffee for inviting me to participate in this stimulating project. I am also grateful to Michael Vickery for his invaluable tutorials on pre-Angkorian history in the last several years, and particularly for his assistance in translating the K. 600 inscription. I finally thank colleagues in Cambodia's Ministry of Culture and Fine Arts, particularly Her Royal Highness Princess Norodom Bopha Devi and His Excellency Chuch Phoeurn. Their support and encouragement have been essential to my Cambodian research.

1. The title Poñ connotes elite status, refers to the founder or donor of seventh- and early eighth-century monuments, and might have served as rulers' representatives in establishing foundations (Vickery 1998, 190–92). The title Kpoñ Kamratān Añ may refer to a pre-Sanskritic local-lineage goddess (Vickery 1998, 152). The term Vrah Kamratān may refer to a pre-Sanskritic local-lineage god, whose name in this case is Mahāganapati. In pre-Angkorian inscriptions, mratān was a high-ranking sub-royal title (Vickery 1998, 190–205). The term yajamāna translates literally as "sacrificer" in Sanskrit, but its Khmer usage remains unclear beyond the fact that this individual was involved in commemorating foundations and installing deity images within those structures (Vickery 1998:158–59).

Bibliography

Abraham, Shinu. 2003. "Chera, Chola, Pandya: Using Archaeological Evidence to Identify the Tamil Kingdoms of Early Historic South India." *Asian Perspectives* 42 (2): 207–23.

Allard, Francis. 1998. "Stirrings at the Periphery: History, Archaeology, and the Study of Dian." *International Journal of Historical Archaeology* 2 (4): 321–42.

Allen, S. Jane. 1998. "History, Archaeology, and the Question of Foreign Control in Early Historic–period Peninsular Malaysia." *International Journal of Historical Archaeology* 2 (4): 261–90.

Andrén, Anders. 1998. *Between Artifacts and Texts: Historical Archaeology in Global Perspective*. New York: Plenum Press.

Basa, Kishore 1998. "Indian Writings on Early History and Archaeology of Southeast Asia: A Historiographical Analysis." *Journal of the Royal Asiatic Society* (Series 3) 8 (3): 395–410.

Bellina, Bérénice. 1999. "La formation des réseaux d'échanges reliant l'Asie du Sud et l'Asie du Sud-est à travers le matériel archéologique (VIe siècle av. J.-C.-VIe siècle ap. J.-C.): Le cas de la Thaïlande et la Péninsule Malaise." *Journal of the Siam Society* 86:89–105.

———. 2003. "Beads, Social Change and Interaction between India and South-east Asia." *Antiquity* 297:285–97.

Bishop, Paul, Dan Penny, Miriam T. Stark and Marian Scott. 2003. "A 3.5ka Record of Paleoenvironments and Human Occupation at Angkor Borei, Mekong Delta, Southern Cambodia." *Geoarchaeology* 18 (3): 1–35.

Bronson, Bennet. 1977. "Exchange at the Upstream and Downstream Ends: Notes Toward a Functional Model of the Coastal State in Southeast Asia." In *Economic Exchange and Social Interaction in Southeast Asia: Perspectives from Prehistory, History, and Ethnography*, ed. K. H. Hutterer, 39–52. Michigan Papers on South and Southeast Asia No. 13. Ann Arbor: Center for South and Southeast Asian Studies, University of Michigan.

Brown, Robert L. 1996. *The Dvāravati Wheels of the Law and the Indianization of South East Asia*. Leiden, Netherlands: Brill.

Chang, Kwang-chih. 1980. *Shang Civilization*. New Haven, Conn.: Yale University Press.

———. 1983. *Art, Myth and Ritual: The Path to Political Authority in Ancient China*. Cambridge, Mass.: Harvard University Press.

Christie, A. H. 1979. "Lin-i, Fu-nan, Java." In *Early South East Asia: Essays in Archaeology, History, and Historical Geography*, ed. R. B. Smith and W. Watson, 281–87. New York: Oxford University Press.

Christie, Jan Wisseman. 1995. "State Formation in Early Maritime Southeast Asia: A Consideration of the Theories and the Data." *Bijdragen tot de Taal- Land- en Volkenkunde* 151 (2): 235–88.

Coedès, Georges. 1942. *Inscriptions du Cambodge*. Vol. 2. Hanoi: École Française d'Extrême Orient.

———. 1968. *The Indianized States of Southeast Asia*. Ed. W. F. Vella. Trans. S. B. Cowing. Honolulu: East-West Center Press.

Colless, Brian E. 1972–73. "The Ancient Bnam Empire: Fu-nan and Po-nan." *Journal of the Oriental Society of Australia* 9 (1–2): 21–31.

Feinman, Gary. 1997. "Thoughts on New Approaches to Combining the Archaeological and Historical Records." *Journal of Archaeological Method and Theory* 4:367–77.

Funari, Pedro Paolo A. 1999. "Historical Archaeology from a World Perspective." In *Historical Archaeology: Back from the Edge*, ed. P. P. A. Funari, M. Hall and S. Jones, 37–66. One World Archaeology 31. London: Routledge.

Funari, Pedro Paolo A., Siân Jones, and Martin Hall. 1999. "Introduction: Archaeology in History." In *Historical Archaeology: Back from the Edge*, ed. P. P. A. Funari, M. Hall and S. Jones, 1–20. One World Archaeology 31. London: Routledge.

Gaudes, Rüdiger. 1977. "Kambodschanishe Hochzeitsbräuche und -legenden." *Jarhbuch des Museums für Völkerkunde zu Leipzig* 31:51–80.

———. 1993. "Kaundinya, Preah Thaong, and the Nāgī Somā: Some Aspects of a Cambodian Legend." *Asian Folklore Studies* 52:333–58.

Groslier, Bernard Philippe. 1966. *Indochina*. Translated by J. Hogarth. Cleveland: World Publishing Company.

Ha Van Tan. 1986. "Oc Eo: Endogenous and Exogenous Elements." *Vietnam Social Sciences* 1–2 (7–8): 91–101.

Hall, Kenneth. 1982. "The 'Indianization' of Funan: An Economic History of Southeast Asia's First State." *Journal of Southeast Asian Studies* 13:81–106.

———. 1985. *Maritime Trade and State Development in Early Southeast Asia*. Honolulu: University of Hawai'i Press.

Ishizawa, Y. 1995. "Chinese Chronicles of 1st–5th Century AD *Funan*, Southern Cambodia." In *South East Asia and China: Art, Interaction and Commerce*, ed. R. Scott and J. Guy, 11–31. Colloquies on Art and Archaeology in Asia No. 17. London: University of London Percival David Foundation of Chinese Art.

Jacob, Judith. 1979. "Pre-Angkor Cambodia: Evidence from the Inscriptions in Khmer Concerning the Common People and Their Environment." In *Early South East Asia: Essays in Archaeology, History, and Historical Geography*, ed. R. B. Smith and W. Watson, 406–26. New York: Oxford University Press.

Jacques, Claude. 1979. "'Funan,' 'Zhenla': The Reality Concealed by These Chinese Views of Indochina." In *Early South East Asia: Essays in Archaeology, History, and Historical Geography*, ed. R. B. Smith, and W. Watson, 371–79. New York: Oxford University Press.

———. 1995. "China and Ancient Khmer History." In *South East Asia and China: Art, Interaction and Commerce*, ed. R. Scott and J. Guy, 32–40. Colloquies on Art and Archaeology in Asia No. 17. London: Percival David Foundation of Chinese Art, School of Oriental and African Studies, University of London.

Johnson, Matthew. 1999. "Rethinking Historical Archaeology." In *Historical Archaeology: Back from the Edge*, ed. P. P. A. Funari, M. Hall and S. Jones, 23–26. One World Archaeology 31. London: Routledge.

Junker, Laura Lee. 1998. "Integrating History and Archaeology in the Study of Contact Period Philippine Chiefdoms." *International Journal of Historical Archaeology* 2 (4): 291–320.

Keightley, David N. 1978. *Sources of Shang history: The Oracle-bone Inscriptions of Bronze Age China*. Berkeley: University of California Press.

———. 1983. "The Late Shang State: When, Where, and What?" In *The Origins of*

Chinese Civilization, ed. D. N. Keightley, 523–64. Berkeley: University of California Press.

———. 1994. "Sacred Characters." In *China: Ancient Culture, Modern Land*, ed. R. E. Murowchick, 71–79. Norman: University of Oklahoma Press.

Kepecs, Susan. 1997. "Introduction to New approaches to Combining the Archaeological and Historical Records." *Journal of Archaeological Method and Theory* 4:193–98.

Kulke, Hermann. 1986. "The Early and Imperial Kingdom in Southeast Asian History." In *Southeast Asia in the 9th to 14th centuries*, ed. D. G. Marr and A. C. Milner, 1–23. Canberra: Research School of Pacific Studies, Australian National University and Singapore: Institute of Southeast Asian Studies.

Lape, Peter V. 2001. "Historic Maps and Archaeology as a Means of Understanding Late Precolonial Settlement in the Banda Islands, Indonesia." *Asian Perspectives* 41 (1): 43–70.

Leone, Mark P., and Parker B. Potter. 1998. "Introduction: Issues in Historical Archaeology." In *The Recovery of Meaning: Historical Archaeology in the Eastern United States*, ed. M. P. Leone and P. B. Potter, 1–22. Washington, D.C.: Smithsonian Institution Press.

Lewis, Mark E. 1999. *Writing and Authority in Early China*. SUNY Series in Chinese Philosophy and Culture. Albany: State University of New York Press.

Lewitz, Saveros. 1973. "Kpuon Ābāh-Bibāh ou le livre de marriage des Khmers." *Bulletin de l'École Française d'Extrême Orient* 60:243–328.

Loofs-Wissowa, H. H. E. 1968–69. "Funanese Cultural Elements in the Lower Menam Basin." *Journal of the Oriental Society of Australia* 6 (1–2): 5–9.

Lunet de Lajonquière, Edward E. 1902. *Inventaire descriptif des monuments du Cambodge*. Vol. 4. Paris: Publications de l'École Française d'Extrême Orient.

Mabbett, I. W. 1997. "The 'Indianization' of Mainland Southeast Asia: A Reappraisal." In *Living a Life in Accord with Dhamma: Papers in Honor of Professor Jean Boisselier on his Eightieth Birthday*, ed. N. Eilenberg, M. C. Subhadradis Diskul and R. Brown, 342–55. Bangkok: Silpakorn University.

Malleret, Louis. 1959. *L'Archéologie du Delta du Mékong*, Part 1, *L'Exploration Archéologique et Les Fouilles d'Oc-Èo*. Paris: École Française d'Extrême-Orient.

———. 1960. *L'Archéologie du Delta du Mékong*, Part 2, *La Civilisation Matérielle d'Oc-Èo*. 2 vols. Paris: École Française d'Extrême-Orient.

———. 1962. *L'Archéologie du Delta du Mékong*, Part 3, *La Culture du Fou-Nan*. 2 vols. Paris: École Française d'Extrême-Orient.

Manguin, Pierre-Yves. 1993. "Trading Ships of the South China Sea." *Journal of the Economic and Social History of the Orient* 36:253–80.

———. 1996. "Southeast Asian Shipping in the Indian Ocean during the First Millennium A D." In *Tradition and Archaeology: Early Maritime Contacts in the In-*

dian Ocean, ed. H. P. Ray and J. F. Salles, 181–96. National Institute of Science, Technology and Development Studies. New Delhi: Manohar.

Morrison, K. D., and M. T. Lycett 1997. "Inscriptions as Artifacts: Precolonial South India and the Analysis of Texts." *Journal of Archaeological Method and Theory* 4.3/4:215–37.

Orser, Charles. 1996. *A Historical Archaeology of the Modern World*. New York: Plenum Press.

Pelliot, Paul. 1903. "Le Fou-nan." *Bulletin de l'École Française d'Extrême Orient* 3:248–303.

Ray, Himanshu Prabha. 1989. "Early Maritime Contacts between South and Southeast Asia." *Journal of Southeast Asian History* 20:1–42.

———. 1994. *The Winds of Change: Buddhism and the Maritime Links of Early South Asia*. Delhi: Oxford University Press.

Sanderson, David C. W., Paul Bishop, Miriam T. Stark, and Janet Q. Spencer. 2003. "Luminescence Dating of Anthropogenically Reset Canal Sediments from Angkor Borei, Mekong Delta, Cambodia." *Quaternary Science Reviews* 22:1111–21.

Smith, Monica L. 2001. *The Archaeology of an Early Historic Town in Central India*. BAR International Series 1002. Oxford: British Archaeological Reports.

Smith, Robert B., and William Watson. 1979. "Introduction." In *Early Southeast Asia: Essays in Archaeology, History, and Historical Geography*, ed. R. B. Smith and W. Watson, 3–14. New York and Kuala Lumpur: Oxford University Press.

Stahl, Ann Brower. 1993. "Concepts of Time and Approaches to Analogical Reasoning in Historical Perspective." *American Antiquity* 58:235–60.

———. 2001. *Making History in Banda: Anthropological Visions of Africa's Past*. New York: Cambridge University Press.

Stark, Miriam T. 1998. "The Transition to History in the Mekong Delta: A View from Cambodia." *International Journal of Historical Archaeology* 2 (3): 175–204.

———. 2001. "Some Preliminary Results of the 1999–2000 Archaeological Field Investigations at Angkor Borei, Takeo Province." *Udaya: Journal of Khmer Studies* 2:19–36.

Stark, Miriam T., and S. Jane Allen. 1998. "The Transition to History in Southeast Asia: An Introduction." *International Journal of Historical Archaeology* 2 (3): 163–75.

Stark, Miriam T., P. Bion Griffin, Chuch Phoeurn, Judy Ledgerwood, Michael Dega, Carol Mortland, Nancy Dowling, James M. Bayman, Bong Sovath, Tea Van, Chhan Chamroeun, and David K. Latinis. 1999. "Results of the 1995–1996 Field Investigations at Angkor Borei, Cambodia." *Asian Perspectives* 38 (1): 7–36.

Stark, Miriam T., and Bong Sovath. 2001. "Recent Research on the Emergence of Early Historic States in Cambodia's Lower Mekong Delta." *Bulletin of the Indo-Pacific Prehistory Association* 21 (5): 85–98.

Vickery, Michael. 1998. *Society, Economics and Politics in Pre-Angkorian Cambodia: The 7th and 8th Centuries*. The Centre for East Asian Cultural Studies for UNESCO. Tokyo: The Toyo Bunko Foundation.

Wang Gungwu. 1979. "Introduction: The Study of the Southeast Asian Past." In *Perceptions of the Past in Southeast Asia*, ed. A. Reid and D. Marr, 1–9. Singapore: Heinemann Educational Books.

———. 1986. "Introduction." In *Southeast Asia in the 9th to 14th Centuries*, ed. D. G. Marr and A. C. Milner, xi–xviii. Singapore; Sydney: Institute of Southeast Asian Studies, and Research School of Pacific Studies, Australian National University.

Welch, David J. 1998. "Archaeology of Northeast Thailand in Relation to the Pre-Khmer and Khmer Historical Records." *International Journal of Historical Archaeology* 2 (4): 205–35.

Wheatley, Paul. 1983. *Nagara and Commandery: Origins of the Southeast Asian Urban Traditions*. Research Papers Nos. 207–8. Chicago: Department of Geography, University of Chicago.

Wolters, Oliver W. 1979. "Khmer 'Hinduism' in the Seventh Century." In *Early Southeast Asia: Essays in Archaeology, History, and Historical Geography*, ed. R. B. Smith and W. Watson, 427–42. New York and Kuala Lumpur: Oxford University Press.

——— 1999. *History, Culture, and Religion in Southeast Asian Perspectives*. 2nd ed. Ithaca, N.Y.: Southeast Asia Program, Cornell University Press.

10

The Materiality of History
Reflections on the Strengths of the Archaeological Record

PHILIP L. KOHL

Archaeological data are often deemed ambiguous, open to alternative or multiple readings of their historical significance. Some strands of current archaeological theory even celebrate these purported limitations of archaeological evidence. The archaeological record, we are told, is always "undetermined," making possible, if not inevitable, multiple and sometimes contradictory interpretations of that past. Taken to an extreme, this postprocessual perspective leads to an intellectual paralysis: archaeological knowledge is uncertain, and one interpretation of the past is as good or as valid as another. Such a verdict is overstated and cannot be sustained. One can and should distinguish plausible from implausible, impossible, or even dangerous reconstructions of the past. As we will see here, however, it remains true that the archaeologist cannot always unequivocally demonstrate or scientifically prove an interpretation grounded in the material culture record. Does such an admission imply that material remains are a more ambiguous and less reliable source for reconstructing the past than the written records of the historian?

This commentary explores the relative strengths and weaknesses of material culture and written sources. Are they qualitatively distinct or complementary? Is one necessarily superior or more informative than the other? To what extent does the same uncertainty of interpretation beset the historical record, particularly when that record is fragmentary and partial? One way to answer such questions is to focus on the *limits* of material-culture ambiguity. That is, while some interpretations cannot be confirmed and must remain provisional, others can be reasonably demonstrated and accepted by a community of scholars familiar with the evidence. The example of the manipulation of archaeological evidence for contemporary political purposes, particularly for the promotion of nationalism or the celebration of one ethnic group over others, is instructive in showing what cannot and what can be said from material remains.

Countless historical and contemporary examples of such manipulation and misuse abound. T. Trautmann and C. Sinopoli (chapter 6) review the creation of a racial theory of Indian civilization and briefly allude to the current quest to locate the homeland of the Indo-Europeans solidly in the subcontinent, counting the Indus Valley civilization as one of the earliest achievements of these pre-Vedic Aryans. Most Western scholars reject this interpretation and see it for what it blatantly is: a fillip to Hindu nationalists. The same assessment can be made for other current efforts to locate the *Urheimat* of the Indo-Europeans on the Ukrainian or south Russian steppes. Such dubious reconstructions are correctly perceived as politically motivated. But can they be disproved? Unfortunately, archaeologists simply cannot solve what is essentially a linguistic and historical problem. In the absence of decipherable texts, the archaeologist cannot positively identify the language spoken by the people whose material remains he or she studies. Score one for material-culture ambiguity.

Nevertheless, there are limits to politically biased readings of archaeological remains. The Nazis found their *Indo-Germanen* in a homeland that encompassed and extended beyond the borders of the German state, using their questionable ethnic identification of material remains as a pretext for military expansion. Archaeology under the Third Reich, of course, represents the paradigmatic example of how past material remains can be manipulated to fulfill contemporary political agendas. Yet even Hitler recognized the limits of such manipulation, castigating Himmler to the effect: "Why do we call the whole world's attention to the fact that we have no past? It's bad enough that the Romans were erecting great buildings when our forefathers were still living in mud huts; now Himmler is starting to dig up these villages of mud huts and enthusing over every potsherd and stone axe he finds . . . We really should do our best to keep quiet about this past" (as cited in Arnold 1992, 36). To Hitler's chagrin and Mussolini's delight, the later Iron Age remains from barbarian Central Europe simply were less impressive than those found in the heart of the Roman Empire; it was impossible to confuse one for the other despite the political imperative to do so.

Let us return to contemporary India. If we are unable on current evidence to discredit totally the identification of the Indus Valley civilization as Aryan, archaeology can positively demonstrate that the Babri

Masjid at Ayodhya was not built over the remains of a Hindu temple dedicated to the god Rama. Although allegations for the existence of such a temple were made, they can and have been shown to be false. Indeed, had such archaeological disclosure been forthcoming in 1992, hundreds of lives may have been saved and a political crisis averted. The point is that material culture evidence is not infinitely ambiguous and manipulable. Alternative interpretations or assessments of the same evidence may be possible, but some reconstructions are capable of being unequivocally demonstrated and others of being disproven. In this respect, the archaeological and historical records are not qualitatively distinct.

The most influential prehistorian V. Gordon Childe (1956, 21–22) thought that at times "archaeological data had to be invoked to correct the ambiguities and errors of the ancient written records." While keenly aware of its inherent limitations, he often preferred archaeological evidence over written sources for the former more clearly revealed an orderly, rational process of ever-increasing human control of nature, the record of technological progress that defined human cultural evolution (Childe 1951, 171, 175). Writing in an earlier age of archaeological theory and method, he remained skeptical of archaeology's ability to reconstruct nonmaterial aspects of social structure and ideology. But as a materialist, he considered such aspects secondary, and he consoled himself with the fact that the material culture record was at least sufficiently informative to demonstrate that social evolution had been made by humans, not by inexplicable natural or supernatural forces. Childe never suffered from an archaeological inferiority complex, resigning himself to the inevitable "tyranny of the text." In a sense, the archaeological record was even superior to the historical record, because the former did not consciously lie or distort what had happened in the past.

Childe's views today seem both dated and overstated and his materialism too vulgar. Using new types of evidence, contemporary archaeologists can reconstruct much more of the intangible features of past societies, including, to some extent, their values and belief systems. It should also be admitted that archaeological data can also deliberately mislead and present essentially the same epistemological or historiographic problems that confront the historian. Is monumental art a sign of power or instability and weakness? Is the Luxor relief of the Battle of Qadesh in 1275 BC any less or more misleading than Ramses II's account of it (cf. Kitchen 1995, 766–67)? Here too the archaeological record is neither superior nor inferior to that provided by written sources. Both the archaeologist and the historian must read between the lines of their evidentiary sources to determine "what happened in history."

The chapters collected in this volume use contemporary archaeological techniques and interpretations and illustrate the much greater strengths of the material-culture record for reconstructing the past, not only complementing what is known historically, but also adding to it and, at times, correcting it. With its use of settlement pattern data and recovery of new types of information, such as paleobotanical remains, today's archaeology can tell us much more about the past than earlier generations of historians and even archaeologists, like Childe, believed possible. The chapters collected here convincingly illustrate this power and demonstrate that archaeological and historical research complement one another and should be used in tandem. P. Lape's chapter (8) explicitly addresses this point. He wants to "transcend the limitations of each kind of data." His research on trade and the advent and role of Islam in the Banda Islands clearly shows how combining both sets of data—the archaeological and the documentary—leads to new "insights beyond what either could provide alone." The Dutch not only possessed overwhelming military force when they conquered the islands in the early seventeenth century, but they were also the beneficiaries of Bandanese factionalism with deep economic and ideological roots.

Examined historically (i.e., developmentally over time), archaeology always appears to have been history's handmaiden, particularly in areas such as the Near East and South Asia. The "tyranny of the text" or the written word prevailed, and the archaeologist was on the defensive, dotting the i or crossing the t to what was already known historically. Archaeology's role was confirmatory, simply documenting tangibly and visually what textual evidence reported. Indeed, this relationship has been so dominant in the southern Levant that A. Joffe alone among the contributors argues for separating the domains of textual and archaeological evidence, to go it alone at least for a while given the current climate of hostility between biblical scholars and critics (chapter 3).

This situation may be unique, and the recommendation consequently extreme. More paradigmatic is the changing relationship between text and archaeology described for South Asia in the chapter by T. Trautmann and C. Sinopoli (chapter 6). The "word" may have been in the beginning, but today such written knowledge is being enriched, even supplanted, by artifacts dug from the soil. The examples from South Asia that they sequentially present reveal clearly how the written and material records complement one another, how our understanding is reduced when only one source of information is available. The Bronze Age Indus Valley civilization remains enigmatic — an empire (Rao 1973), a stateless civilization (Possehl 1998), or a chiefdom (Fairservis 1989) — for many reasons specific to its archaeological record. For example, how to interpret negative evidence — the relative lack of monumental public architecture and absence of royal mortuary evidence? All would agree, however, that written evidence — decipherment of the Harappan script (if it, indeed, constitutes true writing) — would add immeasurably to our understanding of this puzzling Bronze Age culture. Nevertheless, there is a substantial material culture record and much is known about the daily lives, crafts, town planning, and subsistence practices of the Harappans.

Just the opposite situation prevails for the Mauryan empire: textual evidence is abundant, though problematic and one-sided, and archaeological evidence virtually nonexistent. Clearly much basic archaeological work needs to be done. But this example also illustrates how critical it is for both the archaeologist and the historian to be aware of the state of the research of a given problem; that is, to what extent understanding is skewed and partial due simply to lack of research. Systematic, large-scale excavations at Patna (Pataliputra) would immediately transform our understanding of the Mauryan empire but cannot be undertaken since the remains are capped by a modern city. Somehow the Mauryan state must be understood without access to the material remains of its capital city.

The same problem besets A. Joffe's stimulating reconstruction of the tenth and ninth century BC polities in the southern Levant (chapter 3). The state that emerged in this area may have been "a fragile and perishable Potemkin Village," and one that "stimulated both the development of even more peripheral polities and new concepts of identity" (i.e., in his terms, an ethnicizing state). This interpretation, which is at odds with traditional biblical understanding, is original and consistent with the archaeological evidence presented. But, unfortunately, this record is inevitably partial and skewed due to the lack of excavations of the relevant areas of Jerusalem — also unavailable to the archaeologist's spade. In short, it is difficult, if not impossible, to gauge the weakness or strength of the state without access to its center.

When is the absence of evidence really evidence of absence? This problem besets archaeological interpretations essentially for every period. Was there a pre-Clovis horizon in the Americas? Considerable research yielded little convincing evidence — until the excavations at

Monte Verde. And how many Paleo-Indian sites still lie submerged off the Pacific Coast? J. Johns (chapter 5) believes that the absence of material declarations of Islam for roughly its first seventy years or until the inscriptions on the Dome of the Rock in 72/691–2 reflects reality and is not a question of the accidents of discovery or the state of research. Archaeology provides no early evidence for the ideological basis of the caliphate "because there was not yet any state to commission the coins, documents, and inscriptions through which such declarations could be made." The interpretation is perfectly plausible and appears convincing, yet Johns concludes by noting the impossibility of conducting excavations of the relevant early levels of the great mosques in Mecca and Medina, as well as active state discouragement for excavating other potentially relevant late sixth- and seventh-century archaeological sites in Saudi Arabia. Given these limitations, Johns's interpretation simply cannot be tested.

As reported by Trautmann and Sinopoli, archaeologists' contributions to understanding early Buddhist societies and, particularly, the Vijayanagara empire have been substantial. The strengths of the archaeological record for adding new information not contained in historical sources are manifest in these two cases. Archaeological surveys beyond the monastic walls of early Buddhist communities are situating these societies in a broader natural and social environment. Analysis of monumental architecture and the documentation of rural settlements and non-elite activities, including craft and subsistence practices, are revealing the economic infrastructure of the Vijayanagara empire, a picture that could not be gleaned from the extant documentary sources. Both these examples illustrate how much is gained from interdisciplinary collaboration, not just between archaeologists and philologists but also from a variety of disciplines, including the natural sciences.

R. Zettler (chapter 4) emphasizes a similar point in his discussion of the fruitful collaboration among the Near Eastern specialists who formed the Sumerian Agriculture Group to reconstruct the subsistence practices of ancient Mesopotamia. Zettler welcomes the collaboration that brings together Assyriologists, archaeologists, and natural scientists, such as botanists, pedologists, and geomorphologists. Although he sharply criticizes the scenario of an abrupt climatic change with catastrophic social consequences throughout the Near East that occurred around 2200 BC, he applauds H. Weiss's efforts for achieving a more "holistic historical reconstruction" using data derived from many disciplines. His summary of the different contexts in which tablets were recovered at Nippur and other Mesopotamian sites reminds us that many of our documentary sources for understanding the ancient world are not only texts, but also artifacts. That is, these textual sources have been recovered from archaeological contexts that must be understood in order to be properly evaluated. The image of the late third-millennium BC Ur III state as highly centralized, controlling all aspects of the economy and owning all the land, is skewed due to the fact that the tablets for that period, save for those from Nippur, have come exclusively from institutional temple and palace archives that record activities of the state. Conversely, other periods, which appear less centralized with more mixed private and public economic structures, have yielded more tablets from more diverse archaeological contexts, including private houses. Where such sources were recovered is critical for evaluating their significance.

Both W. Wendrich and colleagues' study of the port town of Berenike on the Red Sea (chapter 2) and Li Min's regional study of the Jinan area of Shandong province in northeastern China (chapter 7) show how the combination of archaeological and textual data lead to more balanced and comprehensive historical reconstructions. The former analyzes in considerable detail archaeological materials recovered from the harbor settlement of Berenike, while Li Min's study principally reports data derived from settlement patterns and mortuary evidence. The archaeological artifacts recovered from Berenike only imperfectly "fit" with what is reported in the historical sources; some gemstones and plants recovered at the site are not mentioned in the texts and vice versa. A plausible, if partial, explanation is that some of the materials brought to Berenike were not meant for long-distance exchange but were needed to support the settlement in its isolated, arid setting. The authors convincingly argue that it is precisely the discrepancy between the archaeological and textual information that needs to be scrutinized and explained; in so doing, one more fully understands both the site and the nature of long-distance trade that connected the Mediterranean to the Indian Ocean in Classical times.

Li Min's study reveals how the social history reconstructed from settlement pattern and mortuary data allows for an understanding of daily activities and "the most basic dimensions of human life" and this picture is essential to complement the political narratives related in the historical sources. The archaeological evidence shows how the regional Jinan economy was increasingly integrated into the central imperial economy with the rise of the Qin and Han states. Several aspects of the archaeological record summarized by Li Min are noteworthy: (1) the lack of the use of bronze and the extremely late introduction of iron tools for basic agricultural production; (2) the striking contrast between commoner and elite burials, as seen particularly in the truly immense Western Han M1 burial at Shuangrushan; and (3) the scale of the monumental constructions built without bronze or iron tools. The Long Wall of Qi, which was built before the Warring States period and extended for nearly 620 kilometers (!), must minimally reveal "evidence of territorial control of the region by a powerful political authority lying beyond the regional boundary." These East Asian states, even in periods of imperial breakdown, were extremely powerful and capable of harnessing the labor of numerous dependent subjects.

As already noted, the picture that A. Joffe paints for the tenth- and ninth-century BC Iron Age states that developed in the southern Levant is quite different. These states are small, fragile, and ephemeral. They developed in a less complexly structured social world than that which had characterized the area during Late Bronze times and remained peripheral to the more complex, recovering polity to the south, Egypt, and the culturally but not politically united Phoenician city-states to the north. Levantines struggled for their survival by emphasizing their ethnic distinctiveness, perceiving themselves as having stable territorial boundaries and having descended from common ancestors and possessing their own patron deities. They struggled to survive by embracing the concept of ethnicity, and it is this idea that ultimately proves adaptive and ensures their long-term survival.

This reconstruction is unique in that it explicitly eschews direct reference to the Bible, the overpowering relevant historical (and literary and mythological) source, and purports to be based principally on archaeological and extra-biblical historical evidence. But have its parameters for delineating these Iron Age ethnicizing states really been established independently of what is recorded in the Bible? Can one just forget what is there when one "reads" this archaeological record or, worded differently, would one's "reading" be the same in the absence of knowledge of what the massively important, if problematic, historical source of the Bible relates? The absence of storage facilities at Hazor and Megiddo — negative evidence, in other words — supposedly demonstrates that elites were not "engaged in providing economic and social services to local communities." Rather, this lack of evidence reveals a concern for "establishing a local ideological presence and conducting political affairs." Similarly, the absence of large-scale food-preparation facilities, such as bakeries and breweries, and the lack of standardized ration containers somehow suggests that these Iron Age ethnicizing states were concerned with their own survival and did so by manipulating the concept of ethnicity. Examined critically, such inferences hardly seem straightforward, derived directly from the archaeological record (or here the absence of this record). Joffe's interpretation is stimulating, plausible, and, indeed, probably correct, but the question must be asked whether his reconstruction could have been even further developed by using, as opposed to consciously ignoring, the most important and available textual source — the Bible. Basic criteria of historiography would have to be applied: no literal or uncritical consideration, but an informed, selective one. All the other contributors have demonstrated the positive feedback between textual and archaeological sources, each enriching and complementing the other. The same should be true here.

Why have most archaeologists suffered so long from "the tyranny of the text"? Why is their record seemingly less informative and reliable than the historian's? The nonmaterial ideological world and questions of intentionality and agency may be more difficult to comprehend from material evidence alone, but many contemporary archaeologists attempt to account for them and have greater methodological and theoretical tools to do so than were available in C. Hawkes' day when he presented his famous ladder of archaeological inference and reliability. As we have seen, Childe was not an archaeologist with an inferiority complex; if anything, he placed the onus of documentation and verifiability on the shoulders of the historian. A review of the chapters collected here necessarily leads to a reflection on the relative strengths and weaknesses of archaeological and textual data. The remainder of this essay briefly considers more of these epistemological issues.

Both ancient historians and archaeologists have to contend with the problems of their respective records being representative or containing lacunae or gaps of uncertain dimension and significance. Do the Ur III texts from palace contexts provide a basis for reconstructing the entire state, including the activities of private individuals? How serious is the problem of not being able to excavate the relevant areas of Jerusalem for understanding the nature of the Early Iron Age state that was centered there, or to uncover late sixth- and seventh-century AD sites in Saudi Arabia that potentially could document the earliest years of Islam? Then there is that peculiarly textual problem of deliberate distortion. How do we recognize that a king's boasts or state reports are historically suspect? Real Potemkin villages would represent a material-culture parallel, but these are relatively exceptional compared to the self-serving accounts and propaganda promulgated by rulers and their elite accomplices. Monumental royal art also must be interpreted cautiously, but would anyone be likely to believe that the Pharaoh (or Naram-Sin on his famous victory stele) physically towered several times above his adversaries or dependent subjects? Again, it may be the historical text that is more opaque and difficult to interpret than the tangible artifact.

The only reliable record available to reconstruct prehistory is the archaeological record; consequently, despite its limitations, it is the best source for reconstructing most of the human past. The chapters here, however, have treated periods when both archaeological and historical evidence were available. Over time (i.e., in later periods), the problem of gaps in the historical record diminishes; the historian typically confronts a new problem: an abundance of source materials, leading to selection of what is relevant based upon criteria of significance, a selection that the historian may explicitly and consciously make or not. The historian of modern times, say, the last 250 years or so, may be so overwhelmed with source materials that this selection process becomes exceptionally difficult, and such historians can be evaluated on how well or how poorly they go about it. This problem did not arise with the historical materials discussed in these articles; these sources were more fragmentary, and archaeology was invoked to make more sense of them, to complement them, and often even add critical information on daily life and activities about which these texts were totally silent.

Is there a time when the archaeological record becomes totally redundant, given the abundance of source materials? P. Lape cites the well-known adage that "historical archaeology is an expensive way to find out what we already know about the past." But is that really true—even for well-documented areas during the nineteenth and twentieth centuries? The archaeology of plantations in the American South has added a vital material dimension to our understanding of life on these plantations that was missing from the presumably complete documentary sources. The size of the rooms in which people were forced to live; the foods they ate and materials they possessed; and the difference in the lives of field and house slaves—all are much better understood today as a result of the excavations of plantations. Similarly, French archaeologists (Boura 1998) have excavated battle sites of World Wars I and II and, as a result, have graphically brought home the horrors of those confrontations by unearthing collective tombs and munitions deposits. Aerial photos strikingly reveal the permanent devastation wrought upon the landscape by the lines of immobile trenches that defined the "Great War's" western front. The archaeology of these twentieth-century events is painful but cathartic. It not only adds to what is known historically but also enriches it through its very tangibility.

It is easy to imagine other possible archaeological explorations of the recent past. Would it not be worthwhile, for example, to set up a multidisciplinary project of archaeologists, historians, anthropologists, and other relevant specialists to investigate the material remains of the Soviet Gulag before some of the camps totally deteriorate and vanish and before all the prisoners, camp wardens, and officials it comprised die? The point is that archaeology here would not simply be redundant to what is recorded somewhere in recently opened or still classified files or simply rumored to exist through the circulation of prisoners' oral accounts. How many circles of hell were there? Are they easily distinguishable in terms of their material remains: the size of the rooms, their "amenities," and so forth? The goal would not be to write a revisionist history, either to inflate or to minimize the scale and nature of a system responsible for millions of deaths; rather, it would be to reveal its tangible dimensions, to give it a concrete material reality that would make it truly unforgettable. It is, after all, important that one can still visit Auschwitz, Dachau, Buchenwald, and other camps. The Gulag deserves equal treatment.

In short, archaeology should not be history's handmaiden for any period. The material culture record is our only source of information for most of the human past, the long period of prehistory. Its relevance does not diminish when textual sources first appear. For remote historical periods, we need to use all the sources that are available: historical and archaeological. They mutually enrich each other, as is so clearly demonstrated in the articles collected here. An archaeology of modern times likewise is valuable — not as an expensive means for confirming what is already known, but as an independent source for informing us about the past — the accomplishments and horrors that we have effected upon ourselves. The strengths of the material culture record often compensate for the ambiguities and inadequacies of historical documentation, and that remains true whether one reconstructs the remote or the recent past.

Bibliography

Arnold, B. 1992. "The Past as Propaganda." *Archaeology* 45:30–37.

Boura, F. 1998. "Le poids des morts ou comment s'en débarrasser: Que faire de l'encombrant patrimoine de la Grande Guerre?" *Les Nouvelles de l'Archéologie* 70:1–6.

Childe, V. G. 1951. *Social Evolution*. New York: Meridian Books.

———. 1956. *A Short Introduction to Archaeology*. New York: Collier Books.

Fairservis, W. A. 1989. "An Epigenetic View of the Harappan Culture." In *Archaeo-logical Thought in America*, ed. C. C. Lamberg-Karlovsky, 205–17. Cambridge: Cambridge University Press.

Kitchen, K. A. 1995. "Pharaoh Ramses II and His Times." In *Civilizations of the Ancient Near East*, ed. J. M. Sasson, 763–74. New York: Charles Scribner's Sons.

Possehl, G. L. 1998. "Sociocultural Complexity without the State: The Indus Civilization." In *The Archaic State*, ed. G. M. Feinman and J. Marcus, 261–91. Santa Fe: School of American Research.

Rao, S. R. 1973. *Lothal and the Indus Civilization*. Bombay: Asia Publishing House.

CONTRIBUTORS

ROGER S. BAGNALL

Bagnall is a professor in the Department of Classics at Columbia University, specializing in Greco-Roman history and papyrology. His publications include *Egypt in Late Antiquity* (1995) and *Egypt from Alexander to the Early Christians: An Archaeological and Historical Guide* (co-editor, 2005).

RENÉ T. J. CAPPERS

Cappers, assistant professor of paleobotany at the Groningen Institute of Archaeology, University of Groningen, specializes in archaebotany and Greco-Roman trade. His publications include *The Dawn of Farming in the Near East* (2002) with S. Bottema.

BRADLEY L. CROWELL

Crowell is a visiting assistant professor in the University of Toledo's Department of Philosophy. His dissertation, "On the Margins of History: Social Change and Political Development in Iron Age Edom" (2004), is on the effect of the Assyrian empire on marginal polities.

JAMES A. HARRELL

Professor of geology in the Department of Earth, Ecological and Environmental Sciences at the University of Toledo, Harrell's research focus is on sedimentary petrology and archaeological geology of ancient Egypt. His recent publications include articles in *Journal of Egyptian Archaeology* and *Archaeometry*.

ALEXANDER H. JOFFE

Joffe is an associate of Global Policy Exchange, Ltd. His research interests include early complex societies, archaeology and nationalism, environmental security, and the role of culture in international relations. His publications include *Settlement and Society in the Early Bronze Age I-II Southern Levant: Contradiction in a Small Scale Complex Society* (1992) and recent articles in *Journal of Mediterranean Archaeology* and *Disarmament Diplomacy*.

JEREMY JOHNS

Johns, director of the Khalili Research Centre for Art and Material Culture at the University of Oxford's Oriental Institute, researches archaeology and history in the Islamic Mediterranean, with a special interest in Sicily and Jordan. His most recent publication is *Arabic Administration in Norman Sicily: The Royal Diwan* (2002).

PHILIP L. KOHL

Kohl is a professor in the Department of Anthropology at Wellesley College. His research focuses on Central Asia, the Caucasus, Eurasia, and Iran, with interest in politics and archaeology. He is the editor of *Nationalism, Politics, and the Practice of Archaeology* (1996) and *Bronze Age Civilization of Central Asia* (1981).

PETER V. LAPE

Lape is an assistant professor in the Department of Anthropology at the University of Washington and a curator of archaeology at the Burke Museum. His research focuses on archaeological and documentary analysis in relation to cross-cultural interaction in Island Southeast Asia. He has published articles in *Antiquity*, *Asian Perspectives*, and *World Archaeology*.

LI MIN

Li Min is a PhD candidate in the Department of Anthropology, University of Michigan. His research focuses on the evolution of early states in China and maritime trade in early modern China.

STEVEN E. SIDEBOTHAM

Sidebotham is a professor in the Department of History at the University of Delaware. He is the author of *Roman Economic Policy in the Erythra Thalassa 30 BC–AD 217* (1986), and he also co-edits the preliminary reports of the excavations at Berenike with Willemina Z. Wendrich.

CARLA M. SINOPOLI

Sinopoli, a University of Michigan Department of Anthropology professor, is also the curator of Asian archaeology. She is the director of the university's Museum of Anthropology. She specializes in archaeological research on ceramics, craft production, and early states in India, and she has been engaged in long-term research at the site of Vijayanagara, India. Her most recent book is *The Political Economy of Craft Production: Crafting Empire in South India, c. 1350–1650* (2003).

MIRIAM T. STARK

Stark is an associate professor in the Department of Anthropology at the University of Hawai'i and editor of *The Archaeology of Social Boundaries* (1998) and *An Archaeology of Asia* (2005). Her research interests include ethnoarchaeology and particularly the archaeology of complex societies of Cambodia and the Philippines.

ROBERTA S. TOMBER

Tomber, a visiting fellow in the Department of Conservation, Documentation, and Science at the British Museum, specializes in Indo-Roman trade, Roman period ceramics, and Roman economy. She has published articles in *Man and Environment*, *Journal of Roman Archaeology*, and *Antiquity*.

THOMAS TRAUTMANN

Trautmann is a professor in the University of Michigan Departments of History and Anthropology. His research focuses on the history of India and Orientalist scholarship in India, the history of anthropology, and kinship. His recent books include *The Aryan Debate* (2005) and *Aryans and British India* (1997).

WILLEMINA Z. WENDRICH

Wendrich is an associate Professor in the Department of Near Eastern Languages and Cultures at the University of California, Los Angeles. Her research interests include the social context of crafts organization, ethnoarchaeology, and trade. She is the author of *The World According to Basketry: An Ethno-archaeological Interpretation of Basketry Production in Egypt* (1999).

NORMAN YOFFEE

Yoffee is a professor in the Department of Near Eastern Studies and the Department of Anthropology at the University of Michigan. His most recent publication in Mesopotamian studies and social theory is *Myths of the Archaic State: Evolution of the Earliest Cities, States, and Civilizations* (2005).

RICHARD L. ZETTLER

Zettler is an associate professor in the University of Pennsylvania Department of Anthropology. He has taken part in excavations in Syria and Iraq and has long-term interests in integrating material culture and written sources from Mesopotamian cities. His publications include *The Ur III Temple of Inanna at Nippur* (1992) and, as co-editor, *Treasures from the Royal Tombs of Ur* (1998).

ILLUSTRATION CREDITS

Chapter 2, 4, and 7 figures were originally published in *Journal of the Economic and Social History of the Orient* 46 (1). Copyright © 2003 by Brill Academic Publishers. Reprinted by permission. Figure 2.1 (appeared as fig. 1, p. 48); figure 4.1 (fig. 1, p. 4); figure 7.1 (fig. 1, p. 91); figure 7.2 (fig. 2, p. 92); figure 7.3 (fig. 3, p. 96); figure 7.4 (fig. 4, p. 96); figure 7.5 (fig. 5, p. 99); and figure 7.6 (fig. 6, p. 102).

Chapter 3 figures were originally published in *Journal of the Economic and Social History of the Orient* 45 (4). Copyright © 2002 by Brill Academic Publishers. Reprinted by permission. Figure 3.1 (fig. 1, p. 433); figure 3.2 (fig. 2, p. 441); figure 3.3 (fig. 3, p. 443); figure 3.4 (fig. 4, p. 444).

Chapter 5 figures were originally published in *Journal of the Economic and Social History of the Orient* 46 (4). Copyright © 2003 by Brill Academic Publishers. Reprinted by permission. Figure 5.1 (fig. 1, p. 413); figure 5.2 (fig. 2, p. 415); figure 5.3 (fig. 3, p. 417); figure 5.4 (fig. 4, p. 419); figure 5.5 (fig. 5, p. 420); figure 5.6 (fig. 6, p. 427); figure 5.7 (fig. 7, p. 428); figure 5.8 (fig. 8, p. 429); figure 5.9 (fig. 9, p. 430); figure 5.10 (fig. 10, p. 430); figure 5.11 (fig. 11, p. 431); and figure 5.12 (fig. 12, p. 432).

Chapter 8 figures were originally published in *Journal of the Economic and Social History of the Orient* 45 (2). Copyright © 2002 by Brill Academic Publishers. Reprinted by permission. Figure 8.1 (fig. 1, p. 474) and figure 8.2 (fig. 2, p. 479).

Figure 9.1 was constructed by John Shearer, Anne Dunlop, and Jane Drummond (Department of Geographical and Earth Sciences, University of Glasgow) and originally appeared as figure 3 in *Geoarchaeology* 18 (3): 363. Reprinted with permission of *Geoarchaeology* (2003).

INDEX